DIRECTING for the THEATRE

DIRECTING for the SECOND EDITION THEATRE

by

W. DAVID SIEVERS
Professor of Drama
California State College
Long Beach

WM. C. BROWN COMPANY PUBLISHERS
135 SOUTH LOCUST STREET · DUBUQUE, IOWA 52003

Copyright © 1965
by
Wm. C. Brown Company Publishers

Library of Congress Catalog Number: 65-21887

Manufactured by WM. C. BROWN CO. INC., Dubuque, Iowa
Printed in U. S. A.

"Besides the method, actors must have all the qualities that constitute a real artist: inspiration, intelligence, taste, the ability to communicate, charm, temperament, fine speech and movement, quick excitability and an expressive appearance. One cannot go very far with just the method."

—Constantin Stanislavski
(from *Stanislavsky Directs*, by Nikolai M. Gorchakov. New York: Funk and Wagnalls Company, 1954).

v

By the same author——

FREUD ON BROADWAY

A History of Psychoanalysis
and the American Drama

INTRODUCTION

This book was designed as a text for a college course in the fundamentals of play direction. It follows no one theory or system, but is indebted to many. It would not have been possible without the teachings and example of notable directors such as Erwin Piscator, Thomas Wood Stevens, James Light, F. Cowles Strickland, Samuel Selden, and Stella Adler. The manual draws heavily upon the Stanislavski method, but equally upon Alexander Dean's technical analysis of stage mechanics, which remains a classic book in its field. The creation of inner truth and the technical control of form are not mutually exclusive, but in fact two sides of the same coin. The working director needs to know both approaches, and should never mistake either part for the whole. This manual integrates the two approaches in a way that has been found workable in the educational theatre.

Neither a textbook nor one course in play production can teach the student all he needs to know in order to direct plays. Most successful directors have had previous experience as actors, although a few learned the theatre through playwriting or scene design. In any case, the theatre is a pragmatic art, and theory is only a prerequisite to practice, which begins with short scenes, progresses to one-act plays and ultimately to full-length plays. The audience is the final arbiter and tells the director whether he has been successful. A director learns most about his craft by watching and listening to his audience; coughs, restlessness, and laughter at the wrong places are all signs that he has failed to communicate, while tense silence and crisp bursts of laughter tell him when his cast has communicated the desired effect. Dr. Samuel Johnson observed several centuries ago:

> *The drama's laws the drama's patrons give,*
> *And we that live to please must please to live.*

The qualities which seem essential for the drama director to possess if he is to please his audience include:

1. Showmanship, or an innate flair for the dramatic.
2. Insight into human behavior and psychology.
3. A strong background in dramatic literature, criticism, and theatre history.
4. Knowledge of the crafts of the theatre, including acting, directing, stagecraft, lighting, costuming, make-up, and dance.
5. A background of appreciations in art and music.
6. Organizational skill and the ability to plan ahead.
7. Taste and a sense of appropriateness.
8. Love and respect for people and the ability to work well with them.
9. Energy and dedication to the high purposes of the theatre.
10. Infinite patience.

This manual will concentrate largely upon numbers 1, 4, and 6, suggesting techniques for heightening the student's innate sense of the dramatic, and giving him a body of tested principles upon which to rely until his own creative powers mature. Stanislavski observed that the director needs to know, in addition to all that the actor learns, how to work with (a) the script, (b) the actor, and (c) the technical staff. The author's purpose in this book is to systematize what can be taught about an admittedly elusive and subjective art, and to offer some possible solutions — never unbreakable laws.

Although some of these suggested solutions apply specifically to the educational theatre, this book is by no means limited to any one dramatic level. "Good theatre" — whether on Broadway or the high school stage — happens *when actors and technicians make and hold effective contact with an audience.* How this is planned and accomplished is the director's craft.

Some suggested ways in which this book might prove helpful include its use as a text for a college course in fundamentals of direction for theatre and drama majors, as a text for a course in play production preparing secondary school drama teachers, and for acting-directing workshops at the junior college or college level. Materials in Chapters 3, 6, 7, 8, 9, and 11 may also serve as a basis for a teacher's syllabus of a fundamentals of acting course at the high school or college level. For the many teachers in the secondary schools and junior colleges who are currently directing plays in addition to the pressures of a heavy teaching load, the systematic analysis of the director's problems in this manual may prove a welcome timesaver and source for reference. For the volunteer community theatre director or recreation leader who may find himself called upon to direct a play even though he has had little formal training in theatre art, for the neophyte with the imagination to try out the principles suggested and do further independent reading, this book will furnish a foundation for practical work in the theatre.

At all levels the text is intended to provide the theoretical basis for understanding what the actor and director do in rehearsal. The exercises included (or similar ones) should be performed and critiqued in class as a means of testing and applying the theory. It has been found effective in play direction classes to assign each student director one play to study for the semester, preparing a director's book, writing a full interpretation, and staging selected scenes which contain problems in composition, movement, vocal interpretation, tempo and climax. No attempt has been made in this manual, however, to cover the crafts of scenery design and construction, lighting, costuming or make-up, with which a director should be familiar and which ideally should be included in his course of study prior to his first directing experience.

The director in the nonprofessional or educational theatre must be a teacher at the same time that he is a director. In one sense he performs a more demanding kind of artistry than does the director in the professional theatre, where the actors and technicians are highly skilled. There will be moments of frustration and despair for every director. But when he accomplishes his task well — when he can sit in the back row on opening night and watch as each cue times out perfectly, and actors, lights, scenery, music and costume all fuse their effects to create "theatre magic" for the audience — the results will be incomparably satisfying for the director.

ACKNOWLEDGMENTS

It is with warm appreciation that I acknowledge my great indebtedness to Dr. Kenneth L. Graham, Professor of Speech and Theatre Arts at the University of Minnesota, who served as editorial advisor for the manuscript. I also wish to express my thanks to my colleagues in the Speech and Drama Departments of California State College at Long Beach; to Dr. John H. Green for his reading of the manuscript and the drawing of the ground plan for *The Barretts of Wimpole Street;* to Dr. Leo Goodman-Malamuth, Milton Howarth and Herbert Camburn for their valuable comments on the various chapters. I am also grateful to Dr. Frank Nelson of our English Department for permission to quote from his translation of Ibsen's *Pillars of Society,* and to Dr. Josephine Burley Schultz of the Art Department for assistance in locating art reproductions. Isabel Thomason and Aileen Alvich graciously served as models for the photographs of stage positions, and the latter also did the art work for the drawings and diagrams. Bill Coleman of Long Beach did the photography for the cover and many of the plays illustrated throughout the book. Above all, I am indebted to the many directors and designers who kindly furnished me with pictures of their productions and granted permission to use them as illustrations; those responsible for each picture are acknowledged on pages 380-383, and special thanks are due as well to George Freedley of the Theatre Collection, New York Public Library, to Mrs. Florence Vandamm of Vandamm Studios, and to Eileen Darby of Graphic House, Inc. Where not otherwise indicated, photographs are of productions at California State College at Long Beach.

For permission to quote from plays, I wish to acknowledge my thanks to the following:

Random House, Inc., for *The Diary of Anne Frank* by Frances Goodrich and Albert Hackett, and for *Hedda Gabler* by Ibsen, translated by Eva LeGallienne in the Modern Library Book, *Six Plays by Henrik Ibsen,* Copyright, 1957.

Holt, Rinehart and Winston, Inc., for Robert Whitelaw's translation of Sophocles' *Antigone* in *An Anthology of Greek Drama,* Vol. I, and for Dudley Fitts and Robert Fitzgerald's translation of *Antigone* in *Greek Plays in Modern Translation,* Copyright, 1947.

Little, Brown and Company for *The Barretts of Wimpole Street,* by Rudolph Besier.

Hamilton Russell Corp., London, for *Blithe Spirit* by Noel Coward.

Reinheimer and Cohen for *You Can't Take It With You,* copyright by George S. Kaufman and Moss Hart.

Howard Richardson for his play, *Dark of the Moon.*

Viking Press, Inc., for *Death of a Salesman* and *The Crucible* by Arthur Miller.

Harper and Brothers for *Our Town* by Thornton Wilder.

Robinson Jeffers for his play, *Medea.*

Anderson House for *Winterset* by Maxwell Anderson. Copyright, 1935, by Anderson House.

Samuel French, Inc., for *The Late Christopher Bean.* Copyright, 1932 (under the title *Muse of All Work*) by Sidney Howard, Copyright, 1933, by Sidney Howard, Copyright, 1959, (in renewal) by Polly Damrosch Howard. All rights reserved.

New Directions for *Summer and Smoke* excerpt, reprinted from *Summer and Smoke* by Tennessee Williams. Copyright, 1948, by Tennessee Williams. By permission of New Directions, publishers.

The second edition incorporated valuable suggestions made by Professor Donald D. Fogelberg of the University of Minnesota. I am indebted too to The Tyrone Guthrie Theatre of Minneapolis for permission to use the photograph of *The Three Sisters,* and to Frederic McConnell, director emeritus of the Cleveland Playhouse, for his production photograph of *The Crucible.* The section on the ground plan was expanded with the assistance of Dr. Maxine Merlino, Professor of Art and Theatre Design at California State College, Long Beach, whose drawings of sample ground plans are a contribution which is most sincerely appreciated.

W.D.S.

CONTENTS

The Servant of Two Masters

Chapter 1

THE VALUES AND PURPOSES
OF EDUCATIONAL THEATRE

I. Introduction.

Some critics of modern education have accused play production of being time-consuming, expensive, distracting; it has been called a "frill" and an interference with the "3 R's." The drama teacher today must therefore be prepared to justify his program to principals, deans, school boards, parents, and the public. To do this he should be clear as to the values of educational theatre and the purposes which it may serve; successful drama directors not only understand these values — they believe in them fervently.

II. The heritage of educational theatre.

Many of the greatest minds of western civilization have written for the theatre. Together with the mountebanks and humble entertainers, the theatre has attracted Aeschylus and Sophocles with their majestic vision of man's role in the universe; Euripides with his compassionate humanitarianism; Shakespeare with his vibrant characters and his poetry; Molière, Sheridan and Shaw with their catalytic satire of human foible; Goethe, the last of the universal minds; Ibsen with his still-pertinent challenges to a democratic society; Chekhov, who taught the world how to observe the minute detail that makes up human character; Strindberg and O'Neill who broke beneath the surface of psychological motivation. The humanistic vision and enduring values of these writers are all the

1

more accessible because they are in a form that is irresistibly appealing — the drama, permitting of emotional participation as well as intellectual understanding. The theatre is the most human of all arts, for its subject has always been the life of men and the destiny of Man. For some 2,400 years before John Dewey the theatre has been a means of learning through *doing*, through participation (the very word *drama* comes from the Greek verb *to do*).

A. The classic heritage.

In ancient Athens, where democracy and drama were born, the theatre was held in high esteem as a civic, educational, and religious institution. Aeschylus, Sophocles, and Euripides left mankind a heritage in poetry, dramatic craftsmanship, philosophy, and insight into character which has not become obsolete in 2,400 years. Plato was aware of the educational value of the theatre, observing that ".... dramatic poets are acquainted not only with all arts, but with all things human which bear upon virtue and vice, and also with things divine." The Greeks treasured their theatre to the extent that a group of Athenian prisoners captured in the Peloponnesian War were given their freedom because they could recite some passages from Euripides. In addition Aristotle, the world's first drama critic, ended his days as an educator and tutor to no less a personage than Alexander the Great.

B. The Renaissance heritage.

There is a record of a play acted at Oxford University before Columbus discovered America; by the end of the sixteenth century virtually every school included the study of Greek and Roman dramas.[1] The Renaissance scholars used these plays as a means of reviving interest in classicism, improving the student's speech, and fostering his interest in the study of Latin and Greek. Far from being a "frill," the drama was taken so seriously at Cambridge University that a regulation of 1546 threatened to expel any student who refused to accept a role or to attend a performance. The first native English comedy, *Ralph Roister Doister,* was written by a secondary school teacher for his students to act, and by the Elizabethan era the choirboys of St. Paul's Cathedral and the Chapel Royal were acting with such skill in plays written especially for them by Ben Jonson, John Lyly, and John Marston, among others, that even Shakespeare felt their competition.

C. The American heritage.

Educational theatre in America is almost as old as the colonies themselves. As early as 1702, the students of William and Mary

---

[1]Coggin, Philip A., *The Uses of Drama* (New York: George Braziller, Inc., 1956), p. 79.

College in Virginia staged a "pastoral colloquy" before the governor. During the nineteenth century Greek and Roman tragedies and comedies were regularly performed at many colleges and secondary schools, often in the original language. As a rule these performances were extracurricular, however; the modern integration of theatre arts in the college curriculum began with Professor George Pierce Baker, who taught playwriting in the famous 47 Workshop at Harvard and later at Yale. His students included Eugene O'Neill, S. N. Behrman, Sidney Howard, Philip Barry, Robert Sherwood, and George Abbott — a class that reshaped the American drama. From the impetus given by Baker, the *production* of plays has been gradually recognized as no less worthy of academic credit than the literary study of drama, and courses in acting, directing, stagecraft, lighting and costuming have won acceptance as necessary components in the total program that furthers the liberal arts objectives of the educational theatre.

There are today some 1,500 colleges and universities in the United States which produce educational theatre; the American Educational Theatre Association, which includes some 4,000 members, found in a survey that its own member institutions staged 2,343 productions of 867 different full-length plays during 1961-62; a total audience of 2,666,984 persons saw these productions, in which 85,568 students received an educational experience as participants.[2] Although no complete survey has been made of all the high schools in the nation which produce plays, the National Thespian Society lists some 2,540 affiliated high schools and estimates that their member schools produced some 4,110 major full-length plays during the 1962-63 season.[3]

Even this brief glance at the heritage of the educational theatre should serve to remind directors and teachers of the proud past and high calling of their profession. There should be no need to apologize for the theatre as one of the liberal arts, although in the great re-evaluation of American education since Sputnik, drama teachers have repeatedly been placed on the defensive.

The Gallup Poll recently highlighted the significant role which education plays in forming cultural tastes and habits. Over half of those persons with a college education attended the theatre during 1962, it was found, as compared with only 3 per cent of those with a grade-school education who attended the theatre. The implications

[2]Stambusky, Alan A., "Significant College and University Play Production Patterns in 1961-1962," *Educational Theatre Journal*, XV, No. 2, May, 1963, pp. 163-165.

[3]"Summary of the 1962-63 Thespian Season," *National Thespian Society*. College Hill Station, Cincinnati, Ohio.

for the high school, where the tastes and values of those who do not go on to college are formed, is all too apparent.[4]

With the current emphasis upon technical and scientific education, it is becoming clear that space-age technology could prove to be a monstrous Frankenstein unless it rests in the control of humanistic, liberally educated individuals. More than ever before in history, man needs to draw upon his inner resources and his ability to communicate with his fellow man to achieve an enriched life (or

The Lark, California High School, Whittier, California

any life at all) now that science has given him incredible power and more leisure than his ancestors ever dreamed of enjoying. A clear and unequivocal awareness of the goals of the educational theatre will be of invaluable aid to the drama director in his public relations program, in his justification of his activity to administrators, in his selection of plays, and in his conduct of rehearsals and classes.

---

[4]"Gallup Poll: U.S. Women Narrow Culture Gap," *Los Angeles Times,* April 14, 1963.

III. Values to be derived from play production in schools and colleges.

    A. Values for both participants and audience.

        1. Liberal education in depth and breadth.[5]

           a. Depth of insight into human character and life as reflected in literature. To understand fully the psychology of a character in a well-written play is to know something more about human nature and one's self as well. Directors and actors work backward from effect to cause, discovering motivations or psychological drives sufficient to warrant the outcome described by the playwright. The theatre is thus a living laboratory for the study of psychology in action, and an actor who plays, a director who interprets and (to a less intense degree) a spectator who empathizes with a Willy Loman, a Nora, an Oedipus or a Macbeth cannot help but grow in maturity and insight, identifying with the character at his best to help him deal with his own problems, and perceiving how to avoid the mistakes of the character at his worst. As a tragic character goes to his doom, the actor, director, technician in the wings or spectator in the audience can exclaim, "There, but by the grace of whatever insight I have gained, go I."

           b. Breadth of empathic experience, permitting the student to participate vicariously in the lives and emotions of people from other centuries and distant lands, thereby enlarging his insights and fostering appreciation of history, other nations, cultures, and peoples. Preparing or witnessing a production of *The Crucible, The Lark, The Corn is Green, The Teahouse of the August Moon,* or *Antigone* may lead to further reading in history, literature, biography or anthropology. A student who is well read in the drama has begun the fascinating study of the humanities, which has as its goal the understanding of man and his culture, perceiving his present and estimating his future with the perspective of his past.

           Impressed with the relevance of a production of *Danton's Death* with which Dartmouth College dedicated its new Hopkins Center for the fine arts, Howard Taubman wrote in the *New York Times*:

           If the arts can reveal man in relation to himself, his history, his contemporaries and his environment, and they can do so glowingly and penetratingly, they should be among the

---

[5]These values are superbly illustrated in a series of films which teachers should utilize whenever possible: An Introduction to the Humanities based upon *Great Dramatic Literature*, 12 sound color films by Encyclopaedia Brittanica Films, Inc.

foundation stones of a liberal education. Properly cultivated in the college atmosphere, they may prove of more lasting value to the citizen of tomorrow than the so-called basic courses.[6]

The Emperor Jones, College of Idaho.

2. Appreciation of literature.
   a. The educational theatre at all levels has the responsibility of making available and cultivating an appreciation for good theatre and worthwhile dramatic literature. In the absence of a national theatre in America, the only classic dramas by the Greeks, Shakespeare, Molière, Sheridan, Shaw or O'Neill

---

[6]Taubman, Howard, "Arts on Campus," *The New York Times,* X, Nov. 18, 1962.

that a student is apt to see are in schools and colleges. New friends for the classics are made, however, *only when the plays are excellently staged.*

b. In an era when television is but one of many stimuli competing for the student's attention, anything which encourages the student to read and broaden his literary interests should be welcomed by educators and parents. In bringing literature to life, the theatre has a unique ability to engross young minds and open further doors to the enrichment which is to be found in books.

c. Giving participants and audience the opportunity to experience the struggles, either comic or tragic, of worthwhile characters from the great classics of dramatic literature as well as modern drama whose actions reaffirm the age-old theme of the drama — the dignity of man, the worth of individual life, the spiritual strength of purposeful striving, and the reassurance to be found in the way others have borne their sufferings.

3. Development of critical standards.

The appreciation of good theatre should develop critical standards of judgment which will carry over and influence the student's taste in selecting film and television entertainment. With his knowledge of good theatre as a reference point, he will be better able to recognize superior writing, acting, and production in television and motion pictures and to reject the shoddy and the banal.

B. Additional values for the audience.

1. Audience decorum.

The theatre offers young people valuable training in being a good audience, in listening, showing respect for the performers and observing social decorum which is not offered by a popcorn-munching motion picture audience or a casual, inattentive television audience. Theatre-going should be a special occasion worthy of "dressing up" and paying respectful attention.

2. Sharing an emotional experience with others.

The theatre permits the individual to test his own reactions against those of the rest of the audience and to experience the contagion of laughter or tears with his fellow man. Discussing and evaluating the play, matching impressions with others, and sharing an emotional experience are among the real satisfactions of playgoing. Of all the arts, all but the theatre can be enjoyed in isolation; only for the theatre must man leave his solitude and make common cause with his fellow man.

3. Developing future audiences for the theatre.

   Enjoyment of the theatre, if developed in high school or college, may remain as a leisure-time activity that will bring lifelong satisfactions. And if the professional theatre is to survive in America, new audiences must be created among young people.

4. Enjoyment.

   It is in no way an unworthy goal of the theatre to offer sheer enjoyment to playgoers, to open doors on a world of magic, laughter, and suspense through the sensuous appeal of color, movement, poetry and music — to let the theatre become, in short, a place where our unfulfilled wishes are brought to fruition. If the theatre could not do this it would not have survived these many centuries; if it is to meet its educational goals it must do this — and more.

Antigone, Millikan High School, Long Beach, California

C. Additional values for the participants.

   1. An enriched program for the academically superior student.

      a. Although a very small percentage of high school students can go on to careers in the theatre arts, many of our superior students who are preparing for college will be challenged and enriched by participation in theatre, a total experience involving intellectual, emotional, spiritual, and physical values. Such students will find stimulation in the ideas of the great playwrights, emotional release in rehearsal, and a necessary balance in an academic program heavy with mathematics and science.

b. The theatre is an excellent preparation for future leaders in all walks of life. A remarkably large number of America's leaders in business, the professions, the sciences, and government had "dramatics" under their names in high school and college yearbooks. Parents and educators are becoming increasingly aware of the importance of getting along with others, assuming leadership, and finding expressions for the imagination.

2. Personal development and psychological maturation.

a. For the average student as well as the superior one, the theatre is in an excellent position to foster psychological maturity. Both in casting and in rehearsal, the sensitive director reflects back to the student how he appears to others, how he communicates, and how he affects others. Audience awareness, an essential quality in many professions from sales to diplomacy, is consciousness of self in relation to others. Poise, self-confidence, broader insight, and a sense of personal accomplishment can all be important derivatives of a play production experience. Drama in the school has been called "trying on life for size."

b. As a therapeutic outlet for emotions — particularly hostile ones — the educational theatre makes a significant contribution to mental health. Outside the theatre, there are very few outlets in our culture for aggressive and hostile impulses (except football and boxing); the actor who has expended his bitterness or aggression playing these emotions in a scene will have less need to release them in his personal life.

c. To a greater extent than the audience, the actor identifies with the character he plays, and in so doing often discovers new facets of his own personality, new ideals and goals for his own guidance, and worthwhile lines which when memorized are generally retained long after formal reading assignments have been forgotten.

3. Growth in speech and language arts.

a. Command of voice and diction is one of the most apparent values of an acting experience. Much of this is actually ear training in the awareness of dialect, slang, colloquialisms, careless speech and tensions in the vocal mechanism. Although a rehearsal for a public performance is not the place to do remedial work in speech, many speech problems are primarily emotional and can best be dealt with in a creative atmosphere where the student has the security of playing someone else rather than himself.

b. Vocabulary building and language usage are greatly enhanced by the intimate association with a fine play which goes on during the period of rehearsals. Learning to appreciate the linguistic style, phrasing and choice of words of an outstanding playwright cannot help but influence the student's vocabulary and language habits.

4. Improvement in body movement and coordination.

a. The student's control of his body, gestures and posture, as well as his freedom from tensions, are fostered by the same factors which contribute to improved speech. The wearing of costumes has an almost magic effect in freeing the individual from self-consciousness and awkwardness.

b. Drama, particularly musical drama, offers the opportunity for disciplining the body in coordination, timing, integrating movement with speech, and rhythmic response.

5. Group and social values.

a. Play production satisfies the student's need for group identification and a sense of "belongingness." The most modest backstage assignment in shifting a prop or pulling a curtain contributes to the success of the performance and entitles the student to speak of "our show." The fact that dramatics absorbs and satisfies the emotions of a group makes it a potent weapon against juvenile delinquency.

b. Because play production is a team activity, it demands faithfulness at rehearsals, discipline, a sense of responsibility to the group, precision in performance, and the ability to work constructively with others toward a creative goal.

6. Discovering aptitudes and developing skills.

a. Avocational and recreational skills for use in later life have become more and more essential as the working day decreases. All of the skills of the theatre have leisure-time applications which may lead to satisfying association with community theatre groups — currently multiplying in this country — as well as church, civic and youth groups.

b. In every group of students there will be some with special talents which, if allowed to remain undeveloped, would be a waste of human resources. These students will need guidance and encouragement in planning their future careers.

Bernardine, University of Oregon.

Although the professional theatre, motion pictures and television can absorb but a tiny fraction of those qualified, there is a growing need for teachers of theatre, for directors, technical directors, designers, costumers and children's theatre specialists in community and recreational theatre. In addition to discover a new student with talent as a creative writer would entitle any teacher and any school to a justifiable sense of pride. (Vocational opportunities are treated in Chapter 13).

D. Additional values for the school itself.

If the educational theatre program accomplishes many or all of the foregoing goals, it will have more than justified itself in the curriculum. In addition to these values, however, administrators may have in mind the specific values of theatre in relation to the program of the school itself.

1. Public relations value.

Parents, alumni, and the community need to be aware of the activities and intellectual attainments of the school and its students. An effective theatre program can add immeasurably to the prestige of the school or college in the community. The theatre director or teacher should therefore welcome every opportunity to show the work of his students to parents and the public, not only through major productions but also by means of one-act plays, assembly programs, P. T. A. meetings and evenings of scenes.

2. Interdepartmental cooperation.

   The wise theatre director finds ways to involve other departments in play production activity, thereby broadening the base of student and audience support. Particularly at the high school level, teachers of English, foreign languages and history can assist in play selection, home economics teachers in costuming, industrial arts in scenery construction, art in scenery and poster design, business classes in script typing, publicity and ticket sales, music teachers in the production of operetta, and physical education in dance.

3. Fund-raising potential.

   Although the theatre, in contrast with many school activities, has the potential for raising revenue, the director in the educational theatre must guard against letting this objective take priority over the educational aims listed. All too often, moreover, the theatre facilities are the last to benefit from the funds raised. A well-run educational theatre program, however, need not be a drain on the school budget and can in many cases earn as much as half its production costs over a period of time (exclusive of facilities and staff salaries).

E. Maintaining a balance between academic and activity.

It is apparent that the goals listed cannot all be achieved if the drama director runs his program too permissively, limits his play selection to *The Valiant* and *The Clutching Claw,* fails to challenge his students with reading assignments which enrich their insights into the theatre and the play, or lets rehearsals consume a disproportionate part of the student's time.

Where twenty years ago a drama teacher might have emphasized those goals relating to personality development, the shift today has been made toward those goals which relate to academic growth, appreciation of literature and critical standards. It is interesting to note that the General Goals for Theatre Arts recommended in a recent *Bulletin of the National Association of Secondary-School Principals* are evenly divided between the goals derived from study and appreciation (Numbers 1, 2, 3) and those derived from participation (Numbers 4, 5, 6):

The primary goal of theatre arts in secondary schools is to provide all students with understandings so that they can make intelligent, aesthetic discriminations about all forms of theatre from TV Westerns to legitimate theatre production.

Each student, according to his abilities and interests, should have the opportunity to:

1. *Understand and evaluate the literary form of the play, the dance, or opera, the quality of acting, differences in the uses of speech, lighting and stage design, the staging and choreography, and the costume design.*
2. *Acquire a knowledge and appreciation of dramatic literature, including the skill of reading to visualize staging and acting.*
3. *Become aware of the influence of the theatre arts in his daily life and the influence of theatre as a social force, especially its help in understanding other national and cultural groups.*
4. *Experience a wide variety of theatre, including the best in classic and contemporary production in order to have a basis for making his own independent judgments.*
5. *Discover values derived from participation such as knowledge of avenues of expression, control and use of voice and body, stimulation of the imagination, the discipline of working creatively with others, and how to contribute to the aesthetic experience of others.*
6. *Discover how theatre experiences can help individuals develop and maintain emotional stability.*[7]

In an effort to gain academic respectability, however, the drama teacher must never forget that educational theatre is, above all, *theatre* in an educational framework, not education in a theatrical framework. The nature of the theatre demands that the production of a play be as skillfully staged, acted, designed and lighted as it is possible to make it within the resources of the producing group. A bad production of Shakespeare, a sloppily spoken production of Sheridan or wooden acting in an Ibsen play will not foster appreciation for these classic writers, and may even do education a disservice. When the term "academic theatre" is used, it is generally in a derogatory sense, synonymous with pedantry as a substitute for artistry. Casting a deserving but inept student in a major role in the name of educational growth is fair neither to the student nor to the audience which will pay to see him act. The drama director thus will find himself frequently treading the fine and delicate path between the seemingly contradictory demands of education and good theatre. If he knows his craft and loves the theatre, however, he can be the servant of these two masters simultaneously, as has been proven throughout the vast and vigorous educational theatre in this country.

---

[7]"The Arts in the Comprehensive Secondary School," *The Bulletin of the National Association of Secondary-School Principals*, Vol. 46, No. 275, Sept., 1962, pp. 8-9.

IV. Summary.

Many sound and desirable values which are in keeping with the philosophy of modern education may potentially be derived from play production in the educational theatre, justifying its inclusion in the curriculum of schools and colleges. The theatre arts offer a *total* experience involving intellectual, emotional, spiritual, and physical aspects which contribute to the personal and social development of the individual. All of these educational values accrue most strongly when the drama director is dedicated to producing classic and modern plays of acknowledged literary merit, and to producing them in the most effective manner of which he and his group are capable, bringing the play to life in a way that creates theatre magic. To achieve these goals, there are definite implications for play selection in the educational theatre, which will be analyzed in the next chapter.

A. The heritage of the educational theatre is ancient and honorable.
  1. The classic heritage.
  2. The Renaissance heritage.
  3. The American heritage.

B. Values to be derived from play production in schools and colleges.
  1. Values for both participants and audience.
  2. Additional values for the audience.
  3. Additional values for the participants.
  4. Additional values for the school itself.
  5. Maintaining a balance between academic and activity.

Suggested Reading

ALINGTON, A. F. *Drama and Education.* Oxford: Basel Blackwell, 1961.

"The Arts in the Comprehensive Secondary School." *Bulletin of the National Association of Secondary-School Principals*, 46, 275, Sept., 1962, pp. 1-19.

COGGIN, PHILIP A. *The Uses of Drama.* New York: George Braziller, Inc., 1956.

DAVIS, OLIVE B. "An Integrated Arts Program for the Gifted," *Educational Theatre Journal*, XV, 4, December, 1963, pp. 327-331.

HARTKE, GILBERT V. "Educational Theatre," *Educational Theatre Journal*, VIII, 1, March, 1956, pp. 39-45.

HEFFNER, HUBERT. "Theatre and Drama in Liberal Education," *Educational Theatre Journal*, XVI, 1, March, 1964, pp. 16-24.

HOBGOOD, BURNET M. "Theatre in U. S. Higher Education: Emerging Patterns and Problems," *Educational Theatre Journal*, XVI, 2, May, 1964, pp. 142-159.

HODGE, FRANCIS. "A Symposium on Aims and Objectives in Educational Theatre," *Educational Theatre Journal*, VI, 2, May, 1954, pp. 106-119.

MEARNS, HUGHES. *Creative Power.* New York: Dover Press, 1959.

MOTTER, CHARLOTTE KAY. "A Method of Integrating the High School Drama Program," *Educational Theatre Journal*, XII, 2, May, 1960, pp. 94-97.

————. "The Dramatic Arts, A Comprehensive Teaching Medium," *Educational Theatre Journal*, XIII, 4, December, 1961, pp. 269-273.

SIMOS, JACK. *Social Growth Through Play Production.* New York: Association Press, 1957.

TAUBMAN, HOWARD. "Arts on Campus." *New York Times,* X, November 18, 1962, p. 1.

TAYLOR, HAROLD. "Education by Theatre," *Educational Theatre Journal,* XV, 4, December, 1963, pp. 299-310.

WICKHAM, GLYNNE. *Drama in a World of Science.* Toronto: University of Toronto Press, 1962.

Chapter 2

PLAY SELECTION

I. Introduction.

The previous chapter indicated how critical is the problem of play selection if the educational theatre is to achieve its objectives. It is no less critical in the community theatre or professional theatre, where wrong choices may spell disaster. The drama director must therefore be widely read in dramatic literature, and must keep abreast of the field by reading new plays and rereading old ones. It is a wise practice never to select a play for production on the basis of having once read or seen it, but to read it afresh with the specific production in mind.

II. Criteria for play selection.

In order to maintain his perspective in the face of various pressures from segments of his audience with special tastes, actors with favorite roles, and the many practical limitations in production facilities, the director needs to keep in mind a well-defined set of criteria for play selection. These criteria can be divided into two main categories: those relating to the merits of the play itself and those relating to the practical problems of staging it.

A. The drama itself — is it a good play?
   This should be the overriding consideration in play selection. The director must be able to read a play and evaluate it on the basis of its literary and theatrical values, knowing that his nonprofessional

actors will look better if their vehicle is substantial. Even professional stars often fail to save a weak play; students should not be asked to do so.

It was Aristotle who first observed that there are six major elements by which a play can be evaluated: (1) plot or story, (2) characters, (3) theme, (4) language, (5) spectacle, and (6) melody or music. With the exception of music, which forms a category of its own in our theatre, Aristotle's ingredients can hardly be improved upon:

1. The plot or story.

   The author's story, and how interestingly he tells it, is the skeletal structure of the drama from which the other elements grow. A strong plot — as in melodrama or farce — may overcome weaknesses of characterization, language or theme, and a play without a strong plot — for example *The Cherry Orchard, The Member of the Wedding* — must rely heavily on characterization, theme and language as compensation. Some questions to consider in evaluating a plot include:

   a. Is the story sufficiently large in scope to absorb one, two, or three hours of the audience's time?

   b. Does the story grow believably and logically from its original premises?

   c. Does the action seem lifelike and well-motivated, or far-fetched and contrived by the hand of the author?

   d. Is there sufficient action and change of situation to engage, sustain and finally satisfy the audience's interest?

   e. Are there sufficient obstacles or complications placed between the protagonist and his desire or wants so that the audience can empathize or participate in his struggle?

   f. Are the individual episodes integrally related to the main story? Are they properly prepared for, do they "build" effectively to a climax and then move the story forward?

2. The characters.

   Many classic writers including Shakespeare freely re-used old plots; it was in the richness of the characterizations that their plays rose above their sources. The great dramas of every period survive because their characters are alive — even when their themes become dated (as with Ibsen). It is characterization too which attracts actors to want to play the roles, and which sustains them when their lack of experience or technique might show through in a one-dimensional character. In evaluating character, the factors which should be considered include:

   a. Are the characters recognizable and real — do we believe in them as people who might exist in life?

b. Are the characters interesting as people — colorful, contrasting, memorable, vital — in short, human? Do they have many facets or has the author oversimplified his observations of real people?

c. Do we feel that we know these people intimately by the time the play is over?

d. Is there at least one major character whom we like — with whom we can identify?

e. Is the motivation of the characters logical, convincing — based on a deep insight into human psychology? Does the author illuminate behavior or merely describe it?

3. The language.

Although poetry *per se* has largely disappeared from our realistic theatre, we still look to our best playwrights to use language that is emotionally charged, selected for its eloquence, memorable in organizing ideas more expressively than everyday speech. We remember Arthur Miller's "Attention, attention must be finally paid. . ." and the superbly tooled verbal gems of Oscar Wilde, Giraudoux and Anouilh. These questions regarding language will help distinguish worthwhile plays from potboilers:

a. Do the characters speak with heightened expressiveness?

b. Has the author captured the rhythm, color and even poetry of everyday speech?

c. Are there lines or passages that express ideas worth quoting — lines which make the audience say, "I wish I had said that."

d. Is the choice and arrangement of words fresh and unhackneyed, appropriate for the characters?

e. Will the language help the actors in characterization or stand in their way?

4. The theme or meaning.

What the play is "about," what the author is saying, is quite often the quality which attracts us to the play. We should beware, however, of plays which are weak in the three foregoing ingredients — plot, character and language — relying too heavily on the message, no matter how deeply felt by the author. The great plays dramatize their message, not merely state it. Suffusing the humanistic classics is a theme of the dignity of each individual's life and the value of struggle to overcome obstacles. Many of the murder mysteries so popular in high schools — including *Arsenic and Old Lace* — make light of death and may be questionable choices for this reason. A check list for evaluating the theme of a play might include:

    a. Has the author observed a segment of life with honesty and integrity, and reported his conclusions fairly?

    b. Does the play have something worthwhile to say?

    c. Does the play leave its audience with a sense of affirmation?

    d. Does the play treat human beings, including minority groups, with dignity and respect?

    e. Is the author's theme worth saying? Are there lasting values which would justify the time spent in producing it?

    f. Does the author's theme touch upon universal human experience? Is it true to life? Does he relate specific situations to a larger frame of reference? Does the theme enlarge our view or understanding of life?

5. Spectacle.

We can include here more than Aristotle could have envisioned, broadening his concept to include all those elements which make a play "good theatre."

    a. Will the play come alive on the stage so as to absorb the interest of an audience — will it "play"?

    b. Does the play take full advantage of the theatrical elements of scenery, costuming, lighting, make-up, and music for the aesthetic satisfactions which they can offer?

    c. Are there effective climaxes and curtain lines?

    d. In short, does the play have to be seen on the stage rather than read to be fully appreciated?

B. The practical problems of staging which affect play selection.

Assuming the play under consideration is a good play by most of the aforesaid criteria, there are a number of practical factors which may affect its choice for production. Essential as it is to consider these limiting factors, the director should not settle for a play which merely presents no production problems — it should also be a good play.

1. Is the play appropriate for its audience and participants?

Play selection, particularly at the high school level, is a sensitive and often delicate matter; the drama director should be aware of the potential problems and must share with his fellow educators the obligation to raise the tastes and appreciations of his audience gradually, to overcome intolerance and narrowness, and to foster a humanitarian outlook.

    a. The director must know his audience.

A play that would be acceptable in a sophisticated community could disturb a less urbane one. *Bernardine* or *The Happy Time* might present no problem to a high school in Beverly Hills, yet be a poor choice for a community ten miles away.

The Crucible

b. The director should have the courage of his convictions.
 Some administrators tend to be overly fearful of public relations in their schools. The drama director may need to plan a
 tactful, long-range campaign to convince his administrator
 that an innocuous but safe drama program is not entirely
 fulfilling the responsibilities of the educational theatre. Administrators should rely upon the good taste, judgment and
 integrity of the drama director and not attempt to censor
 or screen each play before it may be produced, nor should
 one crank letter be a cause for panic.

c. To enjoy this freedom from censorship, the director must accept the responsibility for self-censorship and mature judgment.

 (1) His aim must not be to shock, to be daring for its own
 sake, or to make a test case at the expense of his long-
 range objectives.

 (2) The playwright's intent should be a guiding consideration. *The Happy Time* is in keeping with an accepted
 precept of mental health — to give young people a
 sound and unsoiled understanding of sex; the intent of
 The Moon is Blue, on the other hand, seems to be
 merely to titillate.

(3) A controversial play should be defensible for its literary merits. A play that is studied in the English classes of a school presumably would be acceptable on the stage of the same school. The classroom, however, is an environment for reflective analysis and the stage is a public platform. The director should consider the over-all impact which the play might have upon students, parents, administrators and the community; he should educate his audience by easy stages rather than startling jumps. There may be times when his long-range dedication to fostering appreciation for the theatre must take priority over his personal preferences in play selection.

(4) The most troublesome areas in high school play selection are:

(a) Smoking.
(b) Drinking.
(c) Religion — advocating or criticizing any particular faith.
(d) Profanity.
(e) Relations between the sexes.

(5) The director of high school drama should decide whether some few deletions are justified. Certain actions and words often can be omitted without doing violence to the play. The drunken actress, for example, could be eliminated without harm from *You Can't Take It With You;* the drunk scene could not, however, be eliminated from *Come Back Little Sheba.* The martinis are not essential to the success of *Blithe Spirit,* but Simon Stimson needs to be intoxicated in *Our Town.* It is better not to do a particular play than to cut it to the point of destroying the author's intent.

d. Aside from the negative factor of not going too far ahead of community *mores*, the positive qualities which a play should have to make it appropriate for the high school include:

(1). Preponderance of action over static conversation.
(2). Roles that are within the intellectual and emotional range of young actors.
(3). Roles that present the cast an opportunity to grow in maturity.
(4). As many roles as possible so as to give opportunity to a number of students.

e. High school drama directors should not assume that the only way to keep from running afoul of one of the foregoing limitations is to confine themselves to a safe but vacuous list of "high school plays," trashy and trite. The National Thespian Society, which has done much to raise high school production standards, lists among those plays given the most high school productions during 1962-63 many of genuine literary merit: *Our Town, The Curious Savage, The Diary of Anne Frank, The Miracle Worker, I Remember Mama, Pygmalion, The Matchmaker, Teahouse of the August Moon, The Glass Menagerie, The Importance of Being Earnest, The Skin of Our Teeth, The Crucible, Antigone.*

2. Can the play be cast adequately?
   a. Is the distribution of male and female roles suitable for the group?
   b. Are there too many mature roles for a group of young actors?
   c. Does the play's success depend upon one major role's being brilliantly played?
   d. Do the roles present challenge to the actors?
3. Can the play's scenic requirements be handled?
   a. How many sets does the play require?
   b. How complete or realistically detailed must the sets be?
   c. What are the problems of scene shifts and off-stage storage?
   d. Are there sufficient man-hours available to construct the sets?
4. Is the available budget adequate for the play?
   Items which substantially affect the budget include:

   a. Scenery — where a large stock does not already exist.
   b. Costumes.
      (1) If the play is a period play, can the costumes be constructed, rented or taken from stock?
      (2) How large a cast will have to be costumed?
   c. Wigs (usually costly to rent).
   d. Properties.
      Certain drawing room plays require elegant furniture and trim props which may have to be rented or purchased.
   e. Publicity.
      Less well-known plays will require a more extensive publicity campaign than others in order to draw audiences.
   f. Royalty.
      The director must consider it his ethical and educational responsibility to pay the required royalty. There can be no justification for evading this requirement.
      (1) Royalty is rarely a burden and never the major percentage of the total budget. To seek out "Budget Plays" or "Ten-Dollar Plays" at the sacrifice of dramatic merit is a short-sighted policy.

Noah, New York production

(2) The director should write to the play-leasing company well in advance, stating the size of his auditorium and the price of his tickets. The play-leasing companies are usually cooperative in giving minimum royalty quotations where justified.

(3) A play may be copyrighted for 28 years and renewed for 28. If it is more than 56 years old it will be in the public domain and hence royalty-free. Translations, adaptations and musical versions may be copyrighted, however. The royalty for a good new translation of a classic may be almost as much as for a new play, but it is well worth the investment.

5. Is the play available?
Recent releases of Broadway successes play a large part in the programming of many community theatres. The director can never assume that he has the right to produce a play merely because it is listed in a catalogue. Plays are sometimes released to nonprofessionals in one part of the country and not in another. In other cases rights are withdrawn when the play is sold to motion pictures or made into a Broadway musical. It often takes months of correspondence to locate and obtain the permission of the copyright holder. The director *must always* obtain the

permission of the copyright holder or his agent before announcing the play, purchasing scripts or going into production.

6. Does the play fit in with the rest of the season?

    a. A well-balanced season should have variety, appeal to many different tastes, and draw upon the rich heritage of dramatic literature.

    b. A classic should be chosen, when possible, for its timeliness — for the pertinence of its theme or story to the needs and interests of contemporary audiences.

    c. The season should have a balance among serious and light plays, classics and modern drama, plays for the box office and plays for the aesthetic satisfaction of the discriminating.[1]

    d. Plays which make heavy demands upon the technical director or the costumer should be alternated with plays which are less demanding.

    e. Each generation of students should be exposed, during their three or four years in a school, to some of the enduring classics of dramatic literature. A theatre in a high school or college which lets students graduate without having seen Shakespeare, Molière, the Greeks or Ibsen can hardly claim the name of educational theatre.

    f. Play selection should take into account what has been performed recently by all of the theatres in the community.

7. Does the play, finally, appeal to the director, the actors, and the staff, exciting their imaginations and making them want to produce it?

III. Resources for play selection.

To build a season of plays which takes cognizance of the criteria given, the director should be aware of the resources upon which he may draw. He should first of all be familiar with the conventional classification of plays by type.

A. Types of plays.

Although elements of one type may be found in another — and generally are in modern drama — the types following are the most clearly distinguishable:

1. *Tragedy*: a serious work of some significance in which the hero strives to overcome formidable obstacles but in the end is overcome by them.

    Examples: *Hamlet, Winterset*

---

[1]The above criteria are intended for the educational theatre. The community theatre, semiprofessional and professional theatre necessarily place stronger emphasis upon the play's box office appeal. Most commercially successful producers discover, however, that in the long run audiences can be attracted profitably to plays that meet the above criteria of good drama.

2. *Comedy*: a humorous work in which the hero succeeds in overcoming his obstacles.

> Examples: *Twelfth Night, The Philadelphia Story*

   a. *High comedy* or *comedy of manners*: a work which generally draws its characters from the upper strata of society and depends for its humor upon verbal wit.

   > Examples: *The Rivals, The Importance of Being Earnest*

   b. *Low comedy* or *farce*: a work which depends less upon verbal wit than upon physical action, ludicrous situations and unexpected happenings.

   > Examples: *Charley's Aunt, Room Service*

3. *Drama*: a play which is basically serious but does not result in the death of the hero. Most modern plays fall in this category.

   > Examples: *The Glass Menagerie, Tea and Sympathy*

4. *Melodrama*: a serious play, usually with a happy ending, in which there is a maximum of physical action, suspense and overt conflict.

   > Examples: *Angel Street, The Desperate Hours*

5. *Satire*: a comedy involving social criticism and the holding up to ridicule of human foibles and absurdities of behavior.

   > Examples: *The Inspector General, No Time for Sergeants*

B. Categories from which to choose.
   1. Classics.
      a. Greek and Roman
      b. Medieval
      c. Shakespeare and Elizabethan
      d. Molière
      e. Restoration and eighteenth century
      f. Oriental
      g. nineteenth century European
      h. Early American
   2. Modern classics of Europe, including (but not limited to):
      a. Ibsen and Strindberg
      b. Bernard Shaw
      c. Wilde, Coward and English school
      d. Irish school
      e. Chekhov and Russian school
      f. Twentieth century continental writers
   3. The best of the modern American playwrights, including (but not limited to):
      a. Eugene O'Neill
      b. Philip Barry
      c. S. N. Behrman
      d. Paul Green

e. Maxwell Anderson
f. Sidney Howard
g. George Kelly
h. Clifford Odets
i. Lillian Hellman
j. Elmer Rice
k. Kaufman and Hart

l. Thornton Wilder
m. Robert Sherwood
n. William Saroyan
o. Sidney Kingsley
p. Arthur Miller
q. Tennessee Williams
r. William Inge

4. Recent Broadway successes.
5. Contemporary European plays of note.
6. Standard mysteries and comedies.
7. Plays for children.
8. Musicals.
9. One-act plays.
10. Original plays.

Whenever possible, new creative talent should be encouraged by the production of original plays by local or undiscovered writers. In many cases the material may compare favorably with the old-hat plays in the catalogues, and the group will have the satisfaction of staging a *première* and giving a new writer an opportunity to see his work come to life. In junior high school and high school, too, original assembly programs may grow out of creative dramatics to which the entire class contributes, as will be treated in the next chapter.

C. Play-leasing companies.

The director should be on the mailing list of the play-leasing companies so as to receive their latest catalogues, which are helpful

Death of a Salesman. Santa Monica City College, Calif.

in play selection. (See Appendix B for names and addresses of principal play-leasing companies.) Translations and acting versions of classics are often listed by several companies and should be compared before selecting the one to use.

D. Library resources.

1. To keep current, find out what other groups are doing, and draw upon the insights of dramatic criticism, a director should have access to:

   a. *Drama: The Quarterly Theatre Review.* British Drama League, 9 Fitzroy Square, London W1.

   b. *Dramatics Magazine,* published by National Thespian Society, College Hill Station, Cincinnati 24, Ohio. See also publications of The National Thespian Society including: Pearson, Talbot (Editor), *Directory of Three-Act Plays for High Schools.*

   c. *Educational Theatre Journal,* published by The American Educational Theatre Association. See also AETA publications available through executive office, Kennedy Center for the Performing Arts, 1701 Pennsylvania Ave., N.W., Washington, D.C.

      (1) "One Hundred Twenty Plays Recommended for Contest and Festival Use," *Educational Theatre Journal,* October, 1949.

      (2) "Director's Choice: 70 Long Plays for High School," *Educational Theatre Journal,* December, 1949.

      (3) "Director's Choice: 80 One-Act Plays for High School," *Educational Theatre Journal,* October, 1950.

   d. *New York Times,* Sunday Drama Section.

   e. *Players Magazine,* published by National Collegiate Players, Department of Speech and Drama, University of Kansas, Lawrence, Kansas.

   f. *Theatre Arts,* 104 E. 40th St., New York. (Contains a full-length play each month.

   g. *Drama Survey,* 800 Washington Ave. S.E., Minneapolis, Minn.

   h. *Modern Drama,* University of Kansas, Lawrence, Kansas.

   i. *World Premières,* published by the International Theatre Institute and distributed to members of the American National Theatre and Academy (ANTA).

   j. *World Theatre,* quarterly published by International Theatre Institute, and distributed by Theatre Arts Books, 333 Sixth Avenue, New York.

   k. *Tulane Drama Review,* Hill and Wang, 141 Fifth Avenue, New York.

2. To find summaries of plays and suggestions for possible production:

   a. *The Best Plays Series,* edited by Burns Mantle, then Louis Kronenberger, John Chapman and Henry Hewes. Dodd, Mead and Company. The 10 best plays of each Broadway season since 1919, with index covering 1899-1950.

   b. Cartmell, Van H., *Plot Outlines of 100 Famous Plays.* Garden City, New York: Doubleday, 1962.

   c. Lovell, John Jr., *Digest of Great American Plays.* New York: Thomas Y. Crowell Co., 1961.

   d. *New York Theatre Critics' Reviews,* 235 E. 22nd St., New York 10. Reviews by all New York critics of every Broadway opening since 1939. Index, 1940-1960.

   e. *New Play Service* of the American Educational Theatre Association, for original scripts.

   f. Plummer, Gail, *Dramatists' Guide to Selection of Plays and Musicals.* Dubuque: Wm. C. Brown Company Publishers, 1963.

   g. Shank, Theodore, *A Digest of 500 Plays.* New York: Crowell-Collier, 1963.

   h. Shipley, Joseph T., *Guide to Great Plays,* Washington, D. C.: Public Affairs Press, 1960.

3. To locate published full-length plays:
   (In addition to catalogues of play-leasing companies.)

   a. Briggs, Elizabeth, *Subject Index to Children's Plays.* Chicago: American Library Association, 1940.

   b. Drury, F. K. W., *Drury's Guide to Best Plays.* Washington, D. C.: Scarecrow Press, 1953.

   c. Firkins, Ina Ten Eyck, *Index to Plays*: 1800-1926. New York: H. W. Wilson Co., 1927.

   d. ...., *Supplement,* 1935.

   e. *Guide to Play Selection,* 2d Edition, published by the National Council of Teachers of English. New York: Appleton-Century-Crofts, 1958.

   f. Ottemiller, John H., *Index to Plays in Collections*: 1900-1956. Washington, D. C.: Scarecrow Press, 1957.

   g. *Reader's Guide to Periodical Literature,* indexes all plays published in *Theatre Arts* and *Plays.*

   h. Thomson, Ruth Gibbons, *Index to Full-Length Plays*: 1895-1925. Boston: F. W. Faxon and Co., 1956.

   i. ...., *Index to Full-length Plays,* 1926-1944. Boston: F. W. Faxon and Co., 1946.

   j. West, Dorothy, and Peake, Dorothy, *Play Index,* 1949-1952. New York: H. W. Wilson Company, 1953.

4. To locate published one-act plays:
   (In addition to catalogues of play-leasing companies.)
   a. Logasa, Hannah, and Ver Nooy, Winifred, *An Index to One-Act Plays,* 4 Vols., 1924-1948. Boston: F. W. Faxon Company.
   b. Mayorga, Margaret, *Best One-Act Plays.* Yearly volumes since 1937. New York: Dodd, Mead and Co.
   c. See list, Appendix B, of recommended one-act plays and anthologies.
   d. *Plays*: The Drama Magazine for Young People. High school and junior high school plays which are royalty-free to subscribers. Boston: Plays, Inc., 8 Arlington Street.

IV. Summary.

A. The criteria for play selection include the following considerations:
   1. The drama itself — is it a good play?
   2. The practical problems of staging.
B. Resources for play selection.
   1. Types of plays.
   2. Categories from which to choose.
   3. Play-leasing companies.
   4. Library resources.

EVALUATION FORM FOR PLAY SELECTION
(Use 5 x 8 card)

Name of play .... Student's name ....

Author .... Translator (if foreign play) ....

Type of play .... Style of play ....

Full-length ...... One-act .... Number of characters .... Men. ....Women.

Number of sets .... Int. .... Ext. Period of costumes.........................

Levels of theatre for which appropriate ....
                         (children, junior high, high school, college, community)

Play-leasing company .... Royalty ....

Production problems if any ....

....

Theme of play ....

....

Brief summary of plot (use this space and reverse side of card) ....

....

....

Suggested Reading

CORRIGAN, ROBERT W., AND ROSENBERG, JAMES L. *The Context and Craft of Drama.* San Francisco: Chandler Publishing Co., 1964.

HATLEN, THEODORE W., *Orientation to the Theatre.* New York: Appleton-Century-Crofts, 1962.

HEFFNER, HUBERT C., SELDEN, SAMUEL, AND SELLMAN, HUNTON D. *Modern Theatre Practice,* Fourth Edition. New York: Appleton-Century-Crofts, 1959. Chapters 2 and 4.

O'HARA, FRANK, AND BRO, MARGUERITTE. *Invitation to the Theatre.* New York: Harper and Brothers, 1951. Part. I.

LOVELL, JOHN JR. *Digest of Great American Plays.* New York: Thomas Y. Crowell Co., 1961.

PLUMMER, GAIL. *Dramatists' Guide to Selection of Plays and Musicals.* Dubuque: Wm. C. Brown Company Publishers, 1963.

ROWE, KENNETH THORPE. *A Theatre in Your Head.* New York: Funk and Wagnalls Co., 1960. Chapters 6-11.

SHANK, THEODORE J. *A Digest of 500 Plays.* New York: Crowell-Collier, 1963.

STAMBUSKY, ALAN A. "Continuing Trends in U. S. College and University Play Selection: 1962-1963," *Educational Theatre Journal,* XVI, 2, May, 1964.

"Summary of the 1962-63 Thespian Season," National Thespian Society. Cincinnati: College Hill Station.

WRIGHT, EDWARD A. *A Primer for Playgoers.* Englewood Cliffs, N. J.: Prentice-Hall, Inc., 1958. Chapter 3.

Chapter **3**

BACKGROUND FOR THE
DIRECTOR AND ACTOR—
IMPROVISATION

I. Introduction.

Before proceeding to a study of the techniques for staging the formal play, it would be valuable for the neophyte director as well as actor to have experience in another form of theatre art which not only provides a sound foundation on which to build the mechanics of play direction but has invaluable applications in itself for actor training and high school drama classes — the improvisation.

Improvisation has been known to actors at least since the *commedia dell'arte* of the sixteenth century and was probably used by the comic mimes of ancient Greece; it was revived by Stanislavski in an attempt to restore naturalness and fresh responsiveness in an era of stereotyped acting. The improvisation is closer to life than the rehearsed play, retaining the spontaneity and unrehearsed quality which the director of a formal play often must go to considerable pains to recapture. The study of direction therefore most logically begins with a creative approach to the raw material of the theatre — which is life; to study technical rules before the student has learned to bring life to the stage simply and truthfully would be to put the theatrical cart before the horse.

II. The Purposes of Improvisation.

A. As a bridge to the mechanics of direction.

The improvisational method teaches the director and actor to analyze and play the inner dynamics of a situation as though they

31

were in life rather than on the stage — an essential stepping stone to an understanding of play interpretation as treated in Chapter 4. After becoming comfortable in improvisation, the director will be able to assimilate the techniques of formal direction without losing sight of the essence of the improvisation — its naturalness and spontaneity. Ultimately the director will find ways to synthesize the two seemingly contradictory approaches, creative and technical, in his own working method.

B. As creative dramatics and sociodrama.

In recent times improvisation has been adapted with only minor modification as creative dramatics for children.[1] It has found wide acceptance among educators in a variety of classroom uses from kindergarten to junior high school, in recreation and religious education. When the purpose of the improvisation is social problem-solving rather than a purely theatrical experience, it has been called sociodrama or role-playing, and has proved useful in a variety of forms from salesmanship training and industrial relations to teen-age problems, interrace relations and group therapy.[2] For junior and senior high school youth, improvisations offer an excellent means of giving a larger number of students an experience in acting within the classroom without subjecting them to a competitive tryout, an extended rehearsal period and a critical audience. The techniques are applicable in English, social studies and foreign language classes as well as speech and drama.

C. As an aid in actor training and rehearsal.

With more mature students from college acting classes to the famous Actors' Studio of New York, this method of improvisation (also called *étude* by some of Stanislavski's translators) remains a valuable technique in actor training, a useful approach to staging a play if time permits, and a unique means of opening up the inner psychological life of a scene. This chapter will indicate some ways of using improvisation for these purposes. In the hands of a master of inventiveness like Stanislavski, the improvisation produced such brilliant results in final production as those described

---

[1]The reader interested in creative dramatics for children is referred to: Burger, Isabel, *Creative Play Acting*. New York: A. S. Barnes, 1950; Fitzgerald, Burdette S., *Let's Act the Story*. San Francisco: Fearon Publishers, 1957; Siks, Geraldine, *Creative Dramatics*. New York: Harper and Brothers, 1958; Siks, Geraldine Brain and Dunnington, Hazel Brain, *Children's Theatre and Creative Dramatics*. Seattle: University of Washington Press, 1961; Ward, Winifred, *Playmaking With Children*. New York: Appleton-Century-Crofts, 1957; and Kase, C. Robert (Editor), *Stories for Creative Acting*. New York: Samuel French, Inc., 1964.

[2]The reader interested in sociodrama is referred to: Haas, Robert B. (Editor), *Psychodrama and Sociodrama in American Education*. New York: Beacon House, 1949; Moreno, J. L., *Psychodrama*. New York: Beacon House, 1946; Shaftel, George and Fanny, *Role-Playing the Problem Story*. New York: National Conference of Christians and Jews, 1954; Shellhammer, Lois B., "Solving Personal Problems Through Socio-Drama." *English Journal*, 38:503-5, November, 1949.

by Gorchakov.[3] Most important of all, however, one need not be a Stanislavski; anyone can improvise — children do it by the hour.

III. How to use improvisations.

A. Definition of improvisation.

An improvisation is a short scene in which the actors speak and act as they feel, without relying upon previously written dialogue. There may be a simple plot synopsis, but the rest is spontaneous and unrehearsed. It is not performed for an audience; hence it is player-centered. There is no one right or wrong way to play a given improvisation — the objective is to evoke truthful actions and reactions from the players.

B. How to work with actors in improvisation.

1. Warm-up period.

Improvisations cannot begin "cold" but need a period in which the actors talk about what they are going to do and begin to get involved in the situation.

   a. Planning the action.

With inexperienced actors, it is wise to begin with the simplest situations; those involving eating are particularly useful because of their opportunities to use "sense memory." The entire class may choose to go on a picnic, a beach party or a birthday party. In such familiar situations the actors need a minimum of structure; each student should suggest what food he wants to bring — knowing what to bring in an improvisation gives the actor security just as knowing in a scene what inner action to bring gives confidence. In more complex story situations, however, it is important to list on the blackboard the sequence of actions; this should be reviewed after the scene is cast so that each actor will be clear as to what he has to do and when he does it. This technique will be further analyzed under C on page 35.

   b. Casting the improvisation.

(1) At first it is better for students to play roles near to their own age rather than character parts. (This is the reverse of the approach used in creative dramatics with children, who find no difficulty in imagining themselves princes, magicians or wicked stepmothers, whereas more sophisticated actors tend to resort to clichés and artificialities if thrust into character parts too early. In addition some stereotypes that might be acceptable for children lack the sense of truth which is the goal of adult improvisation.)

---

[3]Gorchakov, Nikolai M., *Stanislavsky Directs*. New York: Funk and Wagnalls, 1954.

(2) Reticent students should not be cast in improvisations against their will, but should, if possible, be motivated and made to feel sufficiently secure so that they will volunteer, however hesitantly.

(3) As public performance for an audience is not the purpose of improvisation, what has been called "therapeutic casting" can sometimes be used with good results. The teacher has no reason not to cast a student in the first role for which he volunteers (however unsuited to it he might actually be), although he must guard against the most extroverted students monopolizing the best roles in every improvisation. Often by means of suggestion the teacher can get a student to undertake a role which would be beneficial to his personal development.

c. Planning the setting.

A simple but clear arrangement of the physical setting should be made so that all actors will know where imaginary doors, windows and properties are, and what the rehearsal furniture represents. One of the class may serve as stage manager and set the stage, showing the rest how it is arranged, or the actors in the scene may set their own stage.

2. Playing the improvisation.

The alert teacher will sense when the group is sufficiently warmed up and aware of the situation to play it. Some teachers have followed the practice of giving the actors five minutes backstage to plan the scene, but this seems inadvisable because planned effects are not desired. The warm-up period should culminate naturally in the teacher's saying, "Are we ready? Then let's play it. Curtain." During the playing the teacher or director should:

a. Sit unobtrusively and watch. (In an early improvisation, such as the picnic, he may take part as an actor, but he should gradually ease himself out of performances.)

b. Avoid catching the eye of any actor who looks out at him.

c. Not interrupt for any reason.

d. Bring the "curtain" down before the actors run out of ideas and the scene goes dead.

3. Evaluating the improvisation.

a. As important as the playing is the evaluation period, for it is here that standards are set which influence the actor's future development. Things to discuss during the evaluation (with praise as much as possible rather than negative criticism) include:

        (1) Did we follow our plot synopsis?
        (2) Did we stay in character?
        (3) Did we play the actions truthfully and naturally?
        (4) Did we believe in what we were doing?
        (5) Did we use fully the setting and physical environment?
        (6) Did we listen to each other and respond to our partners?

    b. These standards will discourage breaking out of character, looking out at the director, breaking up each other, and doing stereotyped reactions, all of which should tend to disappear as the group gains confidence and experience in improvisation.

    c. The evaluation should at first be conducted by the teacher or director. Students are often more severely critical of each other than the director would be. As standards of evaluation are set, the teacher can gradually rely more on student comment.

C. How to analyze the action in an improvisation.

    1. Reviewing the story or plot of the scene to be improvised.
This step utilizes a technique which will carry over into analysis of scenes in plays. Here is a simple situation which has been successfully improvised by a beginning acting class in college:

> "Four students are rooming together, and it is the first of the month when the rent is due. Three of the boys have their money ready when the landlady comes, but the fourth boy is not home. They persuade the landlady to come back later, and then they discuss what to do about the fourth boy, who has been late before with his rent money. When he walks in they ask him for his share of the rent, but he is unable to pay. He explains why and asks for an extension. The boys won't agree to pay his share, and decide to take decisive action."

    2. Breaking the situation into its components.

    a. It can be seen that the foregoing situation can be divided chronologically into several sub-scenes or *beats*. These should be listed on the blackboard by the teacher, asking, "What happens first?" "What happens next?" "What is — doing at this point?" The "doing" refers to inner psychological action as well as overt physical action.

    b. A structure something like the following may result for the scene described, which contains *ten beats*:
        (1) The boys want to study for an important test.
        (2) The landlady comes to collect the rent.
        (3) The boys try to stall her off as they haven't all the money.

(4) The landlady agrees to come back later.

(5) The boys try to figure out what to do.

(6) The boys agree that the fourth boy will have to pay now or move out.

(7) Fourth boy arrives to change his clothes for a date.

(8) The others confront him with their ultimatum.

(9) He tries to explain his momentary shortage of funds (the actual reason made up by the actor playing the role).

(10) The boys reject his appeal for an extension and take decisive action (as evolved by the actors themselves).

3. Identifying the beats and actions.

   a. The foregoing story has been divided into a rudimentary plot sequence consisting of ten different events. Each of these little events or developments in the plot is called (in the Stanislavski system) a *beat*. Beats are the smallest subdivision into which the plot can be broken; each beat is a little action done by one or more of the players. (This definition should not be confused with the use of the term "beat" in music, as there is no connection). In *An Actor Prepares,* Stanislavski's translator used the term *Unit* in the sense that *beat* is used here.[4]

   b. A beat is always indicated in terms of a *verb*.
      Note that each of the ten beats in the situation above contains a verb which tells what happens — "comes to collect," "try to stall," "confront," "reject," etc. Verbs convey action; actors can act verbs. Actors cannot play adjectives, which describe qualities; the director should not tell an actor to be "jealous" but should suggest a verb which is an action a jealous person would do.

   c. One character usually dominates each beat. It is "his beat" and the verb expresses his desire or will (although sometimes two or more characters play a beat together). The others in the scene also play beats in terms of verbs, although these generally do not need to be written on the blackboard — it is sufficient that the actor know them or invent them as he improvises. They may include actively furthering the main beat, passively listening, wondering how he can get control of the situation or actively opposing the main beat.

   d. An *action* is a unified group of beats relating to one main verb. It is the character's main *objective* in the scene. The landlady in the illustration *wants her rent money;* that is her

---

[4]Stanislavski, Constantin, *An Actor Prepares* (New York: Theatre Arts Books, 1936), Chapter 7.

action or objective. She furthers her action by several beats. The boys' action is to solve the rent problem and get back to their studies. The fourth boy's action is to do something else with his money. Thus each character has one main action in a scene, composed of several successive beats. The term *objective* as used in *An Actor Prepares* is synonymous with *action* as used here.

D. Suggested situations for improvisation.[5]

1. "Some girls who room together have agreed to devote a whole day to cleaning their apartment and rearranging their closet. After they have started, a boy arrives to call for one of the girls. The others accuse her of accepting a date in order to get out of the cleaning chore. They persuade the boy to stay and help them clean, and one of the other girls proceeds to flirt with him."

2. "A mother and father are waiting up at night for their daughter, who is out very late. The father checks with the police, but the mother tries to keep him from getting alarmed. The daughter finally arrives with her date and explains where they have been. The parents decide what action to take." (Where the solution to an improvisation is left unplanned, it forces the actors to listen and think while playing the scene, taking advantage of some of the elements of sociodrama, which invites the participants to discover the most workable solution to problems for themselves.)

3. "A boy tries to persuade his father to let him use the car that night. The father refuses because the boy hasn't washed the car as he promised to do. The mother intercedes on her son's behalf, and the father scolds her for being too lenient with him. While the argument is in progress, the younger sister offers to help the boy do a quick washing job and they hurry out to get it done."

4. "The youngest daughter of a family loves to enter contests. She has received a telegram to be by her telephone tonight at 9 P.M. for a phone call from New York. She is sure that she has won a contest offering a free trip to Hawaii. She can't wait for the telephone call, and begins to take out suitcases and start packing. Her mother tries to persuade her not to count her chickens, and her father doesn't want to let her go alone even if she wins. When the call comes, she learns she has won fifteenth prize, a year's supply of soap."

[5]For a variety of other situations for improvisation, see Rosenstein, Sophie, Haydon, Larrae A., and Sparrow, Wilbur, *Modern Acting, A Manual.* New York: Samuel French, 1947.

IV. Justification and a sense of truth.

A. Justification.

The actor must learn to *justify* or find a motivation for whatever is given him by playwright or director. After the group has become proficient in improvisation, exercises in justification may be given as a preparation for work on formal scenes. A facility in justification and a fantasy that can readily invent reasonable motivations are highly desirable qualities in an actor.

1. As an exercise in justification, the class should form a circle around the teacher, who asks the students to do whatever he tells them. Simple physical actions are given:[6]
   a. Raising the hands over the head
   b. Standing on one foot
   c. Bending over
   d. Putting hands behind back
2. As the class does each of the foregoing, the teacher says, "Now *justify* what you are doing." Each student must invent a reason for his action and tell the class his justification. Attention should be called to the number of different ways of justifying a given action which can be invented.
3. More important, it should be called to the group's attention that as each student finds a reason or justification for what he is doing, he immediately changes the *way* he performs the action, making it more natural, truthful, less stiff and mechanical. This process of justification goes on throughout the rehearsal of a play, and actors must justify (in terms of their character) the lines of the author and the blocking of the director. The actor should learn to ask himself "Why?" and to find answers within his character.

B. A sense of truth.

Improvisations and exercises in justification have as their goal to foster in the actor a *sense of truth*. The drama teacher who is able to achieve this during class improvisations will find his task much easier in rehearsing a play. Stanislavski defined a sense of truth as follows:

> *Truth on the stage is whatever we can believe*
> *in with sincerity, whether in ourselves or in*
> *our colleagues.*[7]

1. Believing in the make-believe.
   The director should make the world of the improvisation as real as possible for his cast. He should avoid such terms as "supposed

---

[6]See I. Rapoport, "The Work of the Actor," in Toby Cole (Editor), *Acting: A Handbook of The Stanislavski Method* (New York: Lear, 1947), p. 41.
[7]Stanislavski, *op. cit.*, p. 122.

to be" or "pretend" in favor of "it is." He should address the actors in rehearsal by their characters' names rather than their own.

2. Concentration.

   Becoming absorbed in the improvisation or scene is the only sure way to achieve a sense of truth and free the actor from self-consciousness and stage fright. The actor must black out his awareness of audience, director, stage itself, and live in the make-believe world, knowing and using the given circumstances of the improvisation.

3. The *whole cast* contributes to concentration. The surest way to lose one's concentration is to look into the face of a partner and find giggles, smiles or smirks of disbelief. Each actor helps his partner into a sense of truth; to break a partner's concentration is therefore a serious breach of theatre discipline. Actors need the interinfluence of the other members of the cast which leads the whole group toward the inner truth from which strong emotion can flow.

4. Relaxation.

   A prerequisite to achieving a sense of truth, relaxation can be accomplished more readily by becoming absorbed in performing a simple action or by concentrating upon an object than it can by trying to "relax," which is a self-conscious activity. The actor should learn, however, to recognize when there is unnecessary tension in his body, and to use only the amount of tension normally required to perform the action.

5. Exercises to heighten the actor's sense of truth should include work in these four areas:

   a. Sense memory.

      Performing simple actions involving the five senses with the use of only imaginary properties:

      (1) Taste — a juicy steak, castor oil.
      (2) Hearing — screech of brakes, a favorite song.
      (3) Touch — a cat's fur, an unshaven beard.
      (4) Smell — escaping gas, gardenias.
      (5) Sight — a fertile valley, a friend's face.

   b. Weathers and pains.

      Recalling and building simple improvisations around:

      (1) Waiting for a bus in the pouring rain.
      (2) The hottest you have ever been.
      (3) The coldest you have ever been.
      (4) The worst pain you have ever had.
      (5) A trip to the dentist's office.

    c. Kinesthetic activities.
      (1) Play ping-pong with an imaginary ball.
      (2) Shine a pair of shoes.
      (3) Make a bed.
      (4) Put on a nail polish.
      (5) Change a tire.
    d. Emotion memory.
      Strong emotion cannot be reawakened by the actor at will. He can evoke emotions, however, by recalling the sensory impressions associated with a particularly strong emotion. The actor should not be asked to tell how happy or sad he felt, but rather to describe what he saw, heard, smelled, tasted, touched at the time. The happiness or sadness will return of its own accord.

6. Changed circumstances.

    The actor must learn *adjustment* and the ability to respond to changed circumstances without premeditation, as in real life. The outcome and all the cues are known ahead of time in a rehearsed play; it is therefore a valuable exercise for actors to improvise scenes in which one of the characters is privately given a changed beat or circumstances unknown to the rest of the cast, thereby forcing the actors to listen, to respond and to adjust normally to stimuli.

7. Characterization.

    As actors grow secure in improvisation and able to achieve concentration and truthfulness in the foregoing exercises, they are ready to introduce the element of characterization, playing someone quite unlike themselves in improvisations and yet working to *justify* the new characteristics from within. Observation of people should provide the primary source material; some specific areas for observation and analysis of characters are suggested in Chapter 8, which should be used in connection with improvisations for characterization. To heighten the actor's powers of observation and creation of character, exercises can be given in building a character around:

    a. A walk.
    b. A voice.
    c. A gesture.
    d. A painting.
    e. An animal (extracting the characteristic that most suggests a human quality upon which to build a character).

V. **Using improvisations in rehearsal.**

    A. As a rehearsal technique in the staging of a play (particularly useful for high school actors).

1. To get to the inner life of a scene before the author's lines and cues are memorized. The scene should be structured just as in the author's script, listing on the blackboard the sequence of beats which answer the question, "What is .... doing at this point?" The scene may be improvised several times, trying variations of the beats until the most effective ones are found. It should then be easier to stage the play formally with the author's words, retaining the spontaneity and "illusion of the first time."

2. To help the actor get into character.

   As an aid in identifying fully with his character, the actor might play his character in an improvised situation not written in the play: Hamlet as a carefree student at Wittenberg University, Blanche DuBois as the young wife before her husband's suicide, Anne Frank as a schoolgirl before she went into hiding.

3. To visualize "offstage beats," the scenes described by the playwright but which take place offstage. Some scenes which might profitably be improvised as a means of helping the actors respond more fully to the succeeding scenes are:

   a. Amanda's shocking experience at the business college which she thought her daughter was attending (*The Glass Menagerie*).

   b. The day the cracked airplane cylinders are discovered at the factory (*All My Sons*).

   c. Romeo's unsuccessful efforts to woo Rosaline (*Romeo and Juliet*).

   d. Biff's interview with the man from whom he hopes to get a loan and from whom he steals a fountain pen (*Death of a Salesman*).

B. As a means of creating an informal drama for a PTA meeting, assembly or holiday program without using a written script.

1. Some junior high and high school teachers have successfully used this method of letting the class create the program. To avoid prolonged discussion and confusion, a plan such as the following is suggested for building a scene or program improvisationally:

   a. The teacher leads the class discussion to obtain agreement on the over-all theme and story-line of the program, whether original or derived from literature.

   b. An individual or a committee is delegated to work out the sequence of beats and actions in detail.

   c. The cast improvises the plot as structured, enriching and refining the episodes spontaneously.

   d. The class evaluates the results and suggests additions or modifications.

     e. The same cast (or new actors) replay the scene, trying out the suggestions, followed by further evaluation.

     f. Students are assigned to write down the more important lines and cues.

     g. The actors attempt to do the scene the same way each time, so that ultimately some rough blocking can be added and polishing rehearsals conducted as though it had begun with a written text.

  2. To use this method well, however, may take longer than to begin with a written script, and the results will never be as satisfying as when a skilled author supplies the expressive language, characters, situations and structure which, as was seen in the previous chapter, are important factors in selecting a play for public performance.

VI. Retaining the life of an improvisation in formal drama.

  A. It is apparent that an improvisation is not a play *per se,* and could not in its improvisational form be shown to an audience. It is precisely the introduction of the element of the *audience* which makes the difference between informal and formal drama. When creative dramatics or improvisation is done in the classroom it is player-centered and benefits the performers. When an audience is added, a new objective is coupled with the benefits to the participants — communication with spectators. A new pressure is injected — to make the performance as effective as possible within the capabilities of the group. There is a place and a need for both forms in educational dramatics — the pressure-free improvisational experience in the classroom and the deliberately designed pressure of preparing for opening night. The rest of this book is devoted largely to the latter, but the teacher-director should not lose sight of the unique values which each form has to contribute.

  B. Some of the principal differences between an improvisation or creative dramatics and formal drama produced for an audience include the following:

IMPROVISATION	FORMAL DRAMA
1. Several actors may talk at once.	1. Generally one person speaks at a time.
2. Actors need not worry about where they turn their backs.	2. Actors should be seen by the audience as much as possible.
3. Actors may not always be audible.	3. Actors must be heard throughout the auditorium.
4. The effectivenes of an improvisation can never be guaranteed.	4. The director must be able to show the audience the best possible results.

5. The action may be repetitious and wander from the plot.
6. There is no assurance that a life-like scene will also be interesting.
7. The use of the areas of the stage may be uninteresting or monotonous.
8. It would be impossible to light the actors well if they moved spontaneously.
9. The first way of doing an action which occurs to the actor is not necessarily the most dramatic or effective.
10. In casting, every one can participate and roles can be distributed for the benefit of each individual.

5. The author should have eliminated repetitions and digressions.
6. It is the author's task to find interest in his material.
7. The director must compose interesting and varied stage pictures.
8. The careful plotting of position makes possible effective lighting.
9. Through trial and error, the most telling way of playing a scene must be found in rehearsal.
10. In casting, individuals must be given roles commensurate with ability, experience, and suitability, with the largest roles going to the most talented.

C. It can thus be seen that the differences between the lifelike but random form of the improvisation and the set pattern of the formal drama are precisely what make necessary the professions of the playwright and the director.

1. Having experienced improvisations, the student director will be in a better position to appreciate why he must study techniques for arranging the formless into form, for converting the accidental into the calculated. While attempting to retain the naturalness and unpremeditated quality of the improvisation, he must mould the actors into a set pattern which they can repeat at every performance with maximum effectiveness.
2. The breakdown of the improvisation into a series of beats and actions, each identified by a verb, will materially aid the student in making the transition to the director's analysis and interpretation of the play itself, which will be found to be a series of beats and actions artfully woven together by the playwright. This concept will be treated in Chapter 4.

VII. Summary.

The improvisation is a valuable technique for the teaching of acting, in rehearsing a play, and as an insight into the creative life of a scene. Although not in itself a play, the improvisation contains elements that the director must retain or recapture in formal staging.

A. The purposes of improvisation.
   1. As a bridge to the mechanics of direction.
   2. As creative dramatics and sociodrama.
   3. As an aid in actor-training and rehearsal.
B. How to use improvisations.
   1 Definition of improvisation.
   2. How to work with actors in improvisation.
   3. How to analyze the action in an improvisation.
   4. Suggested situations for improvisation.
C. Justification and a sense of truth.
   1. Justification.
   2. A sense of truth.
D. Using improvisations in rehearsal.
   1. As a rehearsal technique in the staging of a play.
   2. As a means of creating an informal drama without a written script.
E. Retaining the life of an improvisation in formal drama.
   1. Changing values when an audience is introduced.
   2. Differences between an improvisation and a play.
   3. Making the transition to formal drama.

Suggested Reading

BOLESLAVSKY, RICHARD. *Acting*: *The First Six Lessons*. New York: Theatre Arts Inc., 1933.

COLE, TOBY (Editor). *Acting*: *A Handbook of the Stanislavski Method*. New York: Lear Publishers, 1947.

GORCHAKOV, NIKOLAI M. *Stanislavsky Directs*. New York: Funk and Wagnalls, 1954.

McGAW, CHARLES. *Acting is Believing*. New York: Rinehart and Company, 1955.

MOORE, SONIA. *The Stanislavski Method*. New York: The Viking Press, 1960.

NEWTON, ROBERT. *Exercises in Improvisation*. Chicago: Coach House Press, 1961.

ROSENSTEIN, SOPHIE, HAYDON, LARRAE, AND SPARROW, WILBUR. *Modern Acting*: *A Manual*. New York: Samuel French, 1947.

SPOLIN, VIOLA. *Improvisation for the Theatre*. Evanston, Ill.: Northwestern University Press, 1963.

STANISLAVSKI, CONSTANTIN. *An Actor Prepares*. New York: Theatre Arts, Inc., 1936.

STRASBERG, LEE. "Acting and the Training of the Actor," in *Producing the Play*, John Gassner, (Editor). New York: Dryden Press, 1953.

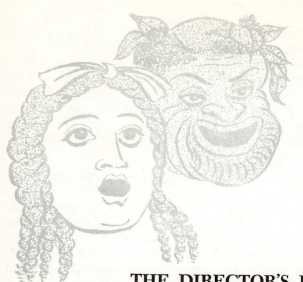

Chapter 4

THE DIRECTOR'S INTERPRETATION
OF THE PLAY

I. Introduction.

Before the director can begin his work with the cast (or even choose a cast intelligently) he needs to evolve and crystallize in his mind an interpretation of the play. This interpretative study may take a week for a light comedy or a year for a classic. A student who does not find this phase of theatre art rewarding and stimulating should go no further in his plan to become a director.

The two basic processes which go on during the director's interpretative study of a play are: (1) to determine what the play means, and (2) to find a form in which to project this meaning to the audience. To accomplish these two aims, the director will need to reread the play many times, each with a different purpose.

II. Determining what the play means.

This is a much more complex process than may at first be apparent. It includes discovering the theme of the play, studying what critics have written about the play, re-creating the background of the play through research, analyzing the characters and their motives, dividing the play into actions and beats, crystallizing the particular emphasis the director wishes to give the production, and preparing the text for production on the basis of this interpretation.

45

A. Discovering the theme or meaning of the play.
1. From what is stated explicitly in the play itself.

Some playwrights are fairly specific as to the meaning of their plays, or at least provide strong clues which the director may take as a significant statement of meaning. Others are less apparent, and the director may have to search for hints, phrases, images, symbols, and key speeches which suggest meaning. Some of the following lines may be revealing in the director's search for meaning.

a. "He had the wrong dreams. All, all wrong. . . He never knew who he was." *Death of a Salesman.*
b. "This is the glory of earth-born men and women, not to cringe, never to yield, but standing, take defeat implacable and defiant, die unsubmitting. . ." *Winterset.*
c. "Greed, Hannah, Greed." *The Late Christopher Bean.*
d. "I love them, Tony. . . I love them deeply. Some people could break away, but I couldn't. I know they do rather strange

Death of a Salesman. New York production

things... But they're gay and they're fun and... I don't know... there's a kind of nobility about them." *You Can't Take It With You.*

2. From what is shown implicitly through the action of the character.

   a. In *The Cherry Orchard*, the characters are emotional, generous, impulsive, but never take positive action to save themselves.

   b. In *The Time of Your Life*, the good people find that there are times when they must rise up and put a stop to evil by whatever means they can.

   c. In *The Crucible* a community is caught by hysteria when its individuals are frustrated and thwarted in their various personal needs.

3. From what the playwright has written elsewhere that may help illuminate the play. For example:

   a. Shaw's lengthy prefaces are unique in dramatic literature for the light they shed upon his plays.

   b. Eugene O'Neill kept a diary while he was at work on *Mourning Becomes Electra* in which he states his purpose in the play: "... to get modern psychological approximation of Greek sense of fate... which an intelligent audience of today, possessed of no belief in gods or supernatural retribution, could accept or be moved by."[1]

   c. A full understanding of Blanche in *Streetcar Named Desire* requires a study of Alma in *Summer and Smoke,* for the two characters suggest the same repressed Southern lady at different stages of her life.

   d. William Inge has written about *Picnic*: "I was fascinated to find out how... the women seemed to have created a world of their own, a world in which they seemed to be pretending men did not exist. It was a world that had to be destroyed, at least for dramatic values."[2]

B. Studying what critics have written about the play and the author.

   1. Before staging a classic or an important modern drama, the director should steep himself in the dramatic criticism of the play. Although literary analysis and theatrical interpretation are not synonymous, the director's insights can be deepened by his study of dramatic criticism; conflicting critical viewpoints can

---

[1]Quoted in Clark, Barrett H., *European Theories of the Drama* (New York: Crown Publishers, 1947), p. 530.

[2]Inge, William, "Picnic from 'Front Porch' to Broadway," *Theatre Arts*, XXXVIII, 4, April, 1954, p. 33.

help bring his own interpretation into focus, and he may discover values in the text which he had overlooked.

2. In the case of Shakespeare an imposing bibliography (see Ebisch and Schuecking, *A Shakespearean Bibliography*, 1931) need not cause the director to shy away. A good reading list might begin with:

   a. A. C. Bradley, *Shakespearean Tragedy*.
   b. H. C. Granville-Barker, *Prefaces to Shakespeare*.
   c. Howard Furness, *The New Variorum Edition of Shakespeare*. (Several now in paperback, Dover Publications.)
   d. E. K. Chambers, *Shakespeare: A Survey*. A Drama book.
   e. Webster, Margaret, *Shakespeare Without Tears*. A Premier paperback.

3. For other playwrights, the *Reader's Guide to Periodical Literature,* the *International Index* and the *New York Times Index* will lead the director to useful critical material. For plays staged in New York since 1939, the *New York Theatre Critics' Reviews* provides the most complete critical summary, but the director should also consult the published work of the leading dramatic critics such as Brooks Atkinson, John Mason Brown and John Gassner. Knowing the critical response to a play may help the director to tighten weak acts, eliminate obsolete references, clarify ambiguities, and anticipate the reactions of his own audience.

C. Re-creating the background of the play through research.

1. Whenever the play is set in any period or environment other than the one in which the director has lived, considerable research will be necessary by the director so he can steep himself in the period and locale. This phase can be one of the most absorbing for the director, and he may make assignments to his cast so that they can share in the research and become familiar with the background of the play. Among the questions that may need to be answered are these:

   a. Who are the people the playwright describes?
   b. Where do they live — in what kind of houses and towns?
   c. What do they do for a livelihood?
   d. How do they dress?
   e. Because of occupation and dress, how do they move and gesture?
   f. What do they eat and drink, and how are they served?
   g. How are their names pronounced?
   h. What is known about their special institutions treated in the play — courts, hospitals, armies, churches?

    i. What else should the director and actors know about them in order to understand the author's play fully?

2. Sources for this particular kind of research.

    a. Talking with people of the same background — Welshmen in the community for *The Corn is Green,* the Oriental community for *Teahouse of the August Moon,* Pennsylvania Dutch for *Papa is All,* police officers for *Detective Story.* Often someone contacted in this way will be willing to serve as "research consultant" for the production and even to lend properties.

    b. Visiting actual locations if practical — the French quarter of New Orleans for *Streetcar Named Desire,* a waterfront for *Anna Christie,* a small Southern town for *Inherit the Wind.*

Inherit the Wind. Manual Arts High School, Los Angeles.

    c. Reading history, biography, manners, customs, and fiction written during or about the period. In preparing *The Crucible,* for example, the director might find it helpful to read Cotton Mather, Perry Miller's *The Puritan Mind,* and Lion Feuchtwanger's *The Devil in Boston.*

    d. Painting, architecture, arts and crafts of the period.

    e. Travel books, postcards and photographs.

    f. Old fashion magazines, Sears-Roebuck catalogues, newspaper advertisements, back issues of *Life,* and family albums for costumes and accessories.

3. The theatrical history of the play.

Knowing the kind of theatre, audience, scenery, costumes and theatrical conventions that were typical of the period in which the play was written and first produced will give the director an understanding of the particular form of the play. For example, familiarity with the painted wings and backdrops in use at the time of *The School for Scandal* or *Fashion* may suggest a stylish modern treatment that requires no delays for scene-shifting. Knowing of the repressive government censorship in force at the time *He Who Gets Slapped* was written in Russia would aid the director in interpreting Andreyev's deliberately vague symbols. Even the knowledge that a particular actor created a certain role may help the director clarify his impressions of the character. Certainly a knowledge of Shakespeare's Globe Theatre is necessary before the director can find a modern equivalent that will permit an unbroken flow of the scenes in Shakespeare's plays.

D. Analyzing the characters and their motives.

The central meaning of a play very often is stated in terms of the main action or goal of the principal character or characters. Before

A modern adaptation of the Globe stage—Oregon Shakespeare Festival, Ashland Oregon.

the director can crystallize his interpretation, he will need to analyze each character in the play, his motivation and his relationship
to all the other characters. A complete analysis of a character should
include all the facets treated in Chapter 8, Characterization.

1. The use of *verbs*.

   Although sound character analysis can be done in many ways,
   directors trained in the Stanislavski method tend to seek out
   verbs which express the basic action or struggle of the characters. This is a practical application of both the Aristotelian system which defines drama as an "imitation of an *action*" and of
   the contemporary, post-Freudian psychology which attempts
   to understand individuals in terms of their basic drives, wants
   or goals and how they are achieved or thwarted.

2. The *spine* of the play.

   Harold Clurman popularized the use of the term "spine" (which
   was Richard Boleslavsky's translation of Stanislavski's term "super-objective"[3]). As Clurman phrases it:

   > ... *what fundamental desire does the plot of his*
   > *play symbolize, what deep struggle gives it*
   > *shape and direction. What is the play's CORE?*[4]

   When he directed Odets' *Night Music* for the Group Theatre,
   Clurman found the spine in the idea that the characters were
   searching for a home. When Robert Lewis directed Saroyan's
   My Heart's in the Highlands, he found the spine in the idea of
   people trying eagerly to give things to other people. The spine
   can thus be defined as the unifying or all-embracing action or
   impulse which motivates the characters and drives them to the
   final denouement. Like the spine of the body, it can be thought
   of as a trunk line which brings together the separate parts and
   carries them forward as a unit.

3. The spine of each character.

   The spine of the play usually bears a close relationship to the
   spine of the principal character or characters. The spines of the
   other characters (also stated in terms of verbs) will bear some
   relationship to the spine of the protagonist, either negatively or
   positively, furthering or blocking the basic action. Examples:

   a. Stanislavski tells how his whole interpretation of *The Imag-
      inary Invalid* was clarified when he realized that the pro-

---

[3]Boleslavsky, Richard, *Acting: The First Six Lessons* (New York: Theatre Arts, Inc., 1933,) Third Lesson.

[4]Clurman, Harold, "Principles of Interpretation," in Gassner, *Producing the Play* (New York: The Dryden Press, 1953), p. 277.

tagonist's spine was not "I wish to be sick," but "I wish to be thought sick."[5]

b. In the article previously referred to, Clurman illustrates the value of verbs rather than adjectives to describe character by examples from Odets' *Awake and Sing*.

(1) Bessie Berger, the mother, constantly wants "to take care of everything." (This is more helpful for the actress playing the part than to be told she is "meddlesome.")

(2) Ralph, the son, wants "to get away from his environment." (This is more helpful for the actor than to tell him he is playing a "young idealist.")

c. Elia Kazan, the noted Broadway director who staged *A Streetcar Named Desire*, has analyzed the spines of the principal characters in a lucid article which should be read by every student director.[6]

(1) Blanche................to find protection.

(2) Stella............to hold onto Stanley.

(3) Stanley..................to keep things his way.

(4) Mitch......................to get away from his mother.

E. Dividing the play into actions and beats.

If the *spine* tells what the character wants in the play (and in life), the *actions* tell the various things he does to achieve his spine, and the *beats* are the detailed ways he goes about furthering his actions. (Actions and beats have already been discussed in connection with improvisations, Chapter 3.) Each action and beat somehow relates to the spine; a group of beats make up an action, and a group of actions make up the spine.

1. Because some of the translators and followers of Stanislavski have used different terms to describe these concepts, the following diagram may prove helpful:

2. Identifying the beats.

When the director has selected the spine of the play and of each of the characters, he is ready to proceed with the detailed analysis of each act and scene, breaking the play down moment by moment into its beats and actions. This is an essential prerequisite to blocking, for *where the beat or action changes, the visual picture should also change.*

a. Separate the beats by drawing a line across the page of the director's book each time the beat changes. For each beat, the director should ask himself, "What is the character trying

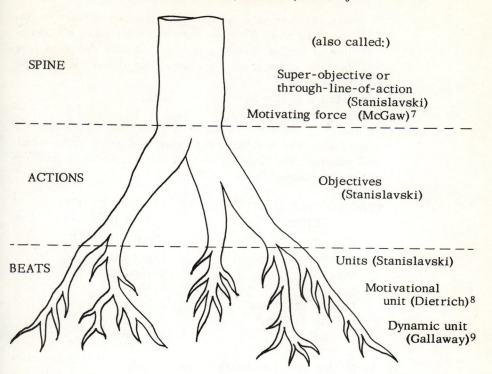

SPINE

(also called:)

Super-objective or
through-line-of-action
(Stanislavski)
Motivating force (McGaw)[7]

ACTIONS

Objectives
(Stanislavski)

BEATS

Units (Stanislavski)

Motivational
unit (Dietrich)[8]

Dynamic unit
(Gallaway)[9]

to do here?" "What does he want here?" "Why is he saying that?" Record the answers to these questions in the margins of the director's book. (Be sure to find the *character's* reasons and not the *playwright's*, which may be entirely external — the need to reveal information to the audience, for example.)

b. How to tell when a new beat begins.
A new beat may begin:

(1) When a new character enters, bringing with him a new want or desire. (Every entrance — the so-called "French scene" — does not mark a new beat; a character may merely participate in the existing beat.)

(2) When a character begins a new approach or gets a new idea.

(3) When another character assumes the initiative. At any given moment, one character is apt to be more aggres-

[7]McGaw, Charles, *Acting Is Believing* (New York: Rinehart and Co., 1955), Chapter 7.
[8]Dietrich, John E., *Play Direction* (New York: Prentice-Hall, Inc., 1953), Chapter 6.
[9]Gallaway, Marian, *The Director in the Theatre.* (New York: The Macmillan Co., 1963).

sive, to dominate, while other characters react or respond to him. When another character takes the initiative or begins "to carry the ball," it may denote a new beat. In older theatre parlance, this determines "whose scene it is."

(4) After a climax has been reached.

c. Selecting strong verbs.

In analyzing what the character is trying to do, the director should wherever possible select strong and active verbs which will stimulate the actor rather than weak, passive or indifferent verbs. Examples:

STRONG AND ACTIVE VERBS	WEAK AND INACTIVE VERBS
to goad	to tell
to defy	to get angry
to needle	to suggest
to tease	to hint
to blow off steam	to inform
to force his hand	to wonder
to "mother"	to be sorry

d. Verbs that reveal *motivation* and *character*.

The director should seek verbs that reveal inner emotional needs and motives — what the character is thinking and feeling rather than what he is saying; the audience will hear the latter for itself. The beats should get beneath the surface of dialogue and express the dynamics which motivate the character to say the given words. The director therefore needs a deep insight into the psychology of human motives, even unconscious motives. If this phase has been done thoroughly, the task of inventing business, movement and picturization will later come easily. For illustration see the examples given from *Romeo and Juliet* and *The Glass Menagerie* in Chapter 8, Characterization.

3. Structuring the beats toward climax.

The director should select beats with a sense of progression, growing from weaker to stronger until a climax is reached. A number of beats can be grouped together until they form one main action which culminates in a strong climax. Then a new main action begins. (Climax is treated more fully in Chapter 9.) To illustrate the concepts of the previous page, *The Diary of Anne Frank* could be broken down as follows into spine, actions and beats; the beats of one scene are given in detail as they might appear in the director's book in preparation for actual blocking.

THE DIARY OF ANNE FRANK
Dramatized by Frances Goodrich and Albert Hackett

SPINE: to hold together as a family and preserve their faith, humor and courage under extreme pressure.

MR. FRANK'S SPINE: to hold his family together and preserve some semblance of normal daily life.

ANNE'S SPINE: to find some meaning for the life she is forced to lead.

THE DIARY OF ANNE FRANK
Act and Scene Breakdown

Act I

Scene 1. (Prologue) Mr. Frank: to keep from breaking down as he sees the room for the last time and tells Miep goodbye.

Scene 2. The two families: to get settled and acquainted.

Scene 3. Anne: to tease young Van Daan. Mr. Frank: to make room for another person and make him feel welcome.

Scene 4. Mr. Frank: to keep Anne from hurting her mother's feelings.

Scene 5. To make Hanukkah a happy festival. Mr. Frank: to keep their courage up when almost discovered by a thief.

Act II

Scene 1. Miep: to cheer them up for New Year's. Peter: to seek Anne's companionship for the first time.

Scene 2. Anne and Peter: to discover their love for each other.

Scene 3. Mrs. Frank: to release her pent-up feelings against Mr. Van Daan. Miep: to bring the good news about the invasion.

Scene 4: Anne: to share her faith with Peter at the moment of crisis.

Scene 5. Mr. Frank: to tell Miep and Kraler that he knows Anne is gone.

(from Act I, Scene 3)

ANNE: to tease young Van Daan.	ANNE: (Enters, dressed in Peter's knickers, jacket and cap.) Good evening, everyone. Forgive me if I don't stay. I have a friend waiting for me in there. My friend Tom, Tom Cat. Some people say that we look alike. But Tom has the most beautiful whiskers...and I have only a little fuzz. I am hoping...in time...
PETER: To get even with her.	PETER: All right, Mrs. Quack Quack! ANNE: Peter! PETER: I heard about you...How you talked so much in class they called you Mrs. Quack Quack. How Mr. Smitter made you write a composition... " 'Quack, Quack,' said Mrs. Quack Quack."
ANNE: To give him the dickens for teasing her back.	ANNE: Well, go on. Tell them the rest. How it was so good he read it out loud to the class and then read it to all his other classes! PETER: Quack! Quack! Quack...Quack... Quack... ANNE: You are the most intolerable, insufferable boy I've ever met! MRS. VAN DAAN: That's right, Anneke! Give it to him! ANNE: With all the boys in the world...Why I had to get locked up with one like you!
MRS. FRANK: to put a stop to the kidding before it goes too far.	MRS. FRANK: Anne, dear...your hair. You're warm. Are you feeling all right? ANNE: Please, Mother. MRS. FRANK: You haven't a fever, have you? ANNE: No. No. MRS. FRANK: ....Let me see your tongue.
MR. FRANK: To restore peace between Anne and her mother.	MR. FRANK: I think there's nothing the matter with our Anne that a ride on her bike, or a visit with Jopie de Waal wouldn't cure. Isn't that so, Anne?

F. Crystallizing in words the particular emphasis, point of view or approach which the director wishes to give the production for his particular audience.

1. The director is ready to do this only after he has done the research indicated into the play itself, the critical commentary, the backgrounds of the play and its theatrical history, the analy-

sis of character, and the breakdown of the play into actions and beats.

2. The director should now summarize his approach in a one-sentence statement that begins with: "This is a play about ———" or "This is the story of ———." The statement should not be a literary or moral theme such as "The wages of sin are death," but a theatrical statement of the basic action or spine of the play as the director feels it.

3. The staging, cutting, scenery, even casting, may hinge upon the way the foregoing sentence is completed. For example:

   a. *The Diary of Anne Frank* could have become oppressive and gloomy if the director's approach had been, "This is a tragedy about what the Nazis did to a group of Jews." Instead, the spine suggested, emphasizing the family feeling, faith and humor, makes for a more touching and human performance.

   b. The Laurence Olivier film of *Hamlet* began with the clear statement that "This is the story of a man who could not make up his mind."

   c. If the director of *Romeo and Juliet* interprets it as the story of "star-crossed lovers," he might conceivably cut the last scene of the reconciliation of Capulet and Montague. If however, he interprets it as "the story of two lovers blighted by family enmity," then the last scene cannot be cut. Today's director, moreover, may see the timeliness of throwing the final accent upon the parents who failed to understand their impetuous, headstrong, "mixed-up teen-agers."

   d. During the Hitler period, Erwin Piscator interpreted *King Lear* for a New York production as the story of an aging authoritarian who attempts to maintain a balance of power by dividing his kingdom.

   e. The Moscow Art Theatre's 1958 staging of *The Cherry Orchard* interpreted it as a comedy foretelling an optimistic future rather than a nostalgic picture of a dying order.

4. No two directors will see precisely the same values in a play nor state their interpretation in the same terms. The director's affinity for certain subjects and environments may be a key to a valid and exciting interpretation. Harold Clurman emphasizes this personal connection between the director and his script. It is this subjective element in play interpretation that makes directing creative and the theatre varied and fascinating. The student director should read some of the best available interpretations which successful directors have written con-

cerning their productions. A suggested list is given at the end of the chapter.

G. Preparing the text for production.

The final phase of the director's interpretative study is the preparation of the text. In the case of contemporary plays from Samuel French or Dramatists Play Service, this may be a relatively simple matter. In the case of classics and translations, however, the editing of the text is a major reflection of the director's insight into the play. Included in this phase are:

1. Developing a feeling for the language of the play.

   Before he can coach the actors in the interpretation of lines, the director will need to discover for himself the special qualities of the language used by the playwright, by:

   a. Appreciating the poetic quality of the dialogue, where applicable.

   b. Feeling the rhythm and tempo of the dialogue, especially if any cutting is contemplated.

   c. Singling out particularly eloquent speeches which the director will want to have pointed.

   d. Deciding, if the play involves dialect, the extent to which it should be used by the actors.

   e. Knowing the meaning and pronunciation of every word used in the dialogue.

2. Selecting the most effective translation in the case of a foreign play. All available translations should be compared, for the translator has a large influence upon our appreciation of an author's style and language — whether it is colloquial or archaic, sprightly or heavy, prose or verse, British or American. Compare these translations and note how different is the feeling conveyed in each case:

(from the opening scene of *Antigone* by Sophocles)

"O Sister-Life, Ismene's, twin
  with mine,
Knowest thou of the burden of
  our race
Aught that from us yet living
  Zeus holds back?
Nay, for nought grievous and
  nought ruinous,
No shame and no dishonour,
  have I not seen
Poured on our hapless heads,
  both thine and mine."[10]

"Ismene, dear sister,
You would think that we had
  already suffered enough
For the curse on Oedipus:
I cannot imagine any grief
That you and I have not gone
  through...."[11]

from Act III of Ibsen's *Pillars of Society*)

"Do not condemn me without bearing in mind how things stood at that time...I came home and found my mother involved in a mesh of injudicious undertakings; we had all manner of bad luck — it seemed as if misfortunes were raining upon us, and our house was on the verge of ruin. I was half reckless and half in despair.

Lona, I believe it was mainly to deaden my thoughts that I let myself drift into that entanglement that ended in Johan's going away."[12]

"Don't condemn me until you remember the situation I was in...When I came home I found my mother involved in a whole series of unwise deals. Then we had a streak of bad luck. We seemed to be caught in a flood of misfortunes and the family business was on the verge of ruin. I was half reckless and half desperate. Lona, I think the real reason I let myself get involved in that affair was to get away from my troubles."[13]

Pillars of Society.

3. Selecting the acting edition to be used by the cast.
   Acting editions should always be compared with the full text so as not inadvertently to choose a chopped-up version which was edited by a squeamish director of bygone days or one with

---

[10]Translated by Robert Whitelaw, in *An Anthology of Greek Drama,* Vol. I. Reprinted by permission of Holt, Rinehart and Winston, Inc.

[11]Translated by Dudley Fitts and Robert Fitzgerald in *Greek Plays in Modern Translation.* Reprinted by permission of Holt, Rinehart and Winston, Inc.

[12]William Archer translation.

[13]Translated by Professor Frank G. Nelson of California State College at Long Beach for a production at this college, and used by permission.

a quite different interpretation of the play. (*The Rivals* and *The Importance of Being Earnest*, for example, have been subjected to heavy-handed editing; Baker's Plays carry the least truncated versions.) Each director will want to do his own cutting and editing.

4. Cutting and editing the text.
Although the copyright laws protect the author's material,[14] the director in the educational theatre who has paid the stipulated royalty fee need not hesitate to make minor cuts or changes so long as they do not violate the author's intent nor destroy the over-all effect of the play. He should not, however, attempt to rewrite the play or insert "gag lines" for local consumption. Legitimate cutting and editing of a text includes the following:

a. Shortening or eliminating scenes that are too long, repetitious or static. A good cut is one which makes a smooth and logical transition, bridging the omitted material within an actor's speech, blending to a later speech of the same actor or to a response by another actor. The director should trust his first impressions — if a scene seemed too long on first reading it, it may also seem so to the audience. When a beat seems to be played out or characters repeating themselves, it is time for a new beat to begin. A cut should *not* be made, however, if the material does any one of the following:

   (1) Furthers the plot.
   (2) Adds significantly to our understanding of a character.
   (3) Contains notable language or humor.
   (4) Provides motivation for a following speech.

b. Deleting lines or phrases which would be objectionable to a particular audience. The director should sense how much profanity would be acceptable in a given context, and should also be sensitive to lines that might give offense to a racial or religious group.

c. Cutting or clarifying lines that are so obscure or archaic that the particular audience would not understand them. It seems legitimate, for example, in staging *The Importance of Being Earnest* in an American school to change Lady Bracknell's exclamation:

   "Untruthful! My nephew Algernon? Impossible. He is an Oxonian."

   to

   "Untruthful! My nephew Algernon? Impossible. He is an Oxford man."

---

[14]The Dramatists Play Service contract with a producing group, for example, stipulates that "The play must be presented substantially in its published form, as per the playbook furnished you."

Shakespeare, especially in the comedies, presents a special problem because of his fondness for the Elizabethan "conceit" or play on words, the meanings of which are often lost on a modern audience. Unless a meaning can be suggested by gesture or pantomime, it often is better to cut the obscure passage. It would be presumptuous to attempt to rewrite Shakespeare, however, and *the director should never substitute a different word in Shakespeare.* (He may, however, consult the Variorum edition and choose from the various folios, quartos and standard editions, the word that seems most meaningful.)

d. Eliminating minor characters or combining several into one. In *Romeo and Juliet,* for example, a director short of male actors can combine the lines assigned to Officer in Act I, Scene 1, Citizen in Act III, Scene 1, and Chief Watchman in Act V, Scene 3. The first and second servants in Act IV, Scene 2, also can be combined with Peter and Gregory or Sampson.

e. Changing the gender of minor characters when appropriate, because of a shortage of either men or women from whom to cast. Merriman, the butler in *The Importance of Being Earnest,* could, for example, become a maid.

f. Reducing the number of scene changes, where it can be done without weakening the impact of the play. The third act of *The Importance of Being Earnest,* for example, could be played in the garden setting of the second act; a few lines would have to be modified, but for a group with limited stagecraft facilities the compromise might be worth making.

g. Placing of intermissions in multi-scene plays where they can be of the most help in scene-shifting, remembering, however, that intermissions should follow scenes of strong suspense or climax.

h. Adding speeches or even scenes from another translation (if a foreign play) or from the full text (if using an acting edition). A translation is often far from literal, and would more accurately be called an adaptation. The director may discover desirable values in speeches which a translator omitted. Even an acting edition of a recent American play may omit speeches which the director might see a value in restoring. The acting edition of *Summer and Smoke,* for example, omits the prologue with the children and the effective father-son dialogue (used as an illustration in Chapter 6, Movement) which are to be found in Williams' full published text.

i. Clarifying the author's intent where confusion might occur. For example, the prologue to *The Diary of Anne Frank* ends with Mr. Frank's reading Anne's diary to Miep. The epilogue begins with a return to this scene, but Mr. Kraler has joined the others. In order to help the audience identify the flashback framework, it might be desirable to bring Mr. Kraler into the prologue just before the reading of the diary begins, so that the prologue ends on the same visual picture with which the epilogue begins.

j. Checking misprints, typographical errors and even incorrect assignment of speeches which sometimes occur in acting editions.

k. Modifying the dialogue where necessary to fit the action and physical blocking. Incidental references to the ghost standing near the piano in *Blithe Spirit* may be changed, if the set is too small to accommodate a piano, to a mantelpiece or buffet. Many times a director will have occasion to change lines such as "Don't just sit there" to "Don't just stand there."

5. The following are examples of judicious cuttings which eliminate nothing essential in plot, characterization, language or motivation, and which make smooth transitions:

a. *Romeo and Juliet*, II, 3.

Friar Laurence

Holy Saint Francis, what a change is here!
Is Rosaline that thou didst love so dear
So soon forsaken? Young men's love then lies
Not truly in their hearts, but in their eyes.
Jesu Maria, what a deal of brine
Hath washed thy sallow cheeks for Rosaline!
How much salt water thrown away in waste
To season love, that of it doth not taste!
The sun not yet thy sighs from heaven clears,
Thy old groans yet ring in mine ancient ears,
Lo here upon thy cheek the stain doth sit
Of an old tear that is not washed off yet.
If e'er thou wast thyself, and these woes thine,
Thou and these woes were all for Rosaline.
And art thou changed? Pronounce this sentence then,
Women may fall, when there's no strength in men.[15]

b. *Summer and Smoke,* by Tennessee Williams, Part II, Scene 5. Although the following lines undoubtedly were written to

---

[15]In cutting Shakespearean poetry, the director should avoid cutting half of a rhymed couplet or words necessary to complete a line of iambic pentameter.

show Alma's beat of "straining to make conversation" to cover up her embarrassment and excitement at seeing John again, a director might feel that the lines are not sufficiently interesting or revealing to warrant delaying the tempo of the scene and could cut as follows:

ALMA: No greetings? No greetings at all?
JOHN: Hello, Miss Alma.
ALMA: Those new glass cases — ah! Such glacial brilliance!
JOHN: New equipment.
ALMA: Everything new but the chart.
JOHN: The human anatomy's always the same old thing.
ALMA: And such a tiresome one! I've been plagued with sore throats.
JOHN: Everyone has here lately. These Southern homes are all improperly heated. Open grates aren't enough.
ALMA: They burn the front of you while your back is freezing.
JOHN: Then you go into another room and get chilled off.
ALMA. Yes — yes — chilled to the bone.
JOHN: But it never gets quite cold enough to convince the damn fools that a furnace is necessary, so they go on building without them.
ALMA: Such a strange afternoon.
JOHN: Is it? I haven't been out.
ALMA: The Gulf wind is blowing big, white — what do they call them? Cumulus? — clouds over! It seemed determined to take the plume off my hat — like that fox terrier we had once named Jacob, snatched the plume off a hat and dashed around and around the back yard with it like a trophy.
JOHN: I remember Jacob. What happened to him?
ALMA: Oh, Jacob. Jacob was such a mischievous thief. We had to send him out to some friends in the country. Yes, he ended his days as — a country squire! The tales of his exploits —
JOHN: Sit down, Miss Alma.
ALMA: If I'm disturbing you — ?
JOHN: No.

III. Finding a form in which to project this meaning to the audience.

When the director has crystallized for himself what the play means both in general terms and in scene-by-scene analysis, he is ready to think of ways to translate this analysis into theatrical impressions that will convey what he wishes his audience to feel. He should have completed all of the steps detailed in II *before* his first production conference with his designer. (See Chapter 10, V, B.) As Gordon Craig has advocated, the director must unify all of the elements of the theatre to create an integrated impact upon the audience. Sometimes the playwright helps the director in this respect; at other times the director must do the creative work of finding a form. Tennessee Williams has anticipated the director's problem and visualized *The Glass Menagerie* in production:

> The play is memory. Being a memory play, it is dimly lighted, it is sentimental, it is not realistic. In memory everything seems to happen to music. That explains the fiddle in the wings.

A. Selecting a *style* for the production.

The director's first problem in projecting the meaning of the play is to find a style which will best express the content and historical period of the play and which can be reflected in acting, scenery, properties, costumes and make-up.

Style can be defined as an expression of (1) the author's personal way of translating life to the stage, and (2) the theatrical conventions in use during the historical period in which he wrote. If "holding the mirror up to nature" can be considered to be the aim of all dramatic art, who holds the mirror, how he holds it, where he focuses it, and the kind of mirror he holds can be thought of as factors which determine style. Because of changing theatrical conventions, what seemed real in one century may seem artificial in another. The extent to which the playwright attempts to photograph or mirror real life gives a basis for a discussion of styles.[16]

1. Presentational styles.

Until the advent of modern realism, actors played directly to the audience; conventions such as asides, soliloquies and enlarged movement were freely used even though they are not normally part of everyday life, and poetic language was used to heighten emotion beyond the powers of normal speech. The play was "presented" to the audience rather than disguised as life itself.

a. *Classic Greek drama.*

Action was centered largely in a circular dancing area with the audience sitting on three sides. Emotions needed

---

[16]For a fuller treatment of styles, see: H. D. Albright, William P. Halstead and Lee Mitchell, *Principles of Theatre Art* (Boston: Houghton Mifflin Company, 1955), Chapters 13, 14, 15; Mordecai Gorelik, *New Theatres for Old* (Samuel French, Inc., 1940); John Gassner, *Producing the Play* (New York: The Dryden Press, 1953), Chapters 3, 4, 5.

Greek theatre at Epidauros.

to be larger than life size, and they were often reinforced by music and choral responses.

b. *Oriental drama.* With no attempt at realism, the audience is well aware that it is watching a stylized distillation of life rather than a picture of life itself.

c. *Medieval theatre.* Wagons or simultaneous platforms furnished a minimum of background while the actors often played to and among the audience.

d. *Shakespearean theatre.* The large forestage made possible intimate contact with the audience, with a number of other acting areas where the audience's attention could shift without pause. The background was largely conventional, with the actual locale described in the poet's words.

e. *Molière, Restoration and eighteenth century drama.* Although painted backgrounds were used, the actors tended to play on the forestage, retaining a frank sense of confiding their emotions and wit to the audience.

2. Representational or illusionistic styles.
   With the advent of the scientific attitude in the nineteenth century together with advances in lighting and stagecraft, the theatre began to strive for an illusion of real life on the stage. The proscenium arch was thought of as a picture frame or "fourth wall," behind which all action was confined.

Reconstruction of the Shakespearean theatre.

a. *Realism*. An attempt to convey the illusion of reality through careful attention to detail, the use of everyday language, and the elimination of asides, soliloquies and direct contact

House of Connelly, Carnegie Institute of Technology.

between actor and audience. The actors presume not to know the audience is present, and the audience presumes to be watching real life. (Ibsen, Galsworthy, Hellman in drama, Stanislavski in acting.)

b. *Naturalism.* An extreme form of realism which attempts to give a complete photograph of reality — a "slice of life" — without eliminating or selecting details or structuring the material into a complex plot. (Zola, Gorki, O'Casey, *Tobacco Road, Dead End.*)

Dead End, New York production.

c. *Selective realism.* A more recent style which selects realistic details as needed without cluttering the picture with a complete depiction of reality. Part of a room, a window or fragment of a wall may be sufficient, hence full walls and ceilings can be eliminated. (*Billy Budd, Darkness at Noon, No Time for Sergeants.*)

The Importance of Being Earnest, University of Minnesota.

d. *Suggestive realism.* The use of realistic detail suggestively. A Gothic arch may suggest a whole cathedral, and with artistic lighting the rest can be imagined. Neutral or black background often used with only those properties, furniture and set elements which are necessary. (*The Lark, The Caine Mutiny Court-Martial.*)

Look Homeward, Angel.

3. Revolts against representationalism.

The twentieth century has seen many efforts to free the the-atre from the limitations of realism and restore greater scope to the playwright and director. Although our theatre today re-mains basically realistic, the trend away from realism is still going on, and realistic elements are often juxtaposed with non-illusionistic styles:

a. *Symbolism.* The use of symbol to convey meaning or emo-tion. Gordon Craig and Adolphe Appia began this "new stagecraft" movement, which attempted to synthesize all of the arts in the theatre, including painting, music, lighting, and dance. (Maeterlinck, Yeats, Andreyev, O'Neill's *Dy-namo, J. B.*

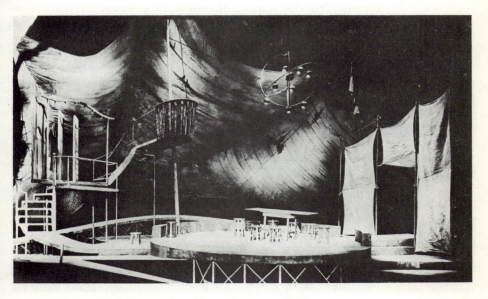

J. B., New York production.

b. *Neo-Romanticism.* A return to the poetic form in costume drama which permits a heightening of effect and language not possible in realism. (Rostand, Maxwell Anderson, Chris-topher Fry.)

Knights of the Round Table, School of Drama, Yale University.

c. *Expressionism.* Purposeful distortion of reality to express inner meaning or the impact of twentieth century mechanization upon the individual. (*The Adding Machine, The Great God Brown, Beggar on Horseback.*)

The Inspector General, University of Nebraska.

d. *Constructivism.* Elimination of external surfaces in order to penetrate to the skeletal construction, showing ramps, levels, steps and joists. (Meyerhold; influence in *Desire Under the Elms.*)

Desire Under the Elms, Stanford University.

e. *Surrealism or subjective realism.* The influence of Freudian psychology in attempting to express man's inner and even unconscious life through dream symbols, psychological distortion, and the "free association"of ideas.[17] (*Hotel Universe, Death of a Salesman, Dream Girl, A Clearing in the Woods.*)

A Clearing in the Woods, New York production.

[17]For a more complete treatment, see the author's *Freud on Broadway* (New York: Hermitage House, 1955).

f. *Stylization.* Enlarging a certain detail or series of details beyond natural proportions. In stylization the audience is conscious of the *way* actions are done as well as what is done. Often used for seventeenth and eighteenth century artificial comedy. (*The Servant of Two Masters, The Matchmaker.*)

Le Bourgeois Gentilhomme, Yale University.

g. *Theatricalism.* Calling the audience's attention frankly to the fact that they are in a theatre rather than watching a slice of life. Deliberate breaking of the "fourth wall," often with the use of imaginary properties, or scenery shifted in view of the audience. (*Our Town, The Skin of Our Teeth, The Visit, Sweet Bird of Youth.*)

The Visit, New York production.

h. *Formalism.* A return to permanent architectural settings based on classic or abstract forms. (Jacques Copeau, "Globe Theatre" staging of Shakespeare, the use of unit sets, and "space-staging.")

The Crucible, Cleveland Playhouse, Euclid—77th St. Theatre.

i. *Epic theatre*. The "learning-theatre," which rejects realism, empathy and illusion in favor of teaching a sociopolitical thesis through the use of narration, projection, slogans, songs, and direct contact with the audience. (Brecht, Piscator.)

The Private Life of the Master Race. Hunter College. Epic Theatre.

j. *Absurdism*. The current attempts by Ionesco, Beckett and in some cases Albee to create plays which on first glance have no rational meaning have been referred to by

Rhinoceros.

Martin Esslin as "the theatre of the absurd." Elements of surrealism and symbolism are utilized along with absurdity and irrationality in order to suggest the meaninglessness of life and the difficulty of human communication. (*Waiting for Godot, The Chairs, Rhinoceros.*)

B. Planning for the most effective use of the theatrical elements.
The elements of the theatre through which the director projects the play to the audience are:

1. Actors
2. Scenery
3. Lighting
4. Properties
5. Costumes
6. Make-up
7. Music
8. Sound
9. Dance

In planning his production, the director should consider how each of these elements can contribute to the whole, reinforce his interpretation of the play, and enrich the enjoyment of the audience. For the director working in the field without training in the backstage crafts and without a scene designer or costumer to help him, a bibliography of reference materials on scenery, lighting, costume, and make-up will be found in Appendix E.

1. Actors.
   a. Preparation for casting.
      As the director analyzes the characters, their spines, actions and beats, he will begin to form specific impressions of the kind of people his playwright has created. Before tryouts he will need to prepare brief paragraphs describing each character. (Refer to Chapters 8 on Characterization and 11 for casting.) It is often helpful for the director to maintain a picture file for make-up studies and as an aid in casting. (Use only candid photographs of real people, not sketches or posed pictures of models or actors.) It would help crystallize the director's images of the characters to find a photograph that suggests each person in the play.
   b. After casting.
      What the director does with his cast after he has selected it is of course the essence of play direction, and is dealt with in all of the succeeding chapters.

2. Scenery
   The director should rely heavily upon his scene designer to find the visual form that will best express the interpretation of the play. He should guard against trying to put ideas into the de-

signer's head or design the sets for him. The director can, however, save the designer many hours of wasted time and later
frustration if at the very beginning of the production conferences
the director supplies the unifying statement of interpretation
and spark that will ignite the imaginations of scene and costume
designers as well as choreographer and composer if involved.
The director should therefore be clear in his own mind on the
following points and be prepared to discuss them at the first
production conference.[18]

a. The kind of background or environment which will make
   the action of the play seem logical and best convey the interpretation of the play to the audience.
b. The style of production that will best express the author's intent for a contemporary audience.
c. The general mood or atmosphere which the scenery should
   convey.
d. Simplifications in setting which might be practical without
   losing the over-all impression desired.
e. Shifting problems, if any.
   The director should be aware of the time that might be necessary for each shift. It is detrimental to the tempo and over-all
   effect of the play to lower the curtain for more than thirty
   seconds to shift scenery. The placement of one or two 10-min-
   ute intermissions may solve the problem, but they cannot
   always be placed primarily to satisfy shifting requirements;
   they must occur only after strong climaxes in the story. Some
   ways which have been found effective in dealing with the
   multi-set play include:

   (1) Permanent settings.
       (a) Multiple sets, with several areas simultaneously
           on stage and shifting accomplished by light. (See
           photograph of *Summer and Smoke*, page 168.)
       (b) Utilizing side areas outside the proscenium arch
           for short scenes if space is available.
       (c) Unit sets. Changes are accomplished by opening
           and closing arches, windows and doors by drapes,
           plugs, etc. Compare the three photographs of
           Romeo and Juliet on the next page, and the two
           of *The Crucible* on pages 20 and 231.

---

[18]This discussion of scenic problems relates primarily to the proscenium stage. Other
possible solutions to visual design include central and flexible staging, which are discussed in
Chapter 12; many times central or flexible staging will prove the best choice for a
director struggling with a lack of technical help or inadequate stage facilities.

(2) Flying the sets.

This method requires a counterweight system and sufficient height above the proscenium arch so that the scenery can be raised out of sight. A small threefold box set can be flown in and then opened up. If there is much furniture to shift, however, an act intermission may be required.

Romeo and Juliet.
(Unit setting) — Act II, Scene 2

(3) Revolving stage.

This method tends to be cumbersome and to require that masking pieces be brought in from the sides.

(4) Wagon stages.

This is a very much-used method in which sets or parts of sets are wheeled into place on low platforms with casters, and all furniture and props are preset. It does, however, require off-stage storage space and may prove noisy in shifting.

Romeo and Juliet.
Act III, Scene 1

(5) Projected scenery.

This method offers exciting possibilities where literal realism is not required. Sufficient distance between projector and cyclorama is necessary (through which the actors cannot move) and a correction must be made for distortion, but designers are finding many ways to use projections effectively, as in the

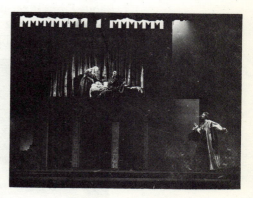

Romeo and Juliet.
Act IV, Scene 5

multi-scene *John Brown's Body* below. See other projections on pages 6 and 89.

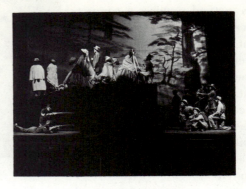

John Brown's Body.

(6) Alternating between forestage and inner stage.
   A curtain (traveller or drop) divides the stage halfway upstage; scenes play on the forestage while the inner stage is being shifted. This is ideally suited for Shakespeare, and is frequently used for musicals. (For a breakdown of *Othello* according to this plan, see page 97.

(7) Black velour curtains.
   In front of an inconspicuous background minimal, suggestive scenic elements can be placed. If the light is kept off the curtains, the audience will be able to accept them as walls. Box sets can even be suggested in front of black velours, using such simple elements as a low wainscoting, door frames, etc. See *The Importance of Being Earnest* on page 68, *The Crucible* on page 73 and *Another Way Out* below which used largely white elements in front of black curtains.

Another Way Out.

(8) Shifting in view of the audience as part of the action. This method can be used with style and ingenuity for the enjoyment of the audience. Minor characters can move furniture, or actors can shift their own sets, as was done in the Lunts' production of *The Visit.* In Frank Whiting's production of *The Taming of the Shrew,* shown below, the screens were reversible and free-standing; the shifting was done rhythmically to music.

The Taming of the Shrew, University of Minnesota.

(9) Space staging.

When a stage is large enough and the light can be carefully controlled by means of a black floor-cloth and black cyclorama, actors can be placed on a virtually bare stage except for platforms and steps and made to stand out three dimensionally against what seems to be an infinitely deep and black background. A shifting pattern of light and shadow can suggest a change of scene. Norman Bel Geddes has utilized space-staging brilliantly in his designs for *Hamlet, Lazarus Laughed,* and *The Divine Comedy.*

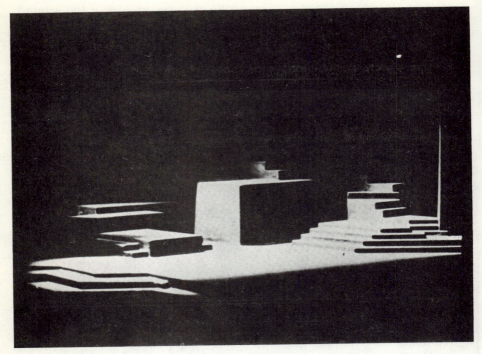

Hamlet designed by Norman Bel Geddes as space-staging,
a New York production.

(10)   Running the flats.
       As a final alternative when none of the foregoing plans
       is feasible, the scenery (flats) can be unlashed, folded
       in sections and carried offstage. The props and furniture
       are carried off after the scenery, then the new props
       and furniture are carried on, and the new flats then
       lashed into place. This method is slow and usually re-
       quires a five-minute intermission. However, ingenious
       design can sometimes work wonders in limited space,
       using double-faced flats which fold in or out to reveal
       a second set. See, for example, J. F. Foster's excellent ap-
       plication of this device to solve the difficult shift prob-
       lem posed by *The Silver Cord*.[19]

(11)   Folding screens or simple units placed in front of a
       basic setting. Note the contrast achieved in this manner

[19]Hewitt, Barnard, Foster, J. F., and Wolle, Muriel Sibell, *Play Production: Theory
and Practice* (Chicago: J. B. Lippincott Co., 1952), pp. 242-245.

by Milton Howarth in two settings for *Cosi Fan Tutte*, by Mozart.

Cosi Fan Tutte, University of Kansas.

Cosi Fan Tutte, University of Kansas.

COMMON MISTAKES IN ARRANGING GROUND PLANS

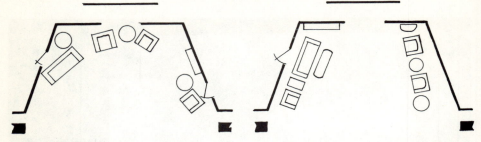

Do not block entrances nor weaken impact of characters' appearance by placement of furniture in front of doors.

Do not force actors to upstage one another by placing furniture at a sharp angle against the side walls.

Do not create a barren effect by too little furniture, wasted space, or forcing the actors to play in a vacuum.

Do not inhibit the actors by cluttering the set with too much furniture.

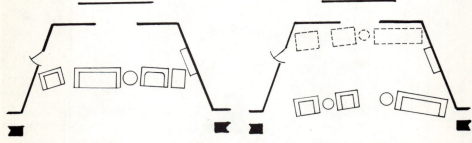

Do not force the actors to remain center stage by crowding furniture to center in a straight line.

Do not force the actors too far upstage or downstage by crowding furniture to either area.

f. The ground plan.

Both the director and the designer are vitally concerned with the ground plan of the set — the designer because it relates to balance, spatial relationships and visual impact, the director because it affects blocking, movement and the playing of the scenes. Before his first production conference with the designer, the director should know his play well enough so that he can discuss these problems intelligently with the designer:

(1) The principal acting areas called for in the play.

(2) The distribution of important furniture in the acting areas to convey a lifelike impression and to avoid the common mistakes shown on page 82.

(3) The possibility of grouping several pieces of furniture as a unit in one area of the stage in order to permit people to talk together, as required by the particular scenes of the play.

(4) The number of actors who have to work together and the physical action required in restricted spaces, on ramps and platforms.

(5) The maximum utilization of the existing space without crowding, and (in the case of quick shifts) the minimum number of set pieces and furniture that have to be shifted.

(6) The best location for doors and windows if they figure prominently in the action.

    (a) There should be an unrestricted view of the door if entrances and exits are important.

    (b) Entrances are most effective through a door on the back wall, exits through a door downstage on the side walls.

    (c) Doors normally swing onstage if they lead to the outside and offstage if they lead to another room. On side walls they are hinged upstage.

    (d) Windows are most effective on the side walls if characters have to react to what is seen through them. A window on the back wall is most effective if the audience must see people through it.

(7) The best location for important properties that figure in the action — the glass collection in *The Glass Menagerie*, for example, and the stove in *Hedda Gabler* illustrated on page 87. (Downstage corners provide the least obstructed view.)

(8) The offstage locations referred to in the script, and where each door leads.

(9) The sight lines in the theatre for which the production is planned, so as not to locate significant furniture, doors or acting areas where they will not be seen from all seats (i.e. in the shaded areas on the following drawings):

Stage Terminology[20]

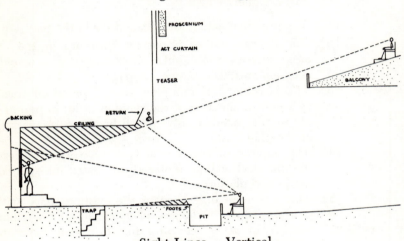

Sight Lines — Vertical

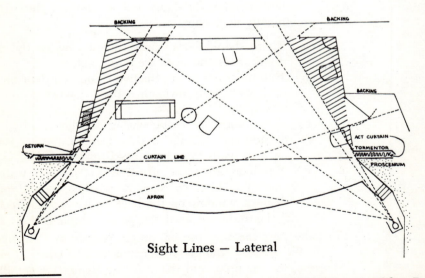

Sight Lines — Lateral

---

[20]Students unfamiliar with stage terminology are referred to Bowman, Walter Parker and Robert Hamilton Ball, *Theatre Language; A Dictionary of Terms in English of The Drama and Stage from Medieval to Modern Times.* New York: Theatre Arts Books, 1961.

After these items are discussed by director and designer, the designer should bring to the next production conference tentative sketches and ground plans (which need not be in finished form). After further discussion and possible modification, the ground plan should be agreed upon (subject only to minor modifications) at least ten days to two weeks prior to the first rehearsal in order to give the director time for his prerehearsal blocking. Although every play presents different problems, here are some conventional ground plans for interiors which may prove helpful to directors and designers:

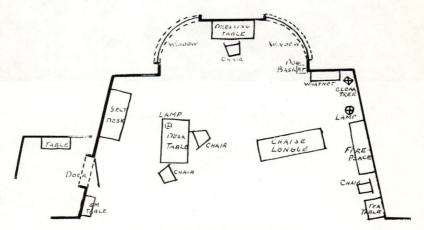

The Barretts of Wimpole Street.
(See photograph of this set on page 150.)

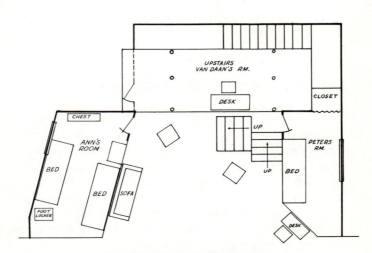

The Diary of Anne Frank
(See photograph of this set on page 111.)

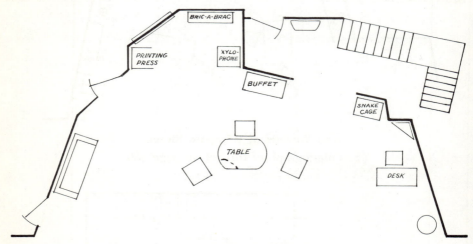

You Can't Take It With You.

3. Lighting

The lighting of the set and the actors is usually conceived as an integral part of the scene design. It is sufficient at this stage of the director's study simply to consider:

a. Is the lighting to be predominantly brilliant or low-key?

b. Is the lighting to be predominantly warm or cool?

c. Will motivated light sources be necessary, i.e., lamps, chandeliers or fixtures?

d. Are there any special lighting problems (such as the beautiful dawn that is referred to in *A Moon for the Misbegotten*,

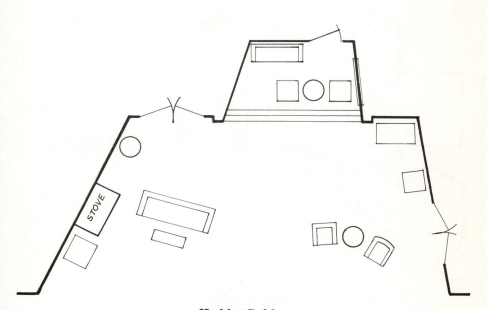

Hedda Gabler

or the need for special flexibility in controlling light and
dark areas in "space-staging" or simultaneous settings).
e. Will the hats (if planned by the costume designer) present
problems in placing lighting instruments so as to get light
onto actors' faces?

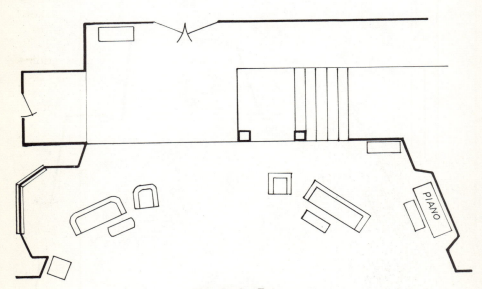

The Little Foxes

4. Properties
   Dressing the stage is, like lighting, a function of design; the use of the furniture, however, needs to be considered by the director in his interpretation. Where a number of authentic properties are required, as for example in *Men in White*, *Detective Story*, *Stalag 17* or *You Can't Take It With You*, the director's research

will not only reveal the kind of properties needed but will often suggest business for the actors using them. The director should be prepared to discuss with the head of the property crew:

a. The kinds of properties needed.
b. Whether "practical" or not, i.e., made to operate in view of the audience.
c. The action involving them.
d. Research sources for information on style and type of props.
e. The placement of the props on stage or by whom carried on.

5. Costumes

Before the costumer can begin his research into the period and the actual creation of designs, he should be clear as to the following points, which the director should be prepared to discuss with him (preferably at the first production conference):

a. How can the costumes help convey the meaning of the play to the audience?

Costuming *Romeo and Juliet,* for example, in the hot colors and bold contrasts of fourteenth century Italy will make its impetuous love story more believable than if it were costumed in Elizabethan high fashion. Molière's *Affected Young Ladies* needs to be costumed in the height of absurd affectation in order to point Molière's satire. Anouilh's *Antigone,* originally played in tuxedos and evening gowns, was made more timely by costuming Creon and the guards in the military uniforms of an Iron Curtain nation.

Antigone

b. In what period should the play be costumed?

Hamlet has been costumed in every period from medieval Danish to World War II G. I. Often a 50 or 100 year variation in the period of the costumes will not disturb the audience and may add to the effect of the production. To modernize an older play may save on costume budget but lose some of its charm or meaning. *The Importance of Being Earnest,* for example, depends upon being costumed in a frothy and artificial elegance; modern young ladies are hardly dependent upon Mama's permission to speak to a young man. *Hedda Gabler,* on the other hand, could be played in modern dress, as the unfulfilled woman Ibsen depicted has not disappeared from our culture.

c. How can the style and general effect of the costumes be integrated with the style, color, and mood of the settings? Should the costumes be literal, enlarged from realism, or fanciful?

d. How can each costume best reflect the character who wears it? In *Summer and Smoke,* for example, Miss Alma's dresses can aid in her characterization by being restrictive and prim. Juliet's costumes, however, need to permit free, impulsive, girlish movement.

e. What problems of quick change are there?

The Diary of Anne Frank offers a record number of quick change problems, requiring careful advance planning concerning which garments can be underdressed and which added; the set designer, too, should be aware that each off-stage area where characters exit needs to be accessible to the wardrobe crew. *Othello* illustrates another quick change problem: Othello's first appearance is in the informal garb of a honeymoon night. He exits and must reappear four lines later formally gowned to appear before the Duke in the Senate.

f. How large a budget is available for costume?

This will in many cases govern the number of extras and bit parts that can be included as well as the number of costume changes for the principals.

6. Make-up

Make-up is as integrally related to costuming as lighting is to scene design. The director's original conception of the characters should include their facial characteristics and the general impression to be conveyed. Where quick changes of make-up are required, this should be taken into consideration in the placement of intermissions. There can be little specific planning for make-up until the play is cast and the facial features of the actors studied, with the following exceptions:

a. Wigs, where needed, should be considered early in the planning because of their high cost.

b. Haircuts of the cast should be checked, and where necessary, actors should be asked not to get haircuts until the performances are over.

c. When forced to cast young players in older parts, the director should be aware of which types of facial structures take character make-up best, and what can be accomplished with beards and mustaches.

7. Music

The decision to use music and to what extent grows out of the director's interpretation of the play, coupled with the practical problem of covering scene shifts. In plays departing from realism, the director is more free to use music. The functions which music may serve include:

a. To provide emotional reinforcement for the actors.

b. To set the period and mood.

c. To bridge from scene to scene.

d. To contribute to tension and suspense.

e. To underscore or punctuate significant moments or climaxes.

f. To lead the audience from realism toward fantasy or expressionism.

g. To fill in the time needed for scene shifts and to cover the noise of shifting.

h. To take the place of the curtain in central staging.

While the actual selection of music can be done later, the director should be conscious early in the planning of the potential contribution music could make to the production.

8. Sound effects.

The extent to which the director wishes to employ realistic sound is related to his conception of style. While some realistic plays such as *The Diary of Anne Frank* require detailed sound plots of recorded effects, others such as *Our Town* are better off with a rather obvious vocal imitation (of the rooster crowing, for example) than an authentic recording. An awkwardly managed sound effect or a late sound cue can, however, destroy the mood of a tense scene — for example, the bellowing of cows in the last scene of *The Crucible*. The director should be aware of sound problems early enough to order special records if necessary.

9. Dance

Plays in the realistic style rarely offer opportunity for dance movement, but many plays which transcend realism offer possibilities for integrating dance within the drama. Among them are *Dark of the Moon, Dream Girl, Peer Gynt, Beggar on Horseback,* and *Happy Birthday.* As one of the theatre's most ancient forms of emotional expression, dance should be used as an enrichment and a means of heightening dramatic effect wherever the style of the play permits. Working closely with a choreographer or dance teacher, the director will want to consider:

a. Ways in which rhythmic movement or movement beyond realism can enrich the production.
b. Space requirements for movement in relation to the ground plan.
c. Problems of casting dancers.
d. Style and quality of movement.
e. Selection of appropriate music for dance.
f. Costumes that permit freedom for dance movement.

10. Other reflections of the director's interpretation of the play.

The Winter's Tale. Experimental Theatre, Vassar College.

As the director arrives at a unified interpretation of the play and crystallizes the "production idea" with his technical staff, he should also try to find an integrated style and treatment of:

   a. Posters and mailing pieces, coordinated with the design of the production.
   b. Promotion and publicity stories, based on those elements in the director's interpretation which best lend themselves to arousing interest in the production.
   c. Program design and program notes if desired.
   d. Lobby displays, growing out of research in the period, the playwright, settings or costumes.

IV. Recording the interpretation in the director's book.

The director's book is the tangible result of all the foregoing study and research. It differs from the stage manager's prompt book in that the former is the projected or anticipated production and the latter the actual record of what is evolved in rehearsal.

Directors vary as to the extensiveness of their directors' books. Max Reinhardt's famous *regiebuch* was so detailed that it could be turned over to an assistant to conduct rehearsals. Mental notes may be sufficient for other directors or for simple productions. For the student of direction, however, a carefully prepared book is not only an assurance that no step has been omitted from his interpretative study, but also a ready source of reference in rehearsal. It should not be thought of as a finished product to which the actors must conform, but only as a tentative basis for conducting rehearsals, subject always to the exciting variations that grow out of a creative rehearsal.

A. Items that should be included in the director's book:
   1. A statement of the theme or meaning of the play as the director interprets it.
   2. Critical commentary on the play.
   3. Background material and research.
   4. Analysis of characters (often with photographs for make-up).
   5. A ground plan of the sets, to scale.
   6. A statement on the style of the production.
   7. The text itself, cut and edited.
      a. When acting editions are used, each page can be pasted with rubber cement onto a sheet of three-hole notebook paper with a center panel cut out to permit reading both sides of the page.
      b. When working from manuscripts, extra wide margins should be left by the typist.
   8. Divisions of the text into actions and beats.
   9. If a multi-scene play, arrangement of scenes into acts and placement of intermissions. (See breakdown of *Othello* on page 97.)
   10. Notations on major and minor climaxes as they occur in the text.
   11. Notations on tempo in the text.

12. Blocking of the scenes.
13. Notations on the use of theatrical elements within the text and summarized at the end — a separate page for props, costumes, music, etc.
14. Bibliography and list of source materials for future reference.

B. For a sample page from a director's book, see following.

Conventional symbols used in marking a director's book include "X" for "cross," a capital letter initial for each character, the terminology of the stage as given on pages 101-2, and simple sketches of the ground plan each time the positions of the actors change substantially.

V. Summary.

The director's interpretative study of a play, involving scholarly, critical, and creative aspects, is the period in which he becomes deeply absorbed with his play, and from which he evolves the ultimate unity of production. Interpretation involves the dualism of creative and technical aspects — internal and external, impression and expression — which will be reflected throughout the analysis of directing problems in succeeding chapters of this book.

The director's study is far from finished, however, when he enters rehearsal; new insights and values will or should emerge as he works with his cast. The processes involved in the director's interpretation are:

A. Determining what the play means. (Internal)
   1. Discovering the theme or meaning of the play.
   2. Studying what critics have written about the play and the author.
   3. Re-creating the background of the play through research.
   4. Analyzing the characters and their motives.
   5. Dividing the play into actions and beats.
   6. Crystallizing in words the particular emphasis, point of view or approach which the director wishes to give the production for his particular audience.
   7. Preparing the text for production.

B. Finding a form in which to project this meaning to the audience. (External)

   1. Selecting a style for the production.
   2. Planning for the most effective use of the theatrical elements:

a. Actors	f. Make-up
b. Scenery	g. Music
c. Lighting	h. Sound
d. Properties	i. Dance
e. Costumes	j. Other reflections of the director's interpretation.

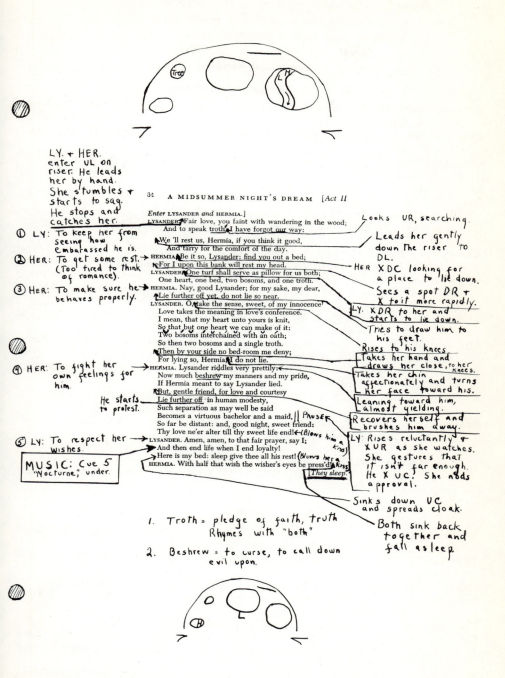

LY. + HER.
enter UL on
riser. He leads
her by hand.
She stumbles +
starts to sag.
He stops and
catches her.

① LY: To keep her from
seeing how
embarassed he is.

② HER: To get some rest.
(Too tired to think
of romance).

③ HER: To make sure he
behaves properly.

④ HER: To fight her
own feelings for
him.

He starts
to protest.

⑤ LY: To respect her
wishes.

MUSIC: Cue 5
"Nocturne," under.

32   A MIDSUMMER NIGHT'S DREAM [*Act II*

Enter LYSANDER *and* HERMIA.]

LYSANDER. Fair love, you faint with wandering in the wood;
    And to speak troth, I have forgot our way:
    We 'll rest us, Hermia, if you think it good,
    And tarry for the comfort of the day.

HERMIA. Be it so, Lysander: find you out a bed;
    For I upon this bank will rest my head.

LYSANDER. One turf shall serve as pillow for us both;
    One heart, one bed, two bosoms, and one troth.

HERMIA. Nay, good Lysander; for my sake, my dear,
    Lie further off yet, do not lie so near.

LYSANDER. O, take the sense, sweet, of my innocence!
    Love takes the meaning in love's conference.
    I mean, that my heart unto yours is knit,
    So that but one heart we can make of it:
    Two bosoms interchained with an oath;
    So then two bosoms and a single troth.
    Then by your side no bed-room me deny;
    For lying so, Hermia, I do not lie.

HERMIA. Lysander riddles very prettily:
    Now much beshrew my manners and my pride,
    If Hermia meant to say Lysander lied.
    But, gentle friend, for love and courtesy
    Lie further off in human modesty,
    Such separation as may well be said
    Becomes a virtuous bachelor and a maid,
    So far be distant: and, good night, sweet friend;
    Thy love ne'er alter till thy sweet life end!

LYSANDER. Amen, amen, to that fair prayer, say I;
    And then end life when I end loyalty!
    Here is my bed: sleep give thee all his rest!

HERMIA. With half that wish the wisher's eyes be press'd!
                                            [*They sleep.*

|| PAUSE

Looks UR, searching.

Leads her gently
down the riser to
DL.

HER XDC looking for
a place to lie down.

Sees a spot DR +
X to it more rapidly.

LY: XDR to her and
starts to lie down.

Tries to draw him to
his feet.

Rises to his knees

Takes her hand and
draws her close, to her
knees.

Takes her chin
affectionately and turns
her face toward his.

Leaning toward him,
almost yielding.

Recovers herself and
brushes him away.

LY: Rises reluctantly +
XUR as she watches.
She gestures that
it isn't far enough.
He X UC. She nods
approval.

Sinks down UC
and spreads cloak.

Both sink back
together and
fall asleep.

(Blows him a kiss)

(Blows her a kiss)

1. Troth = pledge of faith, truth
    Rhymes with "both"

2. Beshrew = to curse, to call down
    evil upon.

C. Recording the interpretation in the director's book.
   1. Items that should be included in the director's book.
   2. A sample page from a director's book.

Suggested Reading

Directors' interpretation of plays:

BENTLEY, ERIC. *The House of Bernarda Alba*, in *In Search of Theatre*. New York: Alfred A. Knopf, Inc., 1953.

BROOK, PETER. "A Realistic Approach to 'Eugene Onegin.'" *New York Times*, October 27, 1957.

CLURMAN, HAROLD. "Some Preliminary Notes for *The Member of the Wedding*," in *Directors on Directing*, edited by Toby Cole and Helen Krich Chinoy. Indianapolis: The Bobbs-Merrill Co., 1963.

GALLAWAY, MARIAN. *The Playboy of the Western World*, in *The Director in the Theatre*. New York: The Macmillan Co., 1963.

GIELGUD, JOHN. "Staging *Love for Love*," *Theatre Arts*, XXVII, 11, November, 1943, pp. 662-668.

KAZAN, ELIA. Excerpts from a notebook on *Death of a Salesman*, in Kenneth Thorpe Rowe, *A Theatre in Your Head*. New York: Funk and Wagnalls, 1960, pp. 44-59.

————. "Notebook for *A Streetcar Named Desire*," in *Directors on Directing*, edited by Toby Cole and Helen Krich Chinoy. Indianapolis: The Bobbs-Merrill Co., 1963.

LEWIS, ROBERT. *My Heart's in the Highlands*, in John Gassner, *Producing the Play*. New York: The Dryden Press, 1953, p. 294.

MILLER, ARTHUR. "A Show Soliloquy," (Kazan's approach to *After the Fall*), *Show Magazine*, IV, 1, January, 1964, pp. 55-98.

REDGRAVE, MICHAEL. *Uncle Harry*, in *Mask or Face*. New York: Theatre Arts Books, 1958, pp. 149-164.

ROBERTSON, TOBY. "Directing *Edward II*," *Tulane Drama Review*, VIII, 4, Summer, 1964, pp. 174-183.

STANISLAVSKY, CONSTANTIN. *Stanislavsky Produces Othello*. Trans. Helen Nowak. London: Geoffrey Bles, Ltd., 1948.

————. *The Seagull Produced by Stanislavsky*. Trans. David Magarshack. New York: Theatre Arts, Inc., 1952.

————. *Stanislavsky Directs*, by Nikolai M. Gorchakov. New York: Funk and Wagnalls Co., 1954.

General:

BARRY, JACKSON G. "José Quintero: The Director as Image Maker," *Educational Theatre Journal*, XIV, 1, March, 1962, pp. 15-22.

CANFIELD, CURTIS. *The Craft of Play Directing*. New York: Holt, Rinehart and Winston, 1963.

CHEKHOV, MICHAEL. *To the Director and Playwright*. New York: Harper, 1963.

deBANKE, CECILE. *Shakespearean Stage Production*: *Then and Now*. New York: McGraw-Hill Book Company, 1953.

GIELGUD, JOHN. *Stage Directions*. New York: Random House, 1964.

GUTHRIE, TYRONE. *A Life in the Theatre*. New York: McGraw-Hill Book Co., 1959.

HAWES, DAVID S. "Preparation for Producing Molière," *Educational Theatre Journal*, XIII, 2, May, 1961, pp. 86-91.

HUNT, HUGH. *The Director in the Theatre*. London: Routledge and Kegan Paul, 1954.

OTHELLO

Production Scheme and Act Breakdown

SCENE # IN TEXT	OUR SCENE #	CONTENT OF SCENE	STAGE AREA	SCENIC REQUIREMENTS
ACT I Scene 1	ACT I Scene 1	Rousing of Brabantio	Full	A street in Venice, before Brabantio's house, with 2d story porch or window, under which Iago can hide.
Scene 2	Scene 2	Summoning of Othello	Shallow	Before the Sagittary Inn.
Scene 3	Scene 3	Hearing Brabantio vs. Othello	Full	Doge's Palace, Senate Chamber.
p. 23 lines 326-422.	Scene 4	Baiting Roderigo to follow to Cyprus.	Shallow	Merely close drape from previous scene.
ACT II Scene 1	Scene 5	Disembarkation at Cyprus	Full	Open place with high platform. Steps to descend from harbor. Things to sit on, bales, trunks.
Scene 2	cut			
Scene 3	Scene 6	Getting Cassio drunk & disgraced	Shallow	Servants carry in table and benches, wine barrel.
		1st INTERMISSION		
ACT III Scene 1	cut			
Scene 2	cut			
Scene 3	ACT II Scene 1	Planting 1st suspicion Handkerchief dropped.	Full	Garden or Patio within Cyprus castle. Place for eavesdropping.
lines 187-226 of III, Scene 4	Scene 2	Bianca-Cassio giving her the handkerchief.	Shallow	In front of drape.
ACT III, Scene 4	Scene 3	Demanding the handkerchief	Full	Same as II, 1, above. Garden or Patio of Castle.
ACT IV, Scene 1	go on, continuous	Epilepsy and Eavesdropping	Full	Same.
		2nd INTERMISSION		
ACT IV, Scene 2	ACT III Scene 1	Confronting Desdemona.	Full	Bedchamber, with heavy practical door, four-poster bed with curtains, drawn now.
lines 198-267 of IV, 2	Scene 2	Iago-Roderigo, needling Roderigo to kill Cassio	Shallow	Before drape.
ACT IV, Scene 3	Scene 3	Willow Song	Full	Same as III, 1. Bedchamber. Curtain around bed now open.
ACT V Scene 1	Scene 4	Killing of Roderigo & wounding of Cassio	Shallow	Street, needs "bulk" for Roderigo to hide behind.
Scene 2	Scene 5	Smothering of Desdemona, and resolution.	Full	Same as III, 1, Bedchamber.

JOSEPH, BERTRAM. *Acting Shakespeare*. New York: Theatre Art Books, 1960.

KNIGHT, G. WILSON. *Principles of Shakespearean Production*. Penguin Books, 1949.

McFARLANE, JAMES W. *Discussions of Henrik Ibsen*. Boston: D. C. Heath & Co., 1962.

McMULLAN, FRANK A. *The Directorial Image*. Hamden, Conn.: Shoe String Press, 1962.

OXENFORD, LYN. *Playing Period Plays*. London: J Garnet Miller, Ltd., 1958.

SAINT-DENIS, MICHEL. *Theatre: The Rediscovery of Style*. New York: Theatre Arts Books, 1960.

VAN DRUTEN, JOHN. "The Job of Directing." *Theatre Arts Anthology*. New York: Theatre Arts Books, 1950.

WATKINS, RONALD. *On Producing Shakespeare*. New York: W. W. Norton and Co., 1951.

WEBSTER, MARGARET. *Shakespeare Without Tears*. New York: McGraw-Hill Book Co., 1942. Premier Paperback, 1957.

Chapter 5

COMPOSITION

I. Introduction.

When the director has completed his interpretative study of the play, made up his director's book, and received a tentative ground plan from the scene designer (or made one himself if he is working without a designer), he is ready to begin his "blocking" of the play. Blocking can be defined as the physical arrangement of the actors on stage and their movement from place to place. The two aspects of blocking are (1) the advance blocking which the director does on paper prior to going into rehearsal, often with a scale ground plan or model and toy soldiers, golf tees, chessmen, stickpins or pipe cleaners bent to represent the actors so that all positions can be plotted and recorded in the director's book, and (2) blocking rehearsals, in which the director tests out his preplanned blocking with the actors; the latter inevitably involves modifying the original conceptions, adjusting, changing, incorporating creative ideas advanced by the cast, and dealing with problems that had not been foreseen on paper. Nevertheless, even the most experienced directors find that preplanning of the blocking is an essential part of their "homework" in order to solve complex problems and save time in rehearsal.

A. Functions of Blocking:

1. To compose effective stage pictures.

   Composition can be defined as the imposition of visual pattern upon random life, the arrangement of the formless into a form that is meaningful and aesthetically satisfying. Even if a cast of outstanding stars were assembled, a director would still be necessary because:

   a. The actors cannot see themselves as they appear from the audience.

   b. It is not practical for each actor to arrange his own groupings with others — his concentration should be within his character.

   c. The actor, like the scenery, properties, costumes and lights, becomes an element in the total composition, and his position on stage at all times is the responsibility of the director; this explains why the profession of direction arose late in the nineteenth century concurrently with the growth of picture-frame realism and the decline of the star system. The director can benefit greatly from a study of great paintings, many of which have approximately the same proportions as the average proscenium opening.

2. To keep the actor's face visible to the audience when he has lines or important reactions.

   The actor's face is generally the most expressive part of his body, and audiences want to see it. (In addition the position of the face can aid or hinder in projection of the voice.) As the dialogue progresses from character to character, the director must serve as a kind of "traffic cop" to make sure that the speaking actor is visible and the others subordinate or appropriately related to the speaker.

3. To move the actors naturally from one picture to another.

   Although this chapter will analyze composition as though the director composes a series of unrelated "stills," the practical application of these principles is always limited by the fact that one picture grows out of the preceding one and leads to the succeeding one. It is through the movement of the actors that the director links the stage pictures and gets the actors where he needs them at any given moment. As movement serves a number of other purposes in addition to linking the stage pictures, it will be treated separately in the next chapter.

B. The director's approach to composition.

There is an old adage that there are two people in every audience for whom the director must plan — the deaf old lady and the blind old man. For the rest of the audience that can both see and hear, effects are doubly strong when one impression reinforces the other. The director thus has two media through which he can communicate with the audience — the visual and the auditory. It would be pedantic to attempt to decide which makes the stronger impression on the audience; we go to the theatre to *see* a play, but many of the greatest playwrights (including Shake-speare) make their strongest appeal through *oral* language. Al-though television separates the electronic components of "video" and "audio," any such separation in the theatre is purely for pur-poses of analysis. This chapter and the one to follow on Movement present the means by which the director organizes or composes the visual picture, and Chapter 7 presents the means of organ-izing the oral pattern.

C. Stage terminology used in blocking (on the proscenium stage).
1. *Stage right* and *left* are always the actor's right and left as he faces the audience.
2. *Downstage* means nearer to the audience. The downstage foot is the foot nearer the audience. To *move down* means to move nearer the audience.
3. *Upstage* means farther from the audience. To *move up* means to move away from the audience.
4. *Cross down right* (abbreviated as XDR) means to move to the downstage right area. XULC means to cross to up left center.
5. *Onstage* means nearer to the center of the stage.
6. *Offstage* means farther from the center of the stage. To move several steps off is to go several steps away from center.

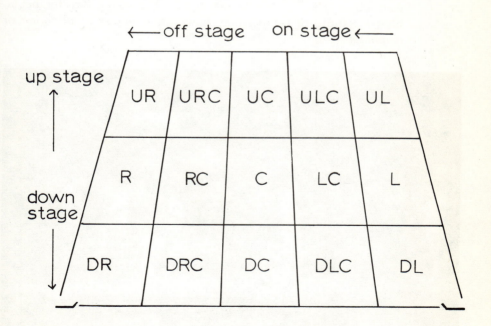

7. *Above* a person or object means on the upstage side.
8. *Below* a person or object means on the downstage side.
9. To *open up* means to turn more of the actor's body to the audience, i.e., from profile to one-quarter, or from one-quarter to full-front. (See body positions, II, A, 1.)
10. To *turn in* means to turn less of the actor's body to the audience, i.e., from one-quarter to profile, or from profile to three-quarter.
11. To *cover* means to stand between another actor and the audience, or between a property and the audience. (There are times when the latter is necessary, as the covering of an oil lamp when it is being turned on.)
12. To *focus* means to look at another actor.
13. To *steal* means either (1) to attract attention illegitimately from one's partner or (2) to move unobtrusively to a new position, also called "easing down" or "dropping down."

D. The requirements of an effective stage composition.

Authorities in the field of painting generally agree that good visual composition should have the following attributes: *unity, balance, center of attention or emphasis,* and *variety.* For the stage we must add two more requirements: it must *tell the story,* and be *functional.* These six qualities are mutually interrelated and affect each other. The simplest to manage for the young director beginning his study of composition, however, is *center of attention* or *emphasis.*

An uncomposed picture (no center of attention)

II. The stage picture should have a center of attention.

The director in one sense may be said to direct not the play itself but the attention of the audience to the play, compelling the spectators to look where he wants them to and anticipating their emotional re-

A composed picture (with a center of attention)

Note variety of body positions:

¼   FF   ¼ ¼   P FF ¼   FF   ¼   ¼ ¾   FF

sponses. Unlike the camera director who can compel the audience's attention by a close-up which excludes everything except what he wishes to emphasize, the stage director must use more subtle and complex means of subordinating that which is less important and directing the spectators' eyes where he wishes them.

Center of attention, or *visual emphasis* is perhaps the most important aspect of composition. An audience can look at only one center of attention at a time. As can be seen from the uncomposed photograph, a picture with no center of attention may confuse or bore an audience. It is even more bewildering when an audience hears a line of dialogue and cannot locate the speaker. We may conclude, therefore, that the center of attention should (with a very few exceptions to be considered under movement) *always include the speaking actor.*

A. Kinds of visual emphasis.

    1. *Single emphasis* is upon one actor at a time, although two actors very close together (as in an embrace) may constitute one center of attention.

    2. *Shared emphasis* permits the audience to dart its eyes quickly from one actor to another in a fast repartee of dialogue. There

should be nothing between the two characters which interrupts the easy shift of the audience's attention from one to the other.

3. *Secondary emphasis* involves the creation of subsidiary centers of attention in addition to the principal one. It is useful in crowd scenes to add variety and interest, but must be held within limits so as not to detract from the primary emphasis. Characters with secondary emphasis may later in the scene become the principal center of attention and should be so placed that attention can go easily to them. Often, too, a character gives a speech about another character who is silent, and the audience often glances briefly at him to see how he is reacting, then back to the speaker.

4. *Multiple emphasis* may be used in crowd scenes such as the prologue to *Carousel,* when there are moments in which there is no center of attention but a variety of groups of more or less equal interest. The audience looks from one to the other

Of Thee I Sing, University of California at Los Angeles (Secondary Emphasis)

as at a three-ring circus; before long, however, the director will need to concentrate the attention of the audience.

5. *Offstage emphasis* is effective for certain moments such as in *The Diary of Anne Frank* when the family is intently listening toward the foot of the steps, or in *Ghosts* when the orphanage burns down. Although offstage emphasis makes a telling picture, it should be used for moments of limited duration.

B. Means of achieving emphasis.

These ten means are not listed in order of importance. A director generally will use more than one at a time, depending upon his interpretation of the scene and the particular set in which he is working. Note how many different means were used by da Vinci in *The Last Supper*. Emphasis can be directed to the actor:

The Last Supper, Leonardo da Vinci.

1. Through the actor's *body position.*

   a. Definition of the basic body positions for the individual actor: (Note: in the following "the footlights" are presumed to be on a straight line between the edges of the proscenium arch, 90 degrees from the center seats of the audience.)

      (1) *Full-front position,* in which the actor's body and head directly face the audience.

      (2) *One-quarter position,* in which the actor's upstage foot parallels the footlights and his downstage foot is brought comfortably back and turned at a 45 degree angle from his upstage foot. This pulls the actor's body around so that more is seen by the audience. His face

is on the same axis as his upstage foot, parallel to the footlights. *The one-quarter position is the "home position" and the actor usually should assume it when working with a partner until directed otherwise.*

(3) *Profile position,* in which the actor's head and body parallel the footlights and both his feet are approximately 90 degrees from the audience.

(4) *Three-quarter position,* in which the actor's downstage foot parallels the footlights and his upstage foot is brought comfortably back, pointing upstage at a 45 degree angle.

(5) *Full-back position,* in which the actor's back is to the audience and he faces directly upstage.

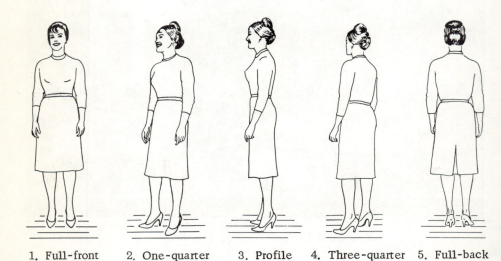

1. Full-front   2. One-quarter   3. Profile   4. Three-quarter   5. Full-back

b. Relative strength of the various body positions:
Other things being equal, the actor in the strongest body position will receive emphasis. An actor in a strong body position can usually dominate regardless of the area of the stage he uses.

(1) Full-front is the strongest position.
(2) One-quarter is next strongest.
(3) Profile is medium in strength.
(4) Three-quarter is a weak position.

(5) Full-back is the weakest position.
(6) Standing is stronger than sitting.
(7) Sitting is stronger than lying down.
(8) Sitting or standing erect is stronger than slouching or leaning.
(9) Body positions can be strengthened or weakened by the direction the head is turned. A full front position can be weakened by turning the head to profile; a three-quarter position can be strengthened by turning the head into profile.
(10) Kneeling, which generally is weak, can best be kept opened by kneeling on the downstage knee and keeping the upstage knee up.

c. Positions of two actors playing a scene together.

   (1) *Shared* means that both actors are in one-quarter positions, equally visible and equally distant from the footlights. *This is a basic position and it is bad theatre manners to deviate from it unless directed to do so.*

   (2) *Profile* means that the two actors are each in profile position facing each other and equally distant from the footlights.

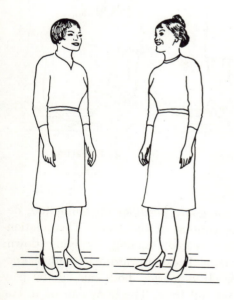
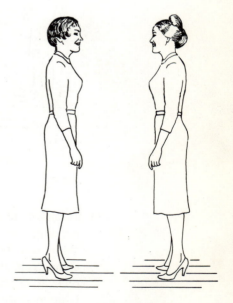

1. Shared   2. Profile

(3) *Upstaging* means that one of the actors is in one-quarter position, upstage of his partner who must therefore turn his head and body to a three-quarter position to face his partner. The *upstage actor* has *taken* the scene and the downstage actor *given* it. Although there are many occasions when the director will want this effect, it is bad etiquette to move upstage of one's partner without being so directed.

(4) *Cheating* means that the actor who has given the scene to his upstage partner cheats by bringing his body and/or face more nearly into profile. He still seems to be facing his partner, and if done within limits the audience cannot detect that he is cheating.

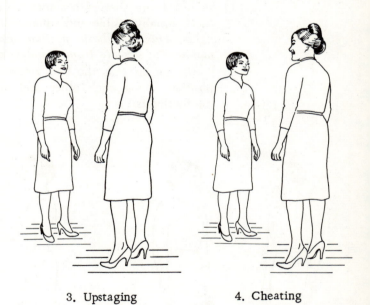

3. Upstaging   4. Cheating

(5) *Variations* of the foregoing positions are unlimited, depending upon the content of the scene. The relationships can be used seated, leaning, or lying down; actors can turn their backs toward each other one-quarter, profile or three-quarter; both can (if the play is nonrealistic) face full front. The body can be in one position and the head in another. Note the number of variations in the picture on page 103.

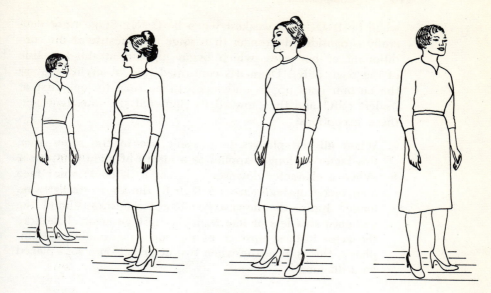

5. Variations of Cheating

2. Through the *area* of the stage.
   The chart pictured indicates the relative strength of areas of
   the stage. Other things being equal, a single actor is strongest

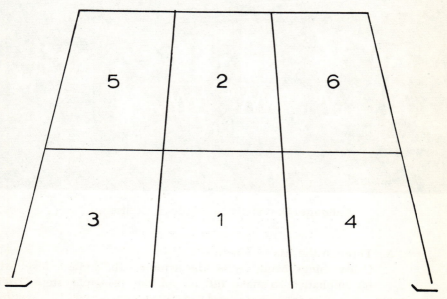

Areas in order of strength.

when he is DC and weakest when he is UL. Stage right generally is considered stronger than stage left because of the conditioning of our eyes, which begin to read at the left side of the page (SR). Dean has confirmed this, observing that as the curtain goes up an audience can be seen to look first at its left (SR) and then toward its right (SL).[1] Note, however, these exceptions:

a. When all the players in a scene are in the same area, this factor no longer applies as a means of giving emphasis.

b. When a character downstage (areas 3, 1, or 4) must face a character upstage (areas 5, 2, or 6) the above strengths no longer apply; the downstage actor is "upstaged" and the audience sees less of him than the upstage actor. Therefore the actor farthest upstage in a group will usually take emphasis; this is also true when two actors sit on a sofa placed on a diagonal.

Antigone. University of Southern California.

3. Through the use of *levels*.

Other things being equal, the actor on the highest level will be emphatic. To make full use of this principle, steps, risers

[1]Dean, Alexander, *Fundamentals of Play Directing* (New York: Farrar and Rinehart, Inc., 1941), p. 133.

and platforms are worked into stage settings wherever justifiable.

Lysistrata.

4. Through the use of *contrast*.
   Other things being equal, the actor who is in some way different from the others will receive emphasis. For example:

   a. If all but one are standing, the seated actor is emphatic.
   b. If all but one are facing out, the actor in profile or three-
      quarter position would be emphatic.
   c. If all but one are in a particular style or color of costume,
      the actor in a contrasting style or color will be emphatic.

The Diary of Anne Frank.

5. Through the use of *isolation*.

   Other things being equal, the actor who is apart from a group — isolated in space — will be most emphatic. Newspaper advertising often uses this principle, surrounding the emphatic words with empty space. The old stock company adage expressed the same concept with the rule "to keep an arm's length from the star."

The Time of Your Life. (Isolation)

6. Through the use of *focus*.

   When other actors focus on (i.e., look at) a particular actor, the audience tends to do the same. The eyes of the actor are therefore a very important means of directing audience attention. The actor should look at the speaking actor unless he has a definite motivation to look away or is asked to do so by the director.

   a. Looking elsewhere than at the emphatic actor is called *counter-focus*. If actor A in *The Happy Time* is the center of attention and B, C, D, G and F are listening to her, E need not focus on A, for example, but may counter-focus on F. If the audience's eye follows from E to F, it will then go where F is looking, which should be back to A. Note the counter-focus in *The Last Supper* by da Vinci.

The Happy Time. (Counter-focus)

B   C   A   D   G   E F

b. Counter-focus will be used by the director to add variety to the composition, to avoid overusing such a strong device as focus for emphasis, to reveal the character's reaction to what is being said, and to link various elements in the composition.

Dark of the Moon. Idyllwild Arts Foundation. (Line)

7. Through the use of *line*.

Lines, either straight or curved, lead the audience's eye like an arrow toward the emphatic figure, which may be at either end, depending upon the focus of the actors in the line.

a. Lines can be supplied by the bodies of the actors, the height of their heads, arms, legs, or by costume elements, such as canes, swords, pikes or rifles.

b. To achieve variety, lines may be diagonal, straight, broken, curved, or the graceful S-curve. See the photograph of *Knights of the Round Table,* page 70. Straight lines are rarely formed in real life except in military situations, formal or public occasions; they must be used on the stage with caution, therefore, in realistic plays.

c. *Repetition* can also be used for emphasis as a variation of line — a number of guards behind a king, a number of butlers behind a dowager, a number of secretaries behind a tycoon, etc. The more minor figures that are used repetitively, the stronger the emphasis upon the major figure. According to Arnheim[2] the eyes tend to move in the direction of diminishing intervals.

The Twin Menaechmi, University of Southern California.

[2]Arnheim, Rudolf, *Art and Visual Perception* (Berkeley and Los Angeles: University of California Press, 1954), p. 23.

8. Through the use of *triangles*.

As an extension of the principle of line, the lines of a triangle tend to lead the eye of the viewer from either side toward the apex. Triangle compositions with the emphatic figure at the apex are therefore a standard form of theatrical grouping.

A Marriage Proposal.

   a. The apex normally is upstage if the emphatic figure is speaking to the others in the triangle.
   b. The apex may be downstage if the emphatic figure has a motivation to face away from the others.
   c. Equilateral triangles seem prearranged and should be avoided except in plays where symmetry is desired.
   d. Triangles can become monotonous if overused and not varied. With nine other means of obtaining emphasis, the director need not rely solely on triangles.
   e. Triangles can be varied by irregular spacing of figures, by the use of counter-focus within the triangle, and by varying the head heights of the figures — some seated, some standing tall, some leaning, and taller actors not placed together.
9. Through *scenic reinforcement*.

Architectural elements in the setting can be used for emphasis; their placement is therefore of concern to the director as well as the designer.

a. An actor gains emphasis when framed in a doorway, arch or window.

b. An actor gains emphasis when related to strong elements such as columns, thrones or masses.

c. An actor gains emphasis when standing where a strong scenic line terminates or where two scenic lines meet. A series of columns or arches may provide repetition to emphasize the actor.

Libel! New York production.

10. Through *lighting*.

Although the modern, realistic theatre has excluded the follow-spot which was conventional several generations ago, the control of light remains a very important means of giving emphasis. The director of a classic, nonrealistic or musical play may use this medium more freely.

a. Unless there are strong factors to counteract it, the most brightly lighted actor will receive the most emphasis.

b. The follow-spot is beginning to find its way back to respectability in such modifications of realism as the road

A Dream Play, University of Illinois.

companies of *Two for the See-saw* and *Sweet Bird of Youth.*

III. The second requirement of a good stage picture is that it should *tell the story,* or picturize the inner relationships in the scene. It should dramatize visually the inherent elements of action and clash at the moment. This is one of the most valuable purposes which composition serves, and the one which makes the story meaningful to the "deaf old lady."

Picturization requires all of the director's conscious artistry, for in life people do not necessarily group themselves into meaningful pictures. Picturization is derived from nature, however, and requires only that the director select and arrange details to further his artistic purpose.

Plays vary in their content to such an extent that picturization cannot be done by rule. To the experienced director stage pictures will come to mind easily as he studies the play. The student director should follow these steps:

A. Break the scene into *actions* and *beats* before picturizing.
   If the director has completed his analysis of the play by action and beat during his interpretative study and marked the beginning of each new beat in the director's book, the composition of the stage picture will be facilitated. Before blocking the scene, the director should ask himself:

1. Who is the dominant figure in this particular beat?
2. What does he want or what is he trying to do in this beat?
   a. Physically.
   b. Psychologically.
3. Who else is in this particular beat, and what do they want?
4. What are the interpersonal relationships in the beat?
   a. Who is the opposition, if any, to the dominant figure?
   b. Toward whom does the dominant figure feel strongly — either strong affection or strong hostility.
   c. What do the others in the scene feel toward the dominant figure and toward each other? Whose side are they on? What are they doing?

B. Relate the characters to each other physically in the stage picture.
   1. People tend to be near those they love, support, defend, protect, want to impress or obtain a concession from.
   2. People tend to stay away from those they dislike, distrust, oppose, reject, or those who make them feel guilty.
   3. People approach those for whom they feel strong hostility, whom they want to threaten or prevent from doing something.
   4. People who are indifferent, afraid to identify themselves, busy with something else, or unrelated to the problem tend to remain apart and can be used to fill in the periphery of the stage picture.
   5. The family is a natural unit. Although its members may quarrel among themselves, they tend to stand together when threatened from the outside.
   6. The actor as a rule needs to be near the person to whom he is speaking.

C. Select the area of the stage in which the particular beat can best be played.
   1. The relative strength of stage areas has already been discussed. The director will often deliberately choose a weak area in which to stage a certain scene (1) for contrast, (2) for variety, so as not to overuse any one area, (3) to make a later scene seem stronger, or (4) to soften the impact of sensational action such as the blinding of Gloucester in *King Lear*.
   2. In addition to strength or weakness, the areas of the stage are considered by many directors to possess inherent emotional values. Alexander Dean[3] was probably the first to formalize this concept, but his rules must not be slavishly obeyed to the exclusion of all originality. Most practising directors would

[3]Dean, *op. cit.*, p. 212.

agree with Dean, however, that (other things being equal) the areas of the stage are particularly well suited for picturizing the kinds of scenes indicated:

a.	Down right	Warm, intimate scenes, love scenes, emotional revelations; also direct narration to the audience, as in *Our Town* and *The Glass Menagerie*.
b.	Down center	Harsh, climactic scenes, quarrels, defiance, explosive moments. Such a strong area must be used sparingly, like *fortissimo* in music.
c.	Down left	Tension, conspiracies, soliloquies, scandals, routine business matters, unsuccessful love scenes.
d.	Up right	Eavesdropping, romance, foreshadowing.
e.	Up center	Royalty, authority, formality, dignity, arbitration between hostile forces.
f.	Up left	Unreality, ghost scenes, horror scenes.

D. Use the furniture in the scene to the fullest advantage in picturization.

In planning the ground plan, director and designer should keep picturization in mind. Even within a given ground plan, however, a piece of furniture can be moved around or repositioned for a certain scene. In many classic plays the director is free to have servants place furniture as needed for each scene.

1. Associate certain furniture with certain characters when appropriate. Some examples:

   a. The dining table to which the family returns after each crisis in *You Can't Take It With You.*
   b. The "dear, honored bookcase" which means so much to Gaev that he weeps over it in *The Cherry Orchard.*
   c. In a production of *Summer and Smoke*, the young doctor never sat at his father's desk (though he leaned on it and put his foot on it) until his father's death brought him to maturity.
   d. The Old Vic production of *Hamlet* used the same principle when Hamlet in a soliloquy sat upon his father's throne, an invasion of his stepfather's prerogative.

2. Use furniture to support the actors in moments of strong emotion. A table can be a buffer between two opponents; a chair can be a crutch in a moment of crisis; how a person feels about social conventions can be shown in the way he handles furniture.

3. People who want to ingratiate themselves or establish rapport usually select low and informal furniture to sit on such as hassocks, stools, a pillow on the floor.

Exercise: See how many different combinations of groupings can be found for two people centered around a sofa.

E. Use the actors' bodies plastically to reveal the emotion that is going on within.

The Miser, Southwest Missouri State College.

1. Dancers are familiar with the opposing principles of:
   a. Contraction-elevation.
   b. Tension-relaxation.
   c. Contact-rejection.
2. For the actor these principles can be applied:
   a. With the head — where it is focused or directed.
   b. With the body.
      Ambivalence or interruption of an activity can be picturized when the head is focused in one direction and the body in another. Leaning forward or backward may express in-

terest or lack of it, reinforcing the visual line to the emphatic figure.

c. With the arms.

Reaching out, threatening, contacting others suggests extroversion; arms related only to self — folded across chest, hands in pockets, on face or in hair — suggests introversion.

d. With the legs.

The degree of formality or informality of the scene is often effectively expressed by actors' legs. The legs of actors seated on the floor may contribute to the line, sequence and unity of the composition. Alfred Lunt in *The Visit* provided a memorable example of legs as an expressive part of the body.

F. Try tentative stage pictures on the basis of the preceding five steps. Look at the composition from out front, refining, modifying and adjusting it for the purpose of:

1. Finding the most interesting way to picturize a given beat or scene, not merely the most "natural" or "normal." Be imaginative within the restrictions of the given scene. Where there is a choice, select the more theatrical or telling picture rather than an equally truthful but less theatrical one. Selection and arrangement make the difference between the artist and the copyist.

2. Avoiding the obvious.

3. Retaining a sense of truth, based on observation of real life and human character. Start with truth and if necessary enlarge it; do not start with the enlargement. Realistic drama requires that stage pictures should *seem* (not necessarily *be*) lifelike and natural.

IV. **The third requirement of a good stage picture is that it should have balance.**

Balance has been defined as "a state of equipoise, as between weights, different elements, or opposing forces; equilibrium." A well-balanced picture is aesthetically satisfying to the viewer, and an unbalanced one disturbing. (This requirement applies mainly to picture frame or proscenium staging. Where there is no frame the spectator is less conscious of balance and imbalance.)

Balance in stage composition is achieved when the elements to the right of center equal those to the left of center. To analyze balance, it is necessary to draw an imaginary line bisecting the proscenium arch and dividing the stage picture into two equal halves. The two halves of the stage can be thought of as a see-saw, with a fulcrum at the center line (which is usually marked on the stage floor at the curtain line). The scene designer will normally provide a balanced set when empty of actors (except when a strong mass of actors is to play an entire scene in one position) and the director should use his actors to maintain this balance.

There are two types of balance, and the director may choose for each scene and each play which type is the more appropriate to use.

A. Symmetrical balance.
  1. This is the simplest form of balance to achieve but also the least interesting. It exists when exactly the same number of actors and scenic elements are on the right side of the center line as are on the left, and with equal spacing, as though a picture of half the stage had been folded over and duplicated on the other half.
  2. Because groups of people rarely divide themselves into equal halves in real life, symmetrical balance seems artificial and calls attention to itself. There are times, however, when the director will find this desirable:
      a. In plays of artificial style, or where there is symmetry in dialogue or content. *The Importance of Being Earnest, The Matchmaker.*
      b. In plays set in periods when symmetry and order were characteristic in music, art and architecture. Greek and Roman, seventeenth century, eighteenth century; operas of Mozart.
      c. In scenes of royalty, great formality, state occasions, equal balance of opposing forces (such as the street fights in *Romeo and Juliet*), courtroom scenes where interest is shared equally by prosecution and defense, scenes involving the church and divine figures.

B. Asymmetrical balance (balance without symmetry).

  Asymmetrical balance is not obtained by duplication of elements on right and left, but by more subtle, interesting and variable means. The net result, however, must be the *impression* that stage right is equal in weight to stage left. "Weight" in this context does not mean the literal weight, size or number of actors, but rather their psychological, aesthetic or emphatic weight. There are therefore no precise rules for arriving at asymmetrical balance; much depends upon the director's cultivating a sense of proportion and aesthetic sensitivity. Factors which affect weight for balance purposes include:
  1. How much visual emphasis is placed upon the character. Each of the ten means of obtaining emphasis can be used for balance. For example:

The Affected Young Ladies, Symmetrical balance.

Armida Abandoned by Rinaldo, by Tiepolo.
Asymmetrical balance.

    a. One actor framed in an arch or against the sky will balance several against neutral backgrounds.

    b. One actor in a strong area or body position will balance several in weak areas or body positions.

    c. One actor standing may balance several seated (or vice versa).

2. How much psychological interest the character has for the audience.

    a. The authority or prestige of the character in the play. Policemen, judges, kings and priests command more weight than average citizens. The same is true of "the boss," the most popular character, the most beloved or most hated.

Prisoners from the Front, by Winslow Homer.

    b. Whether the character is speaking or not.
As a rule, the speaker will command more weight than nonspeaking actors.

    c. The significance of what is said or done.
The suspense or amount of concern the audience feels for what is happening at the moment may add psychological weight to certain characters. A figure suggesting impending action can balance several relaxed figures. In *Amahl and the Night Visitors,* a child taking a step without crutches

is of sufficient interest to balance three kings, a page and the mother.

Amahl and the Night Visitors.

3. How far characters are from the center line.
This is the *principle of the see-saw*.
a. A lighter figure will balance a heavier figure if the lighter one is proportionately farther from center. To balance actors or groups with different aesthetic weight, vary the distance from center, trying roughly to approximate the formula $W \times D = W' \times D'$ — weight times distance from center equals weight on the opposite side times distance from center on the opposite side.

The see-saw principle.

b. When a composition in which one actor balances two or three is thrown off balance by the entrance of a fourth who joins the group, the sole character must move farther from center to restore balance. If a fifth or sixth joins the group, however, he need not move again. There is an old saying that "The eye counts to five."

4. Whether minor figures remain individualized or become a *mass*.

   a. More than three figures placed near each other tend to lose individuality and become a mass, with less weight than the same three individuals might have separately.
   b. Figures overlapping or partially covering one another tend to be thought of as one for purposes of weight.
   c. Mass can be made stronger with secondary centers of attention or counter-focus.

Why Are You Angry? by Paul Gauguin.

5. How much visual interest is added by scenery, furniture, costumes and lighting.

   a. Scenic elements or imposing furniture may add weight to an area of the stage.

b. Brighter colors tend to have more weight than subdued ones. White has more weight than black.

c. Warmer areas in lighting tend to have more weight than cold ones.

6. The principle of the "Golden Section."

Since ancient Greece, experiments in dividing a rectangle into its most pleasing proportions — or where the eye seems to be most comfortably at rest — have resulted in the *Golden Section*. This is a vertical line which may be computed as 38 per cent (a little over one-third) of the distance from stage right and 62 per cent of the distance from stage left. Many famous paintings have their center of attention approximately at the Golden Section, among them Rembrandt's "The Pilgrims at Emmaus," Van Dyke's "King Charles I," Monet's "Haystacks," and Manet's "Lunch on the Grass." The phenomenon of the Golden Section has the following implications for the stage:

a. The Golden Section is an area where the eyes of the spectators come comfortably to rest.

b. It is therefore an effective place for a center of attention.

c. The stage seems in balance when there is a center of attention at the Golden Section and a *lighter* weight balancing it stage left.

d. If the center of attention is stage left, it will take more weight stage right to balance it than if the picture were reversed.

e. Figures stage left seem to have more weight than they would stage right.

This curious fact has been observed by scholars in aesthetics.[4] The right side of a painting (stage left) seems *heavier* in weight (not importance) than the left side (stage right). Paintings which are well balanced with their center of attention at the Golden Section seem off balance when viewed in reverse. Try viewing Monet's "Haystacks" or Raphael's "Sistine Madonna" in reverse. "Haystacks" is printed in reverse on page 129; does it seem off balance? Very likely this phenomenon has to do with the cerebral dominance of persons conditioned to read from left to right. More tension of the eye muscles is required to look to the right (stage left), giving the psychological impression of added weight to figures stage left.

[4]Arnheim, *op. cit.* Gaffron, Mercedes, "Right and Left in Pictures," *Art Quarterly*, XIII, 1950, pp. 312-331. Wolfflin, Heinrich, *Principles of Art History*, New York: Dover Publications, Inc., 1929.

Haystacks in Snow, by Claude Monet.

C. Use of imbalance.

The stage will not always be in balance, either symmetrically or asymmetrically. The uses of imbalance include:

1. Deliberate imbalance.

Times when the director may desire an unbalanced picture include:

a. When the director wants to create tension or a disturbing empathic response in the audience, as in *Angel Street* when the detective is down left and stage right is empty except for the door through which the sinister husband may return at any moment.

b. When the director wants to picturize the upset of forces or imbalance in the story, as in *King Lear* when Lear and the Fool are pitted against the ravages of the storm.

c. When only half of the stage is used for a scene. In a partial stage picture, the audience apparently is willing to ignore the unused half of the stage and concentrate on stage right or left alone, provided there is balance within that area. In this respect the stage is unlike the painting, where the artist almost always uses the entire space available on the canvas.

Monet's **Haystacks** in reverse.

2. Unavoidable imbalance.

Every moment in a production need not present a picture of perfect balance. The requirements of the story and the need for transitions between main pictures may result in frequent imbalance. These moments will be brief, and fortunately are not frozen for all time as in a painting; nor does the playgoer observe with the studiousness of a museum-goer. The stage picture is not static but ever-changing, making its impact unconsciously on the audience. Spectators seem willing to accept transitional moments of imbalance in exchange for a climactic moment of memorable visual impact.

D. Exercises in balance:

1. Analyze the means used by Cezanne to achieve balance in his famous painting, *The Card Players*, and Winslow Homer's *Rainy Day in Camp*.

2. Use actors of relatively the same height and dressed in similar clothing. Work out the following problems in balance:

   a. Two figures DR balanced symmetrically by two figures DL.
   b. One figure URC balanced by two figures DL.
   c. Another figure joins the two in (b) above DL. Rebalance picture.

The Card Players, Paul Cezanne.

A Rainy Day in Camp, Winslow Homer.

d. Three figures sit DR. Find where to place one standing actor UL to balance them.

e. Use the see-saw principle to balance one actor DR in a three-quarter position with one actor DL in full-front position.

f. Try varying (e) by turning the imaginary see-saw on a diagonal instead of parallel to footlights.

g. Use a step unit or level for one actor UL. Balance him with one actor standing DR.

h. One figure stands LC reinforced by two guards. How many figures will it take RC to balance him asymmetrically?

i. Will an actor in one-quarter position URC balance an actor in three-quarter position ULC?

j. Find how many variations of the triangle can be used and still maintain balance.

k. Place five actors stage left in a group with some seated and some standing; balance them with one actor stage right.

l. One figure stands UL and one DR, equidistant from center. Find which body positions each should use to create the best balance.

m. Place one actor in the Golden Section; balance him with three actors stage left.

n. Reverse the composition of (m) and see if any adjustments are necessary.

o. Place a figure UC and use asymmetrical means to balance two groups R and L.

p. Create a picture with deliberate imbalance.

q. Use only half the stage to create a balanced composition of four people.

V. **The fourth requirement of a good stage picture is that it should have unity.**

Unity is achieved when the parts of the composition are so interrelated that the whole composition is viewed as one thing. In a unified composition there is no unimportant or unrelated part, and nothing can be taken away or added without affecting the harmony and completeness of the picture. The director's means of achieving unity include:

A. Controlling the center of attention.
Unity is achieved when there is one dominant center of attention and, if desired, subordinate centers of interest which add variety without distracting from the primary center.

B. Providing "eye-path" or connecting links between figures, groups or centers of attention.

Dean has called this element of composition *sequence;* aestheticians often speak of it as *glance-path.* Its purpose is to provide (1) an easy path so that the audience's eye will move from one actor or group to another, and (2) a compelling path which will not permit the audience to be diverted or distracted along the way.

The director can accomplish this by:

1. An actor placed as a linking or transitional figure between two groups.
2. The focus of the actors.
3. The line of arms, legs and bodies.
4. Line in the scene design.

The Dance Foyer at the Opera, by Edgar Degas.

5. Furniture, properties and even pictures on the wall.
6. Not letting an actor get "hung up" in a strong area during a scene in which he has no lines nor significant reactions.
7. Rhythmic spacing of figures or groups. Where a regular interval is established between groups, other groups will seem unified within the whole if they are spaced at half or twice the distance. (If A and B are four feet apart, B and C might be effectively placed either two or eight feet apart.)

C. Tying down the edges of the composition.
1. Figures placed at the down left or down right edges of the set serve the important purpose of directing the eyes of the audience back into the set. If they should focus out of the picture frame, the audience may find itself doing likewise.
2. A composition with its edges tied down is said to have *stability*.
3. The larger the mass of actors upstage, the more figures that will be needed in the DR and DL corners to provide stability or up-and-downstage balance.

D. Using all the available space interestingly.
1. Related to C is the need to fill up the empty space, not only at the edges of the composition but within the picture itself. Unless used for emphasis, empty stage space may interrupt eye-path and detract from unity.
2. In addition to working for unity, the director should sense the challenge of using his stage space for maximum effect. If the designer has provided levels, steps or interesting upstage areas, it would seem a waste to confine the actors to a shallow downstage plane. Utilizing stage space also permits greater variety in compositions.

VI. **The fifth requirement of a good stage picture is that it should have variety.**

In addition to the four requirements mentioned previously, the most interesting staging of a given scene would be the one which provides maximum variety for the eye.

A. Except where the director wishes to call attention to style through repetition of positions, he should try to find as many different ways as possible, within the context of the scene, in which to group actors. Notice how da Vinci in *The Last Supper* has achieved variety by having no two of the disciples in exactly the same body position.

B. Some bad habits which young actors may unconsciously fall into and which detract from variety include:
1. Lining up in straight lines.
2. Falling into a semicircle around a principal actor.
3. Having equal spacing among a group of actors.
4. Copying another actor's body position — sitting with legs crossed, arms folded, etc.
5. Facing full front to attract greater emphasis than the situation warrants.

VII. The sixth and last requirement of a good stage picture is that it should be functional.

In addition to aesthetic requirements, the composition should meet the functional requirements of actors and director. It should:

A. Permit every actor to be visible (except in large crowd scenes where some will be partially covered or invisible from some seats).

B. Permit easy movement to the next stage picture. The director must consider "where he goes from here" in planning each picture, so that the next actor to speak or move will be in a suitable position.

C. Keep actors clear of a door just before a new character is to enter.

D. Make it easy for the actors to play the scene, helping them to feel comfortable and to find the inner emotion for the scene.

Poor

VIII. Special problems in composition.

    A. Table scenes.

       Scenes around a table present special sight-line difficulties, and the solution used by da Vinci in *The Last Supper* is too symmetrical and formal for a modern, realistic play. In realistic staging, as in everyday life, people would sit on all four sides of a table, and some would therefore turn their backs to the audience and cover their upstage partners. To improve visibility, here are some possible adjustments which can be made:

      1. Use a round table, where appropriate, rather than a square one. Four figures can be placed on diagonals, with the two downstage ones cheating farther apart and the two upstage ones closer together. If a card table must be used, some cheating can still improve sight lines a little.

      2. If a group of people must be seated at a long rectangular table, place it on a diagonal. The most emphatic positions are at the two ends, upstage being the stronger. When all seats are oc-

Better

cupied, the downstage seats are potentially stronger (with cheating of the body) than the upstage seats.

3. The tallest actors should be seated upstage and the shortest (including children) downstage. Actors on the downstage side can help by leaning over the table.

4. The upstage actors can sit on pillows to raise them.

Best

5. The downstage seats should be reserved for characters who enter the scene late or leave early.

6. The actors on the downstage side should be motivated whenever possible to leave the table for some of their lines, or the upstage actors to rise for some of theirs.

B. Courtroom scenes.

1. The logical temptation to put the judge up center should be avoided if the attorneys have important discussions with him.

2. If the jury can be suggested or only partially shown, it will save space.

3. Traditionally the jury box is on the judge's left, with the witness stand between the judge and the jury.

4. The clerk, who is rarely important in the action, should be in a weak position.

5. For a workable ground plan of a courtroom scene, the plan following might be used as a beginning and modified as necessary. (See also page 116.)

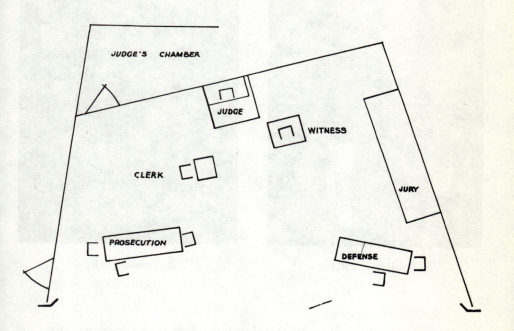

C. Sofa scenes.

When two characters sit on a sofa placed diagonally, the actor farther upstage should sit forward on the sofa and the actor who is downstage leans back.

D. Throne room scenes.

If persons addressing the king must share emphasis with him, the throne should not be on the upstage wall but preferably along the right or left side wall.

E. Love scenes.

For young actors a "covered kiss" is often the best way to avoid embarrassment. The girl turns her head upstage and the boy turns his head downstage. The back of the girl's head will mask the fact that their lips do not actually touch.

Preparation for kiss   The "covered kiss."

F. Crowd scenes.

It is often necessary to achieve separation of the crowd from the emphatic individual who addresses it. The old operatic solution of the crowd in a semicircle around the principal who faces front is no longer believable. Here are some better solutions to the problem:

1. Raise the principal actor on levels (even a table on which he might stand).
2. Isolate the principal figure from the crowd.
3. If the reaction of the crowd is important, the principal down left in a three-quarter position can address a crowd up right for brief scenes.
4. Avoid the same body position for numerous members of the crowd.
5. Avoid too much contrast in costuming the crowd or they will cease to be a mass and create attention as individuals.

The County Election, George C. Bingham. (Effective crowd scene.)

6. The illusion of a larger crowd can be given by:
   a. Keeping the majority of the crowd downstage with a few scattered upstage.
   b. Forming subunits within the crowd — family groups, clusters and pairs, with secondary emphasis upon those most involved.
   c. Having figures lean into the set from doorways and windows.
   d. Using shadows and sound effects to suggest more people.
7. In handling a large crowd it will be helpful to:
   a. Designate leaders for each subunit or cluster of people.
   b. Give members of the crowd specific things to do.
   c. Make sure each member of the crowd knows where to focus.
   d. Keep crowd members out of sight lines to the principal figure.

F. Exercises in composition:
   1. Replay some of the improvisations given in Chapter 3. The instructor should call "Stop" when the composition is poor, and ask a student to adjust the actors' positions until better composition is achieved.

2. Compose the following pictures, attempting to achieve a center of attention, story-telling quality, balance, unity and variety. (For each, select appropriate furniture and invent some lines of dialogue to make the picture meaningful.)

   a. The boss scolding three salesmen in his office.
   b. Grandfather telling some children a story.
   c. A thief confessing to police.
   d. An anxious family waiting for a telephone call.
   e. Three women gossiping about a fourth, who is in next room.
   f. A suitor paying a formal call on the parents of his sweetheart.
   g. A teen-ager asking his parents for the family automobile.
   h. Two men competing for the attention of one woman.
   i. Parents scolding a daughter for staying out late.
   j. Five people conspiring to overthrow their leader.
   k. A doctor examining a sick person while parents wait anxiously.
   l. Two neighbors having a quarrel over the back fence.
   m. Clerks in an office sizing up a pretty new secretary.
   n. Three old friends consoling a bereaved person.
   o. A teacher accusing some students of a theft — one is guilty.
   p. A woman trying to make up her mind in a dress shop with three clerks waiting on her.
   q. Two hoodlums waiting to rob a passer-by.
   r. A peacemaker trying to intercede in a quarrel with relatives.

IX. Summary.

As he watches rehearsals from out front, the director should check his stage pictures to make sure that they meet the criteria of good composition:

A. A center of attention.
   1. Kinds of visual emphasis.
   2. Means of achieving emphasis.
B. Storytelling quality or picturization.
   1. Breaking the scene into actions and beats before picturizing.
   2. Relating the characters to each other physically.
   3. Selecting the area of the stage in which the beat can best be played.
   4. Using the furniture to the fullest advantage.
   5. Using the actors' bodies plastically to reveal inner emotion.
   6. Trying tentative stage pictures, refining and modifying from out front.

C. Balance.
   1. Symmetrical balance.
   2. Asymmetrical balance.
   3. Use of imbalance.
D. Unity.
   1. Controlling the center of attention.
   2. Providing "eye-path."
   3. Tying down the edges of the composition.
   4. Using all the available space interestingly.
E. Variety.
   1. Variety in body positions.
   2. Bad habits to avoid.
F. Functional requirements.
   1. Visibility of the actors.
   2. Easy movement to the next picture.
   3. Clearing doorways before entrances.
   4. Making the actors comfortable in the scene.
G. Special problems in composition.
   1. Table scenes.
   2. Courtroom scenes.
   3. Sofa scenes.
   4. Throne room scenes.
   5. Love scenes.
   6. Crowd scenes.

Suggested Reading

ALBRIGHT, H. D., HALSTEAD, WILLIAM P., AND MITCHELL, LEE. *Principles of Theatre Art.* Boston: Houghton Mifflin Company, 1955, Chapters 23, 25.

DEAN, ALEXANDER. *Fundamentals of Play Directing.* New York: Farrar and Rinehart, Inc., 1941, Chapters 7, 8, 10.

DIETRICH, JOHN E. *Play Direction.* New York: Prentice-Hall, Inc., 1953, Chapters 7, 9, 19, 20.

SELDEN, SAMUEL. *The Stage in Action.* New York: F. S. Crofts, 1946, Chapters 6, 7.

Chapter 6

MOVEMENT

I. Introduction.

In the previous chapter blocking was analyzed as though the play consisted of a series of still compositions. In practice, however, the stage presents a moving picture, flowing from one telling moment to another. As the director begins in his pre-rehearsal blocking of the play to visualize how these major pictures will be composed, his next problem is how to get the actors where he needs them and at the proper time. This chapter will suggest some principles to help the director in making these decisions. Movement can do more than merely connect the various stage pictures, however; the movement of an actor on stage may be in itself a powerful means of communicating meaning — intellectual or emotional — to an audience. Experience with audiences has yielded these traditional rules of movement:

A. A *moving figure attracts* the eye of the audience away from a static figure.

B. The actor therefore should *move only on his own lines,* with the following specific exceptions:

1. When the director *wants* the audience to look away from the speaker, as for example during a routine reading of a newspaper while surreptitious action goes on behind the reader's back.

2. When the movement itself is of sufficient interest to warrant a pause in the dialogue, as for example when all are watching to

see what action a character will take, when no one is speaking, or between the sentences of another actor's speech.

3. When it is necessary to make a *"counter-cross"* or to *"dress stage."*

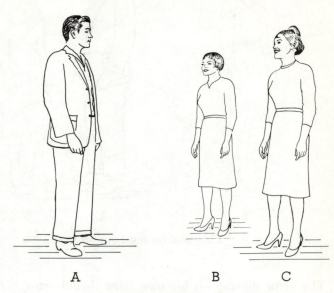

Before the counter-cross

When three characters are grouped together and A crosses in front of B to C, character B should drop down or counter-cross to approximately the place vacated by A; B should begin his counter-cross while he is covered by A. The counter-cross must be done unobtrusively, casually and motivated by the desire to see or hear better what the crossing actor is doing or saying. The purpose of the counter-cross is to restore the balance of the composition and improve the visibility of actors who would otherwise be covered. Actors should "dress stage" without being told.

During the counter-cross

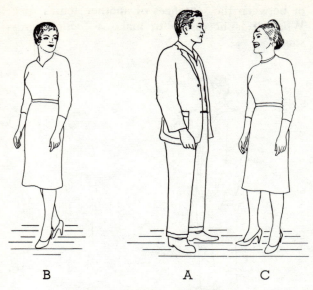

Completing the counter-cross

C. The actor moving on his own lines should cross *below* others, so that part of the line spoken during the cross will not be lost behind another person. There are very few exceptions to this rule; an actor might cross *above* another when:

1. He is playing a servant or stealthy character.
2. When the other person is seated, and the actor will be visible over his head.
3. He can get to a door more directly for an exit, and his partner does not need to face him during the exit dialogue.
4. He is counter-crossing.

D. A cross may be direct or indirect, broken up or continuous, curved or straight, depending upon the lines, the character and the situation.

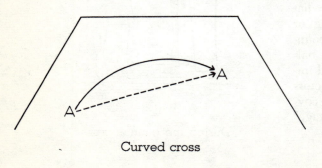

Curved cross

1. A curved cross, in which the actor describes a concave arc, keeps him opened up to the audience longer than does a direct cross.
2. An upstage cross can be broken up with pauses, pivots, turns

and steals to keep from turning one's back to the audience. Inexperienced actors must be cautioned not to walk backwards or to sidle unless a very weak impression is desired; an actor can work his way upstage by a series of zig-zag movements — a motivated step to the right, a pivot, a step to the left, etc.

3. In a normal movement forward, the actor should shift his weight to his downstage leg and step off — a short step — with his upstage leg.

E. Turns should be made *toward* the audience unless the director indicates otherwise (when for example the actor is in the three-quarter position and an open turn would seem roundabout, or when the director wants a particularly weak or rude movement). In making the turn toward the audience, the actor shifts his weight to his upstage foot and steps off with his downstage foot.

F. Every movement *must be motivated,* must have a purpose. Because it is sure to catch the eye of the audience, movement should not be random, aimless or distracting. The inexperienced actor's most common fault is the tendency to make little, purposeless, repetitive movements because of nervousness or insecurity. The actor should use an economy of means, beginning a scene with a *tabula rasa* — a motionless, relaxed body — so that every movement will serve a purpose and convey some meaning. To reverse the familiar adage, the actor should be told, "Don't just do something — stand there." The purposes which movement can fulfill include the following, and one movement may serve more than one purpose simultaneously.

II. The purposes of movement that stem from inner meaning.

In this category are those movements which are chosen because they help the audience experience the inner content of the scene:

A. To give vent to a strong emotion.
When a person is feeling a strong emotion, either happy or unhappy, his impulse is to express the emotion with bodily movement. Explosive lines, exclamations and laments seem to impel the actor across stage space. If the director does not sense this, very often the actor will say, "I feel like moving here." Such a movement may serve the additional value, as we shall see under the technical purposes, of helping the actor achieve the emotional intensity required. *In this and following examples, movements supplied by the director are indicated in italics.*

Example: *Romeo and Juliet,* Act III, Scene 5. Lady Capulet and 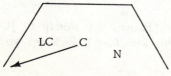 the Nurse are trying to restrain Capulet from his outburst at Juliet.
NURSE: May not one speak?
CAPULET: (*XLC to Nurse*) Peace, you mumbling fool! Utter your

gravity o'er a gossip's bowl; For here we need it not.

LADY CAPULET: You are too hot.

CAPULET: God's bread! (*He shakes off* LADY C'S *restraining hand and XDR, pacing angrily.*) It makes me mad. Day, night, hour, tide, time, work, play. Alone, in company, still my care hath been to have her match'd;

B. To tell the story.

Whole stories can be told with movement alone, as in the dance theatre. Any story can be made more powerful if told through movement as well as pictures and words. Many memorable moments in the theatre are provided solely by movement, as in the last scenes of *The Visit* and *Tea and Sympathy*. Notice how a new development in the story is told through a movement in this scene from *Summer and Smoke*.

Example: DR. BUCHANAN: Be quiet, damn you. (JOHN *heads defiantly for door DL.*) Stay here! And listen to me. (JOHN *stops DLC.*) There is no room in the medical profession for wasters — drunkards — lechers!

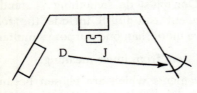

JOHN: (*A few steps towards his father.*) All right, then let me out of it!

DR. BUCHANAN: You were never in it. A medical diploma don't make you a doctor. No doctor fit to be called one would show that sort of — criminal irrespon-

sibility toward his —

JOHN: (Shouting) Then let me out of it!

DR. BUCHANAN: I've sent your things to the Alhambra Hotel. (*XDL past* JOHN *to door.*)

JOHN: Dad! I was with the old lady from seven till three in the morning. (*Sinks onto couch.* DR. *stops in doorway to listen.*) When she — lapsed into coma, I went out for some air. I saw the death of my mother, and ever since then I've had a dread of it that makes me unsuitable material for a doctor. I'm made for the science of medicine but not the practice of it.

DR. BUCHANAN: (Pause) (X *slowly to* JOHN *and puts hand on his shoulder.*) Pick up your things at the Alhambra Hotel and — bring them back to the house. I need you here.

JOHN: Yes, sir. (DR. *looks at his son a moment then turns and goes out.*)

C. To visualize interpersonal relationships as they change. In moments of stress, people move near those for whom they feel strong emotions — negative or positive — and remain farther apart from those to whom they are indifferent.

Example: *The Diary of Anne Frank*, Act II, Scene 3.

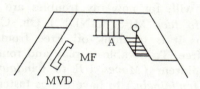

MRS. FRANK: (*X to* MRS. VAN DAAN *and forces the money into her hand.* MRS. VAN DAAN *moves away.*) Give this to Miep. She'll find you a place.

ANNE: (MRS. F. *starts back to put her purse away when* ANNE *comes* DLC *to intervene.*) Mother you're not putting Peter out. Peter hasn't done anything.

MRS. FRANK: He'll stay, of course. When I say the children, I mean Peter too.

PETER: (*Rises from steps.*) I'd have to go if Father goes.

MRS. FRANK: (*X past* ANNE *to* PETER.) He's no father to you. . .that man! He doesn't know what it is to be a father.

PETER: I wouldn't feel right. I couldn't stay. (*He starts slowly up steps to his room.*)

MRS. FRANK: Very well, then, I'm sorry.

ANNE: (*Runs between her mother and* PETER, *and seizes* PETER'S *arm.*) No, Peter! No! (*Turns to her mother.*) I don't care about the food. They can have mine! I don't want it! Only don't send them away. It'll be daylight soon. They'll be caught. . .

D. To visualize transitions in thought or the beginning and end of beats. In this way movement can help the audience follow the development of the character's thoughts and emotions.

Example: *A Doll's House*, Act I.

MRS. LINDE: But dear Nora, what gentleman do you mean?

NORA: Dear, dear, can't you understand? There wasn't any old gentleman: it was only what I used to dream, and dream when I was at my wit's end for money. (*Rises from sofa, XURC.*) But it's all over now — the tiresome old creature may stay where he is for me; I care nothing for him

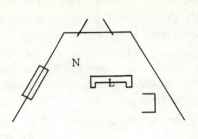

or his will; for now my troubles are over. (*Turns URC to face* MRS. LINDE.) Oh, Christina, how glorious it is to think of! Free from cares! Free, quite free. To be able to play and romp about with the children; (*Moves UR to window and adjusts drape femininely.*) to have things tasteful and pretty in the house, exactly as Torvald likes it! (*Looks out window.*) And then the spring is coming with the blue sky. Perhaps then we shall have a short holiday. Perhaps I shall see the sea again. (*Turns to face* MRS. LINDE.) Oh, what a wonderful thing it is to live and to be happy!

E. To reveal character to the audience.

People reveal themselves by the way they move, and especially by the way they walk.

Example: *Summer and Smoke*, Act I, Scene I.

ALMA: (*As* ALMA *sits on the bench and chatters,* JOHN *slowly circles above her, giving her a "once-over."*) The Gulf wind has failed us this year, disappointed us dreadfully this summer. We used to be able to rely on the Gulf wind to cool the nights off for us.

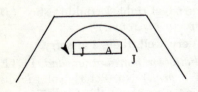

but this season has been an exceptional season.

JOHN: (*Ends DR of bench, puts his foot up on it and scrutinizes* ALMA. *Slowly*). Are you — disturbed about something?

ALMA: (*Fidgeting nervously with her purse.*) That firecracker was a shock.

JOHN: You should be over that shock by now.

ALMA: (*Rises to get away from his gaze, and XDLC.*) I don't get over shocks quickly.

JOHN: I see you don't.

ALMA: You're planning to stay here and take over some of your father's medical practice?

JOHN: (*Sits, sprawling, legs wide apart on bench.*) I haven't made up my mind about anything yet.

F. To establish mood.
1. A tragic mood is suggested by slow, direct, intense movements.
2. A bright mood is suggested by short, quick, vivacious movements.
3. High comedy is suggested by graceful, poised, curved crosses and movement.
4. Melodrama is suggested by tense, fast, direct movements.
5. Farce is suggested by sudden, jerky, incongruous and rapid movements.

Example: *The Barretts of Wimpole Street,* Act I. One of the brothers has just announced that their father expects to go away for two weeks on business. (See ground plan, page 85.)

HENRIETTA: (*Flings arms around* GEORGE'S *neck and kisses him.*) Oh, George! How wonderful! How glorious! Do you polk, George?

GEORGE: Don't be childish!

HENRIETTA: Well, I polk. (*She dances the polka around the room, while humming "Little Brown Jug," all the brothers join in the humming.* OCTAVIUS *claps his hands. The door opens quietly and* EDWARD MOULTON-BARRETT *enters.*)

ELIZABETH: (*Breathlessly, as she sees him.*) Papa — (*an awkward silence.* HENRIETTA *stops dead in the middle of the room.*) Good evening, Papa.

BARRETT: (BARRETT *crosses in a deliberate slow, long cross to fireplace ignoring them all. They are breathless. He turns at the fireplace.*) (*Before fireplace L, in a cold measured voice, looking straight before him.*) I am most displeased.

G. To provide motivation for another actor's next line.
Often two lines seem to follow each other without adequate motivation. Putting an appropriate movement between them may help motivate what follows.

The Barretts of Wimpole Street.
With Miss Julie Haydon as guest artist.

Example: *The Diary of Anne Frank*, Act I, Scene 3. Mr. Frank has just agreed to make room for Mr. Dussel, at Kraler's request. (See ground plan, page 85.)

MR. FRANK: Dussel! I think I know him.

MR. KRALER: I'll get him.

MR. FRANK: (MR. KRALER *goes down stairwell.* VAN DAAN *smacks his hands behind his back and paces angrily DL.* MR. FRANK *notices him.*) Forgive me. I spoke without consulting you. But I knew you'd feel as I do.

III. The purposes of movement that stem from technical or functional necessity.

In this category are those movements dictated by the nature of the theatre itself rather than the inner meaning of the play, and chosen by the director as he visualizes the play as it will look to the audience. Movement given to the actors for technical reasons must, however, *seem motivated* or justified from inner necessity rather than executed mechanically in obedience to the director's wishes. The director should therefore try to suggest to the actor a motivation for each technical movement as he gives it; when he does not have time to do this (and quite often he will not) the actor should try to find his own motivation. Among the technical purposes of movement are the following:

A. To link the important stage pictures and get the actors where they will need to be for succeeding lines or business (to "set up" the next picture).

Example: *The Diary of Anne Frank*, Act I, Scene 2.

MRS. FRANK: What did he mean, about the noise?

MR. FRANK: First (*He XDL to chair below stove. All proceed to take off garment after garment.*) let's take off some of these clothes.

MR. VAN DAAN: (*He XDR to* MRS. VAN DAAN *at sofa.*) It's a wonder we weren't arrested, walking along the streets...Petronella with a fur coat in July...and that cat of Peter's crying all the way.

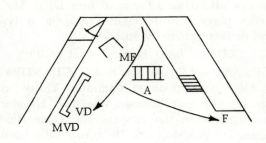

ANNE: (As she is removing a pair of panties.) A cat?

MRS. F R A N K: (Shocked) A n n e, please!

ANNE: It's all right. I've got on three more. (MRS. F. *sit UR chair.*)

MR. FRANK: Now. About the noise...
(*Through a series of technical moves, they are in a position for the picturization of "The Rules about Noise."*)

B. To keep the actors opened up for visibility and projection.
(To control the center of attention and prevent upstaging on important lines.)

Example: *Blithe Spirit*, Act II, Scene 3. (See ground plan, page 223.)

RUTH: Is he highly strung, do you think?

DR. BRADMAN: Yes. (*XDLC and sets medical bag down.*) As a matter of fact I wanted to talk to you about that. I'm afraid he's been overworking lately.

RUTH: Overworking?

DR. BRADMAN: He's in rather a nervous condition — nothing serious, you understand —

RUTH: [*XDC to him.* (*Otherwise he is upstaged for important comedy lines to follow.*)] What makes you think so?

DR. BRADMAN: I know the symptoms. Of course the shock of his fall might have something to do with it, but I certainly should advise a complete rest for a couple of weeks.

C. To open up doorway areas prior to an entrance.

Example: *You Can't Take It With You.* Act I, Scene 2. (See ground plan, page 86.)

TONY: (*XUL to* PENNY'S *desk.*) My mother believes in spiritualism. That's just as bad as your mother writing plays, isn't it?

ALICE: It goes deeper. Tony. (*XDR, to below table.*) Your mother believes in spiritualism because it's fashionable, and your father raises orchids because he can afford to. (*Turns to him DR.*) My mother writes plays because eight years ago a typewriter was delivered here by mistake.

TONY: (*XDR to her.*) Darling what *of* it?

ALICE: And — (*X past him to RC,* GRANDPA'S *place at table.*) and look at Grandpa. Thirty-five years ago he just quit business one day. He started up to his office in the elevator and came right down again. He just stopped. He could have been a rich man, but he said it took too much time. So for thirty-five years, he's just collected snakes, and gone to circuses and commencements. It never occurs to any of them...

GRANDPA: (*Appears UL in doorway which requires the UL area to be cleared previously.*) Hello there, children!

D. To provide variety for the audience.

Many talky or static scenes require that the director add movement purely to relieve the visual monotony for the audience. Long speeches and soliloquies generally require breaking up with movement. The sheer physical necessity to look at another area of the stage will help hold the audience's attention.

Example: *The Importance of Being Earnest*, Act III.

JACK: I fear there can be no possible doubt about the matter. (*X haughtily DLC toward* ALGERNON.) This afternoon during my temporary absence in London

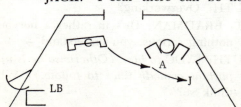

on an important question of romance, he obtained admission to my house by means of the false pretense of being my brother. (*X past* ALGERNON *to fireplace DL*). Under an assumed name he drank, I've just been informed by my butler, an entire pint bottle of my Perrier-Jouet, Brut, '89; a wine I was specially reserving for myself. (*XURC toward* CECILY.) Continuing his disgraceful deception, he succeeded in the course of the afternoon in alienating the affections of my only ward. He subsequently stayed to tea, and devoured every single muffin.(*XDR to* LADY BRACKNELL.) And what makes his conduct all the more heartless is, that he was perfectly well aware from the first that I have no brother, not even of any kind. (*Turns to face* ALGY *DLC*.) I distinctly told him so myself yesterday afternoon.

E. To "dress stage," restore the balance, or otherwise improve the composition.

Example: *Romeo and Juliet*, Act III, Scene 3.

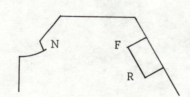

(Enter Nurse to Friar Laurence's cell)

NURSE: (*X to* FRIAR.) O holy Friar, O, tell me, holy friar, Where is my lady's lord, where's Romeo?

FRIAR: There on the ground, with his own tears made drunk.

NURSE: (*X past* FRIAR *to* ROMEO. FRIAR *counters* R *to watch what* NURSE *is going to do.*) O, he is even in my mistress' case, Just in her case!

F. To help the actor express his emotions.

It is important that *the actor feels comfortable in making the movement.* Particularly in scenes of strong emotion, the right movements may stimulate the actor to reach a depth of emotional intensity, and wrong movements may inhibit him and get in his way. The James-Lange theory of psychology may explain the observable fact that actors often are helped through physical autosuggestion to achieve emotional responses. A director who has been an actor himself will intuitively avoid asking his cast to play strong scenes seated or in confining parts of the stage. To achieve a large emotion, the actor needs bodily freedom to move. The movement itself may awaken the emotion. (For an example, refer back to the one given in II, A, to which this purpose is closely related.)

G. To provide a rhythmic pattern through repetition (particularly in plays where style and pattern are desired). A movement or gesture remains in the audience's memory when reinforced by repetition until it becomes characteristic.

Dark of the Moon, Idyllwild Arts Foundation.

Example: *Dark of the Moon,* Act III, Scene 3.

JOHN: (*Leaping up on the rock to face them.*) What hit to you to have Barbara's life?

FAIR WITCH: We ain't jes' winnin her life. We bringin' you back. (*She circles him with an enticing movement of arms, R.*) Bringin' you back to the moonlight and us.

JOHN: (*Turning to brush her off.*) No, you ain't.

DARK WITCH: (*Makes a comparable movement L enticingly.*) To the moonlight, and us.

JOHN: That ain't for me.

FAIR WITCH: Remember John boy, can't you remember. (*Weaving her arms about him.*) Remember those nights up thar in the sky, you in my arms on the screamin' wind — how free we all was then. Can't you remember?

JOHN: (*Moves away DL to edge of rock.*) But hit's over. Hit's finished.

DARK WITCH: Hit's jes' the beginnin'. When you a witch again, (*A movement R.*) you'll see things different.

JOHN: But I'll allus remember, and I'll allus love her.

FAIR WITCH: You'll change yore mind. (*Laughs and disappears over edge of rock.*)

DARK WITCH: We'll be a-waitin'. (*Also laughs and disappears over edge of rock.*)

H. To get laughs.

Business, movement and even "hokum" designed to get laughs can greatly enrich farce and comedy. Inventive directors and actors will find many ways to use movement for comic touches.

Example: *The Rivals,* Act III, Scene 4. Bob Acres has just written a challenge to Ensign Beverley, though he is mortally afraid of a duel. He asks his friend Captain Absolute to deliver the challenge, not knowing that Absolute and Beverley are the same person. As soon as

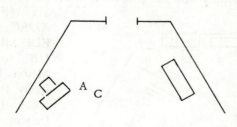

Absolute takes the letter, Acres wishes he had it back.

ACRES: I want you to find him out for me, and give him this mortal defiance.

CAPTAIN ABSOLUTE: Well, give it to me, (*Taking letter*) and trust me he gets it.

ACRES: Thank you, my friend, my dear — (*Lunges to grab the letter back as soon as ABSOLUTE takes it.*) but it's giving you a great deal of trouble.

CAPTAIN ABSOLUTE: Not in the least. (*XDR, putting letter in R hand.*) I beg you won't mention it. No trouble in the world, I assure you.

ACRES: (*Follows DR to ABSOLUTE'S R, reaching for letter, ABSOLUTE transfers letter to L hand.*) You are very kind. What it is to have a friend! You couldn't be my second, could you, Jack?

CAPTAIN ABSOLUTE: Why no, Bob — not in this affair; it would not be quite so proper.

ACRES: Well, then, I must get my friend, Sir Lucius. (*Moves above ABSOLUTE to his L, reaching deftly for letter. ABSOLUTE eludes him, shifting letter to R hand.*) I shall have your good wishes, however, Jack?

CAPTAIN ABSOLUTE: Whenever he meets you, believe me. (ACRES *moves R above ABSOLUTE desperately reaching for letter. ABSOLUTE puts it neatly in his pocket.*) Well, my little hero, success attend you.

I. *To heighten tension or build to climax.*

Although movement is not the only means at the director's disposal for building a scene to a climax, it is one of the very effective ways of heightening dramatic intensity. Climax is covered in detail in Chapter 11.

Example: *The Crucible,* Act I, Scene 2.
(Proctor's wife has just been taken off to prison.)

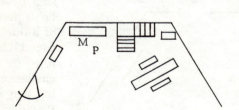

MARY: (*Slowly she XDRC and takes ELIZABETH'S apron UR to fireplace.*) Mister Proctor, very likely they'll let her come home once they're given proper evidence.

PROCTOR: (*Rises suddenly and XUR to her fiercely.*) You're coming to the court with me, Mary. You will tell it in the court.

MARY: (*Edges away from him DR.*) I cannot charge murder on Abigail.

PROCTOR: (*Follows her DR vehemently.*) You will tell the court how that poppet come here and who stuck the needle in.

MARY: (*Cornered, her back to wall, she blurts out in desperation.*) She'll kill me for sayin' that! Abby'll charge lechery on you, Mr. Proctor.

PROCTOR: (*Stops*)...She's told you!

MARY: I have known it, sir. She'll ruin you with it. I know she will.

PROCTOR: Good. Then her saintliness is done with. We will slide together into our pit. You will tell the court what you know.

MARY: (*X past him DLC.*) I cannot. They'll turn on me.

PROCTOR: My wife will never die for me. (*XDLC and grabs her.*) I will bring your guts into your mouth, but that goodness will not die for me.

MARY: I cannot do it. I cannot.

PROCTOR: Make your peace with it. Now Hell and Heaven grapple on our backs, and all our old pretense is ripped away. (*He flings her to the ground.*) Make your peace.

MARY: (*Sobs*) I cannot.

PROCTOR: Peace. It is a Providence and no great change. (*XR to door and opens door looking after ELIZABETH.*) We are what we always were, but naked now. Aye, naked, And the wind, God's icy wind, will blow.

CURTAIN

J. To reinforce or punctuate the dialogue through "pointing" and "throwing away" of lines.

This technical purpose of movement, which provides a means of emphasizing certain lines and subordinating others, is listed last not because it is less important, but only because it requires more detailed explanation. It is actually one of the most important techniques at the director's command; the effective integration of movement with dialogue makes blocking relatively simple and may at times give student actors the appearance of professionals.

1. Movement before, during, or after a line.

Extending the principle that the actor should move only on his own lines (with certain exceptions), it follows that there are logically only *four* possible times for him to move:

a. Before he speaks.
b. After he speaks.
c. While he is speaking.
d. Between phrases within his own speeches.

Exercise: Try the following lines from *The Importance of Being Earnest* each of the four ways and see which is the most effective:

a. JACK: (Kneels) Gwendolen, will you marry me?
b. JACK: Gwendolen, will you marry me? (Kneels)
c. JACK: (Kneeling as he speaks) Gwendolen, will you marry me?
d. JACK: Gwendolen, (Kneels) will you marry me?

a. ALGERNON: (Crosses to Cecily) But, seriously, Cecily, if my name was Algy, couldn't you love me?
b. ALGERNON: But, seriously, Cecily, if my name was Algy, couldn't you love me? (Crosses to Cecily)
c. ALGERNON: (Crossing as he speaks) But, seriously, Cecily, if my name was Algy, couldn't you love me?
d. ALGERNON: (Crossing as he says first part of line) But, seriously, Cecily, (Stops) if my name was Algy, couldn't you love me?

2. "Pointing" and "throwing away."
Experiment with the two foregoing examples will yield the following conclusions:

a. Movement or business *before* the line emphasizes or "points" the *line*. Therefore to point a line, put movement just before it.
b. Movement or business *after* the line emphasizes or "points" the movement. Therefore to point a piece of business or *movement* put an anticipatory line just before it.
c. Movement or business *during* the line emphasizes *neither* and hence weakens both line and business. Therefore to underplay or "throw away" a line, move while speaking it.
d. Movement or business *between* phrases within a speech points the part of the speech that comes after the movement. It is appropriate when a speech is part weak and part strong, and gives a cleaner separation of ideas than to move and speak together.

   (1) When the author repeats phrases for emphasis, the first can often be treated as weak and the second as strong. For example: (Pacing) "What could I have done? (Stops and turns) What could I have done?"
   (2) To point an exit line, move to the exit on the preceding weak line or phrase, turn and point the final line. To say

the final line in the center of the stage gives the actor a long and usually weak cross to the door.

e. These rules are particularly useful in playing *comedy*. An actor can get a laugh either by pointing or throwing away a line.

(1) If the line requires pointing to get a laugh, there should be no movement during it. Movement or business may be put just prior to the comic line. Brief, pointed gestures or business may also be used immediately *after* a comic line for punctuation. For example: fanning, flicking ashes from a cigarette, putting a hat on, sitting down.

(2) A laugh can also be obtained by applying these rules in reverse, i.e., point for a big effect and give the audience a lesser one. For example: "Do you know what I am going to do about it? (Rises pompously) Nothing!"

f. One type of line which may be neither strong nor weak and yet which often takes a forward movement is a question or exclamation directed to a specific character. If the line ends in an emphatic point, it is well to come to a stop before those words.

3. Dividing the dialogue into strong and weak lines.

To apply this principle that the actor should move only on his own weak lines, just before strong ones, or on questions or exclamations to an individual, the director must be able to sense which lines are strong (to be pointed) and which are weak (to be thrown away).

a. Weak or throw away lines are not necessarily poor or valueless lines. They are merely lines that can receive relatively less emphasis than strong ones for the sake of contrast. Weak lines still must be heard clearly by the audience (or if they serve no purpose they should be cut).

b. Movement is not necessary on every weak line; many times vocal techniques alone are sufficient to set apart the strong and weak lines, as will be pointed out in Chapter 9.

Example: Notice the value which these movements give in punctuating a speech from *Blithe Spirit*. (See ground plan on page 223.)

CHARLES: (*Rises, XR to RUTH.*) Once and for all, Ruth, I would like you to understand that (*Stops*) what happened last night had nothing to do with alcohol. (*Turns with shrug, and XDL.*) You've very adroitly rationalized the whole affair to your own satisfaction, but your deductions are based on complete fallacy.

(*Stops DL & faces R.*) I am willing to grant you that it was an aberration, (*XUL apologetically.*) some sort of odd psychic delusion brought on by suggestion or hypnosis.(*Turns to face* RUTH, *UL*) I was stone cold sober from first to last (*moves to UL chair.*) and extremely upset into the bargain. (*Sits vigorously.*)

Exercise: Divide the following speech from *The Importance of Being Earnest* into its strong and weak lines. Jack has just advised Algernon to dine with Aunt Augusta:

ALGERNON: I haven't the smallest intention of doing anything of the kind. To begin with, I dined there on Monday, and once a week is quite enough to dine with one's own relations. In the second place, whenever I do dine there I am always treated as a member of the family, and sent down with either no woman at all, or two. In the third place, I know perfectly well whom she will place me next, tonight. She will place me next Mary Farquhar, who always flirts with her own husband across the dinner table. That is not very pleasant. Indeed it is not even decent...and that sort of thing is enormously on the increase. The amount of women in London who flirt with their own husbands is perfectly scandalous. It looks so bad. It is simply washing one's clean linen in public. Besides, now that I know you to be a confirmed Bunburyist, I naturally want to talk to you about Bunburying. I want to tell you the rules.

IV. How to use movement in blocking a scene.

With the purposes, both internal and external, which movement can serve clearly in mind, the director is ready to proceed to the actual work of blocking the play in his director's book. In his interpretative study of the play as suggested in Chapter 4, the director will have begun to form general impressions of the movement and flow of the play, as well as some fragmentary images of the pictorial composition. On the basis of these impressions, he has discussed a possible ground plan with the designer, who arrives at a final, specific and detailed ground plan to scale. Only then, with a scale ground plan in front of him (sometimes with the aid of toy figures or twisted pipe cleaners) can the director block the play in detail, visualizing every movement and recording the result in his director's book. As he blocks the play, the director may find himself going through something like the following process. He must decide:

A. *Who* is to make the movement.

Analyzing each scene by beats and actions will reveal who takes the initiative or "whose scene it is." This character will most likely have the dominant movement in the beat, the other characters responding to him with reactions or compensating movement. When the beat changes and another character asserts himself, he will take over the dominant movement.

B. *Why* the movement is needed.

(On the basis of one or more of the purposes which have been listed.)

C. *What* kind of movement is needed.

   1. Types of movement.

      a. Changes in body position.

         (1) Facings and facial expression.

         (2) Changes of posture.

         (3) Gestures.

         (4) Turns.

      b. Movement in space.

         (1) Crosses.

         (2) Rises and seatings.

         (3) Contact with other actors — grabbing, pushing, restraining, embracing.

         (4) Contact with scenery or properties.

         (5) Changes of level — ascents and descents.

      c. Business.

         (1) With hand props.

         (2) With character props — fans, cigars, gloves, etc.

         (3) Pantomime.

   2. Emotional values of movement.

      a. Aggressive versus regressive.

         (1) Aggressive movements impel one actor toward another.

         (2) Regressive movements impel one actor away from another.

      b. Possessive versus rejecting.

         (1) Possessive movements impel one actor toward another.

         (2) Rejecting movements impel one actor away from another.

      c. Dominant versus passive.

         (1) Movements which dominate others are strong.

         (2) Movements which yield to others are weak.

    d. Peacemaking or mediating.

    e. Expected versus unexpected.

        (1) Expected movements are often weak.

        (2) Unexpected movements or those which go against the empathic desire of the audience are strong.

    f. Completed versus incomplete.

        (1) Completed movement is generally strong.

        (2) Incomplete movement is generally weak.

        (3) Interrupted movement may be either strong or weak. The actor must make the movement as though he expected to complete it if it were not interrupted by another actor.

    g. Other systems for categorizing movement.

    Many teachers of play direction have their own terminology for the emotional values of movement. Among the most inesting are these:

        (1) Samuel Selden[1] divides movement into three large sets:

            (a) Rising-sinking.

            (b) Approaching-avoiding.

            (c) Nurturing-destroying.

        (2) J. F. Foster[2] divides movement into six categories:

            (a) Opposition.

            (b) Withdrawal.

            (c) "Pounding," a series of aggressive pursuits of another actor.

            (d) Intervention.

            (e) Taking sides.

            (f) Enmeshing, a group of actors hemming one in.

3. Technical values of movement.

    All movement can be categorized technically as either *strong* or *weak* in value. The strength or weakness of the movement should correspond to the strength or weakness of the dialogue with which it is associated unless deliberate incongruity is desired for comic effect.

    a. Strong movements:

        (1) To move from a weaker body position to a stronger one. (From three-quarter to profile or one-quarter, etc.)

        (2) To move from a weaker stage area to a stronger one. (Cross from UL to DL, etc.)

        (3) To rise.

---

[1]Selden, Samuel, *The Stage in Action* (New York: F. S. Crofts and Co., 1946), pp. 67-79.

[2]Foster, J. F., *Basic Stage Movement* (Filmstrip). His categories are similar to those suggested in Milton Smith, *Play Production* (New York: Appleton-Century-Crofts, 1948).

(4) To step forward, onstage or downstage.
(5) To ascend steps or levels.
(6) To move out from behind furniture.
(7) To move in contrast to others.
(8) To move to scenic elements of strength — columns, thrones, arches, etc.
(9) To move to brighter areas in light.
(10) To move out from a group.
(11) To cross from stage left to stage right is stronger than from stage right to left. (Dean[3] concludes that this results from the conditioning of our eyes to read from the left side of the page toward the right. Movement counter to this tendency sets up a resistance in the eye muscles which makes the movement seem more emphatic. An army going off to battle thus is most effective going from SL to SR, returning in defeat from SR to SL.)

b. Weak movements:

(1) To move from a stronger body position to a weaker one.
(2) To move from a stronger stage area to a weaker one.
(3) To sit (or if sitting to slouch or lie down).
(4) To step back, offstage or upstage.
(5) To descend in level (except that descending steps may be strong if it brings the actor to a strong downstage area).
(6) To move behind furniture.
(7) To move along with others.
(8) To move away from scenic elements of strength.
(9) To move to a darker area of the stage.
(10) To merge into a group.

4. Style of movement.
   a. Realistic, literal movement.
   b. Enlarged realistic movement.
   c. Stylized movement, calling attention to itself.
   d. Symbolic movement or movement heightened beyond realism.

5. The amount of movement.
   The mood of the play will govern the amount of movement that is appropriate.

   a. Tragedy or drama requires relatively less movement.
   b. Comedy, farce and melodrama require more movement.
   c. Talky, static plays require more movement for variety.

---

[3]Dean, Alexander, *Fundamentals of Play Directing* (New York: Farrar and Rinehart, Inc., 1941), pp. 229-230.

6. The size of the movement.
   Factors which affect the size of movement include:

   a. The character making the movement — whether expansive or inhibited.
   b. The size of the auditorium to which it must be projected.
   c. The width and depth of the setting.
   d. The length of the lines which must be integrated with the movement. See Strickland[4] for an interesting exercise in getting across the width of the stage on four lines.

7. The tempo of the movement.
   Movement must advance rather than impede the tempo of the scene. Factors which govern the tempo of movement will include:

   a. The intensity of the inner emotion which motivates the movement — how anxious the character is to further his beat by making the movement.
   b. Where the movement comes in relation to a climax.
      As scenes build to climax movement becomes progressively faster or slower, depending on the nature of the scene.
   c. The interest which the movement will have for the audience — how long it will "hold."

D. *Where* on the stage the actor should move.
On the basis of the factors analyzed in Chapter 5, Composition, the director will decide where he wants to group his actors.

1. The director should work from one main picture to another.
   He visualizes a strong or climactic moment, noting with sketches in his director's book where each actor should be for the most effective composition.
2. He then *works backwards,* going back several lines or even pages in order to find an appropriate line on which to move each actor where he later needs him.

E. *When* the actor should move.
The selection of the actual line on which to move is done on the basis of the principles given on pages 157-159, which discuss movement in relation to dialogue.

1. The director (or the actor himself at rehearsal) will find a line which seems appropriate, i.e., a weak line, a question, exclamation or anticipatory half of a strong line.
2. It should be long enough to get the actor where he needs to go.
3. *It need not be the same place as indicated in the stage directions of the acting edition.* The director should consider the value of

[4]Strickland, F. Cowles, *The Technique of Acting* (New York: McGraw-Hill Book Co., 1956), Chapter 2.

using these directions but need not feel constrained to unless
they serve a purpose; these movements were originally devised
for other settings, ground plans, actors, size theatre, and possibly even another interpretation of the play.

4. It should not contribute to a repetitious pattern of movement.
(See V following.)

F. *How* the actor should move.

The movement visualized by the director and performed by the
actor must be done in character, naturally and spontaneously. The
movement should feel right to the actor, should be properly integrated with the dialogue, and should be rehearsed until the actor
can make the movement without looking where he is going or making it seem studied. Some traditional techniques for making movement appear natural and keeping the actor opened up to the audience include these:

1. Gestures.
   a. Almost all gestures are made with the upstage hand or arm.
   The most common exceptions are saluting and shaking hands,
   which traditionally are done with the right hand whether
   it is upstage or downstage.
   b. In handing a prop from one person to another, the actor
   reaches for it with his upstage hand, then changes it to his
   downstage hand to pass it on, rather than crossing his body
   with the upstage arm (except in a comic characterization of
   an awkward person).
   c. Gestures that cover the face, particularly the mouth, should
   be carefully managed so as not to interfere with projection.

2. Sitting and rising.
   a. The actor should sit and rise in character. How the legs and
   feet rest while sitting is an important element in characterization. If the character is graceful and poised, he will sit
   with his upstage leg forward and his downstage leg drawn
   back.
   b. In approaching a chair, the actor can feel for it with the
   back of his leg rather than having to turn around and look
   before he sits.
   c. When a chair is placed facing partly upstage, the actor can
   still sit in it without being upstaged; he can cheat his body
   and sit sideways in the chair, bringing his face into profile for
   most of his lines.

3. Entering and exiting.
   a. The actor should always close a door after entering or exiting
   except when directed otherwise.

b. If the door is on the side wall, it should be opened with the upstage hand and closed with the downstage hand. If the door is on the rear wall, it is opened with the arm nearest the hinges and closed with the arm which is toward center stage.

c. The actor should anticipate an entrance cue in sufficient time to arrive in position on the word cue except when directed otherwise.

d. When two characters enter together, the speaking one usually enters last.

e. A butler stands on the upstage side of a door in announcing someone.

f. Don't let the audience's first view of an actor be of his back, unless some special purpose is served thereby. The actor should try to avoid facing upstage on his entrance even if all the other actors are upstage of him.

g. The actor should not anticipate where people or objects will be on stage. Unless the room is well-known to him, the actor should hesitate in the door area long enough to survey the room.

h. At rehearsals the actors should pay particular attention to the outline of the set marked on the floor. They should enter where the door will actually be, pantomiming opening and closing it if necessary rather than drifting in and out or walking through walls.

i. An effective exit is made by getting the actor near the door on the *speech prior to his last,* so that after his last line he can disappear promptly. It is usually quite weak to walk to an exit with no lines to say or after the exit speech is finished; the only exception to this would be when a character's decision to leave is of more significance than his lines. Almost never would an actor have occasion to exit on someone else's lines.

4. Economy of movement.
The actor should learn to stand still, not rocking back and forth nor fidgeting from leg to leg. Meaningless movements, gestures or repetitive mannerisms soon begin to distract the audience. The actor should also guard against bobbing his head up and down while speaking or bending from the waist for emphasis.

5. Miscellaneous.
a. When an actor looks out a window, he should establish the off-stage object in such a position that he does not turn his back on the audience.

b. In turning on and off lights, deliberate covering usually is necessary; the actor's body should cover the business, with the actor keeping his hand on the switch or lamp until the lights come up or down.

   c. In handling a telephone, the actor should keep it farther from his mouth than usual in order not to muffle his voice.

V. The pattern of movement.

As the individual movements fall into place in relation to dialogue, a pattern of movement begins to emerge. The pattern will need to be refined, clarified and polished over a period of weeks, new points added for enrichment and awkward moments fixed. Except in highly stylized plays, the audience should not be conscious of pattern.

A. Means of achieving a varied and natural pattern of movement:

   1. Actors should avoid repeating the same movement.

     (One cross to window in the speech from *A Doll's House* on page 148 — would be effective. A second cross might be boring. Many ideas for movement in a scene will have to be rejected by the director simply because they have already been used in the same scene.)

   2. Avoid spacing the movements too regularly.

     (A pattern of turning away for two lines and then turning back on the third would soon become monotonous.)

   3. Avoid a series of movements which are all equal in strength.

     (As will be seen in the study of climax, a scene should either build toward climax or relax after it. Movement within a beat should therefore become progressively stronger or progressively weaker.

   4. Avoid two persons moving in exactly the same or exactly the opposite direction at the same time, unless a particular comic effect is desired. (In real life two people rarely move in parallel, and to use such movement on the stage gives a studied or pre-arranged impression.)

B. Means of achieving a stylized or self-conscious pattern:

   1. In stylized plays such as *The Importance of Being Earnest* or *The Matchmaker*, the foregoing four "things to avoid" can be done deliberately and with studied repetition. (A movement or piece of business needs to be done three times for the audience to be fully aware of it.)

   2. Pattern suggests conformity and as such can be used for telling effect, both comic and serious.

     (For example, each of the sons in *Life with Father* enters for breakfast and kisses his mother. The youngest breaks the pattern by sliding down the bannister into the room. In *Tea and Sympathy* the boys habitually check the pay phone as they pass it, to see if a nickel has been left in the return hopper — a delightful "touch" supplied by director Elia Kazan.

C. Movement in constricted space.

Confining sets present particular problems concerning the avoidance of monotony in the movement pattern.

The following scene from *Summer and Smoke*, Act I, was played in a constricted set which utilized only one third of the stage, in order that the park and the doctor's office could be simultaneously visible. Notice that the placing of the mother on a bench DL makes it possible for Alma to come at her from a variety of positions and

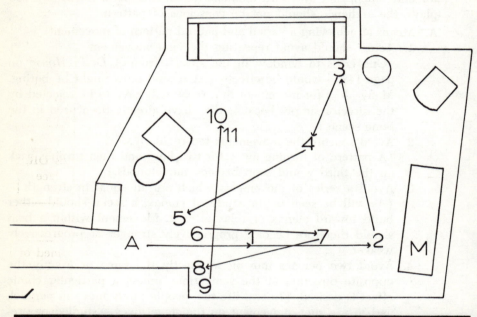

Summer and Smoke.

keep herself visible. If the mother had been upstage, it would have weakened every one of Alma's emphatic moments.

Alma is speaking to her mother, who has the mentality of a child. Her mother has accused her of being in love with the boy next door (which happens to be true).

(1) XDC toward mother who sits on DL bench.	
(2) stops DL.	
(3) Alma XUC	
(5) Moves wearily away toward DR.	
(7) XDLC toward mother.	
(9) Turns to face mother.	
(11) Wheels to face mother, URC.	

ALMA: If ever I hear you say such a thing again, if ever you dare to repeat such a thing in my presence or anybody else's, then it will be the last straw! You understand me? Yes, you understand me! You act like a child, but you have the devil in you. And God will punish you — yes! I'll punish you too. I'll take your cigarettes from you and give you no more. I'll give you no more ice-cream either. Because I'm tired of your malice. Yes, I'm tired of your malice and your self-indulgence. People wonder why I'm tied down here! They pity me — think of me as an old maid already! I'm young. Still young! It's you — *it's you*, you've taken my youth away from me! I wouldn't say that — I'd try not even to think it —if you were just kind, just simple! But I could spread my life out like a rug for you to step on and you'd step on it, and not even say "Thank you, Alma!" Which is what you've done always — and now you dare to tell a disgusting lie about me — in front of that girl!

Closes door DR behind Nellie who has gone out, and wheels to face her mother.	
(4) Comes DC a step to threaten her.	
(6) Stops DR, turns to face mother.	
(8) Ashamed of what she said, she turns away, DR.	
(10) XURC.	

VI. Summary.

The neophyte who may feel overwhelmed by the intricacies of movement should be reassured that no director ever completely sets his blocking prior to rehearsals or in one rehearsal. Blocking grows organically over a period of many rehearsals as a result of the creative interaction of actors and director. No two directors will block a scene with exactly the same movement, and no principles given in this chapter are to be considered inviolable. It is, however, constantly amazing that experienced directors and actors will so often instinctively agree on where and when to move. The techniques of movement grow out of the widely accepted concepts that: (1) a moving figure attracts the eye of the audience away from a static figure; (2) with certain exceptions, actors should move only on their own lines; (3) the speaking actor should cross below other standing actors; (4) a curved cross keeps an actor opened up longer than does a direct cross; (5) turns should be made toward the audience; (6) every movement must be motivated.

A. The purposes of movement that stem from inner meaning.
   1. To give vent to a strong emotion.
   2. To tell the story.
   3. To visualize interpersonal relationships as they change.
   4. To visualize transitions in thought or the beginning and end of beats.
   5. To reveal character to the audience.
   6. To establish mood.
   7. To provide motivation for another actor's next line.

B. The purposes of movement that stem from technical or functional necessity.
   1. To link the important stage pictures and get the actors where they will need to be for succeeding lines or business.
   2. To keep the actors opened up for visibility and projection.
   3. To open up doorway areas prior to an entrance.
   4. To provide variety for the audience.
   5. To "dress stage," restore the balance or otherwise improve the composition.
   6. To help the actor express his emotions.
   7. To provide a rhythmic pattern through repetition.
   8. To get laughs.
   9. To heighten tension or build to climax.
   10. To reinforce or punctuate the dialogue through "pointing" and "throwing away" of lines.

C. How to use movement in blocking a scene.
   1. Who is to make the movement.
   2. Why the movement is needed.
   3. What kind of movement is needed.
   4. Where on the stage the actor should move.
   5. When the actor should move.
   6. How the actor should move.

D. The pattern of movement.
  1. To achieve a varied and natural pattern of movement.
  2. To achieve a stylized or self-conscious pattern.
  3. Movement in constricted space.

Exercise: Work out the blocking and movement for the scene from *A Midsummer Night's Dream* given in Appendix D.

Suggested Reading

ALBRIGHT, H. D., HALSTEAD, WILLIAM P. AND MITCHELL, LEE. *Principles of Theatre Art.* Boston: Houghton-Mifflin Co., 1955, Chapters 9, 23.

BATTYE, MARGUERITE. "Stage Movement" in *Acting and Stage Movement*, by White and Battye. New York: Arc Books, 1963.

DEAN, ALEXANDER. *Fundamentals of Play Directing.* New York: Farrar and Rinehart, 1941.

REINHARDT, PAUL D. "Movement in Period Plays," *Educational Theatre Journal*, XIV, 1, March, 1962.

SELDEN, SAMUEL. *The Stage in Action.* New York: F. S. Crofts & Co., 1946, Chapters 3, 8,

STRICKLAND, F. COWLES. *The Technique of Acting.* New York: McGraw-Hill, 1956, Chapter 2.

Chapter 7

VOCAL INTERPRETATION

I. Introduction.

Just as the director composes visual pictures that are meaningful and aesthetically satisfying, so he must also compose oral patterns, using as his means the voices of the actors. Chapters 5 and 6 were designed to train the director's eyes. This chapter is concerned with training his ears and heightening his ability to hear how his play should sound.

It is by now a commonplace to say that American actors do not spend enough time working on voice. Anyone who has heard European actors knows that their voices are more pleasing, flexible and useful as a means of expression. Whether he likes it or not, the director in the American educational theatre will find he is a voice coach, among his many other duties.

He and his actors should take as their goals to make the voice an instrument for conveying:

A. Audibility
B. Intelligibility
C. Emotional impact

No matter how much an actor feels his part, the audience will be moved only to the extent that he succeeds in communicating his feelings, and his voice is one of his principal means of doing this. He will not move or delight an audience either, unless he can be heard and understood. The vocal techniques presented in this chapter should be thought of not as substitutes for the actor's true emotion, but as means by which the director can help his actors express the meaning of the play and their own true emotions.

II. Interpretation of lines.

Included among the techniques which the director uses in coaching actors in the interpretation of lines are those which help the actor (1) express the meaning of the lines, (2) express the serious or humorous emotional content of the lines, (3) build the scene to climax, and (4) achieve variety. It must first be assumed that the actor understands clearly his beat or action — what he is trying to do psychologically that motivates him to say the particular lines at the given moment. He must also know to whom the lines are said, what they mean, and how he feels about the things he is saying. If the actor understands all these in theory and still is unable to interpret the line effectively in practice, the director may help him by reference to one or more of these technical devices for oral communication:

A. Emphasis.

    1. The word which when emphasized unlocks the meaning of a phrase is called the *key word*. Every phrase or thought-group of words should have a key word, just as every speech should have a key sentence and every scene a key speech.

    2. The student actor should underline key words and sentences in his script with one, two or three lines to indicate the amount of emphasis. A key word generally is emphasized by a rise in pitch and elongation of the vowels. Notice how meaning can be altered by shifting emphasis within a sentence.

        a. *I* don't think there is much likelihood, Jack, of you and Miss Fairfax being united (but others apparently do think so).

        b. I don't *think* there is much likelihood, Jack, of you and Miss Fairfax being united (but I may be wrong).

        c. I don't think there is *much* likelihood, Jack, of you and Miss Fairfax being united (but there is a faint chance).

        d. I don't think there is much likelihood, Jack, of *you* and Miss Fairfax being united (but she will marry someone else).

        e. I don't think there is much likelihood, Jack, of you and *Miss Fairfax* being united (when you are engaged to someone else).

        f. I don't think there is much likelihood, Jack, of you and Miss Fairfax being *united* (but it needn't stop your loving each other).

        Exercise: Stanislavski once suggested that his actors underline all the emphatic words of a scene in their scripts and then play an improvisation in which they speak only the words they had underlined.

3. Pointing.

Even a routine reading of prose requires emphasis on key words for understandability of meaning. In dramatic dialogue, however, it is necessary to give even greater weight to particular words or phrases for emotional impact or for humor. This is called "pointing" the word or phrase. Pointing may employ any combination of the following techniques:

a. A rise in pitch or a fall in pitch.
b. A rise in volume or a fall in volume accompanied by more intensity. The latter can be very effective, as radio actors proved by achieving great intensity without increasing volume.
c. A slowing down in tempo.
d. A pause before the word or sentence.
e. Movement or gesture before the word or sentence.
f. Elongation of the vowel sounds.

4. Throwing away. (Subordination)

The reverse of "pointing" is "throwing away" and it is an equally valuable technique, for without it there would be no contrast, no black to offset white. (The principle of strong and weak lines was discussed in connection with movement, Chapter 6, Sec. III, J.)

a. "Throwing away" means to minimize the importance of a phrase or sentence through a casual, flippant or disinterested reading of the line. It does *not* mean to mumble the line so that it cannot be understood. It is merely a way of telling the audience that the line is relatively less important than other lines in the speech. Means of throwing away a line include these five possibilities:

   (1) A level pitch.
   (2) More rapid tempo.
   (3) Moving during the line.
   (4) Reduction in volume.
   (5) Less emphasis or intensity.

b. The change from throwing away to pointing need not occur at the ends of sentences, but wherever the thought changes. Several weak sentences can be phrased together or joined with a weak introductory phrase in a strong sentence for greater contrast and naturalness.

Exercise for pointing and throwing away:

GWENDOLEN: Ah! That accounts for it. And now that I think of it I have never heard any man mention his brother. The subject seems distasteful to most men. Cecily, you have lifted a load from my mind. I was growing most anxious. It would have been terrible if any cloud had come across a friendship like ours, would it not? Of course you are quite, quite sure that it is not Mr. Ernest Worthing who is your guardian?

—*The Importance of Being Earnest*, Act. II.

B. Inflection.

Inflection is a change in pitch within a word itself. The pitch may glide upward or downward during a vowel tone, or step upward or downward between syllables.

1. The possible inflections are:
   a. Rising——
   b. Falling——
   c. Circumflex — rising and falling within the word. ∧
   d. Inverted circumflex — falling and rising within the word. ∨

2. Some possible interpretations derived from inflection include the following:

   a. A rising inflection creates suspense for the words yet to come; it implies incompletion, uncertainty or interruption: "Oh?" "Today. . ." "Who?" "I believe. . ."
   b. A falling inflection implies finality, completion, certainty. "Well!" "Sure!" "Yes." "There!"
   c. A circumflex inflection gives melody and added emphasis to certain words: "Tomorrow" "Unforgettable" "Well!"

3. A *pitch pattern* results when any one inflection is used repetitively. One of the most common faults of inexperienced actors is the use of a rising or falling inflection at the end of every line. Such a pitch pattern results in deadly monotony, and must be broken up by attention to the meaning of the phrases in relation to each other.

C. Oral punctuation and phrasing.

The actor should become aware that the punctuation marks required in written English do not always correspond to phrasing of thought units in oral communication. When reading lines for meaning charged with the character's personal emotion, the actor will discover:

1. Every period does not require a falling inflection or a pause. A rising inflection should be used at the end of a sentence which is one of a group of ideas that make up a unit or which build to a pointed line.

Example: LADY BRACKNELL:

I hope not, Algernon.

It would put my table completely out. →

Your uncle would have to dine upstairs:

Fortunately he is accustomed to that.

2. Within a long sentence, a rising inflection may be used when the actor needs to pause to take a new breath or when he is pausing for emphasis.
3. A question mark is not always indicated by rising inflection.
4. A comma sometimes but not always indicates a pause; if it is so used, it usually is preceded by rising inflection.
5. A colon or semicolon generally suggests more to follow, hence takes a rising inflection.
6. An exclamation point usually takes a falling inflection.
7. Dashes or dots usually take a rising inflection, indicating broken sentences or incomplete thoughts.
8. In Shakespeare or poetic dialogue, the end of a line does not necessarily mean the end of a thought; the run-on line requires either a level or rising inflection so as not to suggest finality.
9. The number of words which the actor should phrase together depends upon:
   a. The thought unit itself.
   b. The emotional state of the character.
   c. The relative importance of the words in relation to the whole speech.
   d. The breath control of the actor.
   e. The tempo of the scene.
D. The use of the pause.
   There is no more effective single technique in acting than the full use of the pause. Charles Macklin, the famous eighteenth century English actor, is supposed to have described his three kinds of pauses as, "the pause, the long pause, and the grand pause." In a recent production of *Mary Stuart*, the distinguished actress, Eva Le Gallienne, used what seemed to be the longest example of a "grand pause" on record as she looked Mortimer up and down wondering if he could be trusted. Yet every moment of it seemed charged with the tension of Elizabeth's probing eyes.

   1. In using the pause, the actor should keep in mind:
      a. A pause will hold as long as the situation and the actor can justify it.

b. A pause points the line or movement which comes immediately after it.

c. A pause implies suspense if the audience cares what comes next.

d. A pause should be preceded by a rising inflection.

e. A pause is more effective, as a general rule, *within* an actor's speech than *between* two actors' speeches. In the latter case, it may seem that the second actor is merely slow in picking up his cue. (See Chapter 9, page 221.)

2. An actor may enrich a pause with the little musical noises which are natural to everyday speech but which the playwright often fails to indicate in words: chuckles, grunts, hmmmm, sighs, etc.

3. An actor should pause at the end of a line in poetic dialogue only when the thought is complete or when he can create suspense thereby.

Example: Listen to Eva Le Gallienne in *Hedda Gabler, ANTA Album* I, Decca DL 9002. (Excerpt reprinted in Appendix D.)

E. Connectives between phrases.

To help achieve variety and to interrelate the lines with the emotions motivating them, it is often helpful for the young actor to think to himself the connective phrases that the author might have put between sentences. Sometimes the relationship between lines can be clarified by the mental use of such connectives as:

1. "On the other hand."
2. "And by the way."
3. "As a matter of fact."
4. "Now wait a minute."
5. "To prove what I just said."
6. "And so here's what I've decided."
7. "And to top it all."
8. "You won't believe this."
9. "I've got a new idea!"

F. "Topping" and "Undercutting" in building to climax.

In constructing the dynamics of a scene so that it seems "to go somewhere" and doesn't become monotonous, the director will want to pay particular attention to the surge and ebb, the rise and fall of emphasis, both within the individual actor's speeches and between actors' speeches (see Chapter 9, Tempo and Climax). Successful ensemble acting is based on the true give-and-take that makes possible topping and undercutting.

1. Topping.

   When one actor's line is given with a certain emphasis or force, the next line should be given with somewhat more emphasis or force in order to "top" the previous one. This may be done by:

A rise in pitch.	A decrease in tempo.
An increase in volume.	An increase in intensity.

2. In a progression or build-up to climax, it is important for each actor to sense just how much force is necessary to top the previous line or actor. Too little will be monotonous, and too much will cause the build-up to reach its high point too soon, leaving no place to go for the remaining lines. In a series of lines requiring building, it is important to begin low and to keep the dynamics fairly constant within the individual lines.

3. Undercutting.

   Equally valuable in dynamics is a deliberate drop under the level of the previous line. It may be done as gradually as topping, or the actor may undercut abruptly so that a new build-up to climax can begin. It is also a useful technique for comic effect by understatement. Undercutting can be accomplished by:

A fall in pitch.	An increase in tempo.
A decrease in volume.	A decrease in intensity.

Exercises for topping and undercutting:

a. In reading the following aloud, have the actors top (T) and undercut (U) as indicated:

	PHEBE:	Good shepherd, tell this youth what 'tis to love.
	SILVIUS:	It is to be all made of sighs and tears:
T		And so am I for Phebe.
T	PHEBE:	And I for Ganymede.
T	ORLANDO:	And I for Rosalind.
U	ROSALIND:	And I for no woman.
T	SILVIUS:	It is to be all made of fantasy,
T		All made of passion, and all made of wishes,
T		All adoration, duty, and observance,
U		All humbleness, all patience and impatience,
T		All purity, all trial, all obedience;
T		Am so am I for Phebe.
T	PHEBE:	And so am I for Ganymede.
T	ORLANDO:	And so am I for Rosalind.
U	ROSALIND:	And so am I for no woman.

— *As You Like It*, V, 2.

b. For a skillful example of topping and undercutting in a soliloquy listen to John Gielgud's reading of "Ye Elves of

Hills" — *The Tempest,* V, in *The Ages of Man* recording. The text is given in Appendix D.

c. Analyze the topping, undercutting and building to climax on the recording of *Death of a Salesman.* A scene near the end of Act I (side 2, one inch from the inside, Decca DX-102, 9007) is reproduced in Appendix D without punctuation. Mark in the script the rising and falling inflections at ends of sentences, the topping and undercutting, key words and pauses.

4. Repeated words.

A particular case where topping or undercutting is almost obligatory is a line of dialogue in which the same word or phrase is repeated several times: "Stop, stop, stop," or "I won't. . . I won't. . .I won't." It would be fatal to deliver all three words or phrases with exactly the same emphasis. The director or the actor must decide to build them up or down.

G. Variety.

The human voice is one of the most beautiful of musical instruments, capable of almost unlimited adjustment. Yet monotonous reading of lines is one of the drama director's most persistent problems. The actor should be helped constantly to find new shades of meaning and vocal values in order to avoid monotony. If he has just done a particular thing vocally, that is sufficient reason for not doing it again soon. Achieving vocal variety requires practice largely in ear training.

Monotony has two causes: (a) the actor's failure to see or feel the moment-by-moment changes in his character's thoughts, motives and emotions, and (b) inability to use fully the technical means for reflecting these changes to the audience. There are technically only four elements that can be varied, corresponding to the four physical properties of sound:

1. Pitch.

Generated by the larynx and controlled by the ear, pitch changes are the most significant means of increasing the actor's expressive range. Low pitches generally are associated with deeply felt emotion, sincerity, authority, depression. High pitches are associated with excitement, anxiety, flippancy, and hysteria. Great dynamics of pitch change are associated with volatile, emotional, giddy and superficial people. Less variety in pitch is associated with stable, laconic or repressed individuals.

a. The student actor must be cautioned not to force his pitch down in the hope of acquiring a baritone voice, as undesirable strains and artificialities will result.

b. He may, however, increase his pitch range by relaxation, by working at a piano, and by breaking up his script — marking places where pitch should change by either:

(1) A glide (inflection) upward or downward during a sound.

(2) A step upward or downward between sounds.

Exercise to increase pitch range and awareness of the potential for pitch dynamics:

Read the following speech, starting with normal pitch, going as low as you can comfortably go, rising until in the middle of the speech you are at your highest pitch, then descending again to the lowest at the end.

Start with normal pitch:

LADY BRACKNELL: Come her. Sit down. Sit down immediately. Hesitation of any kind is a sign of mental decay in the young, of physical weakness in the old.

Lowest
Apprised, sir, of my daughter's sudden flight by her trusty maid, whose confidence I purchased by means of a small coin, I followed her at once by a luggage train. Her unhappy father is, I am glad to say, under the impression that she is attending a more than usually

Highest
lengthy lecture by the University Extension Scheme on the Influence of a Permanent Income on Thought. I do not propose to undeceive him. Indeed I have never undeceived him on any question. I would consider it wrong. But, of course, you will clearly understand that all communication between yourself and my

Lowest
daughter must cease immediately from this moment. On this point, as indeed on all points, I am firm.

— *The Importance of Being Earnest,*

Act III.

2. Volume.

The principle of *crescendo* and *diminuendo* gives music much of its climactic effect. In drama too, within the permissible range required for projection, volume changes are a significant means of achieving dynamic and emphatic performance. They must be accomplished with corresponding increase in breath support.

Exercise: Try the foregoing exercise from *The Importance of Being Earnest,* beginning as softly as possible, reaching its loudest on the sentence ending with "Thought," and diminishing until it is again soft at the end.

3. Tempo.
Although it is a commonplace to say that a fast tempo is used in comedy and a slow one in tragedy, the fact is that both comedy and tragedy require a considerable variety of tempi in order to hold the audience's attention. Dynamics of tempo are useful chiefly as a means of communicating shades of meaning and signalling to the audience which ideas are more important and which less important. A symptom of nervousness in the young actor is the desire to hurry through his lines.

a. *We tend to slow down on emphatic or important lines.* This is one way of "pointing" a line.
b. *We tend to speed up on less important or casual lines.* This is called "throwing away" a line (See Movement, Chapter 6, Sec. III, J.)

Exercise:
Try the exercise from *The Importance of Being Earnest*, beginning as slowly as possible, gradually accelerating tempo until it is most rapid on the sentence ending "Thought." Then slow down again.

Try the speech again after marking the emphatic lines, slowing down for those marked and speeding up for those unmarked.

4. Quality.
The fourth variable, quality, depends upon the particular resonance used. Quality is a reflection of characterization perhaps more than the other three, and is equally a mirror of inner emotional states. The way the actor holds tension in his lips, cheeks and jaws will influence quality, as do tone placement in mouth, head, or chest, and the physical dimensions of the actor's skull, neck, mouth and thorax.

Although there are many variations of quality possible in reflecting changing emotional states within a basic characterization, some of the most familiar vocal qualities have been classified as follows:

a. Aspirate or breathy.
b. Gutteral or throaty.
c. Pectoral or chesty.
d. Nasal.
e. Orotund or "with a round mouth."
f. Pharyngeal, back of throat and neck.

g. Strident.

h. Quavering.

i. Falsetto.

Exercise for variety in quality.
Try the speech from *The Importance of Being Earnest,* using a different form of resonance or quality on each sentence.

Review exercises for variety.

Now try the speech from *The Importance of Being Earnest,* reading it intelligently for meaning but incorporating as many changes of pitch, volume, tempo and quality as are appropriate.

Listen to Judith Anderson's recording of *Medea,* an outstanding illustration of variety in pitch, volume, tempo and quality as well as emotional truth (Decca-DAU-12). The text of an excerpt from Act I is included in Appendix D.

Read the famous "Speech of The Nose" from Rostand's *Cyrano de Bergerac,* Act I, which offers opportunity for maximum variety.

H. Rhythm.

Added variety and interest can be given to speech by rhythm, which is the *regular recurrence* or ebb and flow of intensity.

1. Inner rhythm.
Stanislavski defines inner rhythm as "...the acceleration or diminishing of the *inner intensity* — the desire to realize the problem and to execute the inner or outer physical action."[1]

The inner rhythm of a speech will grow out of the playwright's construction of the scene, its language, its emotional content, and the emotional rhythm of the characters who play the scene.

2. Outer rhythm.
To capture the inner rhythm of the scene, the director and actor should be conscious of external keys to rhythm:

a. The spacing and frequency of key words and stress.

b. The distribution of long and short syllables.

c. The spacing and frequency of pauses.

d. The spacing and frequency of climaxes and diminuendos.

e. The meter of the speech, if in poetry.

3. Meter.
In poetic drama the actor must be aware of the additional problem posed by meter, which is the regular spacing of accented

---

[1]Gorchakov, Nikolai M., *Stanislavsky Directs* (New York: Funk and Wagnalls Co., 1954), p. 323.

and unaccented syllables. The actor should read the lines with an awareness of and a rhythmic response to the meter, but *should never let meter take priority over meaning.*

    a. The most frequently used meter, especially in Shakespeare, is iambic pentameter [five feet to a line, with a foot consisting of a short, (˘) then a long (´) syllable].

Thĕ clóck | strŭck nine | whĕn í | dĭd sénd | thĕ núrse.

    b. Occasionally in reading Shakespeare it is necessary for the sake of meter (provided meaning is not obscured for the listener) to make an extra syllable in a word ending in "ed" when normal usage would contract it.

Ĭ múst | ŭpfíll | thĭs ó | sĭer cáge | ŏf oúrs
Wĭth bále | fŭl wéeds | aňd pre | ciŏus-júic | eď flów'rs.

    c. Shakespeare felt free to vary his meter, substituting other meters where sense demanded, and the modern actor should likewise feel free from a slavish metronome-like fidelity to meter while attempting to capture the full beauty of Shakespeare's musical lines.[2]

I. Playing comedy.

  1. The actor should *point* his comedy lines. This involves a combination of subtle techniques which telegraph the audience exactly when to laugh.

    a. By opening up more in body or facial position for the comic line.

    b. By getting to the punch quickly once the joke begins to be caught.

    c. By giving special emphasis and particularly clear articulation to the last few words of the sentence which contains the humor.

    d. By preceding the word or words that contain the humor with a pause or piece of business.

    e. By moving on a preceding line and standing still on the comic line.

  2. The others in a scene must help the actor get his laughs by:

    a. Feeding the straight lines rapidly, clearly, and with a serious, interested expression.

    b. Not moving, gesturing or reacting during the comic line, so as not to distract the audience. After the line is said, the

---

[2]For an excellent analysis of meter and rhythm in speaking Shakespeare, see Dorothy Birch, *Training for The Stage* (London: Sir Isaac Pitman & Sons, Ltd., 1952).

other actors may help crystallize the laugh by punctuating it with reactions of their own.

3. The actors should *hold for laughs.*

Holding for a laugh means to pause while the audience is laughing and unable to hear the next line. A well-timed laugh breaks suddenly and the welcome sound of laughter crests quickly, then subsides gradually.

a. The actor should *never* deliver a line through a laugh. He may continue his movements or pantomime, or he may simply wait, remaining in character and in the scene. It is a theatrical convention that the cast waits while the audience laughs as long as it chooses.

b. When the laugh has almost *but not quite* died out, the actor resumes his lines, repeating if necessary any words lost during the laugh.

III. Mechanics of Voice and Speech.

The techniques of interpretation given presuppose that the actor will bring to rehearsal a relatively well-controlled vocal mechanism. All too often this is not the case, however, and the director will have to give the actor basic drills to work on outside of rehearsal and as a warm-up before a performance. It is important for the director in the nonprofessional theatre to understand the mechanics of voice and speech, the essentials of which are given on the following pages, together with exercises for the student's drill and practice.

A. Relaxation.

Because so many of the student's voice problems come from tensions and misplaced strains, it is important to begin vocal drills with exercises for relaxation. The anxieties and heightened tensions associated with acting before an audience tend to inhibit the natural processes upon which voice is based, and it is in voice that a tense actor will first betray himself.

Exercises:

1. For general relaxation:
   a. Adding tension gradually, beginning with right foot, until entire body is as tense as possible. Then release all tension suddenly.
   b. Bouncing like a rag doll, letting arms and head flop loosely.
   c. Concentrating upon an object such as a pattern in a student's clothes, an off-stage sound, a remembered piece of music, or the ten best movies seen this year.
   d. Running a mental check list through the body, noticing if muscles are relaxed.

2. For specific relaxation of the mechanisms of voice:
   a. Yawning.
   b. Rolling the head in a circular movement as far forward, right, back, and left as posssible.
   c. Contracting all the muscles of the neck and then releasing the tension suddenly; repeat with face muscles, then abdomen.

B. Breath control.

It is essential for the actor to realize that the impulse to speak and the strength of voice originate in the breathing mechanism and *not in the throat,* nor even in the lungs themselves, which are passive and must be activated by the muscles surrounding them.

1. Inasmuch as sitting, slouching, having a pile of books on one's lap or wearing tight garments inhibits deep breathing, the student should begin the study of breathing in a relaxed but erect posture.

2. Help the student locate the diaphragm, which is a membrane of muscle and sinew separating the chest cavity from the abdominal cavity. It lies horizontally, is somewhat dome-shaped when relaxed and is attached to the sternum in front, the lowest ribs at the sides, and the spinal column in the back. Place your hands at the base of the ribs and notice the action of the area around the waist during these four processes:

   a. Normal inhalation.
   To take in air, a larger area must be created in the chest cavity into which the air can go. To accomplish this, the diaphragm tenses, pushing down on the abdominal cavity and outward on the base of the rib cage, while muscles lift and expand the rib cage. Air will rush into the lungs to fill the vacuum created by the expanding of the area around and below the lungs. Normal inhalation is effortless and slow, taking about the same length of time as normal exhalation.

   b. Normal exhalation.
   When the diaphragm relaxes, the pressure from the abdominal viscera forces it upward. At the same time the muscles expanding the rib cage relax and the weight of the rib cage forces it to fall slightly by gravity. The result is that air is forced from the lungs. Normal exhalation is a relaxation.

   c. Inhalation for stage speech.
   Inhalation for speech must be done more actively and rapidly than normal. There is greater movement outward and downward with the diaphragm, and the rib cage expands at the sides and front. If the actor is hunched over, he is more limited in the amount of air he can inhale than if he is erect

on his spine. In continuous speech, inhalation must be much more rapid than exhalation, and is therefore done as a rule through the open mouth rather than the nose.

d. Exhalation for stage speech.

All speech in English (except an audible gasp) is done on the exhalation of the breath stream. To accomplish this, a steady, controlled pressure is exerted on the diaphragm by the abdominal muscles, and other muscles contract the rib cage. All the muscular movements are greater than in quiet breathing. They must continue to sustain an even pressure on the lungs until the sentence or phrase is complete.

Exercises to strengthen the muscular control of the breathing mechanism:

Inhale and exhale normally and easily without speech. Place one hand in front and one at the side at the base of the ribs. Notice the movement of the hands, which should be outward on inhalation and inward on exhalation. Now place the right hand on the clavicle (collarbone) and leave the left hand at the diaphragm. As you perform these exercises make sure the left hand moves but not the right.

Inhale a good supply of air for speech and exhale it evenly on a sound such as "Ah" or "s. .s. .s."

Inhale as much air as possible, making sure the hand on the diaphragm moves outward. Exhale as you count from one in a steady, controlled tone. As you practice, the number to which you can count on one breath should be increased. Stop when the tone begins to waver.

Lie on the floor and place several heavy books on the diaphragm. As you lift the books on inhalation, the diaphragm will be strengthened.

Practice panting like a dog (for brief periods only, or the increased oxygen will make you dizzy).

Do a controlled laugh, with a new impulse from the diaphragm on each "ha."

Begin with a soft "Hey" and grow louder, supporting each sound with a fresh supply of air.

In none of these exercises should there be visible movement of or tension in the shoulders or clavicular area.

It was an old tradition with actors that the great curse speech from Bulwer Lytton's *Richelieu* should be said on one breath, as Edwin Booth was reputed to be able to do. Try it without a pause for inhalation:

"Mark, where she stands! — around her form I draw
The awful circle of our solemn church!
Set but a foot within that holy ground,
And on thy head — yea, though it wore a crown —
I launch the curse of Rome!"

C. Phonation.

The purpose of the controlled air stream described is to set in vibration the vocal cords, located in the larynx. As most of the muscular adjustments of the larynx are autonomic rather than conscious, it is sufficient for the actor to be aware of the following general concepts:

1. Pitch is generated by the vibrations of the vocal cords.
2. The vocal cords are lengthened when they are relaxed and shortened when they are tense. As in a piano, longer strings give lower pitches than shorter strings.
3. Tension in the throat and neck muscles is therefore the principal obstacle to optimum pitch production. There is little the actor can do at will with his larynx, except to insure a relaxed and tension-free set of muscles surrounding the vocal cords.
4. Hoarseness is the result of strain in the vocal cords, produced either by too much tension in the neck or too little breath support when loud volumes are attempted.
5. Pitch variation is controlled largely by the ear. An actor's variety in pitch can be increased only by ear training. It is not necessary to be able to sing on key in order to recognize intervals in pitch and reproduce them.

Exercises for Pitch Level:

At a piano, sing up and down the scale to find the range of tones that can be sung. The individual's natural level is approximately one-quarter of the distance up from the lowest note to the highest (including falsetto).[3]

For those who do not find it easy to sing on pitch, count using a rise in pitch for each number. Each number should rise only one easy interval rather than a big jump. Descend in pitch the same way.

D. Resonance.

The sound generated at the larynx consists of a fundamental pitch and its overtones. The latter are weak in volume, however, and re-

---

[3]The student attempting to find his natural pitch level should refer to Grant Fairbanks, *Voice and Articulation Drillbook,* 2d ed., (New York: Harper and Brothers, 1960), Chapter 11.

quire reinforcement which is supplied by resonating chambers which amplify the sounds. The sounding board of a piano, violin, or the tube of a clarinet gives the distinctive sounds to these instruments that permit us to identify them even when playing the same fundamental pitch. In the human voice, the resonators which give its distinctive quality are:

1. The pharynx (the back of the throat behind the tongue and the uvula) which is a conical tube extending from the larynx to the nasal cavities. With an elaborate set of muscles, the pharynx can modify its size and shape in a great number of combinations in order to provide the best size resonator for the various pitches produced by the larynx. The walls of the pharynx are lined with mucous membranes, which when relaxed and lubricated with saliva provide a rich tone, and when tense and dry cause a harsh or strident tone.

2. The mouth, which has both hard and soft reflecting surfaces. Its size can be varied by action of the lower jaw and by the variations of tongue positions. The hard palate (the roof of the mouth at the front) is the best sounding board off which to reflect sounds for carrying power or projection. The instruction to "bring the sound forward in the mouth" refers to this noticeably superior projection when tones are resonated in the front of the mouth as opposed to those resonated in the back. The larger the mouth cavity, the lower the pitches that can be resonated. A tight jaw therefore inhibits both resonance and projection.

3. The nasal cavities, unlike the mouth and pharynx, are not variable. Only three sounds in English, m, n, and ng, are resonated in the nose, although some actors, such as Basil Rathbone, have noticeable nasal resonance on other sounds.

4. The sinuses, which like the nose are not adjustable, add only a small amount of resonance.

5. The chest, particularly the bronchial tubes and trachea, act to reinforce lower pitches.

Exercises for Resonance:

With good breath support, sing the sound of "ah" first with the mouth normally open, then gradually wider and wider until it is almost a yawn. Notice the enrichment of the tone.

Resonate the same tone of "ah" in the mouth, the sinuses and the chest. This is often called mask, head and chest resonance. Practice the vowel combinations, oo, oh, ah, ai, ee (u, o, a, e, i) until you find your optimum placement and most pleasing resonance. Always precede such exercises with relaxation, yawning and breathing exercises. Add to these vowels the consonants *p* and *b,* which, because they are plosives, seem momentarily to increase the pressure in the pharynx and to inflate sagging passages: oop, ope, ahp, ape, eep, etc.

Notice the change in a well-resonated tone when you (a) close off the nose, (b) press your hand on your throat, (c) pat your chest vigorously, (d) strengthen or weaken the breath support, (e) make the same sound forward in the mouth and at the back of the throat, and (f) make the same sound with the neck and pharyngeal muscles contracted and then relaxed.

For character parts, practice resonances which are deviations from the norm: breathy, throaty, nasal, tight-jawed, wavering from the lack of breath, gravelly, gutteral. To avoid hoarseness, be sure to use no more extra tension than necessary, and to support the tones with greater breath than usual.

E. Articulation (enunciation).

The tones produced by the larynx and reinforced by resonance are vowel tones until the articulatory mechanism produces the consonants which are needed to form words. Because some of the consonant sounds are very high in frequency, they do not have as much carrying power for projection as do vowels. Many times when a spectator says, "I couldn't hear the actors," it would be more accurate to say that he heard vowel sounds but not the consonants, particularly the final consonants necessary for understandability of the words. Lip laziness is the most serious cause of poor projection, and the actor must acquire greater than normal vigor and precision of his articulatory mechanism, which is made up of:

1. The tongue.
   This extraordinarily complex and sensitive bundle of muscles is capable of rapid, subtle and infinitely variable adjustment. Although the movements are governed primarily by the ear, the actor needs to be conscious of tongue placement and to guard against letting the tongue hump up at the back of the throat and obstruct the projection of tones.
2. The teeth.
   Loss of teeth or the acquisition of dentures requires the actor to relearn his tongue placement to make sounds against the teeth.
3. The lips.
   Like any other muscles, those activating the lips can be strengthened, made more responsive and precise through exercise and practice. The actor trained on the stage may find he must reduce his lip activity slightly when appearing before the TV

or motion picture camera, but the actor trained in the understated articulation of these media will be handicapped on the stage.

4. The soft palate.

A kind of curtain at the back of the throat, the soft palate controls admission of sounds into the nasal cavities. A sluggish soft palate will create nasal speech or may blur the two sounds produced by contact of the soft palate and the back of the tongue, K and G.

Exercises for Articulation: (For other exercises, refer to Fairbanks, *Voice and Articulation Drill Book.*)

Precede the vowel sequence of oo, oh, ah, ai, ee, with consonants which exercise:

The lips — b, p.
The tongue — t, d, r, l.
The soft palate — k, g, also nga.

Perform these exercises with exaggerated lip and jaw movements. Try consonants after the vowels, then both before and after.

Gradually increase the speed of the phrase, "Tilly-vally, Lady;" without losing precision.

Read the following, prolonging the vowel sounds and making the consonants as precise as possible:

Morris Carnovsky as King Lear.

Blow, winds, and crack your cheeks! rage! blow!
You cataracts and hurricanoes, spout
Till you have drench'd our steeples, drown'd the cocks!
You sulph'rous and thought-executing fires,
Vaunt-couriers to oak-cleaving thunderbolts,
Singe my white head! And thou, all-shaking thunder,
Strike flat the thick rotundity of the world,
Crack Nature's moulds, all germains spill at once,
That make ingrateful man!
—*King Lear*, III, 2.

Listen to and analyze the articulation of Katharine Cornell and Brian Ahern in *The Barretts of Wimpole Street*, ANTA Album II, Decca DL 9009.

F. Projection.

Voice in the theatre must be enlarged beyond the requirements of everyday conversation. Yet it must seem natural and conversational even while achieving audibility in the farthest seats of the theatre (with the exception of some of the acoustically atrocious high school auditoriums which student voices can rarely fill without strain).

Mere shouting should not be confused with projection. Projection is required for both loud and soft tones, including stage whispers. Instead of saying "Louder," the director may help the student actor to project better if he works with him to achieve:

1. A stronger and more intense emotional reinforcement for the line — not merely to want to say something but to want to communicate it urgently and forcefully. The best motivation for projection is from *within*.
2. Stronger support of the tone through breath control.
3. Placement of the voice forward in the mouth, reflecting tone off the hard palate and upper teeth.
4. Wider opening of the mouth to let the sound out rather than keeping it dammed up.
5. More vigorous action of the lips and tongue in forming consonants, particularly final consonants.
6. An opened-up body position (at least one-quarter position) so that the actor's voice stream is directed toward the auditorium.
7. Even greater articulatory emphasis for intimate or whispered tones. Much greater force of breath is necessary to sustain the aspirate quality.

IV. **Problems of pronunciation.**

A. Standards of pronunciation.

Correct pronunciation involves the choice of which vowels and consonants to use and which syllable to accent. Pronunciation makes a decided impression upon the listener, and generally identifies the speaker as to:

> Educational background
> Regional background
> National background

For this reason the actor must choose an appropriate speech pattern as part of each characterization.

1. Standard "stage speech."

   During the nineteenth and early twentieth centuries the American stage was dominated by British influence, and standard speech for the American actor was British diction. The folk playwriting of Eugene O'Neill, Clifford Odets, Paul Green, and others, however, made native American dialects necessary on the Broadway stage. The British tradition still prevails in the speech of the Lunts and Katharine Cornell, and is appropriate to plays by such writers as Noel Coward, Christopher Fry and Bernard Shaw.

   For an example listen to the Katharine Cornell recording of *The Barretts of Wimpole Street* or Noel Coward and Margaret Leighton in *Blithe Spirit,* (Caedmon TC 10693).

2. General American pronunciation.

   There are today three general categories of American speech: Eastern, Southern, and general American. Unless performing a dialect play, actors in the educational theatre should use the best speech of their own geographic region which is:

   a. Free of local idiosyncracy.
   b. Understandable to the audience.
   c. Not affected so as to call attention to itself.
   d. Consistent with the rest of the cast.

3. Further refinements within the three categories, i.e., New England, New York and variations of Southern, are necessary only when plays are localized in a particular area. The sound of R is perhaps the most characteristic identification of the region of the speaker.

4. Uncouth or crude speech.

   When the character being portrayed lacks education or refinement, the actor's speech should reflect this. Otherwise, however, mistakes in pronunciation grate on the ear and are inexcusable in a classic play. Some of the most familiar errors in pronunciation include:

   a. "Git" and "jist" for "get" and "just."
   b. Leaving off final "ng" in words like "going" and "doing."
   c. The "e" sound in "friend" (not "frind") and "gentleman" (not "gintleman").
   d. Corruptions such as "gonna" and "wanna," whatcha," "awright."
   e. Elisions of the final consonant of one word to the beginning of the next. "Long Gisland."
   f. Commonly mispronounced words such as "toward" (not "to-ward"), "athlete" (not "athalete"), "poor" (not "pore"), and, heaven forbid, "the-ater" for "theatre."

5. Pedantic speech.

It is equally incorrect, however, to overarticulate such unemphatic words as "the" and "a," which are correctly pronounced "thuh" and "uh" in connected speech. To do otherwise makes the speaker sound pedantic. Unless the character being portrayed is affected or speech conscious, the actor should not emphasize all words equally or give weak words and syllables too much weight.

B. Dialects.

1. Many of the most important twentieth century plays are written in a dialect. Where a director can find actors who can manage the dialect, it will enrich the performance and add authenticity. Included in this category are *Juno and the Paycock, Desire Under the Elms, The Field God, Summer and Smoke, Golden Boy, The Corn is Green, The Happy Time.*

2. It is always better to use too little dialect than too much. Never let dialect get in the way of understandability, nor use it if the entire cast cannot achieve a uniform and consistent dialect. Do *not* use a foreign dialect if the play is a translation from a foreign language.

3. Mastery of dialect is largely ear training. It can be accomplished best by listening to the speech of natives of the region or country and, where feasible, tape recording it. When this is not possible, authentic recordings of the dialect (made by natives, not simulated by actors) should be studied; some sources of authentic dialects on phonograph records are suggested in Appendix C. A unit on dialects should be included in the training of the actor to give him as wide a repertory of dialects as possible.[4] In listening to dialects, the ear should be trained to concentrate on:

   a. Sound substitutions (which can be identified much more easily if the actor and director know phonetics).
   b. Variations in pronunciation and accent.
   c. Melody and inflection patterns.

V. **Summary.**

The actor's voice is one of his most powerful means of communication with an audience. It must serve the three purposes of audibility, inteligibility, and emotional impact. The director must have a highly attuned ear that is sensitive to voice and speech, and must know the techniques that can help the actor express the meaning of the play and his own truthful emotions, building scenes to climax and achieving vocal variety.

---

[4]It may be helpful to refer to Herman, Lewis H. and Marguerite S., *Foreign Dialects: A Manual for Actors, Directors and Writers* (New York: Theatre Arts Books, 1958), and the same authors' *American Dialects: A Manual for Actors, Directors and Writers* (New York: Theatre Arts Books, 1959).

Vocal techniques which the director can use to help the actor include the following:

A. Interpretation of Lines.
   1. Emphasis.
   2. Inflection.
   3. Oral punctuation and phrasing.
   4. The pause.
   5. Connectives between phrases.
   6. Topping and undercutting in building to climax.
   7. Variety.
   8. Rhythm.
   9. Playing comedy.
B. Mechanics of Voice and Speech.
   1. Relaxation.
   2. Breath control.
   3. Phonation.
   4. Resonance.
   5. Articulation.
   6. Projection.
C. Problems of Pronunciation.
   1. Standards of pronunciation.
   2. Dialects.

Suggested Reading

AGGERTT, OTIS J., AND BOWEN, ELBERT R. *Communicative Reading*. New York: Macmillan Co., 1956.

ANDERSON, VIRGIL A. *Training the Speaking Voice*. New York: Oxford University Press, 1942.

BIRCH, DOROTHY. *Training for the Stage: The Technique of Acting*. London: Sir Isaac Pitman and Sons, Ltd., 1952.

FAIRBANKS, GRANT. *Voice and Articulation Drill Book*, Second Edition. New York: Harper and Brothers, 1960.

GRASHAM, JOHN, AND GOODER, GLENN G. *Improving Your Speech*. New York: Harcourt, Brace and Company, 1960.

HERMAN, LEWIS H., AND MARGUERITE S. *American Dialects: A Manual for Actors, Directors and Writers*. New York: Theatre Arts Books, 1959.

...........*Foreign Dialects: A Manual for Actors, Directors and Writers*. New York: Theatre Art Books, 1958.

KAHAN, STANLEY. *Introduction to Acting*. New York: Harcourt, Brace & Co., 1962.

KLEIN, RUTH. *The Art and Technique of Play Directing*. New York: Rinehart and Company, 1953.

LEE, CHARLOTTE I. *Oral Interpretation*. Boston: Houghton Mifflin Co., 1952.

STANISLAVSKI, CONSTANTIN. *Building a Character*. New York: Theatre Arts Books, Robert M. MacGregor, 1949.

WOODBURY, LAEL J. "The Director's Use of Rhythm," *Educational Theatre Journal*, XIV, 1, March, 1962, pp. 23-28.

WOOLBERT, CHARLES H., AND NELSON, SEVERINA E. *Art of Interpretative Speech*. New York: Appleton-Century-Crofts, Inc., 1956.

Chapter **8**

CHARACTERIZATION

I. Introduction.

Helping the actors to build effective characterizations is one of the director's major responsibilities. The criticism most frequently heard from the average playgoer is that an actor is or is not "convincing" in his part. Although the director's work in this realm will be made much easier if he casts skillfully, "type-casting" in the educational theatre would not always be desirable even if it were always possible.

In the days of the old stock companies, it usually was simple enough to divide all the roles of a play into the standard categories: lead, ingénue, juvenile, (the "straight" parts), and character man, character woman, heavy, comic, and general utility (the "character" parts). Today, however, playwriting and acting have changed in keeping with the great advances in our knowledge of psychology, and in most contemporary drama all the parts are "character" parts — there are no "straight" roles. One of the indispensable tools of the director in the theatre today is an insight into human behavior, whether intuitive or acquired through study. In fact, the applied psychology learned as a derivative from an acting or directing experience is one of the strongest justifications for theatre art in the educational curriculum at any level.

Helping the actors in characterization usually involves the director in the following steps: (1) finding the right conception of the character, and (2) finding ways to project this conception to the audience.

II. The conception of character.

The director's initial concept of the characters in the play should be a part of his interpretative study as described in Chapter 4. His concept of each role will have a strong bearing upon his discussions with the costume designer, his description of the parts at tryouts, and his selection of the cast. When the cast is complete and assembled for the first round-table readings, the director should discuss the characters in detail, clarifying his concepts, referring to lines in the play, and (where applicable) showing the cast the costume sketches. At this first phase of characterization, the director's emphasis should be upon the psychological factors, the inner aspects which will contribute to the actor's understanding of the character. The following psychological factors may be pertinent:

A. The character's major drive or goal in life and in the play (his "spine").

As discussed in Chapter 4, some modern directors such as Elia Kazan and Harold Clurman find it helpful to begin with the central motivational force that impels the character through the action of the play. While some plays lend themselves better than others to this scheme of analysis, it would always be valuable to consider first the dynamic rather than the static aspects of character — the *verbs* rather than the *adjectives* that relate to the character and which answer questions such as these:

1. What does he *want* most, what are his needs and drives, what is he *doing* in the play? Hedda Gabler states her own spine quite specifically when she exclaims, "I want for once in my life to have power to mold a human destiny."

2. What is he willing or able to do to get what he wants? How conscious is he of his own true motives in doing what he does? How badly does he want his objectives and how vigorously does he pursue them?

In choosing verbs to answer these questions, it should be kept in mind that:

a. The verbs relate to the character as if he were in life rather than serving a dramatic purpose. The actor should try to get inside the character, rather than looking at him objectively as the playwright may have. The author's purpose may have been to show how corrupt a man is or to reveal information to the audience; this is not the character's own purpose, however.

b. *The choice of verbs is in itself characterization.* Insight into the character is revealed by the choice of the most appropriate actions and beats. If, for example, the actress playing Juliet's nurse chooses as her action in Act II, Scene 5, "to tell Juliet what Romeo said," it will be much harder to make the scene come alive than if she chooses a more *characteristic* action: "to tease little Ladybird about her first boyfriend." Again, it would be more helpful for the actress playing Amanda in *The Glass Menagerie* to choose the beat "to pretty up for a Southern gentleman caller," rather than to think of the scene in terms of "to get ready for a dinner party." The first is specific in terms of Amanda's character, the second is general.

B. The character's background.

Although in many plays the author has no time nor need to develop each character fully, the actor should consider the following factors which influence personality:

1. The character's family.
    a. Father and mother: what influence did each have on him?
    b. His brothers and sisters, if any, and his relationship to them.
    c. The type of discipline he was subjected to as a child.
    d. Affection, overprotection or rejection in childhood.
    e. The economic status of the family.
    f. Religious attitudes of the family.
    g. Any special situations in the family such as divorce, drinking, illness.
2. The character's innate intelligence.
3. The character's educational background.
    a. Level achieved.
        Education is most clearly revealed on the stage by patterns of speech, grammar and pronunciation.
    b. Adjustment to school and peers.
    c. Interests and activities.
4. The character's political and sociological environment. The effect which war, occupation, pioneering, disillusionment, travel or the political temper of the times may have had upon him.

C. The character's adjustments to his background and the forces that moulded him.

1. Social adjustments.
    a. His manners.
    b. The kind of friends he has.
    c. Participation in social activities and organizations.
    d. The role he plays in a group.
    e. Feelings about minority group status, if applicable.
    f. Dating, courtship and attitudes on sex.

    g. His home and how he lives.

    (Even the kind of car a person drives is, in our society, a comment upon his personality.)

    h. Hobbies and interests.

    i. His ideals, beliefs, and political opinions.

      (1) His heroes.

      (2) His hates.

2. The character's marriage, if applicable.

    a. His choice of mate.

    b. His success in marital adjustment.

    c. His children and their relationship to him.

3. The character's vocation and career.

    a. The kind of work he does.

    b. How he feels about his work.

    c. How he got where he did.

    d. Whether he spends most of his time indoors or outdoors.

4. The character's emotional adjustments.

Reactions to stress or conflict; the kinds of outlets utilized when under pressure, and the amount of pressure tolerable (often called the "frustration-tolerance level").[1]

ADJUSTMENT	EXAMPLE OF A CHARACTER WITH THIS ADJUSTMENT
a. Immature adjustments	
(1) Adjustments by defense mechanisms:	
Compensation	Melody, *A Touch of the Poet*
Rationalization	Chris, *Anna Christie*
Aggression	Joe Bonaparte, *Golden Boy*
Self-righteousness	McLeod, *Detective Story*
Masochism	Ephraim, *Desire Under the Elms*
Sadism	Oscar, *The Little Foxes*
Alcoholism	Doc, *Come Back, Little Sheba*
Narcotics	Mary, *Long Day's Journey Into Night*
(2) Adjustments by withdrawal:	
Negativism	Larry, *The Iceman Cometh*
Fantasy	Laura, *The Glass Menagerie*
Regression	Blanche, *Streetcar Named Desire*
Suspicion and hostility	Queeg, *Caine Mutiny Court-Martial*

---

[1] This personality inventory adapted from George F. J. Lehner, *Explorations in Personal Adjustment* (New York: Prentice-Hall, 1949).

(3) Adjustments by repression:

Anxiety	Rosemary, *Picnic*
Phobias	Evelyn, *Guest in the House*
Compulsions	Biff, *Death of a Salesman*

(4) Adjustments by physical symptoms:

Psychosomatic illness	Coney, *Home of The Brave*
Hysteria	Alma, *Summer and Smoke*

b. Mature adjustments:

(1) Dealing successfully with one's emotions	Rev. Harmston, *The Climate of Eden*
(2) Awareness of self	Papa, *The Happy Time*
(3) Sense of humor	Jacobowsky, *Jacobowsky and the Colonel*

Exercises to foster understanding of character:

1. Ask the actor to write an imaginary biography of his character in the play, supplying all the details necessary for a full life story consistent with the information given by the playwright. See Crafton and Royer[2] for an effective illustration of the value of a biography.

2. Suggest improvisations in which the actor plays his character in situations not in the play. (Refer back to suggested uses of improvisation, Chapter 3, Section V.)

3. If the actor fully understands his character and his spine, he should be able to sustain it in situations totally extraneous to the play. Try these juxtapositions in improvisation:
   a. Othello faced with Hamlet's dilemma in avenging his father.
   b. Macbeth married to Ophelia.
   c. Hedda Gabler married to Torvald Helmer.
   d. Stanley Kowalski trying to find a man for his sister, Laura.

III. The projection of character.

Important as the foregoing psychological factors are in helping the actor to understand his character, it is only through physical factors — those so-called "externals" which an audience can see or hear — that an actor can project his character. The director should therefore discuss with the cast the physical aspects of character, not only as an outgrowth or expression of inner psychological needs and wants but also as an influence which affects the inner psychological state. (Laura's limp, for example, in *The Glass Menagerie*, is a physical factor which

---

[2]Crafton, Allen, and Royer, Jessica, *The Complete Acted Play: From Script to Final Curtain* (New York: F. S. Crofts and Co., 1946), p. 167.

has strongly influenced her feelings of inferiority and wish to escape through fantasy; every person has some feelings about his physical health and appearance.) The psychological and physical aspects of character are thus mutually interrelated and interdependent; neither aspect alone can lead the actor to a complete characterization. The director should call the actor's attention to the following physical aspects of character:

A. The character's age.

Too much emphasis is sometimes placed on the age of a character. In the educational theatre it is often sufficient to fix the character's age within a ten or twenty year span. Young actors all too often characterize anyone over forty with all the quavering voice and palsied movements of ninety. There is no substitute for detailed observation of people at various ages.

Summer and Smoke.

B. The character's bodily appearance.
  1. His health.
  2. His facial expression.
    a. Use of the eyes.
    b. Muscular set, particularly around the mouth.
    c. Make-up as an expression of character.
      (1) Complexion.
      (2) How the strains of life are reflected in lines and shadows.
      (3) Beards or whiskers, if any.
      (4) Street make-up, if a woman.
      (5) Moulding of the features and bone contour.
  3. His size and height.
  4. His hair and hair styling.
  5. His clothing.
    a. How he wears it.
    b. How he handles it.
    c. Style and quality of clothing.
  6. His posture, as an expression of age, health, and inner feeling.
C. The character's movements.
Using the body interestingly to depict character includes consideration of the following:

  1. His walk.
This is one of the most revealing aspects of character. Stanislavski spends almost an entire chapter on it in *Building a Character*. Finding and using a character walk is not only revealing to the audience but also helpful to the actor in getting into character.

  2. His gestures.
A gesture which is used so often that it becomes identified with the character is called a "master gesture" or as Michael Chekhov termed it, "psychological gesture" or (PG).[3]
Gestures may be either:

    a. Completed or left incomplete.
    b. Vigorous or weak.
    c. Compulsive or controlled.
  3. His use of "character props."
A property chosen by the actor or director because it helps establish character is called a "character prop." Included in this category are pipes, fans, canes, purses, gloves, watch chains, cigars, etc.
  4. His energy level or vitality.

---

[3]Chekhov, Michael, *To The Actor: On the Technique of Acting* (New York: Harper and Brothers, 1953), Chapter 5.

D. The character's voice.

    1. As we saw in Chapter 7, the vocal means by which the actor can characterize include:

        a. Pitch.

        b. Volume.

        c. Tempo.

        d. Resonance or quality.
Refer back to the suggested list of voice qualities or resonances, pages 181-182.

    2. His speech.

        a. Articulation — careless or precise.

        b. Pronunciation — standard or colloquial.

        c. Dialect, if applicable.

E. The character's rhythm.
The way in which movement, voice and gesture are integrated and repeated produces a characteristic rhythm. Some rhythmic possibilities include:

    1. Jerky or smooth (staccato or legato).

    2. Volatile or even-tempered.

    3. Impulsive or deliberate.

    4. Ponderous or light.

    5. Broken or continuous.

Exercises in the use of physical aspects of character:
Directors and actors as well as students of make-up will find it very useful to collect candid photographs of people's faces, such as those that appear in *Life, Look,* and newspapers; use only firsthand sources, not posed models, sketches or pictures of actors in character. In building a character, try to find a photograph of the face of the person as you visualize him.

Develop a character and sustain it in an improvisation based entirely upon one physical element:

    A facial expression (from a painting, photo or actual person).
    A costume (refer to Stanislavski's brilliant illustration of this in *Building a Character*).[4]
    A walk.
    A gesture.
    A prop.
    A vocal or speech mannerism.
    A dialect.

---

[4]Stanislavski, Constantin, *Building a Character* (New York: Theatre Arts Books: MacGregor, Robert M., 1949), Chapter 2.

Observe an animal and select certain elements that suggest human qualities. Build a human character around these elements and sustain it in an improvisation. (The notable actor, Morris Carnovsky, who played the father in *Golden Boy* on Broadway, for example, is said to have built his character around the walk of a bear.)

IV. Helping the actor find his character.

After the round-table readings in which characters are discussed from both psychological and physical aspects, the director begins blocking rehearsals, and for a brief period physical position on the stage and movement take priority over characterization. Even at this early phase, however, the director should keep in mind that blocking is *character in action;* helping the actor to choose the right physical actions, beats, and accompanying movement may go a long way toward helping him find his character. *Give him movement that is in character and he will begin to be the character.*

After the blocking is set, the director is free to concentrate on characterization. He may find the actor at a loss as to where to begin selecting usable elements from the long list of psychological and physical aspects of his character. Fortunately, however, there are some reliable guideposts so that the director and actor need not lose too much time groping for the character. The following considerations all tend to narrow down the possibilities and make the choice easier:

A. What the playwright reveals about the character.
The playwright's intent is the final authority in all questions of interpretation. Playwrights vary widely, however, in the depth of their psychological insight, and their intent is not always transparent. Some acting editions include a two or three line description of each character which is often on a superficial level: "She is 17, a typical college student, cute, vivacious." Such descriptions, particularly when they include the word "typical," are generally of little value; if the playwright has not given this student cute and vivacious things to say and do, the actress will have a hard time making her cute and vivacious. Of much more value in analyzing the playwright's intent are the following:

1. What the character *does* in the play.
Capulet in *Romeo and Juliet,* for example, loses his temper not only at Montague but also at Tybalt, the Nurse, and violently at Juliet. He tells Paris that he wants his daughter to wait two more years before marrying, but the next day he agrees to her marriage in three days and then advances it to a day earlier. These actions reveal more about Capulet's character than if

Shakespeare had written in the *Dramatis Personae*, "Capulet — a hot-tempered, impulsive father."

2. What the character *says* about himself.

   Although a character's own evaluation of himself may not be the way the author intends the audience to see him, there often are valuable clues in what a person says about himself. In *The Glass Menagerie*, for example, the gentleman caller analyzes himself with these words:

   > . . . .I believe in the future of television! I wish to be ready to go up right along with it. Therefore I'm planning to get in on the ground floor. In fact I've already made the right connections and all that remains is for the industry itself to get under way! Full steam — (*His eyes are starry*). *Knowledge* — Zzzzzp! *Money* — Zzzzzp! — *Power!* That's the cycle democracy is built on!. . . .I guess you think I think a lot of myself!

3. What *other characters* say about him and how they react to him.

   It is often of great value for the actor to see his character through the eyes of the others in the play, and a playwright sometimes puts his most penetrating observations of character into the mouths of others. It is Biff, for example, who gives the final appraisal of his father in *Death of a Salesman*: "He had the wrong dreams. All, all, wrong."

   Because of the importance of clues such as these — often said when the character himself is offstage, the director must caution his actors against the all-too-common tendency not to read or listen to those scenes they are not in. Such an actor might, for example, miss the graphic picture of himself which Blanche gives of Stanley when he is offstage in *Streetcar Named Desire*:

   > He eats like an animal, has an animal's habits! Eats like one, moves like one, talks like one! There's even something — sub-human — something not quite to the stage of humanity yet! Yes, something — apelike about him, like one of those pictures I've seen in — anthropological studies!

4. What the *playwright says* about the character in stage directions, prefaces, articles and other published works.

   From such brief stage directions as "His eyes are starry" in the example in #2 above to the lengthy character analyses in the prefaces of Bernard Shaw, the words of the playwright provide one of the best keys to the character. It is only when the playwright is ambiguous, sketchy or noncommital that the director and actor must fill in the gaps from other sources. An actor playing General Burgoyne in Shaw's *The Devil's Disciple* could hardly complain of a lack of information after reading Shaw's seven-page character analysis, complete with documentation and such Shavian sentences as this:

> .... but his peculiar critical temperament and talent, artistic, satirical, rather histrionic, and his fastidious delicacy of sentiment, his fine spirit and humanity, were just the qualities to make him disliked by stupid people because of their dread of ironic criticism.

B. The growth of the character during the play.
1. The question of whether characters "grow" or develop during the course of the play or whether they are the same at the fall of the curtain as they were at the rise is an old one in dramaturgy. Kenneth Macgowan[5] suggests a list of characters that are no different at the end than they were in the beginning: Hamlet, Willy Loman, Liliom, Cyrano, Candida, Captain Boyle.
2. On the other hand, many characters develop during the play, both physically and psychologically: King Lear, Anne Frank, Liza Doolittle, Blanche Dubois, Juliet, Nora.
3. Macgowan suggests that the development of character may be like a photographic negative which can be "developed" to bring out what was originally latent. This is more in keeping with modern psychology than some of the sentimental dramas with their too-easy conversions of character.
4. In other plays, particularly mysteries, the character does not change but merely reveals more of himself to the audience, which may change in its reaction to the character.
5. The director and actor should analyze the play from the standpoint of character growth in order to determine how much development can be made convincing and consistent, and at what stage of his growth the character is during each scene of the play. If, for example, the actress playing Nora in *A Doll's House* does not establish the doll-like, fragile qualities in Act I, she will have nothing to rise above in the last act.
C. The style of the production.
The director must find a way to harmonize the style of the characterizations with the style of the settings and costumes so as to achieve unity. The same character would be portrayed quite differently within a realistic setting than, for example, in expression-

---

[5]Macgowan, Kenneth, *A Primer of Playwriting* (New York: Random House, 1951), p. 78.

ism or theatricalism. A classic play proscenium-staged with historical authenticity would require different styles in characterization than the same play done on the open stage or in suggestive, skeletonized sets. The same character would appear quite differently if treated by Chekhov, Shaw, Williams or Wilder. The differences growing out of style may include:

1. The amount of detail that is necessary or desirable.
   Anouilh's Antigone takes time, for example, to admire the golden, feminine curls of her sister, Ismene; Sophocles' Antigone does not.

2. The broadness or subtlety of the characterization.
   Auntie Mame, for example, is characterized more subtly than her Restoration counterpart, Millamant.

3. The size of gesture, movement and other elements of characterization. Actors feel more like making expanded gestures the moment they change their street clothes for period costumes (which free them from the necessity to reproduce literal reality). Period and stylized productions require a heightening of emotion and an enlarging of gesture and other elements of characterization. Maurice Evans' modern-dress G. I. *Hamlet,* for example, required smaller, more naturalistic characterization than his prior period-costume production.

4. The extent to which hand props and character props can appropriately be used.

   The fussy lawyers and notaries in Molière, for example, can legitimately develop broad character business with inkwells, quills and scrolls which would seem entirely overdone for a lawyer in a modern play.

D. What the actor must supply for himself.
   When the director has helped the actor to narrow down the possibilities and define fairly clearly what he is looking for in characterization, much of what remains must be done by the actor himself. The director can guide him to at least three possible sources of aid:

   1. *Observation* as a basis for building a character.
      The young actor need not be told to "go out and live" in order to find his character, but rather "go out and *look.*" There is source material everywhere around the actor if he will but look for it — on the bus, on the campus, in the park. Stanislavski tells of finding ideas for characterization from his own experiences, from his friends, from pictures, stories or simple everyday incidents.

a. When the actor finds someone who suggests his character to him, he should try to do more than imitate the individual. He should watch the individual long enough to *empathize* with him — to begin to feel as he does. He should then bring the details back to rehearsal and try them.

b. The actor may find a walk from one individual, a voice from another, a facial mannerism from a third, and fit them all into a composite characterization.

c. The actor should avoid observation of other actors. This is secondhand; he should go directly to the source, which is in life. Young actors should be discouraged particularly from going to the movie version of a play which they are rehearsing.

d. The most obvious solution is most apt to be a cliché or stereotype and should be avoided. All policemen are not Irish, nor do all Italians gesticulate wildly. While looking for an Irish policeman or a gesticulating Italian, the actor may overlook a dozen more interesting policemen or Italians.

e. The actor should work to achieve a wide *variety* within the framework of his character. He should show as many facets and moods of his character as possible. To escape the charge made by one critic that an actor "...ran the gamut of emotions from A to B," he should work for both technical and emotional variety to hold the audience's interest.

2. Research.

Where applicable in the case of historical or actual characters, the actor can help himself to identify with the character through research. The best sources are:

a. Biography.

b. History.

c. Paintings.

(These are particularly valuable for costume, facial expression, stance and gesture. Even when the character is fictional, paintings can help the actor steep himself in the period and perhaps find a portrait that suggests his character.)

3. Intuitive identification with the role.

In the final analysis, whatever the playwright fails to supply and the actor's observation and research fail to uncover, the actor must invent for himself.

a. The actor should turn to his intuition and imagination to fill in all the gaps left by the playwright, who quite often will not mention where a character has just come from when he

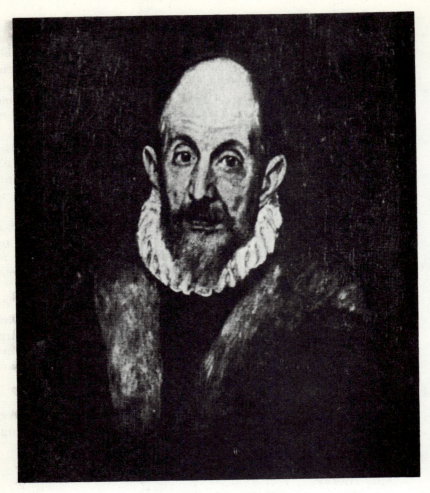

Portrait of a Man, El Greco.

enters, what he does between scenes, or essential information about minor characters.

b. The actor should create such a full inner life for his character that by opening night he knows the character better than does the director (or possibly the playwright). As this identification or empathy between the actor and his character grows deep, the director should respect it and not ask the actor to do anything which he feels his character would not do.

c. The actor's imagination is more intuitive than intellectual. He may know how Caesar or Lear feels, not because he clearly imagines life in ancient Rome or prehistoric Britain, but because he has felt or feels the same way himself. When he identifies himself with his character, he will have no trouble getting into character and playing the part.

V. Helping the actor get into character.

When the actor has a clear concept of the character and has done the necessary observation, research and imagination to give him a specific idea of how to project the character through external elements, there comes a time — usually after the blocking is set — when he must try to get into character and play the part. All too little is known about this psychological process of assuming someone else's personality (called "introjection" in psychology), but it is usually apparent to the spectator and should be quite obvious to the director when the actor is deeply "in character" and when he is not.

At this stage of the rehearsals, getting into character is not so much an intellectual process as an emotional one of identification with his character. An unconscious element is undoubtedly involved to such an extent that it might be compared with autosuggestion or hypnosis. The actor should not at this point try to review consciously biographical detail such as "I am thirty-six years old and had an unhappy childhood..." but should rather put himself figuratively in the character's shoes, acting and reacting as he knows his character would. The director can give the actor considerable help in this process:

A. By creating a favorable rehearsal environment which fosters *experimentation*. Effective characterization often grows spontaneously out of a period of *trial and error*, in which the actor deliberately "tries on for size" the various facets of his character. The director must give the actor sufficient freedom so that he feels like daring and experimenting. The director can, for example:

1. Encourage the actor to explore, create for himself, bring new ideas to rehearsal. The director should respect these contributions of the actor and integrate them into the whole where possible.

   The finest recent statement of how an actor explores within himself at rehearsal until he finds something usable is in Sir Laurence Olivier's discussion of his approach to *Othello*, which should be required reading for every student of acting. On this point Sir Laurence says:

   > *During rehearsals I try things out very extravagantly — ways of using my hands, my eyes, my body. It's a kind of self-flagellation that I've given myself practically all*

> *my life — early grasping this nettle of making a fool of myself.......Often an accident happens, often a turn of pose and a gesture and a stance and a position, an attitude — suddenly you say "Well, that's the man: I feel it is. That's him."*[6]

2. Discover the aptitudes, resources and personalities of the actors as individuals. Search for a spark within the actor that can be brought out and strengthened. (Remember that if the actor cannot give what the director wants, the director must adapt his conception of the role to something the actor *can* give.)
3. Help the actor to build a little bit at a time, finding things that work and growing from small moments of truth to larger moments.
4. When an actor hits upon a moment in the rehearsal that is just right, single it out after the rehearsal for praise and later reference. "Remember how you played the speech about the farm? — that was just right. Use that same quality in the last scene."
5. Keep a concentrated and disciplined rehearsal so that actors can remain in character during a scene. *Try to stop them as infrequently as possible* during the rehearsals when they are groping for a character.
6. Speak to the actors during rehearsal by the names of their characters.
7. Encourage improvisation and trial-and-error. Often an actor can hit upon a character through an improvisation or a bit of spontaneous invention. Anne Bancroft used an Irish accent in *The Miracle Worker* not for authenticity but because she discovered it helped her overcome her own New York dialect.

B. By getting the actor into the character or the character into the actor. The director should realize that the actor may approach his character in one of two ways — working from the inside out or from the outside in; the actor can bring the character down to himself, or he can bring himself up to the character. The best method is the one that works for the individual actor.

1. Working inside out.
Stanislavski rightly emphasizes the value of starting with the inner impulses, the spine of the character or "through line of action" and letting the character grow organically outward, adding external elements as the actor goes along. No matter how extreme a "character part" he is playing, an actor puts a good part of himself into every role he plays. A mild-mannered actor

---

[6]Olivier, Sir Laurence, "The Great Sir Laurence," *Life,* LVI, May 1, 1964, p. 88.

who is successful in playing sadistic villains must have a streak of sadism in him somewhere. Although critics may glibly say that "He wasn't acting Iago, he *was* Iago," the fact is that the actor can use only his own emotions to play a part. Iago's emotions do not exist in actuality, and become real only to the extent that the actor can arouse in himself the same (or analogous) emotions that the fictional Iago is supposed to have felt. An actor is therefore not likely to play a role successfully that is wholly outside his capacity to empathize with or comprehend.

2. Working outside in.

Other actors find it easier to start outside with a clear image of the character and work inward, consciously selecting a voice, a walk, or gestures just as they select their color of grease paint and crepe hair to portray their character. Stanislavski was well aware of the effectiveness of this second method, and it would be entirely in error to identify his name solely with the method of working inside out. Stanislavski devoted virtually his entire second volume, *Building a Character* (based on the curriculum of his second year students at the Moscow Art Theatre) to external means of creating character with the aid of costume, movement, voice, walks and rhythm. In this book he states:

> ....*external characterization can be achieved intuitively and also by means of purely technical, mechanical, simple external tricks.... The only proviso is that while he is making this external research he must not lose his inner self.*[7]

Although Stanislavski most likely was not familiar with the psychological theory of James and Lange, many of his experiences as an actor confirm the principle that the emotions can be awakened by physical activity, i.e., if an actor assumes a sagging posture and a tired old man's voice, he will soon feel tired and spent inside; if he stands with legs wide apart and chest erect he will feel cocksure, probably more quickly than if he waits for these feelings to grow from within and alter his external stance. In other words, both Stanislavski and James-Lange imply that the actor should take advantage of *autosuggestion* in getting into character.

C. Other ways for the director to help the actor get into character.

1. By making sure the actor gets into character before his entrance and sustains it until well past the exit.

---

[7]Stanislavski, *op. cit.*, p. 7.

Although some experienced actors pride themselves on their ability to joke with the stage crew until a moment before an entrance cue and then walk on in character, most actors (and certainly student actors) need a quiet period backstage at rehearsal as well as performance in which to get into character through pacing back and forth with the character's walk, thinking the character's thoughts, bringing to mind the image of the character or a moment in his life.

2. By letting the actors use parts of a costume or a prop at rehearsal to help them get into character.

Often the psychological act of wearing or using something pertaining to the character will help the actor feel his part at rehearsal. Although it is an unfair burden on the costume staff to expect a whole cast to be in costume before dress rehearsal, there are many times when it would be extremely helpful if the actors could work with shawls, cloaks, high heels, floor-length rehearsal skirts, canes, hats, swords, purses, gloves, etc., long before dress rehearsal.

3. By suggesting to the actors that they use a "sub-text" or think the character's thoughts.

Another valuable kind of autosuggestion is to think the character's thoughts silently while other actors are speaking, during pauses in one's own speech, or offstage while waiting for an entrance cue. Henning Nelms calls this the "silent script"[8] and Stanislavski called it the "sub-text."

Here is an example of what might be an actor's sub-text from *Death of a Salesman*, Act II. Willy is trying to talk his boss into taking him off the road and giving him a local job.

HOWARD'S SUB-TEXT	TEXT
	WILLY: (with increasing anger) Howard, all I need to set my
That's more than your commissions last week..	table is fifty dollars a week.
	HOWARD: But where am I going to put you, kid?
	WILLY: Look, it isn't a question of whether I can sell merchandise, is it?
	HOWARD: No, but it's a business, kid, and everybody's gotta pull his own weight.

---

[8]Nelms, Henning, *Play Production* (New York: Barnes and Noble, 1950), p. 134.

I can't carry you for
charity. .

WILLY: (desperately) Just let
me tell you a story, Howard —
HOWARD: 'Cause you gotta
admit, business is business.

WILLY: (Angrily) Business is
definitely business, but just
listen for a minute. You don't
understand this. When I was a
boy — eighteen, nineteen — I
was already on the road. And
there was a question in my mind
as to whether selling had a future for me. Because in those
days I had a yearning to go to
Alaska. See, there were three
gold strikes in one month in
Alaska, and I felt like going out.
Just for the ride, you might say.
HOWARD: (barely interested)
Don't say.

Then get back on the road
and let me get back to work.

Oh no, not that Alaska story.
How many times have you
told me that?

VI. Putting the character into the play.

Crafton and Royer[9] suggest this title for the final phase of characteriza-
tion.The actor's search for a character has led him into introspection
and a highly personalized center of attention. If he stops here, however, he will be playing in a vacuum, isolated from the others in the
scene. The director's final step in characterization, therefore, is to integrate the individual characters, and the actor's final step is to redirect
his concentration away from himself and onto the centers of attention
that his character would have — the things that are said and done by
the others in the scene.

A. Responding spontaneously and in character.

After the actor's characterization has been crystallized and "set,"
he will find a new freedom to listen, to concentrate, to respond
to the stimuli of the scene not as himself but in character. He will
discover that some of the other actors have also built effective characterizations to which he can respond. He will discover new implications in the dialogue and new ideas for business. He will find himself reacting in ways that he had not planned or premeditated. It
is then that the scenes begin to come to life, to "play." Stanislavski
thus explained this exciting experience in the life of an actor:

---

[9]Crafton and Royer, *op. cit.,* p. 171.

Thus a characterization is the mask which hides the actor-individual. Protected by it he can lay bare his soul down to the last intimate detail.[10]

B. Sustaining and modifying the character.

In the final phase of rehearsals, the director's attention will be on tempo and climax, on tightening the play and polishing its form. The actor must be prepared for this, and must know his character so well that he can sustain it through rehearsals that are primarily technical. If he is fully in character, a request to pick up cues faster, to increase the tempo or to top his partner should be a simple matter to justify from within; it should present no threat to his character. There may even be occasions when the director must ask him to modify his characterization for the sake of contrast with other characters, to create a better sense of integration (as for example when minor figures become too attention-catching), or to step the whole play up to a performance level big enough to project to the back row of the theatre.

VII. Summary.

One of the director's major responsibilities, particularly in the educational theatre where type-casting is not always possible or desirable, is to guide the actors in building effective characterizations. The two steps in this process are: (1) finding the right conception of the character, and (2) finding ways to project this conception to the audience.

A. The conception of character.
1. The character's major drive or goal in life and in the play (his "spine").
2. The character's background.
3. The character's adjustments to his background and the forces that moulded him.

B. The projection of character.
1. The character's age.
2. The character's bodily appearance.
3. The character's movements.
4. The character's voice.
5. The character's rhythm.

C. Helping the actor find his character.
1. What the playwright reveals about his character.
2. The growth of the character during the play.
4. What the actor must supply for himself.
3. The style of the production.

---

[10]Stanislavski, *op. cit.*, p. 28.

D. Helping the actor to get into character.
 1. By creating a favorable rehearsal environment which fosters experimentation.
 2. By getting the actor into the character or the character into the actor.
 3. Other ways for the director to help the actor get into character.
E. Putting the character into the play.
 1. Responding spontaneously and in character.
 2. Sustaining and modifying the character.

Suggested Reading

ALBRIGHT, H. D. *Working up a Part*. Boston: Houghton Mifflin Company, 1947, Chapter 6.

BOLESLAVSKY, RICHARD. *Acting: The First Six Lessons*. New York: Theatre Arts, Inc., 1933. The fourth lesson.

CARNOVSKY, MORRIS. "Design for Acting: The Quest of Technique," in Corrigan and Rosenberg, *The Context and Craft of Drama*. San Francisco: Chandler Publishing Co., 1964, pp. 299-322.

CHEKHOV, MICHAEL. *To the Actor: On the Technique of Acting*. New York: Harper and Brothers, 1953, Chapter 5.

CRAFTON, ALLEN, AND ROYER, JESSICA. *The Complete Acted Play: From Script to Final Curtain*. New York: F. S. Crofts and Co., 1946, Chapter 17.

EUSTIS, MORTON. *Players at Work*. New York: Theatre Arts, 1937.

FUNKE, LEWIS, AND JOHN E. BOOTH. *Actors Talk About Acting*. New York: Random House, 1961. (Abridged) Avon Paperback, 1963.

McGAW, CHARLES. *Acting is Believing*. New York: Rinehart and Co., 1955, Chapters 7 and 8.

OLIVIER, SIR LAURENCE, interview on his approach to *Othello*, *Life*, LVI, 18, May 1, 1964, pp. 80A–103.

SELDEN, SAMUEL. *First Steps in Acting*. 2nd Edition. New York: Appleton-Century-Crofts, 1964. Chapters 5 and 6.

SIEVERS, W. DAVID. *Freud on Broadway: A History of Psychoanalysis and the American Drama*. New York: Hermitage House, 1955.

STANISLAVSKI, CONSTANTIN. *Building a Character*. New York: Theatre Arts Books; Robert M. MacGregor, 1949.

————. *Creating a Role*. New York: Theatre Arts Books, 1961.

Chapter **9**

TEMPO AND CLIMAX

I. Introduction.

The necessity for structuring the tempo and climax of a performance arises from the nature of the theatre itself. In real life, events may happen tediously, repetitiously or over extended periods of time. To hold the attention of an audience in the theatre, however, there must be an intensification and condensation of reality. Moreover, our restless age of playgoers, conditioned by the trigger-happy tempo of television, come to the theatre in a more impatient mood than playgoers of Shakespeare's day or even Shaw's. Some aspects of tempo and climax have been referred to in the chapters on Composition, Movement and Vocal Interpretation. Although the director plans his tempo and climaxes during his preliminary interpretative study of the play, his actual work with the cast to achieve performance tempo and climax is one of the last phases prior to dress rehearsal — after the blocking, movement, characterization and inner truth are well established.

II. Tempo.

Tempo may be defined as the speed at which new impressions or ideas *seem* to occur for the audience's benefit. The word *seem* is essential,

---

[1]Dietrich, John E., *Play Direction* (New York: Prentice-Hall, Inc., 1953), p. 176.

because pure speed is by no means the same thing as what John Dietrich has called "the impression of speed."[1] The test of good tempo in the theatre is whether the audience is continually interested (they manage to let the director know by coughing and rustling when they are not). The impact of the author's ideas and his skill in arranging them will determine how rapidly the director must present these ideas in order to hold the attention of the particular audience for whom he is directing the production. When, for example, the final curtain falls on Arthur Miller's *The Crucible* at 11:45 P.M. and audiences are surprised at the time because it had not seemed like a long play, the director has done his work well.

A. Ways to speed up the tempo of a play.

To convey the impression of speed, the director can use one or a combination of the following methods:

1. To decrease the time between new impressions.
   a. By cutting. (Refer to Chapter 4, Sec. II, G.)
   b. By getting to the next new impression more quickly.

2. To add more impressions.
   a. By creating interest in moments that might have been glossed over.
   b. By variety in movement, composition and individual actors' performances.

3. To intensify the impressions.
   a. By heightening the climaxes; climax thus becomes a means of achieving tempo just as tempo becomes a means of building to climax.
   b. By having the actors do what they do more fully, want their objectives more keenly, and make their emotional reactions, either serious or comic, more intense.

B. Inner factors which affect tempo:

1. The frequency of new beats, new impressions, new stage pictures, the entrance of new characters, or new complications in the plot. When a beat is played out, it is time to begin a new one. The director should attempt to gauge the frequency of the new impressions during his interpretative study of the play; if the playwright has not timed the progression of new impressions effectively for a contemporary audience, judicious cutting should be done at that time — before the actors learn their lines.

2. The rhythm and speed of responses of the characters.
3. The intensity of the individual beats or scenes themselves.
4. The content and significance of the play itself.
   Ideas that are trivial or superficial should be hurried briskly over rather than dwelt upon, so that the audience does not have time to react with "So what?" or "Who cares?"
5. The form and style of the play.
   Realism offers the director less opportunity to use contrived tempi than do the broader styles. Mysteries and plays with a strong plot or built-in suspense can afford to move very deliberately, whereas talky plays need to be kept on the move. Tragedy and serious drama have a slow tempo that grows out of the inner development of the action, whereas farce usually acquires momentum and ends up at breakneck speed (lest the joke wear thin).
6. The frequency of major and minor climaxes and their progressive or cumulative effect, growing from weaker to stronger as the play progresses.
7. The vigor and animation of the actors themselves.
   A vigorous actor can pick up a scene merely by walking on stage.

C. External factors which affect tempo:
   1. Picking up cues promptly.
      a. The normal response to a cue is for the actor to inhale his breath and be ready emotionally so that he can begin to talk the instant the last word of the cue line is spoken. If the actor waits until he hears the cue word before getting ready to respond, there will be an undesirable pause which when multiplied throughout the play will noticeably affect tempo.
      b. The jumped or overlapped cue.
         There may be times when it is desirable for one actor to begin speaking before the previous one has finished, sacrificing the understandability of a few words for the cumulative emotional impact.
      c. The broken line.
         When one character is to interrupt another, the first actor should use rising inflections, and the second actor should break in promptly so as not to make necessary the adding of additional words.

Example: *The Late Christopher Bean*, Act. II.

(Ada, who has gone to Abbie's room to try and steal her portrait, returns while Susan is on the phone.)

The Late Christopher Bean.

Prompt pick-up of cue at places marked with *

SUSAN: (Into phone) Just a minute. I'll call him.

MRS. HAGGETT: (Turns to Ada) (*) Did you get it?

ADA: (Gasping, her hand on her heart) (*) No!

DR. HAGGETT: (*) She didn't catch you?

SUSAN: (*) Pa!

Jumped cue. (Ada answers DR.'s question without waiting for SUSAN'S line.)

ADA: ⟨ No. But if the biscuits hadn't been burning she would have caught me. I was just lifting it off the hook when I looked over my shoulder and there she stood with her head in the oven.

SUSAN: (*) Pa!

Jumped cue.

MRS. HAGGETT: ⟨ We'll just have to try again. We'll eat dinner quiet as if nothing happened. I'll send her out on an errand. Come on, Ada. We'll finish setting the table.

SUSAN: (*) When you're done plotting and whispering over there, New York's calling Pa.

MRS. HAGGETT: (*) New York — *again?*

SUSAN: (*) I can't get the name. It sounds to me like Knoedler & Company.

DR. HAGGETT: (*) I won't speak to him!
I won't speak to no more from New York!
Tell him I'm out! Tell him I've gone away!
Tell him —

SUSAN: You can tell your *own* lies, Pa!

DR. HAGGETT: (*) All right, I will. (Takes phone)

> Broken line. SUSAN must interrupt DR. promptly, or may jump cue slightly.

2. Finding more key words to emphasize.
Inexperienced actors often hurry through a speech when, if they would slow down and emphasize key words for their full significance, they could in effect convey the impression of speeding up, i.e., there would be more points of interest for the audience.

Example: *The Importance of Being Earnest,* Act II. Read this speech first rapidly and without special emphasis:

GWENDOLEN: Well, to speak with perfect candor, Cecily, I wish that you were fully forty-two, and more than usually plain for your age. Ernest has a strong upright nature. He is the very soul of truth and honor. Disloyalty would be as impossible to him as deception. But even men of the noblest possible moral character are extremely susceptible to the influence of the physical charms of others. Modern, no less than Ancient History, supplies us with many most painful examples of what I refer to. If it were not so, indeed, History would be quite unreadable.

Now read the speech giving emphasis to the key words indicated:

GWENDOLEN: Well, to speak with perfect *candor,* Cecily, I wish that you were fully *forty-two,* and more than usually *plain* for your *age. Ernest* has a *strong upright* nature. He is the very *soul* of truth and *honor. Disloyalty* would be as *impossible* to him as *deception.* But even men of the noblest possible *moral* character are extremely *susceptible* to the influence of the *physical charms* of *others. Modern,* no less than *Ancient History,* supplies us with *many* most *painful* examples of what I *refer* to. If it were not *so,* indeed, *History* would be quite *unreadable.*

3. Pointing and throwing away lines.
As was demonstrated in Chapter 7, Vocal Interpretation, Sec. II, A, the pointing and throwing away of lines is a most valuable

technique not only for variety but for the tempo of the play. Unemphatic or trivial lines can be "thrown away" by speeding up the delivery, and emphatic lines can be "pointed" by slowing down.

Example: *The Importance of Being Earnest,* Act. I.

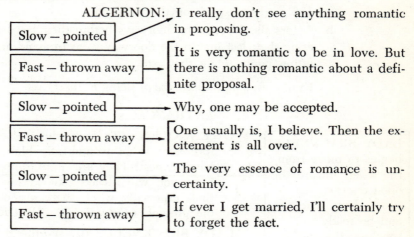

ALGERNON: I really don't see anything romantic in proposing.

Slow — pointed

Fast — thrown away — It is very romantic to be in love. But there is nothing romantic about a definite proposal.

Slow — pointed — Why, one may be accepted.

Fast — thrown away — One usually is, I believe. Then the excitement is all over.

Slow — pointed — The very essence of romance is uncertainty.

Fast — thrown away — If ever I get married, I'll certainly try to forget the fact.

4. Using pauses effectively.
   a. The pause must be filled with meaning, revealed through facial expression, gesture or movement; otherwise it should come out.
   b. The pause is more effective *within* one actor's speech than *between* actors' speeches. By beginning to speak, the actor shifts the audience's attention to him and he may then pause for full effect. If he pauses before he speaks, the audience may not be sure what is happening or whether someone has forgotten a line.

Example: *The Importance of Being Earnest,* Act. I.

WRONG: LADY BRACKNELL: Do you smoke?
              JACK: (Pause) Well, yes, I must admit I smoke.

RIGHT: LADY BRACKNELL: Do you smoke?
              JACK: Well . . (Pause) yes, I must admit I smoke.

   c. Exceptions to the foregoing:
      (1) Cases where a group are focused on one character, whose reactions are of such interest to the other characters and to the audience that the pause before he speaks will "hold" — St. Joan in the trial scene, for example.

(2) Direct questions to an individual, who precedes his answer with a movement or piece of business designed to heighten the audience's interest in his answer.

5. Avoiding delays on entrances and exits.

    a. Actors should anticipate entrance cues so as to be in position and ready to speak on the word cue.

    b. Actors should cross to doorways before their last line, delivering their last line in the doorway so as to avoid an uninteresting pause while they exit.

Examples: *The Importance of Being Earnest,* Act. I.

ENTRANCE:

> LADY BRACKNELL begins to move from the wings toward the open doorway, so as to see them, react and be ready to speak on the cue.

GWENDOLEN: (To Jack who is kneeling before her) What wonderfully blue eyes you have, Ernest! They are quite, quite blue. I hope you will always look at me just like that, especially when there are other people present. (*Enter LADY BRACKNELL*)

LADY BRACKNELL: Mr. Worthing! Rise, sir, from this semi-recumbent posture. It is most indecorous.

EXIT:

JACK: I can produce the hand-bag at any moment. It is in my dressing-room at home. I really think that should satisfy you, Lady Bracknell.

> She X to doorway.

> Turns at doorway to face Jack.

LADY BRACKNELL: Me, sir! What has it to do with me? You can hardly imagine that I and Lord Bracknell would dream of allowing our only daughter — a girl brought up with the utmost care — to marry into a cloak-room, and form an alliance with a parcel? Good morning, Mr. Worthing! (LADY BRACKNELL sweeps out in majestic indignation.)

6. Using movement to heighten the tension of a scene.

In addition to the value of movement in punctuating, pointing and throwing away lines, movement that is restless, agitated or rapid can help to sustain the tempo of a scene that might otherwise be talky or tedious.

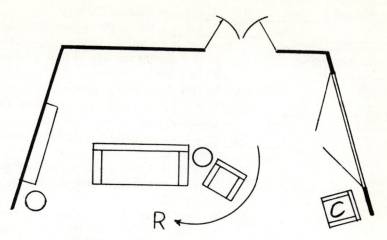

Example: *Blithe Spirit,* Act II, Scene 1.

XDC in perplexed meditation.	RUTH: Did you feel quite well yesterday — during the day, I mean?
	CHARLES: Of course I did.
Turning to face him.	RUTH: What did you have for lunch?
	CHARLES: You ought to know, you had it with me.
Paces DR.	RUTH: Let me see now, there was lemon sole and that cheese thing.
	CHARLES: Why should having a cheese thing for lunch make me see my deceased wife after dinner?
	RUTH: You never know. It was rather rich.
	CHARLES: Why didn't you see your dead husband then? You had just as much of it as I did.
XUR above sofa.	RUTH: This is not getting us anywhere at all.
	CHARLES: Of course it isn't; and it won't as long as you insist on ascribing supernatural phenomena to colonic irritation.
	RUTH: Supernatural grandmother.
	CHARLES: I admit she'd have been much less agitating.
XUC a few steps.	RUTH: Perhaps you ought to see a nerve specialist.
Rise indignantly.	CHARLES: I am not in the least neurotic and never have been.

XULC toward him.	RUTH: A psychoanalyst, then.
XDC past her.	CHARLES: I refuse to endure months of expensive humiliation only to be told at the end of it that at the age of four I was in love with my rocking-horse.
	RUTH: What do you suggest?
Sits DC.	CHARLES: I don't suggest anything, I'm profoundly uneasy.
XC to above his chair and feels his head.	RUTH: Perhaps there's something pressing on your brain.
	CHARLES: If there were something pressing on my brain I should have violent headaches, shouldn't I?
	RUTH: Not necessarily. An uncle of mine had a lump the size of a cricket ball pressing on his brain for years and he never felt a thing.
Springs up and XDR to fireplace.	CHARLES: I know I should know if I had anything like that.

7. Finding a *variety* of tempi within the play and taking every opportunity suggested by the text to change the tempo.

    a. Make sure that the first ten minutes of the play, when audiences are adjusting their eyes and ears to the stage, do not move too rapidly. If valuable expository points are lost, later scenes may lack significance; if the first scene moves too fast, later scenes may seem to drag by contrast.

    b. Avoid a "let down" after a particularly fast or effective scene by pacing the succeeding scene faster than might otherwise be necessary.

    c. Suspense can be created by a deliberately slower tempo than the audience would expect of the characters under given circumstances.

    d. The director should help the actor decide in each scene whether he is to pick up the tempo of the others or whether the rhythm of his character requires him to play at a different tempo than the rest in the scene.

    e. Sudden changes in speed can be used to good effect in creating variety and sustaining an audience interest.

        Example: *The Late Christopher Bean*, Act II. (No pauses except where || indicated.)

SUSAN plays at a deliberately slower tempo than DR. H.	SUSAN: (Comes downstairs, frightened.) What is it, Pa? What do you want?
	DR. HAGGETT: Have you seen any old pictures of Chris Bean's lying around?

Fast, building to a shout.	SUSAN: (Relieved) Oh, is that all?
	DR. HAGGETT: ↲ "Is that all? Is that *all*?" Don't talk like a fool!
	SUSAN: Pa, what's come over you, hollering this way?
	DR. HAGGETT: Answer my question.
	SUSAN: Yes, of course I have.
Simultaneously	MRS. HAGGETT: *What!*
	DR. HAGGETT: *Where?*
	SUSAN: Last time I seen 'em they was in the barn.
He is fast, hurrying her. She can build suspense by using a slower tempo.	DR. HAGGETT: In the *barn?*
	SUSAN: Yes, Pa.
	DR. HAGGETT: How many?
	SUSAN: I don't know rightly. || Eight or ten, I guess.
	DR. HAGGETT: *Eight* or *ten!*
	SUSAN: Yes, they was in the old box stall.
	DR. HAGGETT: I'm in and out of that barn all day long. Taking the Ford out and putting it up again. *I* ain't seen no pictures! || When did you see 'em last?
	SUSAN: It couldn't have been so long ago. || I remember showing 'em to Warren Creamer.
Angry now, SUSAN picks up faster tempo and each tops the other.	DR. HAGGETT: Aha! Then that's what's become of 'em. Warren Creamer's stole 'em.
	SUSAN. He *ain't*. He *wouldn't*.
	DR. HAGGETT: They was in the barn. You showed 'em to Warren. They ain't there now and I'd have seen 'em. Warren *must* have stole 'em.
	SUSAN: No!
	DR. HAGGETT: You get Warren over here this minute. No! Here! I'll get him. (Crosses to telephone at desk.)
	SUSAN: Pa! Please — (He snatches up the phone.)
Topping both of them.	MRS. HAGGETT: ↲ (Suffocating) *It ain't no use,* Milton.
	DR. HAGGETT: Why ain't it?

Sudden change to slow tempo for climax and variety.	MRS. HAGGETT: ‖ Warren didn't steal 'em. DR. HAGGETT: How do you know he didn't? MRS. HAGGETT: I ‖ burnt 'em. DR. HAGGETT: ‖ You *what?* MRS. HAGGETT: ‖ I put 'em on the bonfire and burnt 'em. DR. HAGGETT: ‖ All eight or ten? MRS. HAGGETT: ‖ I'd have thought there was more.

D. Planning for tempo and achieving it in rehearsal:

1. Keep in mind the desired tempo when planning the blocking and movement of the play.

   a. It will be difficult later to speed up a scene which has been blocked with deliberate or long movements.

   b. Inner factors which affect tempo should be a part of the director's original interpretation and planning of the production.

2. Wait until near the end of the rehearsal period to put pressure on the actors to pick up cues and achieve external tempo.

   a. Working for speed too soon may force actors to hurry artificially and overlook necessary motivations and responses.

   b. When the foundations are well laid and performances are truthful and well motivated, it will be relatively simple to tighten up the pickup of cues and take out unnecessary pauses.

   c. Remember that a fast tempo requires the actors to articulate more precisely than does a slow tempo.

3. A revision or final tightening of the tempo may be necessary after the director has observed audience reaction at the preview or first performance.

   a. Where restlessness or coughing is noted, the tempo may need to be speeded up.

   b. Where points are missed by the audience, the tempo may need to be slowed down.

   c. Holding for laughs will greatly affect the actual speed of the performance: though seeming to move rapidly, many minutes will be added to the playing time of a successful comedy.

Exercises for tempo:

Have actors read aloud the foregoing selections from *The Importance of Being Earnest, The Late Christopher Bean,* and

Blithe Spirit, working to achieve effective tempo by the technical means indicated.

Listen to the recording of Eva Le Gallienne in *Hedda Gabler* (ANTA Album of Stars, Volume 1, Decca DL 9002). Follow the script of one scene as given in Appendix D, marking the tempo of each line in the margin with F. for fast and S. for slow. Note the variety of tempi which Miss Le Gallienne uses brilliantly with both technical mastery and inner justification.

Try the following speech from *The Merry Wives of Windsor* using as many variations of tempo as possible:

MRS. PAGE: (Enters with a letter) What, have I 'scaped love letters in the holiday time of my beauty, and am I now a subject for them? Let me see. (Reads)

> 'Ask me no reason why I love you; for, though Love use Reason for his physician, he admits him not for his counsellor. You are not young, no more am I. Go to then, there's sympathy. You are merry, so am I. Ha, ha! then there's more sympathy. You love sack, so do I. Would you desire better sympathy? Let it suffice thee, Mistress Page — at the least, if the love of soldier can suffice — that I love thee. I will not say, pity me, — 'tis not a soldier-like phrase; but I say, love me. By me,

> > Thine own true knight,
> > By day or night,
> > Or any kind of light,
> > With all his might
> > For thee to fight,
> > > John Falstaff.'

O wicked, wicked world! One that is well-nigh worn to pieces with age to show himself a young gallant! Why, he hath not been thrice in my company! What should I say to him? I was then frugal of my mirth. Heaven forgive me! Why, I'll exhibit a bill in the parliament for the putting down of men! How shall I be reveng'd on him? For reveng'd I will be, as sure as his guts are made of puddings.

III. Climax.

Climax and tempo are closely interrelated and generally occupy the director's attention at the same time in the rehearsal period. It is the surge and fall of intensity in the drama that creates in the audience the impression of a fast tempo, and it is often through the dynamics of tempo that a build-up to climax is achieved.

A. Definition of climax.

Climax can be defined as a moment of high dramatic interest. The term comes from the Greek for "ladder," and suggests that there are various rungs or steps by which the actor progressively ascends to and descends from a high point. Minor climaxes are the highest moments of individual beats or scenes, act climaxes are the moments of greatest impact in each act, and the major climax of the play is the highest point in the action of the entire play.

1. Climax is a relative device and would not be meaningful to an audience without contrasting moments of falling intensity. As "anticlimax" has become a derogatory term, it is better to borrow from music and call a contrasting moment of subsiding intensity a "diminuendo." This will be analyzed more fully under the principle of subordination later in the chapter.

2. *Climax* should be distinguished from *crisis,* for the terms are not interchangeable. Crisis is a term in dramaturgy which refers to the *turning point* in the lives or destiny of the characters. This moment is not necessarily climactic in its theatrical effect, but as the audience reflects back on it, it was a time when the die was cast for the ultimate denouement — perhaps a moment of quiet or even casual decision such as Hamlet's fateful, "No, Up, sword, and know thou a more horrid hent." (Act III, Scene 3.) Edward A. Wright makes clear this distinction between crisis and climax when he states, "It is that crisis in the dramatic action of the play which leads directly to the climactic moment and makes it inevitable."[2]

B. Finding climaxes in the script.

1. Before attempting to block a play, the director should select and mark in his director's book those moments of highest dramatic intensity.

2. Climaxes may grow out of either:

a. Calculated and conscious decision.
"Till then, I banish thee on pain of death..." (*King Henry IV,* Part 2)

---

[2]Wright, Edward A., *A Primer for Playgoers* (Englewood Cliffs, N. J., Prentice-Hall, Inc., 1958), p. 92.

b. Uncontrolled or unpremeditated emotional outbursts.
"Yea, noise? Then I'll be brief. O happy dagger! This is thy
sheath; there rest, and let me die." (*Romeo and Juliet*)

3. Make sure that at least one climax is selected for:
   a. Each long speech or soliloquy.
   b. Each beat.
   c. Each scene.
   d. Each act. } (The larger units should contain several minor climaxes and a major climax arranged in cumulative order.)
   e. The play itself.

4. The director must know how strong each climax should be in relation to earlier and later climaxes, in other words, where a particular climax fits in the over-all pattern of surges and falls. Boleslavsky likened this to an awareness of the floors at which the elevator stops in its ascent to the top.[3]

5. Where the author has failed to provide a climax for each beat, scene or act, the director and actors will have to superimpose and motivate a build-up to climax; otherwise the beat or scene will not "get anywhere."

C. Inner factors which can create a climax.

1. The emotional progression of the actors. The actors grow in their emotional involvement in the situation, giving vent to more and more intense emotions until the most powerful level is reached at the moment in the play selected as the climax by the director. The actors need to hold some of their emotional strength in reserve for this moment, rather than reaching their climax too soon and creating an anticlimax or a plateau. If actors had sufficient inner resources and perfectly expressive voices and bodies, they would need little help from the technical elements listed following. Most often in the educational theatre, however, the director will need to use external techniques to help the actors bring out with the necessary intensity the emotions which they feel.

2. A moment of insight, discovery or recognition which comes to the character, and which can create a climax without necessarily requiring a forceful emotional intensity, provided there is complete understanding of the implications of the moment and the actor permits himself to be deeply affected by them. Such moments are often most telling when they drop quietly under the previous build-up.

---

[3]Boleslavsky, Richard, *Acting: The First Six Lessons* (New York: Theatre Arts, Inc., 1933), 6th lesson.

Example: *Our Town,* Act III. (The climax of the play.)

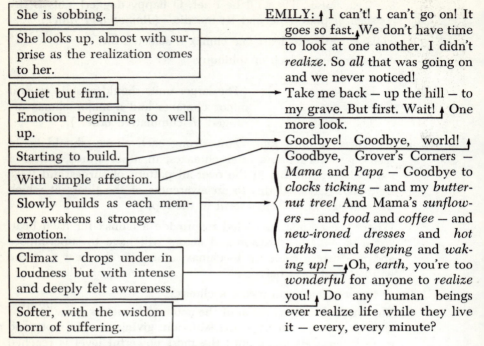

	EMILY: ↑ I can't! I can't go on! It
She is sobbing.	goes so fast. ↑We don't have time
She looks up, almost with surprise as the realization comes to her.	to look at one another. I didn't *realize.* So *all* that was going on and we never noticed!
Quiet but firm.	→ Take me back — up the hill — to my grave. But first. Wait! ↑ One
Emotion beginning to well up.	more look.
	→ Goodbye! Goodbye, world! ↑
Starting to build.	Goodbye, Grover's Corners —
With simple affection.	*Mama* and *Papa* — Goodbye to *clocks ticking* — and my *butter-*
Slowly builds as each memory awakens a stronger emotion.	*nut tree!* And Mama's *sunflowers* — and *food* and *coffee* — and *new-ironed dresses* and *hot baths* — and *sleeping* and *waking up!* —↑Oh, *earth,* you're too
Climax — drops under in loudness but with intense and deeply felt awareness.	*wonderful* for anyone to *realize* you! ↑ Do any human beings
Softer, with the wisdom born of suffering.	ever realize life while they live it — every, every minute?

D. External techniques which can create a climax.

   1. Composition. (Refer back to Chapter 5.)

      a. By using the strongest possible emphasis or center of attention. The strongest body position of the emphatic character(s), the most powerful area of the stage, levels, focus, line, etc., can all contribute to a visual stage picture of climactic power. The element of contrast is vital, making it necessary to save these strong elements for the climax and deliberately use weaker body positions, areas, levels, etc., for scenes preceding the climax. What means were used by the director to compose a visual climax in the accompanying photographs and those on pages 67, 73, 89, 111, 113?

      b. By saving the most telling picturization to dramatize the strong emotions within the characters at the moment of climax. For example, a climax was achieved through picturization in Act III of O'Neill's *A Moon for the Misbegotten* in the California State College at Long Beach production when the drunken Tyrone tries crudely to drag Josie toward her bedroom after she has already offered him her love; she shakes him loose so forcefully that he fall back down the steps. The actor playing Tyrone landed on his hands

Othello.

and knees, and stayed on the ground like an animal during the next two speeches, crawling on all fours toward the porch to grovel for the whiskey bottle.

c. By disturbing the balance of a well-balanced composition, or by restoring the balance after it has been upset. The father's entrance in Act I of *The Barretts of Wimpole Street*, for example (see page 150), upsets a balanced composition and thereby adds to the climactic effect of his entrance. In the last scene of *Romeo and Juliet*, to illustrate the opposite, the unbalanced composition is restored to symmetry as Capulet and Montague clasp hands in reconciliation over the dead bodies of their children.

The Crucible

d. By adding more characters to the picture so that their reactions can reinforce the climax. Shakespeare was intuitively aware of this principle of the director's art, and provided lines in *Romeo and Juliet* to motivate the addition of as many townspeople as the director has room and budget for during the street scene after the death of Tybalt, for which Romeo is banished.

2. Movement. (Refer back to Chapter 6.)

a. By making a strong movement or series of strong movements just before the climactic line, such as crossing from a weak area to a strong area, or opening up from a weak body position to a strong one. (See list of strong movements given in Chapter 6, page 162, and example from *The Crucible*, page 156.)

b. By increasing the size, duration or vigor of a movement as the scene builds to climax.

c. By increasing the speed of movement as the scene progresses. In the example from *The Late Christopher Bean* given on page 220, Dr. Haggett's cross to the telephone at the climax of the scene would be much more rapid than his cross to Susan at the beginning of the scene.

d. By decreasing the speed of movement for contrast.
Danny in *Night Must Fall*, for example, bustles briskly about the stage getting Mrs. Bramson things she wishes — books, candy, etc. In the climactic moment when he picks up the pillow to smother her, he moves with deliberate, extremely slow rhythm.

e. By increasing the number of people moving.
The shipwreck scene, for example, in Act I of *The Tempest*, can be built to climax by having more and more people — sailors and passengers — run across stage in alarm.

f. By suddenly stopping all movement.
The entrance of the father in the midst of an impromptu polka in *The Barretts of Wimpole Street* illustrates the effectiveness of this technique.

g. By gesture.
Just as with the other techniques used in building to climax, gesture must be utilized sparingly, so that the actor does not reach the largest extension of his arms too soon but saves it for the climactic moment. The repetition of a gesture weakens its climactic effect. Thus in the example on page 230 from *Our Town*, if Emily plans to extend her arms in a large gesture on "Oh, earth," she must use a smaller gesture on "Goodbye, world!"

3. Voice. (Refer back to Chapter 7.)
There is a natural tendency to use the four variable properties of voice together — i.e., pitch tends to rise and tempo to decrease when volume increases. However each can contribute to climax separately and the actor can use one or more of the following in different parts of a speech that must build to climax:

a. By changes in volume.
A progressive increase in volume is one of the most frequently used techniques for building to climax. Again the actor must guard against using his loudest volume too soon and being unable to top himself at the climax. In a long speech that must build to climax by means of volume, the actor should try to find places to drop back — growing momentarily softer — and begin the build anew. A sudden decrease from loud to low, intense delivery can also be climactic in effect.

Exercise: *A Midsummer Night's Dream,* Act III, Scene 1.
Trying to maintain pitch, tempo and quality constant, read the speech as indicated to build to climax with volume alone.

Start with normal volume and grow progressively louder on each word indicated.	PUCK: ↑ I'll *follow* you, I'll lead you about a *round,* Through *bog,* through *bush,* through *brake,* through *brier*:
Drop back to softer vol.	Sometime a *horse* I'll be, sometime a *hound,*
Build louder on each.	A *hog,* a headless bear, sometime a *fire;* And *neigh,* and *bark,* and *grunt,* and *roar,* and *burn,*
Climax — loudest.	Like *horse, hound, hog, bear,* ↑ *fire,* at *every turn.*

b. By changes in pitch.
A rising pitch usually accompanies a surge in anger or joy and a loss of emotional control; a falling pitch usually accompanies a climactic moment based on suppression of emotion, threat or decision. Too much rise in pitch, particularly in women's voices, may cause shrillness, and hence pitch is limited in its usefulness in building to climax.

Exercise: Read Puck's speech from *A Midsummer Night's Dream* again, trying to maintain volume, tempo and quality constant and using a progressively higher pitch on each word indicated.

c. By changes of quality.

Quality is the most variable of the four properties of voice, and the one that most closely mirrors inner content. In moments of climax, the voice may reflect an authoritative, exultant, or explosive quality reinforced with chest or full-mouth resonance, or it may reflect a strained, tense or desperate quality with strident, aspirate or throaty resonances.

Exercise: Read Puck's speech from *A Midsummer Night's Dream* again, trying to maintain constant volume, pitch and tempo, and using a different quality descriptive of the content and progressively more mischievously exultant on each word indicated.

d. By changes of tempo.

The cumulative effect of a progressively increasing tempo is also widely used for climax when motivated by emotional pressure, haste or anticipation. When the climax is motivated by authority, emphasis or deeply felt decision, the tempo would progressively decrease or slow down suddenly.

Exercise. Read Puck's speech from *A Midsummer Night's Dream* again, trying to maintain volume, pitch and quality constant and growing progressively faster in tempo.

e. By topping in vocal intensity.

Topping and undercutting as techniques in building to and from climax have already been covered in Chapter 7, pages 177 and 178. When two or more actors have a give-and-take of lines which must build to climax, topping is essential; it can happen only when there are teamwork and interplay between the actors building the scene. In a long speech or soliloquy, the individual actor can use the same principle in topping himself.

Exercise: Read Puck's speech from *A Midsummer Night's Dream* again, trying to make each key word in a sequence top those that precede it.

f. By the use of the pause.

As we have seen, the pause is a highly effective way of pointing the line or business which comes immediately after it. Falstaff's climactic "By the Lord, I knew ye as well as he that made ye," after he has been caught lying about the Gadshill robbery in *King Henry IV* can be made more effective if the actor takes full advantage of a pause after "By the Lord," while the audience is held in suspense watching the keen-witted old man as his shrewd mind invents an outrageous lie to top them all. A pause can also contribute to a climax when there is much animated talking and noise which is suddenly stopped cold at the climax, as for example, in the famous entrance of the Kirbys in *You Can't Take It With You,* in which they surprise the madcap family in a variety of outlandish activities. (See page 86.)

4. Reinforcement from other theatrical elements.

Although any of the theatrical elements can contribute to or reinforce a climax — scenery, for example, in *No Exit* when the bricked-up window is revealed, or costume in the return of the bloody, soaking-wet Shadow in *Winterset*, the elements most frequently used to heighten a climactic moment are:

a. Lighting.

When the form or style of the play permits, a climax can be made visually powerful by a stronger accent of light on the emphatic character(s) and a dimming down of the other areas of the stage. Some plays can also take advantage of special lighting effects at climactic moments — the colorful dawn in the last act of O'Neill's *A Moon for the Misbegotten*,

A Moon for the Misbegotten.

the whirling nightmare of lights in *The Adding Machine,* and
the flashes of lightning in the storm scenes of *King Lear.*

b. Sound effects.

The storm scene of *King Lear* receives additional reinforcement from the thunder and wind, and there are many other
plays in which sound effects can be used to heighten climaxes.
The final, unforgettable climax in *The Diary of Anne Frank*
is accomplished almost entirely by sound effects — the
screeching brakes of the secret police, the heavy boots
ascending the stairs, and the splintering of the door.

c. Music.

Motion pictures, television and radio rely much more heavily
upon music in achieving climaxes than does the theatre; in
the former media the human voice is heard over the same
loud-speaker system as the music, and the audience is not
conscious of any discrepancy between the two as is sometimes the case in the theatre when the music is not of high
fidelity. As will be seen in Chapter 12, in central staging
music becomes in many cases a substitute for the curtain and
as such can be used to heighten climactic moments coming
near the end of an act. Even in the proscenium theatre, however, there are times when music can appropriately be used
to heighten, underline or punctuate the climaxes, provided
there is something in the text with which the director can
justify the use of poetic license. In *Summer and Smoke,* for
example, the overtones of symbolism suggest the appropriate use of two musical themes, a sensual and a spiritual
leitmotif which surge to climax in many of the scenes and
then diminuendo to serve as a bridge into the next scene.

E. The principle of economy of means.

Throughout the foregoing analysis of the means of building to
climax, both inner and external, it will be observed that there was
implicit the principle of economy of means.

1. Saving the biggest effect for last.

In arranging minor and major climaxes, the director must save
his most powerful effect for last. If an actor gives too much emotional intensity to the Act I climax, he may have nothing left
with which to top himself for the Act II and Act III climaxes.
Having experienced the first act climax, the audience will not be
satisfied with the same level of intensity for the next act — unless
there is growth there will seem to be anticlimax and monotony.
As an example, study Judith Anderson's handling of this problem in her masterful recording of *Medea* (Decca, DAU-12).

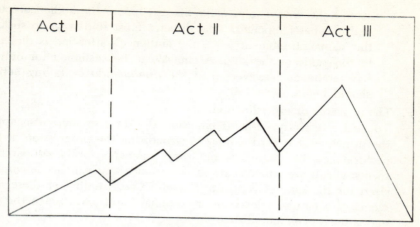

An Ideal Pattern for a Play's Climaxes.

2. Deciding how many steps there are in the progression to climax. F. Cowles Strickland notes that King Richard repeats the word "down" five times in his descent speech from *Richard II*, Act III, Scene 3.[4] If the actor descends all the way on the first few "downs," he will have no movement left with which to make the final "down" climactic. Similarly Capulet threatens Juliet four times (*Romeo and Juliet*, Act III, Scene 5) and the actor must grow in intensity so that the fourth threat is the most powerful.

3. Relating the number of steps in the progression to the blocking and movement.

   If the scene reaches its climax through a discernible number of intermediate steps, the physical blocking should as far as possible reflect this. The director should begin the progression in a weak area of the stage or with weak body positions, so as to give the scene room to build. If, for example, there are three intermediate steps in the build-up to climax, the director might use three movements; if he wishes the actor DRC for the climax, he might start the actor UL so that he can make three crosses — UR, DLC, and DRC.

4. Sustaining the climax when it is achieved.

   Having built up to the climax, it is important to sustain the high level of intensity long enough for its impact to be fully felt by the audience. Samuel Selden points out, for example, that in the climax of the play scene of *Hamlet* the king might cry, "Give me

[4]Strickland, F. Cowles, *The Technique of Acting* (New York: McGraw-Hill Book Company, Inc., 1956), p. 80.

some light: away!" and make his exit before the audience could realize what happened.[5] The director must find ways to sustain this climactic moment while the audience's attention is directed to the panic of the king. A climax can be sustained for only a few moments, however; then the *diminuendo* or falling action should begin.

F. The principle of subordination.

To deal effectively with his climaxes, the director must also apply the principle of subordination. In structuring the progression of the performance, he must seek out those moments, beats, or parts of scenes which are subordinate in importance and can be de-emphasized for the sake of contrast. The effective handling of these moments of a casual, relaxed or transitional nature will make the climaxes seem even more intense.

1. A build to climax is most powerful when it starts low, with a subordinate scene that can be "thrown away," played lightly or unemphatically. The inexperienced director sometimes tends to stress everything and work for too many climaxes; this would be the equivalent of playing an entire symphony *fortissimo*.

2. After a climax has been achieved, there should be a subsiding of intensity or *diminuendo* to another subordinate moment before a new build-up begins.

3. The *diminuendo* or subsiding action generally takes much less time than the progression to climax and, it is to be hoped, the audience's interest does not drop as low as it was at the beginning of the scene.

4. A *diminuendo* can be accomplished by:

   a. A sudden drop from climax to a subdued, contrasting moment.

   b. A gradual descent or relaxation of tension through a reversal of the techniques used to build the scene — i.e., a decrease of intensity, weaker visual emphasis and picturization, weaker movement, vocal undercutting, decreases in volume, tempo, subdued theatrical elements such as lighting, sound or music.

Example of the principles of climax and subordination. *Winterset,* Act III.

The final speech of Esdras, the father of Miriamne, as he and his son bend over her dead body and that of her beloved, Mio, is itself a resolution to the play rather than the climax (which was created by the attempted escape and machine-gunning of the lovers). Within the final speech itself, however, there must be a strong climax of recognition or awareness.

---

[5]Heffner, Hubert C., Selden, Samuel and Sellman, Hunton D., *Modern Theatre Practice* (New York: Appleton-Century-Crofts, 1959), p. 301.

Choking back his tears, he starts softly with the realization of a new truth.	ESDRAS: ↱Well, they were *wiser* than you and I. To die when you are young and untouched, that's *beggary* to a *miser* of *years*, but the *devils* locked in synod
Growing somewhat stronger.	{ *shake* and are *daunted* when men set their lives
Drops back, with gentle wisdom.	{ at hazard for the *heart's love,* and *lose.* ↱ And these, who were yet children, will weigh more than all a city's elders when the experiment
Builds with a sudden surge.	is reckoned up in the end. ↱Oh, Miriamne, and Mio — Mio, my son — know this where you lie,
Clear and strong, "Why didn't I see it before?"	*this* is the *glory* of *earth-born men* and *women,* not to *cringe,* never to *yield,* but *standing,* take defeat *implacable* and *defiant,*
Minor climax.	die unsubmitting. ↱I wish that I'd died so,
Then drops back with resignation.	long ago; before you're old you'll wish that you had died as they have. ↱On this star,
Begins major build-up, growing emphatic.	in this hard star-*adventure,* knowing not what the fires *mean* to right and left, nor whether a meaning was *intended* or *presumed,* man can *stand up,* and look out *blind,* and say:
As a powerful cry of protest.	{ in all these turning *lights* I find no *clue,* { Only a *masterless* night, and in my blood { no certain answer, ↱yet is my *mind* my *own,*
Tops himself, in restrained triumph.	yet is my *heart* a *cry* toward something *dim*
Strongly pointed as climax of speech	{ in *distance,* which is *higher* than *I* am { and makes me *emperor* of the endless *dark*
Diminuendo begins.	{ *even* in *seeking!* ↱What odds and ends of life
With quiet control of his emotions.	men may live otherwise, let them live, and then go out, as I shall go, and you. ↱Our part
Gently and softly he bends over his daughter.	is only to bury them. Come, take her up. They must not lie here.

Exercises for Climax:

Work out the pattern of the build-up to climax of the scenes given in this chapter from *The Late Christopher Bean, Our Town, A Midsummer Night's Dream,* and *Winterset,* using (1) composition and movement alone, (2) vocal techniques alone, (3) both together.

Analyze the progression to climax in the scene from *Death of a Salesman* given in Appendix D. Compare with the Thomas Mitchell recording (Decca DX 102).

Block the scene from *A Midsummer Night's Dream* given in Appendix D, selecting a number of minor climaxes and moments of subordination as well as a major climax.

Stage the final scene of *The Importance of Being Earnest* given in Appendix D, using all appropriate techniques to build the play to its climax.

IV. **Summary.**

The need for structuring the tempo and climaxes of a performance is inherent in the nature of the theatre itself. Although a director must plan his tempo and climaxes in his preliminary blocking, he generally should wait until the last phase of the rehearsal period to tighten the tempo and heighten the climaxes. Tempo and climax are interrelated and have as their purpose to give to the audience the impression of speed and cumulative dramatic intensity.

A. Tempo.
   1. Ways to speed up the tempo of a play.
   2. Inner factors which affect tempo.
   3. External factors which affect tempo.
   4. Planning for tempo and achieving it in rehearsal.

B. Climax.
   1. Definition of climax.
   2. Finding climaxes in the script.
   3. Inner factors which can create a climax.
   4. External techniques which can create a climax.
   5. The principle of economy of means.
   6. The principle of subordination.

Suggested Reading

BOLESLAVSKY, RICHARD. *Acting: The First Six Lessons.* New York: Theatre Arts, Inc., 1933. Lesson 6.

DIETRICH, JOHN E. *Play Direction.* New York: Prentice-Hall, Inc., 1953, Chapter II.

HEFFNER, HUBERT C., SELDEN, SAMUEL, AND SELLMAN, HUNTON D. *Modern Theatre Practice.* New York: Appleton-Century-Crofts, 1959, Chapter 8.

KLEIN, RUTH. *The Art and Technique of Play Directing.* New York: Rinehart, 1953.

STRICKLAND, F. COWLES. *The Technique of Acting.* New York: McGraw-Hill, Inc., 1956, Chapters 5, 6, 7.

WRIGHT, EDWARD A. *A Primer for Playgoers.* Englewood Cliffs, N. J., Prentice-Hall, Inc., 1958, Chapter 3.

Chapter 10

GOING INTO PRODUCTION

I. Introduction.

Play production is today being carried on in small high schools where one teacher "does everything" and in large universities where all production supervision is by a staff of faculty members. The neophyte director should not stand in awe or fear at the number of tasks that need to be performed for a smoothly running production; in many cases he will find help from unexpected sources if he will but seek it.

A. The ideal.

A well-organized production team is indispensable, whether it be in high school, college, community playhouse or on Broadway. Ideally the team spirit that was listed among the values of educational theatre in Chapter 1 can be fostered when a group of individuals come together to do creative work under effective leadership with clearly defined duties and lines of authority. This chapter therefore outlines the duties of a fairly extensive staff such as might be found in a large college or university drama department.

B. The practical.

The director without a fully equipped theatre, a trained scene designer and costume designer to work with or ample student crews to draw upon, will be forced to adapt some of the concepts presented in this chapter to his particular needs. Many high school teachers faced with a vast and formidable auditorium or gym-

242

nasium would be wiser to turn to some of the forms of simplified, central or flexible staging described in Chapter 12, thereby greatly reducing their production problems and the need for backstage staff. Many, too, will find that they can recruit volunteer aid from other faculty members, students and townspeople for stagecraft, costuming, make-up and properties if they are adept at channeling the energies of these volunteers by means of well-organized, enthusiastic leadership. For a person in such a position, this chapter may serve as a valuable check list of tasks to be done, even though he may have to keep changing hats and supervise them all himself. His selection of the play as discussed in Chapter 2 and his interpretation of the play as discussed in Chapter 4 will also affect the extent of the staff and backstage crews required. For the specific duties of each backstage staff member and crew head, see Appendix A.

II. The production staff.

A. Producer.

1. In the professional theatre the producer raises the money, obtains the rights to the play, hires the director and the cast, rents the theatre, and owns the production. In the educational theatre there is as a rule no producer; most of the production duties are assumed by the director.

2. In the community theatre, the board of directors or its chairman often assumes many of the producer's responsibilities.

3. In England the "producer" is what we call the "director," and the "manager" is what we call the "producer."

B. Director.

1. The director is responsible for staging the play, coaching the actors and integrating the entire production. In order to achieve a unified impression upon the audience, the director must be the final authority in all matters related to the production. Too many cooks have spoiled more than one theatrical broth.

2. The foregoing statement does not, however, preclude the director's using his authority sparingly and applying the best psychological principles of leadership, which include welcoming and encouraging creative contributions from others, consulting with his staff before making decisions, explaining his reasons rather than being arbitrary, respecting the special talents and training of his staff, and giving the entire team a sense of participation in the creative process.

C. Technical Director.

1. The technical director is responsible for coordinating backstage activities that relate to scenery, lighting, properties, and sound.

2. He may or may not serve as *scene designer* as well. Ideally he should, so that he can design with limitations of space, facilities, budget and manpower in mind, and see the scenery through the construction and painting phases to final dress rehearsal. If the scenery is designed by someone else, he should work closely with the technical director to translate his concepts into realization.

3. The technical director is responsible for the operation of the scene shop, including the purchase of materials and equipment.

D. Lighting Designer.

Lighting is often done by the technical director or by a *lighting designer* who works closely under his direction in planning and executing the lighting.

E. Costumer.

1. The costumer is responsible for all costumes worn in the play, including accessories such as gloves, jewelry, swords and wigs. The costumer may also be the *costume designer;* if the designs are done by someone else he should work closely with the costumer. In a modern realistic play costumes are usually not designed but selected and assembled by the costumer for the approval of the director.

2. It is often a natural extension of the costumer's duties to assume responsibility for *make-up*. The head of make-up is responsible for planning or designing all make-ups and hair styling, selecting colors of grease paint and powder, obtaining supplies, and supervising the make-up of the cast at each dress rehearsal and performance. Although actors traditionally make themselves up, they should be checked by the head of make-up each night before powdering.

F. Choreographer.

When a production involves dance or stylized movement, a choreographer works closely with the director.

G. Musical Director.

When a production involves live music, a musical director will work closely with the director. When recorded music is used, a music consultant will also be of invaluable aid to the director in selecting recordings.

H. Business Manager.

The business manager is responsible for expenditure of funds, keeping the production within its budget, handling ticket sales and receipts. In the absence of a staff business manager the director will generally assume these functions. A business manager usually handles or oversees student crews responsible for:

1. Publicity
2. Ticket sales and reservations (Box Office Staff)
3. Program editing
4. Bookkeeping

III. The production crews.

In the educational theatre, the director, technical director, lighting designer, costumer and business manager often are members of the faculty. The following are responsibilities usually assumed by students:

A. Stage Manager.
    1. The immediate right-hand man of the director, the stage manager is the most responsible position generally held by a student on major productions and the best stepping stone to direction. During dress rehearsals and performances he assumes complete charge backstage. There may be several *assistant stage managers*, depending on the complexity of the production, for such tasks as getting crowds on and off, cueing lights or sound, prompting, or maintaining quiet on the opposite side of the stage from the stage manager.

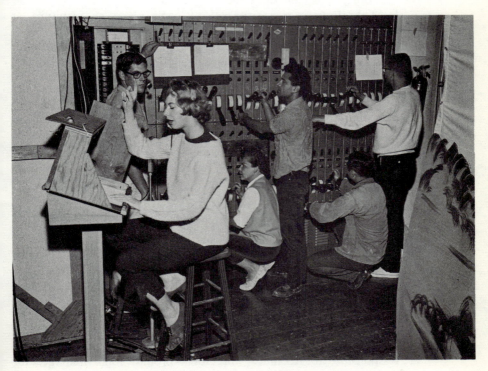

Stage Manager gives warning to light crew.

2. Responsible to director; also the technical director for the operation of scene-shifts.

B. Property Crew Head and Crew.

1. Responsible for the gathering, handling, shifting and returning of all properties, which include three categories:

   a. Furniture.
   b. Trim props (those items desired by the designer to decorate the set, including drapes, rugs, lamps, pictures, bric-a-brac).
   c. Hand props (those items handled by the actors). When gloves, hats, etc., are discovered or left on stage, they are considered costume props, to be furnished by the costume crew but shifted by the prop crew. As soon as the actors are free of books, important hand props (those handled a good deal by the actors) should be brought to rehearsal — or rehearsal substitutes provided — so actors can practise the use of them and save time at dress rehearsals.

2. Responsible to:

   a. The director for approval of each hand prop as to size, workability and general effect.
   b. The designer for approval of each piece of furniture or trim as to color, style and period.
   c. The stage manager for placement, shifting and striking of all props and furniture during performance.

C. Stage Crew Head and Crew.

One crew may perform all of the following duties or may be subdivided into three separate crews. The head of the stage crew is often designated as *technical assistant* or shop foreman.

1. Responsibilities:

   a. Scene construction crew.
      Responsible for building the scenery.
   b. Scene painting crew.
      Responsible for painting the scenery.
   c. Stage crew.
      Responsible for shifting scenery when more than one set is used. A *curtain man* will usually be designated from this crew. Where a counterweight system is used, this crew is often divided into:

      (1) Grips — those handling set pieces on the floor.
      (2) Flymen — those operating the counterweight system.

2. Responsible to: technical director (through stage manager for shifts during performance).

D. Lighting Crew Head and Crew.
   1. Responsible for hanging the lights, operating the switchboard, shifting any electrical floor units, and where necessary, operating follow spots.
   2. Responsible to: technical director or lighting designer who works under him during planning phase; responsible to stage manager during performance.
E. Costume Crew Head and Crew.
   1. Responsible for gathering all costumes and accessories; some costumes may be constructed from designs, others may be rented, borrowed, bought either new or from salvage stores, or loaned by the cast. Fitting, alteration, cleaning, pressing and returning costumes are part of this crew's duties. In addition some college theatres check out costumes to each actor before every performance and check them in afterwards. In other theatres, the actor is made responsible for his costume once it is issued to him except for repairs and cleaning. On large costume productions the crew can be divided into:
      a. Costume construction crew.
      b. Wardrobe crew.
         During dress rehearsals and performances helps actors into costume, helps with quick changes, does emergency repairs, cleaning and laundry.
   2. Responsible to: costumer; (wardrobe crew reports to stage manager for quick changes).
F. Make-up Crew Head and Crew.
   1. Responsible for supervising all make-ups, applying make-up to those actors unable to make up themselves, hair and wig dressing, purchasing supplies, maintenance and clean-up of make-up and dressing rooms.
   2. Responsible to: Costumer or head of make-up.
G. Sound Crew Head and Crew.
   1. Responsible for obtaining and operating all sound effects, including recorded music. Simple sound effects such as door slams can be done by a member of the prop crew, but more complex productions may require a sound crew divided into:
      a. Manual.
      b. Recorded.
   2. Responsible to: technical director or director in planning; stage manager during performance.
H. Publicity Crew Head.
   1. Responsible for promotion and publicity of the play, including preparation of newspaper releases, radio and TV spots, publicity

photographs, advertisements, posters, mailing pieces, banners and marquee signs.

2. *Poster and Program Designer* is often an art student who designs one unified layout for poster, mailing piece and program cover under the supervision of a member of the art faculty, and subject to the approval of the director of the play.

3. *Program Editor* is responsible for obtaining all names (spelled correctly) for the program, acknowledgments, credits, program notes and coming events; checks printer's proof.

4. Responsible to: director, usually through business manager.

I. Box Office Staff.
1. Responsible for reservations, ticket sales, and depositing of funds.
2. Responsible to: business manager.

J. House Manager.
1. Responsible for obtaining, training and supervising the ushers. In charge of lobby and auditorium before and during performance.
2. Responsible to: director, often through business manager.

IV. The relationship between cast and crews.

A healthy relationship between the cast and the crews will do much toward insuring high morale backstage and a smoothly running production.

A. Recognition for the crews.
The unsung heroes of play production are the backstage crews, who rarely receive the acclaim of the public. The director and the actors should take every opportunity to give recognition and appreciation for the contribution of the crews. There is no place in the educational theatre for a "star complex" in an actor or condescension toward the crews. Actors soon learn how dependent they are upon the support of the crews for a smooth performance. Actors should call crew members by their names rather than "Props" or "Wardrobe," and social activities should always involve both cast and crews.

B. Working together for the success of the production.
It should be explained to crew members by the responsible faculty supervisors that their *raison d'être,* their purpose for being backstage, is not an end in itself but rather one of service — to make sure that the actors go onstage able to do their best work and with all of the things they require. Because the success of the performance ultimately depends upon the ability of the actors to perform before a live audience where mistakes are irrevocable, crew members should support their cast, help them in every way possible

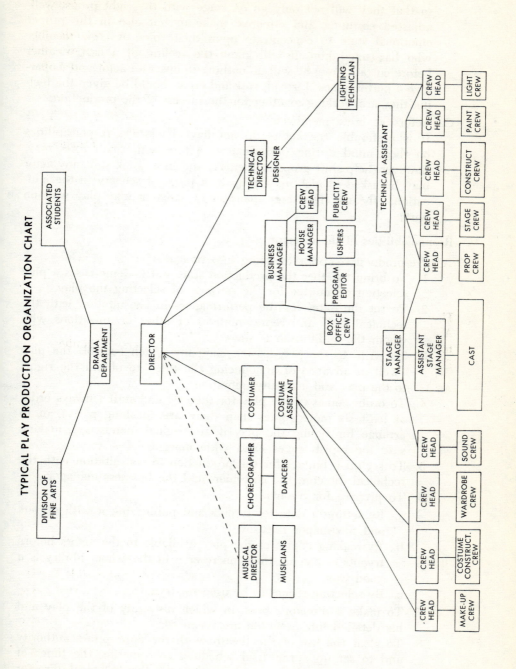

TYPICAL PLAY PRODUCTION ORGANIZATION CHART

so that they will not only go on stage with the right props, well-adjusted costumes and effective make-up but also in the proper emotional state to concentrate upon their roles. A crew member who has acted himself will know the feeling of a cast member before curtain time; he will do nothing to upset an actor and jeopardize a performance. Instead, cast and crew should be given the feeling they are working together for the success of the production.

C. Actors as crew members.

It is preferable the actors do not have backstage responsibilities on their mind during performance. Actors with small roles may, however, help shift props or scenery, and in a quick shift any actor may be asked to pick up a prop or a piece of scenery in the educational theatre. The stage manager or assistant may play walk-on parts.

V. Responsibilities of the director.

A. Pre-production (prior to going into rehearsal).

1. To bring together the production staff and in some cases a play selection committee for the purpose of selecting the play.

2. To set the dates for the performances in consultation with the technical staff and representatives of other organizations with whom the auditorium is shared.

3. To write to the play-leasing company which controls the play (well in advance of announcing the title) to obtain the rights to the play and a royalty quotation.

4. To order copies of the play for the cast and staff (always order at least six more copies than there are speaking parts), or to arrange for typing the play if an original manuscript, making sure the typist leaves extra wide margins.

5. To set up a budget for the production in consultation with the technical director, the costumer, and the business manager.

6. To prepare for tryouts.

   a. By setting a date for tryouts and publicizing it with posters and newspaper releases.

   b. By making copies of the play available to the actors before tryouts — placing them on reserve in the school library is a good way.

   c. By selecting scenes to be used for tryouts.

7. To make a director's book in which his study of the play and his detailed interpretation are recorded.

8. To clear the use of the theatre with the appropriate authority and to set up a rehearsal schedule, coordinating the times of all technical and dress rehearsals with the technical director and costumer.

9. To schedule a series of production conferences with the technical director, costumer and other members of the staff after all have had a chance to read and study the script.

B. Production conferences.

The director takes the initiative in bringing together all the responsible staff and crew heads for planning conferences. Most of the headaches of production stem from decisions made when everyone who is affected has not been consulted.

1. First production conference.

(Note: in the following, the term "designer" is meant to include the technical director if the two are not the same person.)

    a. Director presents his interpretation of the play and his concept of style for the production (see Chapter 4). The staff may react to the director's interpretation or present their own interpretations. After a full and open discussion, a common interpretation should be agreed upon. Although the director is the final authority he should try to incorporate as much as possible the concepts and feeling for the play contributed by the staff.

    b. The common interpretation should include a consideration of mood, style, and ways in which the author's intent can be reinforced by setting, lighting, costumes, properties, music and actors.

2. Second production conference (at least one week later).

    a. After designer has had adequate time to prepare sketches, the director calls a second production conference with the designer, costumer, and lighting technician.

    b. Designer presents his preliminary sketches, ground plans and/or models to the staff. They are evaluated from the following aspects:

        (1) Over-all impression and mood.

        (2) Effectiveness in furthering the author's intent and the agreed-upon interpretation.

        (3) Placement of principal acting areas and ground plan.

        (4) Feasibility of execution and shifting.

    c. Although the director is vitally concerned with the ground plan and the size, placement and usability of furniture while the technical director (when different from the designer) is concerned primarily with executing and shifting the sets with a given number of dollars and man-hours, the designer should as far as possible have his wishes respected as regards:

(1) Color (3) Composition of the total visual picture
(2) Form (4) Choice of materials

d. On the basis of the foregoing factors, the final decision to accept, modify or redo the designs is made by the director after adequate discussion, exploration of alternatives, and respect for the integrity of the designs which can be modified only so far without destroying the basic intent of the designer.

3. Third production conference (at least 2 - 3 weeks prior to the first rehearsal).

a. Designer submits revised designs, color sketches and/or models, and scale ground plans to the staff.

b. Director, designer, technical director, costumer and choreographer (where applicable) agree in final detail upon the settings. A color rendering should be made available to the costumer.

c. Overlay tracings of the ground plan should be given to the director, stage manager, property crew head and lighting technician by the technical director, who also supervises the laying out of the ground plan on the floor of the stage or rehearsal hall with paint or masking tape prior to the first blocking rehearsal.

d. Costumer submits costume sketches (if a period play) or discusses the costume requirements of the play with the director (if a modern dress play). Any possible clashes in color or design between settings and costumes can be noted and remedied at this time.

e. The director should rely upon the costumer's more thorough research and knowledge of:

(1) The period and the fashions worn at the time.
(2) Color, style and silhouette which would be appropriate.
(3) Combinations of colors for characters who have scenes together.
(4) Choice of fabrics.
(5) Cost of construction or renting.

f. The director's concern with the costumes includes:
(1) The general impression of the costume and the reflection of the character who wears it.
(2) The freedom of movement and gesture which the costume permits for the stage business the director has in mind.
(3) The time required for quick changes of costume.

4. Further production conferences.

The director should continue to confer with the technical staff, either together or individually, until all questions are resolved. *These conferences should not be held during rehearsal,* however, when the director should be free to concentrate on his cast. The director should make sure that he covers each item on this check list if applicable:

a. Discusses the costumes in further detail with the costumer (in some cases the physique of the actors cast in the roles may alter the final design). When designs are not used, each character should be discussed in detail and what he is to wear in each act listed on the costume plot. In the latter method, the costumer will assemble the costumes over a period of weeks; some directors prefer to see and approve each costume before the first dress rehearsal.

b. Confers with the business manager to make sure that:
   (1) Tickets have been ordered in ample time.
   (2) Copy approved for publicity releases.
   (3) Design of poster, mailing pieces and advertisements approved.
   (4) Publicity photographs scheduled and date coordinated with costumer and actors concerned.
   (5) Program copy and layout approved, and proof checked at last possible moment.
   (6) Royalty check sent to play-leasing company in ample time.
   (7) Production photographs scheduled at time agreeable to staff.

c. Confers with head of prop crew on hand props, particularly those involved in the action of the play, and makes sure that crew head has conferred with designer on each item of furniture and trim needed.

d. Confers with lighting technician to discuss in detail the mood, intensity, acting areas, and motivation for the light.

e. Confers with the make-up crew head to discuss in detail the make-up of each character and coordinating it with the lighting so that the color of the light does not destroy its effect.

f. Confers with the sound effects crew head to discuss in detail each sound effect, how it will be made, and where it begins and ends.

g. Coordinates the schedule for the use of the stage, making sure that the technical director and lighting technician have adequate time on stage for setup and technical rehearsals. The director often can work successfully in a rehearsal hall if he has planned ahead with this in mind.

h. Makes sure that everyone is informed as changes occur during rehearsal. The stage manager can help in this liaison, notifying the prop crew head of new props added or changed placement of props.

VI. Summary.

A well-organized production team, with each person clear as to responsibilities and lines of communication, is indispensable to successful play production. The director's position requires him to delegate as many responsibilities as possible but to retain the final authority for integrating the work of the staff, crews and cast.

A. The production staff:
 1. Producer.
 2. Director.
 3. Technical director and/ or scene designer.
 4. Lighting designer.
 5. Costumer.
 6. Choreographer.
 7. Musical director.
 8. Business manager.

B. The production crews:
 1. Stage manager.
 2. Property crew.
 3. Stage crew.
 4. Lighting crew.
 5. Costume crew.
 6. Make-up crew.
 7. Sound crew.
 8. Publicity crew.
 9. Box office staff.
 10. House manager.

C. The relationship between cast and crews.
 1. Recognition for the crews.
 2. Working together for the success of the production.
 3. Actors as crew members.

D. Responsibilities of the director:
 1. Pre-production.
 2. Production conferences.

Suggested Reading

BORUM, MAY ROSE, AND McGEE, BARRY. *Stage Production.* Los Angeles: Los Angeles City College, 1956.

GRUVER, BERT. *The Stage Manager's Handbook.* New York: Harper and Brothers, 1953.

HALSTEAD, WILLIAM P. *Stage Management for the Amateur Theatre.* New York: F. S. Crofts, 1937.

SHAFFER, JAMES F. *The Director, The Actor and the Stage.* Portland, Oregon: Allied Publishers, 1956.

SPONSLER, WHITNEY R. *A Manual for High School and College Theatrical Administration.* Hollywood: American Legitimate Theatre Service, 1956.

Chapter 11

REHEARSING THE PLAY

I. Introduction.

No matter how great the talent of the director or his understanding of the principles covered in previous chapters, the success of his production will depend to a great extent upon his ability to conduct orderly and organized rehearsals in which he applies his theory and insight. If the director is relatively inexperienced, then he will have all the more need for a systematic rehearsal procedure.

II. Casting the play.

This is perhaps the most critical time for the ultimate success of the play. The director should carefully prepare for this period so as to get the best possible cast and still leave each candidate with the feeling that he has had a fair chance and that the director has not played favorites.

A. Preparation for casting.
   The director should prepare the following in advance of tryouts:
   1. A description of each character with both physical and psychological requirements (see Chapter 8, Sec. 2-4). This should be presented to the group orally or on ditto sheets at the beginning of tryouts.
   2. Announcement of date and place of tryouts.
   3. A form to be filled out by candidates and used by director (see sample illustrated).

255

4. Scripts of the play obtained in sufficient time for tryouts, with copies made available in library.
5. Tryout scenes, selected for:
   a. Variety of moods demanded in roles.
   b. Limit of three or four characters in each scene.
   (Some directors announce the tryout scenes ahead of time; others prefer not to.)

B. Methods of casting.
   1. Open tryout method.
   Although this method is the most prevalent, it may be necessary to supplement it by other methods.

   a. Any student enrolled in the school or resident of the area is eligible to tryout. A three to four minute scene is read from the stage by candidates. The first evening is devoted to a weeding out of the unsuitable and the working up of a list of "possibles" who are then placed on a "Callback" list for the second night. The decision as to whether to give each actor a thorough hearing or a quick screening the first night must depend upon the number of applicants. A valuable technique to break the ice used by Bert Holland of Santa Monica City College is to let all candidates pair up and go out for fifteen minutes to read the scene aloud before auditioning.
   b. Callbacks.
   The "possibles," sometimes as many as 3 - 4 for each major role, are called back for final readings which must be conducted more thoroughly and under less pressure than the first readings. The director now must consider how well people are matched who will be playing scenes together. (For romantic scenes, check the height of the lovers; check for family similarity and contrast if applicable.)
   c. Final readings.
   The director should assemble his final choices around a table for another reading and careful scrutiny before announcing his cast. At this time he can fill in minor roles with some of the runners-up for the leads. He should make sure that anyone accepting a role understands and agrees to the obligations and responsibilities demanded, and that his schedule will permit his rehearsing at the time others in the same scenes are free.

   2. Closed tryout method.
   When a play is to be cast from a particular class or membership group, closed readings are held. This method requires that the director consider very carefully the potential of the group or

CALIFORNIA STATE COLLEGE
LONG BEACH
Drama Department

CASTING SHEET

Name ....Present Address............................. Phone...................

Date ....Age........ M........ F........ Ht................Year in School..............

Color hair .... Do you dance? .... Sing? .... Voice Range..................

Other specialty ....High School ....
(Fencing, musical instruments played, etc.)

Foreign Languages spoken .... Dialects ....

No. of units for which you are enrolled this semester .... Home town ....

Are you enrolled for 1 unit credit in Drama Activity?...............If so, check crew you
would prefer to work on should you not get a major role:

............Stage Management   ....Costumes   ....Lighting

............Make-up   ....Set Construction   ....Properties

............Set Painting   ....Publicity

Please fill out your program this semester in detail, putting an X in each square when you have a **class or any outside work or commitment** that would interfere with rehearsal. We will build rehearsal schedules from this, so **fill in completely.**

	MON.	TUES.	WED.	THURS.	FRI.	SAT.
9 - 10 a.m.						
10 - 11						
11 - 12						
12 - 1 p.m.						
1 - 2						
2 - 3						
3 - 4:30						
4:30 - 6						
7 - 8 p.m.						
8 - 9 p.m.						

Please use back of this sheet to **list** your **experience** in dramatics:

****DO NOT WRITE BELOW THIS LINE****

Juvenile........Ingenue........Character........Leads........Comedy........Heavy........Other......

Appearance: Interpretation: Emotion:

Speech: Sense of Comedy: Ability to Take Direction:

Voice: Variety: Possible for Role of.......................

class before selecting a play. In high school, the class can participate in the casting process by analyzing the characters physically and psychologically and suggesting students who might possibly be suitable.

3. Personal audition and interview method.

   Most professional productions are cast by private interview and reading, often in the director's office. For the nonprofessional theatre, however, this method is too time-consuming and not conducive to the feeling that the actors have been given fair and equal consideration. Often, however, a director will have to supplement open tryouts by personal auditions to complete his cast when the open tryouts fail to produce the certain type or quality of actor needed.

4. Use of other techniques to supplement the foregoing.
   a. Memorized selections.

      In the case of Shakespeare or other material that is difficult because of its language, the director may expedite tryouts by asking all applicants to memorize a given soliloquy.
   b. Improvisations.

      For high school students and actors with previous experience in the Stanislavski method, the reading tryout can be supplemented by an improvisation based on a situation in the play, or one even indirectly suggested by it, permitting the director to see the actors react spontaneously, freely and with an emotional truth that rarely can be shown in a first reading. The improvisation needs to be carefully structured as described in Chapter 3 to avoid the tensions of this type of tryout.
   c. Physical movement.

      Where the play requires style and heightened body control from the actors, this should be checked as part of the tryout by asking the actors to cross the stage, bow, turn, fall, or sit to a musical rhythm which can be played on the piano or with a drum.

5. What to look for in casting.
   a. Some spark in the actor's personality which suggests the character.
   b. The actor's voice and speech, particularly projection, variety, clarity, and suitability for the role.
   c. The actor's physical appearance and its appropriateness for the role.
   d. The actor's emotional intensity and sense of truth.
   e. How the tryout audience responds to his reading. If a comedy, did he get any laughs?
   f. The actor's sense of timing if the role is a comedy one.

g. The actor's stage presence and poise.

h. The actor's flexibility and ability to take direction.

i. Conflicts in the actor's schedule which might have a bearing on his attending rehearsals.

j. Special aptitudes required such as playing a musical instrument, singing, dancing or fencing.

k. In the case of minor roles, it is often sufficient to have only one or two specific requirements in mind, and to use ingenuity in taking advantage of the particular personalities of the actors available.

l. The theatrical requirements of the role.
Whether a character is tall or short, blonde or brunette, deep voiced or high voiced, is often of less importance than whether he fulfills the theatrical requirements of the role as intended by the author. The director should have these requirements in mind during casting, and should return to them as he guides the actors in characterization. The kind of empathic response which he desires the audience to have to the character may have direct bearing on the choice of actors. Among the theatrical requirements, which can be fulfilled in more than one way by more than one "type" of actor, are:

(1) Positive identification. The audience must like him, find him sympathetic and want him to win. He must inspire confidence.

(2) Negative identification. The audience must dislike him, find him unpleasant, irritating, disgusting, or hateful.

(3) The audience must find him pathetic.

(4) The audience must find him comic. His purpose is to "get laughs."

(5) He must dominate other characters in the play. As this factor is relative, the strength or weakness of the other characters will determine how much strength it will take to dominate them.

(6) The character must be a foil or contrast to another character. Demetrius and Lysander in *A Midsummer Night's Dream*, for example, need to be as different physically as possible — what might be called relative characterization — in order that the audience can distinguish between them during the confusions of a night in a dark forest. In this play too, it is essential that Hermia be shorter in stature than Helena.

A Midsummer Night's Dream.

(7) The character is intended to supply atmosphere or local color.

(8) The character's only purpose is to convey information — messengers, for example — or perform other utility functions. Clarity of voice and diction may be the primary requisites of the role.

(9) The character may not be fully characterized by the playwright, and the actor must supply what the playwright omitted. Through astute casting the director can sometimes enrich his production by taking advantage of the special attributes of his actors.

(10) A special quality of dignity or maturity may be needed to avoid getting laughs in the wrong places. Lodovico, for example, in *Othello* is a relatively minor role in the last act, but he speaks the final speech of the play, and the director should save a strong and mature actor for this role.

C. The double cast.

High school directors must decide whether or not to double cast. College or community theatre directors rarely use this method.

1. Its advantages are that more students can participate in a production, and the roles are covered in case of the illness of an actor.

2. Its disadvantage is that it requires more of the director's time, doing in effect double coaching, and often results in a less polished performance than with a single cast. If the system is used, each actor should be required to attend every rehearsal, observing and learning while his alternate is being directed. Both actors should work in part of each rehearsal.

D. Understudies.

In the nonprofessional theatre, an actor often prefers not to devote the time to preparing a role which he is not assured of playing. As college students are less prone to communicable diseases than high school youth, understudies are generally not needed. At the first hint that an actor may be seriously ill, however, the director must have an understudy stand by. It is amazing how rapidly an actor can learn a part when the rest of the production has taken shape, provided the stage manager has carefully recorded all blocking.

E. Precasting.

Although the director must have one or more possible actors in mind when he selects a play which has a particularly demanding leading role, it is fatal to the morale of an educational or community theatre if it is suspected that the director has made promises or commitments to actors prior to tryouts. Someone much better may turn up at tryouts, and in any case actors must not feel that there is no use trying out, or that a little clique will always get the best parts.

III. **The rehearsal schedule.**

As soon as the play is cast, the director should list all the conflicts in time which his actors may have — hours when it is impossible for them to rehearse — and on the basis of this work out a rehearsal schedule adequate to his estimate of the difficulties of the play.

A. Factors that affect the making of a rehearsal schedule:

1. The schedule should be coordinated with the technical staff and the master calendar for the use of the theatre. (Where the stage can be used only on certain nights, it is best to schedule the large group scenes on those nights.) Opening night should not be left uncertain, but fixed from the beginning.

2. The rehearsal schedule should be duplicated and distributed to all concerned — to the cast at the first rehearsal and to technical

staff and crew heads. In high school the rehearsal schedule can be sent home to parents.

3. Rehearsals should be scheduled regularly and as close together as possible, to preclude the forgetting that occurs during a long interval. The rehearsal schedule must, however, be realistic and take into consideration the maturity, outside pressures and class requirements of student actors.

   a. Daily rehearsals are the most efficient.
   b. Three times a week is minimal.
   c. Less than three rehearsals a week is an inefficient plan.

4. The total number of rehearsals needed will depend upon the difficulty of the material and the experience of the cast.

   a. Four to six weeks, with five rehearsals a week, is minimal for the average modern play with no special difficulties.
   b. Six to eight weeks may be necessary for Shakespeare and other classics, musicals and plays with special problems.
   c. Three to four weeks, with three or four 2-hour rehearsals per week, may be necessary for the average one-act play.

5. What can be accomplished in one rehearsal depends upon the size and experience of the cast, their fatigue level, the difficulty of the material and the stimulation which the director can provide. A suggested allocation of time in the college theatre is:

7:00 P.M. to 7:20	Warm-up (running lines, reviewing or getting familiar with new material).
7:20 P.M. to 8:15	Concentration on new material to be worked on.
8:15 P.M. to 8:25	Break.
8:25 to 9:00	Review and refine new material just worked on.
9:00 to 9:30 or 10:00	Repeat new material to fix it in actors' memory, or review previously learned material.

   a. A suggested high school rehearsal schedule would compress the foregoing into two hours, 3:30 to 5:30 or 7 P.M. to 9 P.M.
   b. The director should be sensitive as to when the cast can be pushed, when they are fatigued, when they are on the verge of a creative discovery. When they are emotionally spent, the director should switch to less strenuous scenes. A play can also be over-rehearsed until the actors grow stale.

6. The director should schedule actors for particular scenes as needed, especially in a large cast play, and not expect busy students or working adults to give up time when not actually needed.

Scenes involving certain characters or groups can be scheduled together on certain nights for more efficient use of the actors' time. (For example, the Friar scenes in *Romeo and Juliet* can, for the early weeks of rehearsal, be scheduled on nights when Benvolio, Tybalt and Mercutio are not present, and vice versa.) The director in the nonprofessional theatre is forced to be flexible in building his schedule around the conflicts, classes and work commitments of his cast.

7. When the director finds that private coaching is necessary or that an actor is embarrassed to be coached in front of the group, individual sessions should be scheduled outside the regular rehearsals. Actors should not be pampered into expecting this, however, because of the demands made upon the director's time during the rehearsal period.

8. *Every rehearsal should have a purpose,* and both director and cast should bring something new to try out at each rehearsal. The purposes of each phase of the rehearsal period are shown in the suggested rehearsal schedule and explained in Section V in order to give the director an overview of the necessary steps between casting and opening night. The director must plan for what he hopes to accomplish at each rehearsal (though he need not necessarily announce his plans to the cast), adapting his strategy as he sees how the cast is progressing and how many rehearsals are left. Too often young directors arrive at rehearsal merely to "run through" an act, which, if it lacks a purpose, may prove to be merely running.

9. The principle of "the juggler."

    A scene that is not completely mastered cannot be left unrehearsed for more than two or three days without ill effects. The director uses the principle of the juggler, throwing one ball (Act I) into the air, then adding a second one and keeping two going alternately, then adding a third and keeping all three going simultaneously.

B. *A suggested rehearsal schedule.*

On the basis of the aforesaid principles, the following is suggested as a rehearsal schedule that has been found workable (with modifications) at the college level for such modern full-length plays as *The Diary of Anne Frank, The Time of Your Life,* and *Summer and Smoke.* (Where a play is in a number of scenes rather than three acts, it is best to divide it into thirds for rehearsal purposes, based upon length rather than number of scenes.)

SUGGESTED REHEARSAL SCHEDULE

WEEK		PURPOSE	PERIOD
1st	Monday	Open tryouts	Casting
	Tuesday	Callbacks	"
	Wednesday	Final casting	"
	Thursday	Reading of whole play	Familiarization
	Friday	Reading, discussion and analysis of play	"
2nd	Monday	Reading, discussion and analysis of play	"
	Tuesday	Block Act I	Exploration
	Wednesday	Review Act I	"
	Thursday	Block Act II	"
	Friday	Act I for characterization and business	"
3rd	Monday	Review Act II	Exploration
	Tuesday	Act I for enrichment	"
	Wednesday	Act II for characterization and business	"
	Thursday	Act I **WITHOUT BOOKS**	"
	Friday	Acts I and II for enrichment	"
4th	Monday	Block Act III	"
	Tuesday	Polishing Act I	Discovery
	Wednesday	Act II **WITHOUT BOOKS**	Exploration
	Thursday	Review Act III for characterization	"
	Friday	Run Acts II and III for polishing	"
5th	Monday	Act III for business and enrichment	"
	Tuesday	Act I for tempo and climax	Formalizing
	Wednesday	Act II for polishing	Discovery
	Thursday	Act III **WITHOUT BOOKS**	Exploration
	Friday	Run Acts II and III for continuity	Discovery
6th	Monday	Run Act I and II for tempo and climax	Formalizing
	Tuesday	Run Act III for tempo and climax	"
	Wednesday	Act III and scenes that need polish	"
	Thursday	Run through of entire play with hand props	Integration
	Friday	Run through of entire play for final polishing in rehearsal hall — stage used by technical crews	"
	Saturday	Technical rehearsal for lights (without actors)	"
7th	Sunday	1st Dress Rehearsal	"
	Monday	2nd Dress Rehearsal with make-up	"
	Tuesday	Preview Dress Rehearsal	"
	Wednesday	Opening Night	Performance
	Thursday	Performance	"
	Friday	Performance	"
	Saturday	Performance	"

(When performances are repeated the following weekend, a line-rehearsal is recommended as a refresher the day preceding.)

IV. General principles of rehearsal.

At the first rehearsal, it generally is desirable to make sure that the cast is familiar with the *traditions of the theatre* and understands the standard of discipline which the director will expect of them during the weeks to come.

A. *Traditions of the rehearsal.*

The rehearsal period is a special time in the daily life of theatre artists, a time for serious and concentrated creative work. To keep the theatre a place of awe and wonder, and make rehearsals efficient, an actor should either know or be told:

1. Come to the rehearsal prepared to work — physically, mentally and emotionally. (This includes bringing your script and a pencil to early rehearsals.)
2. Be prompt at all rehearsals and calls.
3. Share scenes rather than stealing them — each actor looks better with a strong partner. Never upstage your partner unless so directed.
4. Don't move, gesture or face out front on another actor's line except as directed.
5. After the director stops to fix a line or piece of business, begin the rehearsal again by repeating the cue line or lines just before the one corrected so that the change can be rehearsed.
6. Counter-cross and dress stage without being told.
7. Stay in character — never talk under your breath or attempt to "break up" another actor. If you forget a line, remain in character and say to the prompter, "Line."
8. Don't give another actor a direction — let the director do that.
9. Learn your lines at home or offstage, not while everyone waits onstage. Learn the lines precisely and give cues consistently — don't rewrite the play or *ad lib*.
10. Protect your health, particularly when overtired or overheated.

B. Learning lines.

1. Inexperienced actors may need to be shown how to study lines, associating each line with its preceding cue. Some actors memorize best one way, some another, depending on individual differences and whether their visual or auditory memory is stronger.
   a. One workable method is to use a blank piece of paper to cover up the line itself and reveal only the cue; the actor says the line, then uncovers it to see if it was correct.
   b. Another method is to have someone "cue" the actor, reading his cues and watching the script to see that he reads his lines correctly.

    c. Some actors have found it helpful to read their cues into a tape recorder, allowing pauses for their own lines to be spoken.

    d. When several actors have a long wait backstage, they can use the time profitably to "run lines," throwing each other their cues as quickly as they can without interpreting the lines.

2. It is unwise for the director to either expect or permit actors to learn their lines until after an act has been blocked. To do this would be learning by rote. Lines are easier to learn and retain when they are part of a "Gestalt," associating (1) cue, (2) line, (3) motivation, and (4) movement — all to be learned together.

3. The director should set a deadline for memorization of each act, and at this rehearsal scripts *must* be put aside whether or not actors are fumbling for lines. As a rough guide, the deadline for an act might well be after its third rehearsal, and deadlines for the other acts at least a week apart.

4. At the rehearsal when the actors lay their scripts aside for the first time, the director will have to be patient, expecting little if any progress from his cast in characterization, emotion, tempo or climax.

C. Understanding the actor.

When the cast assembles for the first reading, it will be a diversified collection of individuals whom the director must weld into a unified whole by opening night. The inanimate objects with which the director affects the audience — the scenery, lights, costumes — can be made to do what he wants; yet the greatest impact upon the audience is made by an element that is far more complex, difficult to understand and elusive in control — the human beings who make up the cast. The director in the nonprofessional theatre must devote a major portion of his time to the problem of working with the actors, coaching them to give the performance he and they desire.

However experienced the actors or inexperienced the director, the latter has one great advantage — he can see the actors from out front as they cannot see themselves. The director need not be a better actor than his cast, but he must know how to communicate with them — how to talk the actor's language and to recognize the actor's problems. Here are some observations derived from the psychology of directing which may help the young director work more effectively with his actors:

1. Actors vary widely in their previous theatrical experience, in the methods which they use, and in the vocabulary with which they

are used to having the director communicate with them. There
is no reason why the director should use the same method or
terminology with all.

2. Actors vary widely in their psychological background, emotional
maturity, freedom and sense of security. They will also vary
widely from rehearsal to rehearsal in their freshness or fatigue,
emotional stability and interest in the problem at hand. There are
some characteristics, however, which almost all actors share:

   a. Actors want to give a good performance. There is a high
   degree of *motivation* in the theatre. The director must use
   this and keep it alive.

   b. Actors want to have confidence in their director. They need
   to look to him as a source of support, trusting that he can
   guide them to a successful performance.

   c. Actors have heightened ego needs and are hypersensitive (or
   they would not be actors). They want to be praised by the
   director and assured that they are making progress. It is a
   sound rule to *praise the actor in front of the cast but criticize
   him in private*. There are exceptions to this, however: the
   overconfident actor who makes no progress until he is "taken
   down a peg," and criticism which can be made general and
   applied to the whole cast.

   d. Actors need to be accepted by the group, to feel "belongingness' as a part of the team, no matter how small a role they
   play.

   e. The shakier an actor is, the more he needs to be told that he
   is "coming along." A kind of panic can set in if an actor feels
   that the director is worried about him as the weak link in the
   cast. Often the director must do a bit of acting himself to
   convince an insecure actor that he can do the job if he will
   just believe in himself.

   f. Actors need to be given something specific to think about
   at the end of a rehearsal so that they can bring something
   new to try at the next rehearsal. A healthy feeling with which
   an actor should leave rehearsal is that he accomplished something today and knows what specific problems to work on
   for tomorrow in order to polish his performance even more.

3. The actor needs inner *freedom*.
   For the most effective use of his body, voice and emotions, the
   actor must free himself from tensions. Unlike the musician,
   the actor is his own instrument, an instrument which must be
   tuned to respond to the most subtle command of its player's will.
   Freedom can be achieved by:

a. Relaxation and muscular discipline.

Dance movement, athletics and physical coordination all build upon and aid in the development of relaxation. In performance, however, the actor is most apt to achieve relaxation through a control of his attention — through concentration.

b. Concentration.

(1) The actor's attention must not waver or drift out to the audience. It should be confined to the circumstances of the scene.

(2) If the actor thinks the character's thoughts, he will respond in character and with truthful emotion. He should not say to himself, "I am pretending to be Hamlet," nor "I am Hamlet," nor even, "If I were Hamlet. . .," but rather, "If that stupid idiot Polonius bothers me again I'll make him wish he hadn't."

c. Spontaneity.

Although the actor has rehearsed for weeks, he must respond as though each moment were occurring for the first time. He must avoid anticipating or premeditating reactions, attempting rather to create "the illusion of the first time."

4. The actor must play with a *sense of truth.*

He must make the audience believe in the truth of what he is saying and doing. Whether or not the actor's emotions are *actually* truthful, an audience of course has no way of knowing. It can evaluate only the impression of truth; but the spectator can be certain when the actor has evoked real emotional responses in him (the spectator) through empathy.

a. Acting can be said to have a sense of truth when it is convincing and believable, when it rings true, when it corresponds with the audience's impression of how people would respond *if* the situation were actually taking place.

b. Although a master of acting technique might convince an audience of his sense of truth even though he were entirely devoid of feeling, the simplest and surest way for the young actor to seem convincing is for him really to respond truthfully. This is sometimes referred to as the Stanislavski or inner method of acting, because it is based upon what the actor discovers within himself rather than depending upon what previous actors have done to solve the same problems. The great advantage of the inner approach in the educational theatre, as many directors such as Professor Frank M.

Whiting have observed,[1] is that it works for the student actor; though he may lack technical skill, he can call upon his own freshness, vigor and emotions.

5. The actor must *motivate* whatever he does on stage.
   a. He should do nothing on stage without a purpose, or with what appears to be only a technical purpose.
   b. In life human behavior is motivated by stimuli from within and from the outside. Although we do not always explain our motives and are sometimes not even conscious of our true motives, we seldom behave without some motivation.
   c. When no motive is supplied by the playwright or the director, the actor must find his own, consistent with his character.
   d. Actors who have difficulties in motivation are often so busy searching themselves introspectively that they fail to listen to what their partner is saying.

6. The actor must gain *access to his own emotions* and be able to reawaken them at will.

An emotion aroused by accident is of little value compared with an emotion for which the actor finds some stimulation or preparation within himself, within the context of the scene, or within what his partners in the scene say or do. If he controls his concentration, he can then reawaken the same emotion at each performance. Exactly how the actor taps his own emotional resources is, in the final analysis, his own business — as long as it gets done. He may use one or more of the following approaches:

   a. Emotion memory — the recollection of personal experiences which affected him in the past, and which can be reawakened by bringing to mind specific sensory images associated with the emotion.
   b. Imagination — being able to visualize how the individual would feel if he were in the given circumstances.
   c. Substitution of analogous emotions — never having committed a murder, for example, the actor may substitute a murderous impulse he once felt toward a buzzing mosquito.[2]
   d. Autosuggestion or empathy for the character — having identified with the character, the actor lets the circumstances stimulate him as if he were the character. The actor's own identity is thus merged with that of the character. Stanislavski was

---

[1]Whiting, Frank M., *An Introduction to the Theatre* (New York: Harper and Brothers, 1954), p. 138.
[2]This and many other valuable suggestions are contained in a slim book which students and teachers of acting will find rewarding: Boleslavsky, Richard, *Acting: The First Six Lessons* (New York: Theatre Arts, Inc., 1939), p. 44.

aware that fine acting often draws from hidden resources and stands "on the threshold of the subconscious."

7. The actor must establish *relationships* to others.
The actor who focuses his attention exclusively within himself and his emotions has misinterpreted the Stanislavski system. His character does not exist in a vacuum, but has relationships to all of the other characters in the play.

    a. The actor should know how his character feels about the others in the play — what they say and do at all times when he is on stage. He should know what he is doing on stage even when he has no lines. All too often a director might stop a scene, ask an actor what he is doing and be told (if the actor were candid), "Waiting for a cue." The actor who does this cuts himself off from the chance to be stimulated by what others are saying and doing so that when he gets his cue he will be emotionally ready.

    b. The actor should let himself respond truthfully and in character to the moment-by-moment action and dialogue. He can do this only if he *listens* and *reacts*. The director may have to cut down responses that distract from the speaker, but it is easier to do this than to spark life in an unresponsive actor.

    c. The actor who listens, responds and contributes to the interaction of the group not only helps his partners and builds rapport in the ensemble but also helps himself to prepare for his own emotional responses. Stanislavski called this "communion." An actor may even ask his partner for a reaction at a given moment so as to provide him with further motivation.

D. Understanding one's self as a director.

Directors, like actors, vary widely in background and training. There have been famous directors who were autocrats; others use passive, laissez-faire methods. Every director has yearned, as did Gordon Craig, for actors who would be "super-marionettes," responsive to every string pulled by the sole and supreme creative force, the director. Lest we forget, however, Craig was never a practising director in the educational theatre.

1. The director must assume that a communication failure between himself and his actors is a two-way street, and he may be as much at fault as his actors.
2. The director's goal should be the best possible production with the least amount of stress and strain at rehearsals.
3. He should not use his cast as outlets for his own frustrated impulses as an actor or need to be important. There is no place in

the educational theatre for a director's temper tantrums. Moss Hart describes George S. Kaufman's modest method of directing professionals in *Act One*:

> "...he seemed to allow the actors to use him as a sounding board. He watched and listened, and without seeming to impose his own preconceived ideas of how a scene should be played, he let each actor find a way of his own that was best for him; and slowly, with no more than a whispered word here and there, the scenes began to take on a directorial quality and flavor that was unmistakably his."[3]

4. The director in the educational theatre must be a teacher at the same time that he is a creative artist. This involves, as much as possible, telling the actors the reason for the instructions he gives them, so that they will learn and grow as actors as well as giving a particular performance.

5. The director should not betray to his cast his own anxieties, doubts or fears for the success of the production.

6. A study in educational psychology[4] revealed that among the traits which pupils most objected to in their teachers were the following; the findings may have a valuable application for drama directors:

   a. Failure to explain and make clear.　　e. Quick temper.
   b. Lack of discipline.　　　　　　　　　 f. Impatience.
   c. Favoritism.　　　　　　　　　　　　　 g. Sarcasm.
   d. Unfairness.

7. The director's enthusiasm and confidence will be contagious. He can inspire the cast only to the extent that he himself feels enthusiasm for the play and confidence in his cast.

8. Professional modesty is an essential ingredient in the director. He will have done his work successfully if the reviews praise every actor in the cast, even though they scarcely take notice of the "direction."

E. Creating an environment in which the actor can do his best work. Rehearsals should be thought of as a very special time for actors and director to come together, not as students and professor or inferior and superior, but as creative artists working together on a common task.

1. There should be freedom at rehearsals, an easy rapport and permissive environment which will encourage trial and error

[3]Hart, Moss, *Act One* (New York: Random House, 1959), p. 315.
[4]Mursell, James L., *Educational Psychology* (New York: W. W. Norton and Company, 1939), p. 282.

without fear of failure. Even a certain amount of "horsing around" may help the actors achieve spontaneity and release.

2. There must be sufficient discipline at rehearsals, however, so that time is not wasted by late arrivals, interruptions, or distractions by those offstage.

3. Directors and actors vary in their attitude toward visitors at rehearsals. A stranger in the auditorium can introduce tensions in the cast; but in rehearsing comedy the sound of a chuckle from out front may provide welcome encouragement. In any case the house lights should be kept off during rehearsal.

4. The director himself must set an example of promptness and decorum at rehearsal. If the actors learn that the director is not ready to rehearse at the appointed time, they will soon grow careless themselves. Actors can hardly be expected to make progress if the director tells them to "run over their lines" in case he is late or fails to appear.

5. In the educational theatre actors should be encouraged to listen and watch when they are not onstage. Arthur Byron, a fine old actor who was president of Actors' Equity Association, once heard a grievance from a delegation of extras who had been kept waiting to rehearse their scene. He replied to them, "But that is how I learned to act!"[5]

V. The Periods of Rehearsal.

Rehearsing a play falls into fairly well-defined periods or phases, and the director needs to be aware of which period he is in — or should be in — so as not to move too soon to the next one or spend too much time on one particular phase to the neglect of the others.

A. Familiarization Period. (Reading the Play.)
1. Creative aspects.
When the actors assemble for the first reading after casting is completed, there should be a considerable relaxation of tensions. The cast should know that it was chosen because it was the best possible one in the director's judgment. The task of digging into the content of the play begins.

a. Round-table readings.
The director will devote at least one and possibly as many as three days to reading the play. The director will discuss with the cast:

(1) His interpretation of the play, its theme, style and impact.

---

[5]Goodman, Edward, *Make Believe: The Art of Acting* (New York: Charles Scribner's Sons, 1956).

(2) His concept of the characters and their interrelations.

(3) The spine, main actions in each act, and the changing beats.

Round-table Reading.

b. Seeing the whole before it is broken up into parts.
    The director should help the cast to see the totality of the play, the relation of each character to the whole. Each actor should listen to the reading of scenes in which he himself may not appear; he may not hear these scenes again until dress rehearsal.

c. Sharing with the cast the director's research into the period and background of the play.

d. The actors should feel free to ask questions on the meaning of words, phrases and speeches.

2. Technical aspects.
   a. The director will show the cast the scene designs, ground plans, and costume sketches, making sure that all are familiar with the ground plan of the set.
   b. The director will check the rehearsal schedule with the cast, adjusting it for any conflicts, and distribute the schedule as finally agreed upon.
   c. No technical comments on how to read lines should be given during this period.
   d. The actors should underline the name of their character in their script each time they have a line, and note on the rehearsal schedule each scene in which they appear.

B. Exploration Period. (Blocking the Play.)
As the actors find out what the play is about and who their characters are, they begin to explore means of revealing these concepts to the audience. During this period the "blocking" or setting of physical positions on the stage is done, i.e., the director gives to the cast the composition and movement which he has preplanned (as discussed in Chapters 5 and 6). This is a time of trial-and-error, and the actor should be encouraged to try and experiment without paying any penalties for error. Both actors and director must contribute to the establishment of a favorable environment for creative work, keeping an open-minded attitude and a willingness to explore.

1. General Principles:
   a. During blocking rehearsals the actors should take time to write down all of their crosses, rises, sits, and positions opposite the lines on which they move.
   b. One act is the most that should be blocked in one rehearsal, and sometimes even less. The act should be repeated several times so that the actors will remember whatever has been discovered in the rehearsal.
   c. Time in communicating with the cast will be saved if the director sits on the forestage rather than in the auditorium.
   d. The director should not expect results at this period. He is merely defining the problem and planting the seeds which will produce future solutions. Allow time for the incubation to take place.
   e. The director should expect to deviate somewhat from his preplanned blocking because of (1) unforeseen problems, (2) his own spontaneous invention of better composition or movement, and (3) the creative contribution of his actors. Nothing is more deadly for an inventive actor than the feeling that he must be a patient and obedient puppet while the

Blocking rehearsal.

director plods through his book revealing sacred and inviolable solutions to all problems. Between this extreme and that of the director who comes to rehearsal without any preplanned blocking, there is assuredly a judicious middle of the road.

f. As soon as the blocking of a scene is completed, the director should begin to urge actors to learn the lines of the scene. Complicated business with props, in fights and love scenes, should be postponed until books are out of the way.

2. Getting what the director wants from the actors.
This is actually the heart of play direction. Each director evolves his own method of working with actors, depending upon his background and training, the experience and training of the cast, the style and type of play, and the time remaining before opening night. A director may use different methods with different actors in the same scene, with different scenes and certainly with different plays. A continuum might be constructed to show directorial methods from complete permissiveness to complete authoritarianism:

Ideally the director should start at the left of the continuum, trying the most creative approach, allowing it sufficient time to work, before going on to the right. The last step at the right should be thought of as a last resort near opening night or with inexperienced actors. It should be kept in mind too that *when the director can't get what he wants from an actor, he may have to take what he gets and adapt it,* modifying his original interpretation and finding something within the actor's personality which can be substituted.

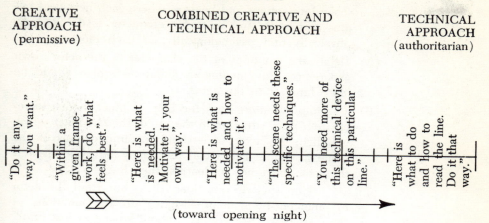

CONTINUUM

(toward opening night)

a. Creative approach.

To rough in a framework or pattern for each scene and let the actors find the detailed moment-by-moment blocking. This method works best for serious and emotional drama, but requires experienced actors.

(1) Draw out through questions and discussion the actor's own interpretation of the scene. If it differs greatly from the director's, plant some questions in the actor's mind which may bring him to the desired interpretation. "How do you account for your behavior in the third act?" "What does your character want in life and in each act of the play?"

(2) Discuss the director's interpretation with the actor — the emotions and reactions of the character. Make sure the actor understands the inner aspects of the scene. Many faults of expression derive from a faulty understanding of what is to be expressed. Help the actor to live within the make-believe circumstances and to become aware of the full implications of the scene for his character. Sometimes outside readings can be suggested which will illuminate the play. The actor playing James Tyrone in O'Neill's *A Moon for the Misbegotten*, for example, must be thoroughly familiar with the same character in *Long Day's Journey Into Night*.

(3) Suggest avenues of observation for the actor — where he can go to find the character or emotion for which he is searching.

(4) Make sure the actor understands the breakdown of the scene into actions and beats — where each new beat begins and ends, and what his character is doing, both physically and psychologically, at each moment.

(5) Relate the emotions of the character to the actor's own experience. Find analogous situations which would be more familiar to the actor.

(6) Use improvisation, with the help of other actors, to re-create a prior situation in the life of the character which will help the actor understand the implications of the scene at hand. The scene itself may be improvised if the actors have not yet learned their lines.

(7) By asking specific questions, draw out from the actor his moment-by-moment insight into the emotions of the character. "Are you glad about what you just said?" "Why did you do that?" "What are you thinking while he is speaking?" With actors trained in the Stanislavski system, whole scenes may be improvised in which the actors speak out loud their inner thoughts — the "sub-text." (For an example of a sub-text, see Chapter 8, page 212.)

(8) In classic or poetic plays where language may be a barrier to understanding, ask the actor temporarily to re-phrase a speech in his own words.

(9) Make sure the actor knows the meaning of each line and word, to whom each line is addressed, and the motivation for the line.

(10) Indicate a general area of the stage for a scene and let the actor find his own movements within this framework. "This scene should play around the desk — see what feels comfortable to you."

b. Combined creative and technical approach.

To suggest to the actors specific positions and movements *along with their motivation,* helping the actors to justify and make their own the technical requirements of the scene. In the educational theatre this synthesis of inner and outer techniques will often prove the best approach.

(1) Suggest that somewhere in a particular speech the actor will want to rise or cross; let him find the exact spot for himself.

(2) Try a line or movement several ways and see which feels most comfortable to the actor or which looks better from out front.

(3) In big scenes of emotional climax, let the actor improvise his own movements as he feels them. Later they must be "set," repetitious movements eliminated and weak moments fixed.

(4) Tell the actor, "We need a movement here; what would your character do?"

(5) Tell the actor, "We need to have you cross DR to the fireplace. Can you find a motivation for yourself?"

(6) Give the actor both the specific movement and the motivation. "I think your character would turn away here because of his guilt feelings about what has just been said to him." "Try crossing to the mirror DR and adjusting your hair before saying the next line."

(7) Discuss with the actor what *effect* is desired. Use positive suggestion to help the actor visualize the technical result. An idea is more easily learned if it seems to come from the actor rather than the director. As F. Cowles Strickland expressed it, "Never tell an actor anything if you can make him think of it himself."[6] He cites as examples of this:

(a) Telling other actors to react to the humor of a particular line may make the speaker of the line aware for the first time that it is potentially funny.

(b) Telling an actor that his lines should come quickly because his partner is trying to build the scene to a climax may give the partner the first inkling that his scene is climactic.

(8) Use the physical to evoke the emotional. The so-called James-Lange effect is based on the power of the physical action to awaken emotion through autosuggestion. If the actor can't feel a particular emotion, give him physical business, movement, body positions or gestures which are characteristic, and the truthful *doing* may evoke the *feeling.*

(9) Show the actor the mood, feeling and intensity desired without actually reading the lines for him. The director may improvise *around* the lines, paraphrasing the words or verbalizing the "sub-text" so that the actor will see the potentialities in the scene without being able to imitate directly what the director did.

---

[6]Strickland, F. Cowles, "Directing Amateurs," *Theatre Arts Monthly,* July, 1937, pp. 566-567.

c. Technical approach.

To give the actors the detailed blocking of positions, movement, crosses, turns, rises and seatings, letting the actors
motivate or justify them for themselves as rehearsals progress.
This method is the fastest, the best suited to comedy and
stylized productions, and is necessarily used in summer
stock companies.

(1) The technical approach to movement in relation to
strong and weak lines is a great timesaver and frees
the actor from having to solve problems that are best
handled from out front by the director.

(2) Crosses, counter-crosses, turns, rises and sits can be
communicated to the cast verbally and generally do
not need to be shown.

(3) With more than four actors on stage at once, composition will present serious problems and the director
dare not wait to face the actors in rehearsal without
prior blocking of the scene in his director's book.

(4) Discuss with the actor in general what technical means
he might use to achieve the effect he realizes is needed.
(See Chapter 7.) Refer to possible:

(a) Changes in tempo, volume, pitch and quality to
achieve variety.

(b) Key words that need more emphasis.

(c) Pointing of lines by movement, gesture and pauses.

(d) Transitions and where they should occur.

(e) Topping and climax, and where they should occur.

(5) Tell the actor specifically where to use a technical device such as emphasis, inflection, pause, or variety in
tempo, volume, pitch and quality. Wherever possible
give him the *motivation along with the mechanics*.

(a) It is better to tell an actor, "Take a moment to
think of an answer," rather than "Pause here,"
and more helpful to say, "You're ashamed to look
him in the eye and so you turn away," rather than
simply, "Turn away."

(b) The *question method* described by L. H. Mouat[7]
is a very useful one for correcting misplaced emphasis. If the actor says, "I *went* to the door," instead of "I went to the *door*," the director can
ask him, "Where did you go?" His answer, "to the

─────────

[7]Mouat, L. H., "The Question Method for Teaching Emphasis in Oral Reading,"
Quarterly Journal of Speech, XXXV, 4, December, 1949.

door" will have the correct emphasis, and this can be pointed out to the actor.

(c) Use positive rather than negative comments. "It needs more variety in pitch," is preferable to "It's monotonous," and "It needs more warmth," preferable to "It leaves me cold."

(d) It sometimes helps an actor enlarge his performance if the director stands at the back of the auditorium and calls his cues to him so that he will feel motivated to project his replies.

(6) If the director has a keen ear or sense of mimicry, he he may try showing the actor two possible ways of playing a certain line — the way the actor has been doing it and the way the director thinks it should be done. He may then ask, "Which way was more effective?"

(7) When the director gives an actor a mechanical direction or piece of blocking the actor should try to find his own inner justification or motivation for the action, rather than to question the direction. The actor should thus be a flexible tool for the director, knowing that he is an element in the director's composition of stage pictures and vocal climaxes which he cannot see or hear from out front. He should be willing to accept a movement, position, or line reading for purely technical reasons, and only after he has made every effort to justify it should he ask the director for help if it still doesn't feel right.

(8) As a last resort when other techniques have failed or time has grown short, the director may legitimately try reading the line or doing the business for the actor. This technique presupposes (a) that the director is himself a competent actor and (b) that the actor will watch with an open mind and have enough technical awareness to recognize what the director is doing.

(a) Demonstration is an accepted method of teaching physical skills, and is perhaps the quickest way to convey a desired effect to the actor. Physical actions, movement, and the integration of lines with business lend themselves best to demonstration, but even line readings sometimes have to be given to the actor. Properly done this technique needs no apologies. Students of "the method" will be surprised to discover that Stanislavski himself used demonstration.[8]

(b) If the director is not sure of his acting technique, however, he is better off not trying to demonstrate than doing it and lamely apologizing afterwards, "That wasn't exactly right, but you get the idea."

Adjusting blocking from out front.

C. Discovery Period. (Books out of hand.)
As soon as the blocking is set, the director should begin working with the actors for characterization, following the suggestions given in Chapter 8. The actor should be encouraged to try various psychological and physical elements to help him get into character.

1. Creative aspects.
   a. After the motivations and characterizations are grasped intellectually, the blocking set, and the lines learned, there will, ideally, be a rehearsal when the actor gets fully into character, is able to release the appropriate emotion, and the scene "plays."
      (1) The moment of discovery for a particular scene is sometimes sudden — a kind of "Eureka!" growing out of a flash of insight.

[8]Gorchakov, Nikolai M., *Stanislavsky Directs* (New York: Funk and Wagnalls Company, 1954), p. 259 and pp. 300-306.

(2) A high degree of concentration is necessary for the "Eureka" to take place. Creativity often happens at white heat. The actor must stay in character at these rehearsals and try to avoid breaking his or his partner's concentration.

b. When the moment of creative discovery comes, make sure that the actor is praised after the scene is over and made aware of the fact that he has found something right for the performance.

c. As the actor begins to find what he wants to do with several scenes as indicated in the foregoing, the director should clarify for himself and the actor which scenes yet remain to be worked on, narrowing down the number as rehearsals progress.

d. As actors respond to each other in this period, new motivations will occur to them and to the director. Little moment-by-moment motivations and responses should be added to fill up empty or dead spots, mechanical or inadequate reactions.

e. An informal talk with an actor during a break or after rehearsal often may be a better way of suggesting what is needed than to stop the rehearsal. The director should begin to make written or mental notes for this purpose. With experience he learns when it is better not to stop the actors and when to stop them.

2. Technical aspects.

a. Add business and pantomime that enrich the scene and strengthen characterization.

b. When the actor still has not found what the director wants, technical suggestions must necessarily be given — relating to key words, points to be "hit," variety in voice, topping and undercutting, transitions.

c. When books are out of hand for a particular scene, actors may begin to work with rehearsal props (easy-to-find substitutes which may be in the prop room). These props often assist in the discovery of the inner emotion. Character props (canes, capes, etc.,) will help the actor get in character.

d. The first few times the actor tries a scene without book, the stage manager should be instructed to make detailed corrections. Otherwise actors often will let lines become fixed in their memory incorrectly. Later on the director may choose to permit minor modifications except where the rhythm, meaning or comic effect is weakened. In Shakespeare and other poetic drama lines must be letter perfect.

284 ~ *Rehearsing the Play*

D. Formalizing Period (Polishing Rehearsals.)
This is the phase in which the director gives the production its final shape in terms of tempo, climax and the strength of the individual actors' performances. At this point the director often finds himself pushing the actors, demanding of them emotional intensity which they do not know they have and sustained levels for which they may lack the physical stamina and discipline. Though he may feel himself a taskmaster, a slave driver at this phase, the director's profession requires that he not settle for anything less than the absolute best which he can get out of his cast. If there are moments of resentment at the director's needling, exhorting, demanding, they will all be forgotten in the aura of opening-night success. This idea is aptly expressed by Anouilh in his delightful play, *The Rehearsal*, when an actress complains to her director:

> Hortensia: You're manipulating us like puppets! I warn you, we won't stand for it much longer!
> Count: Count yourselves lucky that I don't bawl your heads off. There's no inspired production without tears. A play produced by a polite man rarely smacks of genius....[9]

1. Creative aspects.
   a. At this stage actors will benefit from going through a scene without interruption, letting the cumulative effect stimulate them to further growth. However many details can be fixed more efficiently as they happen rather than later from notes. Faced with the dilemma of "to stop or not to stop" a scene, the director can:

      (1) Alternate between detail rehearsals to stop and polish and continuity rehearsals in which the scene is repeated without stops so it can build to climax.
      (2) Use "sideline coaching," as Kenneth Graham has termed it: (i.e., without stopping the scene the director makes adjustments in composition, especially of large groups, and comments to the actors in a way that does not break them out of character).

   b. Now that the actors know their own lines and business, they should be encouraged to *listen* to their partner, react in character, and maintain eye-contact and rapport with the ensemble. Scenes come to life when they have group interplay rather than star acting — what Stanislavski called "stage

---

[9]Jean Anouilh, *The Rehearsal*, in *Five Plays*, Vol. I (New York: Hill and Wang, 1958), p. 216.

inter-influence." The actor must also be sure to give his partner adequate resistance in scenes of conflict.

c. The actors must find a common style for the production. Each should watch the rest of the cast and attempt to find a style that is consistent. At this stage it is most helpful to rehearse with substitute costumes or makeshifts, to approximate the effect that will later be created by trains, capes, long skirts; rehearsing with the right kind of shoes is particularly helpful.

d. The actor must heighten his emotions in proportion to the theatre in which they are to be projected, not by forcing artificially, but by making the emotion itself stronger, by wanting something more intensely, by drawing upon extra resources of vitality.

e. Although many teachers of the Stanislavski method tell actors not to work for "results," the director must constantly keep results in mind. (*An Actor Prepares* is, after all, not *An Actor Rehearses*.) The rehearsal process means working for results, setting them when they are right, and anticipating the effect these results will have on the audience. Stanislavski's noted pupil, Vakhtangov, once said to Chekhov when asked the secret of his success as a director, "I never rehearse without imagining that the theatre is already full. The imaginary audience is always there, from the very first rehearsal to the last."[10]

2. Technical aspects.

a. As the director nears dress rehearsal, his emphasis must grow increasingly technical. His concern should be with getting scenes up to tempo and with heightening climaxes. His approach now is apt to be:

> "Keep what you've got — it's good — but make it even stronger."
> "Take out the pauses."
> "Pick up cues faster."
> "Wait! Now! Hit it!"
> "It's dragging. Faster."
> "I lost that word."
> "Top him!"

b. As the cast achieves what he has been seeking, the director should "set" or "fix" the scenes (in the sense of applying a fixative so that the scenes will keep their form intact) by letting the actors know immediately after a scene when

---

[10]Chekhov, Michael, *To the Director and Playwright* (New York: Harper, 1963), p. 54.

it is just right, and perhaps repeating it immediately to solidify it in the actors' memories.

c. The actors must learn to play with control and consistency, so that emotions are the servant rather than the master, and so that the scene can be played the same at each run-through. When an actor says, "Don't worry, I'll get it right at the performance," the director has cause to worry aplenty. Too much emotion is as much a cause for worry as too little; even through real tears the actor must get his words out clearly and on cue.

d. The director should check the vocal projection of the actors from the back of the auditorium to make sure they can be heard and understood. The actors should use full voice to see if they can sustain the role vocally without hoarseness or strain. (If hoarseness or sore throat develops, the actor should "save his voice" and the director may have to help him breathe correctly and relax his throat.)

e. Scenes and acts will be at varying degrees of completion. Act I will be ready to formalize and set while Act II is still in the Discovery Period and Act III in the Exploration Period. In the final week before dress rehearsal, the director should concentrate on Act III while at the same time keeping the other acts alive by run-throughs.

f. As the play takes shape, the director will see which scenes or which actors need more intensive work. This period is the director's last chance to work with his cast and to correct whatever is necessary.

g. The director should polish, revise and perfect each detail, anticipating as much as possible the problems which the introduction of scenery, props and costumes will add.

h. As a practical necessity, the director may have to settle for less than he had conceived, abandon some ·ideas that did not shape up, relax the pressure on some actors who may be doing their best yet are falling short, and make a choice as to which elements are most amenable to improvement so as to make the best investment of the time remaining before opening night.

E. Integration Period. (Dress rehearsals.)

1. Creative aspects.

a. The director should not expect the best performance from the actors at the first dress rehearsal when they are getting accustomed to lights, scenery, props and costumes. It sometimes happens that the technical elements, particularly costume, stimulate an actor to a new inner quality of performance. Often, however, the actors are so busy adjusting to new elements that both inner emotion and external tempo suffer temporarily.

b. There should be at least one dress rehearsal, however, when all the technical elements are integrated so that the actors can restore their inner concentration and bring the play up to performance level.

c. During the dress rehearsal period the actors might profitably restudy their scripts, which they may not have glanced at for several weeks; they may discover new shades of meaning or lines that they have been misreading.

d. The old adage that "a bad dress rehearsal means a good opening night" is far from reliable; it all depends on whether the things that went wrong at the dress rehearsal are fixed before the opening. Nothing should be left to chance on opening night nor any new technical elements introduced that the actors have not rehearsed with; wishful thinking is no substitute for painstaking rehearsal.

e. At the end of the last dress rehearsal, the director should leave the cast with a feeling of confidence.

2. Technical aspects.

a. The director should work with the technical crews as much as possible without the cast in order to save the actors' energies and have all technical elements "set" and perfected before the actors work with them.

b. Technical elements should be added in the following order:
   (1) A rehearsal for the actors with all hand props.
   (2) A rehearsal for the actors with the scenery and furniture (sometimes where necessary without using costumes).
   (3) A "costume parade" (if a costume play) in order to view and check each actor's costumes before dress rehearsal and get him used to wearing and moving in them.
   (4) A "dress rehearsal" using scenery, costumes, props, and lights.
   (5) A second dress rehearsal with all aforesaid elements plus music and sound.
   (6) One or two final dress rehearsals using all elements plus make-up.

c. During dress rehearsals the director should interrupt as little as possible — where necessary to fix light or sound cues that are wrong, but rarely, if ever, for purely acting problems. The director instead should make copious notes to be given to the cast afterwards. A telephone from auditorium to stage manager is invaluable.

d. Integrating the technical elements and the actors into a unified production requires that the director remain calm during dress rehearsals and in control of a group of tense and perhaps overtired actors and crews.

    (1) When a cue goes wrong, the director should be able to note specifically what was wrong about it and how it can be fixed. Temperamental directors often communicate the fact that they are displeased but not how to remedy the error.

    (2) Although there is a constant temptation to break this rule, it is a wise practice to go through channels during dress rehearsal — communicating with the electrical and stage crews through the technical director, through the costumer on costume matters, and with the cast and prop crew through the stage manager. Conversely, technical director and costumer should not instruct cast except via director.

    (3) When the hour grows late and people are overwrought, making notes to discuss the next day is the best way to deal with apparently insoluble problems.

e. At one of the last dress rehearsals, the curtain call should be planned and rehearsed. The mood of the play will determine the kind of curtain call, from "gag" calls in a farce to a dignified "tableau" call in a tragedy. It is traditional to allow the audience to show its appreciation to the live actor, but in the educational theatre curtain calls should be ensemble calls rather than solo bows, and only those who appeared in the play should be in the curtain call (the audience would not recognize backstage crew members, vital as their contribution was). The end of the last dress rehearsal, however, is a good time for the cast to give a "hand" for each of the crews and the stage manager.

f. If the play is a comedy, the cast should be reminded to *hold for laughs,* and how to do this correctly. Where feasible, a preview audience invited to the last dress rehearsal will give a sample of laugh reactions and help the cast set their timing.

g. In going over final notes with the cast before the last dress rehearsal, it is often a good idea to remind them of the *traditions of the theatre.* In addition to the specific rules pertaining to smoking backstage, etc., there are theatre traditions which give a cast a sense of pride to know they will be expected to honor:

h. *Traditions of the performance.*

 (1) Every audience — large or small — is entitled to the best performance you are capable of giving.

 (2) "The show must go on." Neither fog, snow, rain nor flood, sick babies nor flat tires are valid excuses for failing to be on stage on time. A trouper never lets his fellows or his audience down.

 (3) Be in your dressing room at least one hour before curtain.

 (4) Never peek out front nor appear in the lobby areas in costume or make-up.

 (5) The stage manager is in absolute authority backstage, but it is each actor's personal responsibility to make his entrance on time. Never leave the area where you can hear the play without the permission of the stage manager. When the stage manager calls "Places," respond immediately.

 (6) Actors — respect the backstage crews; your performance depends on them. Although there are costume and prop crews assigned, this does not relieve the actor of personal responsibility to take pride in his costume, to keep it clean, to obtain his hand props and return them to the designated place.

 (7) Crew members — respect the actors; the performance depends on their emotional control, concentration and confidence. Do nothing that will interfere with these factors.

 (8) Absolute quiet backstage is a necessity for the audience's enjoyment and the participant's work; never do anything that might distract a performer.

 (9) Never break out of character when in view of the audience; keep the show going somehow — in an emergency *ad lib* a line or help a partner who forgets a line.

 (10) There is no place in the theatre for alcoholic beverage in any form.

 (11) Leave personal problems at the stage door. Stanislavski best expressed this when he wrote in "Toward an Ethics for the Theatre":

> *Never come into the theatre with mud on your feet. Leave your dust and dirt outside. Check your little worries, squabbles, petty difficulties*

> *with your outside clothing — all the things that ruin your life and draw your attention away from your art.*[11]

F. Performance Period.

    1. Creative aspects.

        a. On opening night, the director must avoid the appearance of nervousness at all costs. He should give the cast quiet reassurance that he has confidence in them. Giving detailed notes or having a cast meeting for a pep talk only serves to make actors nervous. They should be free to concentrate upon their individual roles.

        b. The second performance is the time when there is often a let-down, and the director might well have a pep talk to fix loose ends, remind actors to pick up cues and polish things that weren't right on opening night.

        c. On every succeeding performance, the actors should be kept alert and disciplined by the director's watching the performance and bringing back notes, comments and praise for a scene that went particularly well. He should continue polishing the reading of lines, the pointing for laughs and the adjustment of tempo to the audience response. The director's presence in the auditorium has a desirable effect upon the morale of cast and crew, discouraging "fooling around," carelessness, *ad libbing,* or a let-down after opening night. Even with the best of intentions, actors tend to lengthen their pauses in dramatic scenes or add comic business which they find audiences enjoy though it may distract from the dialogue. The director will want to keep his production in its original shape by discouraging these tendencies — or an even worse one, the addition of "gags." For the director to condone this or fail to deal firmly with it would be to open a Pandora's box which might undo all the painstaking work of rehearsal.

    2. Technical aspects.

        a. The director by now should have every performance responsibility assigned to crew heads. Nothing makes a production staff more nervous than a director's last-minute fiddling with lights or scenery. The director should ascertain that his cast and crew heads are in the building on time, and leave them free to do their rehearsed tasks. The director may

---

[11]Stanislavski, Constantin, *Building a Character* (New York: Theatre Arts Books: MacGregor, Robert M., 1949), p. 244.

want to check certain make-ups before actors powder, but should have no other responsibilities during performance.

b. The director may occupy himself with the comfort and seating of the audienec. He should watch or be within ear-shot of the performance every night in case of emergency.

H. Post-production period.

Responsibilities of the director after the production closes include:

1. To give the cast and particularly the crews his expression of appreciation and praise for a job well done.

2. To make sure the production is struck promptly for the next group using the stage.

3. To make sure that all borrowed items of properties, furniture and costume have been returned.

4. To make sure that production pictures, programs, publicity materials and all technical plots are collected for preservation in scrapbooks or prompt books.

5. To assemble from the staff the final figures on the cost of the production and revenue from ticket sales.

6. To evaluate objectively the success of the production, taking into account all available evidence from audience reaction (of primary value) and such evidence as ticket sales and critics' reviews, which while less reliable cannot be discounted.

VI. Suggested standards for play production evaluation.

Although evaluating a production becomes highly complex with many subjective factors interwoven, a set of criteria for evaluation such as the following may be helpful to the director in his own personal growth and in attempting to appraise the theatrical value of the production for all concerned:

A. Audience response.

1. Did the audience indicate by its laughter, absorbed silence, or rustling and coughing, that it was entertained, moved, held in suspense, or bored? If the director is alert to these subtle but unmistakable clues, he will learn far more about the success of the production than he will from flattering intermission well-wishers. What actually happened in the auditorium — did the production communicate to the audience and did the audience respond to it as intended? Many critics fail to report this paramount fact, and give only personal impressions, oblivious to the audience around them.

2. Did the ticket sales and box office revenue indicate that the public wanted to see the play and gave it favorable word-of-mouth publicity?

B. Choice of play.

Did the play prove to be a wise choice in terms of audience interest, educational values, abilities of the cast and staff to do it justice?

C. Standards of acting.

1. Did the actors realize the playwright's intent and bring the material to life?
2. Did the actors play with a sense of truth, motivating their actions and gaining access to their own emotions?
3. Did the actors create convincing, believable and consistent characters?
4. Did the actors play and respond together as an ensemble and with a unity of style?
5. Could the actors be seen, heard and understood?
6. Did the actors supply vocal and visual variety, tempo and climax?
7. If a comedy, did the actors point their laughs effectively?
8. Was there a freshness and imagination in the conception and execution of the performance?
9. Was there growth and heightened accomplishment by the individual performers (pertains particularly to the educational theatre)?

D. Standards of the technical elements.

1. Did the scenery appropriately reflect the playwright's intent and contribute to the total aesthetic impression? Were the shifts of scenery handled quickly and quietly?
2. Did the costumes seem appropriate for the characters, the playwright's intent and the requirements of the actors for movement? Did they make a positive contribution to the total aesthetic impression?
3. Did the lighting contribute unobtrusively to the total aesthetic impression and give adequate visibility to the actors?
4. Did the make-up express the characters and appear convincing?
5. Were the other elements — properties, sound effects and music — appropriate and did they make a positive, unobtrusive contribution?

E. Standards of direction.

1. If the answers to most of the foregoing questions are affirmative, the director has done his work well. Many laymen are not aware of "direction" and it is just as well that they should not be. Even to the trained eye, it is often impossible to distinguish among the contributions of director, actors and designer. If the

director has coordinated all the elements of the production effectively, there will be a unity of impression that permits the audience to become absorbed in the play.

2. Did the director, in addition, supply an imaginative, perceptive appreciation of the playwright's intent, and reflect this inventively and effectively in the production, with good taste and sensitivity?

3. Were the ensemble elements of tempo, crowd scenes, fights effectively handled?

4. Was the director efficient in his handling of rehearsals and economical in his requirements for budget and man-hours? (The audience will not be able to assess this aspect, but the participants will be well aware of it.)

5. Finally, the best test of direction is the absence of negative factors — if no glaring moments were noticeable to the audience in which actors stumbled over lines, a performer was conspicuously unable to meet the demands of the role, cues were missed, laughter came in the wrong places, or an element of scenery, props, costumes, lighting or make-up attracted attention to itself or was allowed to distract from the performance.

VII. Summary.

The success of the play will depend to a great extent upon the director's ability to conduct systematic rehearsals and to discover ways of drawing out the creative abilities of his cast while at the same time giving the play a technical form and shape which will make it most effective to the audience.

A. Casting the play.
   1. Preparation for casting.
   2. Methods of casting.
   3. The double cast.
   4. Understudies.
   5. Precasting.
B. The rehearsal schedule.
   1. Factors that affect the making of a rehearsal schedule.
   2. A suggested rehearsal schedule.
C. General principles of rehearsal.
   1. Traditions of the rehearsal.
   2. Learning lines.
   3. Understanding the actor.
   4. Understanding one's self as a director.
   5. Creating an environment in which the actor can do his best work.

D. The periods of rehearsal.
　1. Familiarization Period. (Reading the play.)
　2. Exploration Period. (Blocking the play.)
　3. Discovery Period. (Books out of hand.)
　4. Formalizing Period. (Polishing rehearsals.)
　5. Integration Period. (Dress rehearsals.)
　6. Performance Period.
　7. Post-performance Period.
E. Suggested standards for play production evaluation.
　1. Audience response.
　2. Choice of play.
　3. Standards of acting.
　4. Standards of technical elements.
　5. Standards of direction.

Suggested Reading

Working with actors:

"Directing Amateurs," series of articles by Valentine Windt, F. Cowles Strickland, Alexander Dean, Bernard Szold, Frederick Burleigh and Edwin Duerr, *Theatre Arts Monthly,* July, October, November, 1937.

EUSTIS, MORTON. "The Director Takes Command," *Theatre Arts Monthly.*
　I. "Guthrie McClintic," February, 1936.
　II. 'Max Reinhardt, Robert Sinclair," March, 1936.
　III. "John Murray Anderson, Harold Clurman," April, 1936.

————. *"The Man Who Came to Dinner* with George Kaufman Directing," *Theatre Arts Monthly,* XXIII, 11, November, 1939.

GORCHAKOV, NIKOLAI. *Stanislavsky Directs.* New York: Funk and Wagnalls, 1954.

HART, MOSS. *Act One.* New York: Random House, 1959.

HOPKINS, ARTHUR. *How's Your Second Act?* New York: Samuel French, 1948.

ISAACS, HERMINE RICH. "First Rehearsals: Elia Kazan Directs a Modern Legend," *Theatre Arts Monthly,* XXVIII, 3, March, 1944. Reprinted in *Theatre Arts Anthology.* New York: Theatre Arts Books: Robert M. MacGregor, 1950.

LANE, YOTI. *The Psychology of the Actor.* London: Secker and Warburg, 1959.

MOUAT, L. H. "The Question Method for Teaching Emphasis in Oral Reading," *Quarterly Journal of Speech,* XXXV, 4, December, 1949.

Rehearsal Techniques, Cincinnati: The National Thespian Society, 1948.

SHAW, GEORGE BERNARD. *The Art of Rehearsal.* New York: Samuel French, n.d.

SIEVERS, W. DAVID. "The Play Rehearsal Schedule and its Psychology," *Quarterly Journal of Speech,* XXX, February, 1944.

WEBSTER, MARGARET "Credo of a Director," *Theatre Arts Monthly,* May, 1938.

Inner technique:

CARNOVSKY, MORRIS. "Design for Acting: The Quest of Technique," in Corrigan and Rosenberg, *The Context and Craft of Drama.* San Francisco: Chandler Publishing Co., 1964.

CHEKHOV, MICHAEL. *To The Actor: On the Technique of Acting.* New York: Harper and Brothers, 1953.

COLE, TOBY (editor). *Acting: A Handbook of the Stanislavski Method.* New York: Lear Publishers, 1947.

FUNKE, LEWIS, AND JOHN E. BOOTH. *Actors Talk About Acting*. New York: Random House, 1961. (Abridged) Avon Paperback, 1963.

GOURFINKEL, NINA. "The Actor Sets to Work on His Part," *World Theatre*, VIII, 1, Spring, 1959.

LEWIS, ROBERT. *Method or Madness?* New York: Samuel French, Inc., 1958.

MAGARSHACK, DAVID. *Stanislavsky on the Art of the Stage*. New York: Hill and Wang, 1961.

McGAW, CHARLES. *Acting is Believing*. New York: Rinehart and Co., 1955.

MOORE, SONIA. *The Stanislavski Method*. New York: The Viking Press, 1960.

STANISLAVSKI, CONSTANTIN. *An Actor Prepares*. New York: Theatre Arts, Inc., 1936.

————. *Creating a Role*. New York: Theatre Arts Books, 1961.

External technique

DEAN, ALEXANDER. *Fundamentals of Play Directing*. New York: Rinehart and Co., 1941.

FRANKLIN, MIRIAM. *Rehearsal: The Principles and Practice of Acting for the Stage*. 4th edition. Englewood Cliffs, N. J.: Prentice Hall, Inc., 1963.

FUNKE, LEWIS, AND JOHN E. BOOTH. *Actors Talk About Acting*. New York: Random House, 1961. (Abridged) Avon Paperback, 1963.

KAHAN, STANLEY. *Introduction to Acting*. New York: Harcourt, Brace and Co., 1962.

OLIVIER, SIR LAURENCE. Interview on his approach to *Othello*, *Life*, LVI, 18, May 1, 1964, pp. 80A-103.

SEYLER, ATHENE, AND STEPHEN, HAGGARD. *The Craft of Comedy*. New York: Theatre Arts, Inc., 1946.

STANISLAVSKI, CONSTANTIN. *Building a Character*. New York: Theatre Arts Books: Robert M. MacGregor, 1949.

STRICKLAND, F. COWLES. *The Technique of Acting*. New York: McGraw-Hill Book Co., 1956.

WHITE, EDWIN C., AND MARGUERITE BATTYE. *Acting and Stage Movement*. New York: Arc Books, 1963.

Chapter 12

CENTRAL STAGING

I. Introduction.

The popularity of central staging has made possible a renaissance in the community theatre movement since World War II. Today a drama director can hardly afford to be unfamiliar with the techniques of central staging, often called arena staging or theatre-in-the-round. If he knows the principles of good theatre as applied to the proscenium stage, he can easily adapt them to playing in the round. All that has been covered in Chapters 4, 7, 8, 9, and 11 relative to the director's interpretation, voice, characterization, tempo and climax, and the rehearsal process can be applied to central staging, as can many of the principles of movement. It is in composition, some aspects of movement and the handling of the technical elements of theatre that central staging most differs from proscenium staging. The student director may find it frustrating to unlearn all that he has been taught about up and down stage, relative strength of stage areas, and pictorial composition, but he will find it easier to adapt to central staging than would a director trained in the round and adapting to proscenium staging.

II. Advantages and disadvantages of central staging.

A. Advantages.

1. It can be done by a group which has no proscenium theatre. Lack of a home is no longer an insurmountable obstacle to a

community or school group which wants to start a theatre. Stores, auto sales rooms, tents, ballrooms, gymnasiums, classrooms, museum and exhibit halls and even forbiddingly large proscenium stages have been successfully converted to central staging.

2. It greatly reduces a group's budget for scenery. Volunteer man-hours necessary to build sets are also minimized, a considerable advantage to groups without classes in stagecraft.

3. It may represent a far more satisfactory solution for a director in the high school theatre than to struggle against overwhelming odds on an oversized proscenium stage with obsolete lighting equipment, inadequate technical help and budget, in an auditorium which is difficult to be heard in and which is never filled for a dramatic presentation — and in which the director cannot get sufficient rehearsal time because other groups share the facilities.

4. Audiences like it. It offers an intimacy and contact with the actors which many people prefer to the long distances between performers and spectators in the balcony of professional playhouses. Motion picture and television "over the shoulder shots," have accustomed spectators to back and three-quarter views of actors.

B. Disadvantages.

1. It is not equally well suited to all types of plays, as the possibilities for spectacle are greatly reduced. Some of the magic of the theatre is missing. Most directors of theatre-in-the-round would concede that modern comedies and realistic dramas are the best choice for central staging, although period comedies of manners have been successfully center staged. Imaginative directors, such as Pat Brown of the Magnolia Theatre in Long Beach, find it challenging to prove to the contrary, but many directors believe that plays in the following categories would offer a more fully satisfying theatrical experience on a proscenium stage:

a. Plays which depend upon spectacle and background for localizing environment, creating mood and atmosphere, such as *A Midsummer Night's Dream, The Teahouse of the August Moon,* and *Saint Joan.*

b. Plays which because of their subject matter require aesthetic distance between audience and performer. *The Rose Tattoo,* for example, may prove embarrassing in the intimacy of central staging. When emotions are deeply stirred, as in *Our Town,* spectators prefer not to see or be seen by others in the audience.

     c. Plays which were written for direct contact with the audience by means of asides, soliloquies and narration (inasmuch as the contact can be with only a quarter of the audience at a time).

     d. Multi-set plays which require detailed realistic treatment, or which have many scenes necessitating shifting during blackouts.

2. It requires a high degree of concentration on the part of the actors, for some of their conventional securities — prompter, footlights, and turning away from the audience — are unavailable. Actors must play with a sense of truth and attention to detail, act with their whole bodies and always remain in character, oblivious to the faces they can recognize in the audience.

3. Costumes, make-up and properties must be carefully prepared and authentic, as they are subject to scrutiny from all sides.

4. Entrances and exits are often less effective than on the proscenium stage.

5. Illusion is frequently more difficult to achieve, and certain stage effects present knotty but not insoluble problems — shootings and killings, disappearances, playing musical instruments, for example.

6. Changes of setting, particularly quick changes between scenes, are difficult to manage.

7. Good lighting may require more instruments and more careful planning than on proscenium stages.

8. There is less likelihood that a young person will be convincing in an older role, and central staging therefore may impose some limitations on casting.

III. Problems of Blocking.

A. Composition.

The director accustomed to one stage picture in the proscenium theatre will have to get accustomed to planning each scene for the benefit of all four sections of his theatre. There are no strong and weak areas of the stage and there should be no preferred seating for the audience. The director should spend part of every rehearsal in each section of his auditorium.

1. Emphasis.

Of the ten means of obtaining emphasis discussed in Chapter 5, Composition, the only ones practicable in central staging are:

     a. Level — of limited value because (1) it is hard to motivate the use of levels in the average interior set, (2) the elevation on which the actor stands may itself block visibility

The Iceman Cometh, Arena Stage, Washington, D. C.

of part of the stage for some in front row seats, and (3) the elevated actor must still turn his back on at least a quarter of the audience. When feasible, however, levels can increase emphasis on the actor.

b. Focus of the actors.

c. Contrast, particularly between standing and sitting. Whenever possible actors with few lines should be seated and those with the majority of the lines should be standing.

d. The speaking actor will not always be the center of attention for all parts of the auditorium. *Reaction* of other actors to what is being said therefore becomes more important than in proscenium staging — for it is all some spectators may be able to see at the moment.

2. Visibility.

Problems of emphasis in proscenium staging become in central staging simply problems of making actors visible. Each section of the auditorium should be able to see at least one actor's face at all times.

a. Scenes with two people:
   (1) Walden Boyle emphasizes the value of an actor's working with his back to an aisle in order to give the best visibility to the largest number of spectators.[1]
   (2) Both actors should not face the same direction at the same time.
   (3) Playing with space between two actors makes better visibility than when they are close together. Keep the actors as far apart as can be justified, and find ways to pull them apart once they have closed in.
   (4) Except when playing with back to an aisle, actors should avoid facing each other directly when possible. One or both of the actors should step sideways and open up, facing his partner with a one-quarter position rather than full-front — what Kelly Yeaton calls "twisting the pairs,"[2] so that part of the audience sees each actor over the other's shoulder.

Poor   Better

"Twisting the pairs"

[1]Boyle, Walden P., *Central and Flexible Staging* (Los Angeles and Berkeley: University of California Press, 1956).
[2]Yeaton, Kelly, "Arena Production," in Gassner, John (Editor), *Producing the Play* (New York: The Dryden Press, 1953). Also section on "Simplified Staging" in same volume.

(5) Scenes between two people on a sofa present special problems. A sofa forces both people to face the same direction, turning their backs on the same section of the audience. The director must find ways to overcome this by having one actor sit on an arm of the sofa, put his feet up and sit sideways, swivel his body around, etc.

b. Scenes with three people:

Such scenes are easier to handle than twosomes. An open triangle works well, providing each part of the auditorium with a view of at least one actor's face.

c. Group scenes:

(1) Keep as many minor characters seated around the periphery as possible, to motivate the principal character's moving to direct speeches to them.

(2) Eliminate or combine minor characters to reduce the number on stage, as each person adds to the problem of keeping the principals visible.

(3) Where large crowds are required (as in *An Enemy of the People*) use level to make the speaker visible — letting him stand on a bench, table or prop rock.

(4) Minor figures who can appropriately sit or lie on the floor aid in visibility.

(5) Minor figures may stand in the aisles, or even, as in a New York arena staging of *Julius Caesar*, behind the spectators.

B. Movement.

All of the purposes of movement given in Chapter 6 which stem from inner meaning apply equally well to central staging, and all of the purposes which stem from technical or functional necessity apply with the exception of preventing upstaging and dressing stage or restoring balance. The primary purpose for which the director must use movement in central staging, however, is to vary the composition so that each section of the audience sees each principal actor's face for part of every beat, scene or long speech.

1. The "pig on a spit" theory.

While the actor must face each section of the auditorium during a scene, he must not do this mechanically or rotate from one section to the next in sequence like a pig on a spit.

2. A better way of thinking of the actor's movement is suggested by the term coined by Margo Jones,[3] "making the rounds." During a long speech — a telephone conversation for example — the actor must find motivation for turning his body in all directions.

---

[3]Jones, Margo, *Theatre-in-the-Round* (New York: Rinehart and Co., 1951).

3. Movement in central staging must, as in proscenium staging, be motivated from within the character. As more movement is required, more inventiveness on the part of the actor in creating justified movement is necessary. It is especially important to find motivation to move away from other people even while talking to them (based on the principle of strong and weak lines).

4. A stage picture cannot be held for as long as it might be in proscenium staging. Kelly Yeaton has said that "No grouping is bad if it doesn't last long."

5. Furniture needs to be placed at the outer edges of the acting area in order to motivate movement centrifugally from center toward the perimeter.

6. The principle of moving on one's own lines applies in central staging as well as in proscenium, except when a character's re-action to what is being said can be made as interesting as the words themselves.

7. Entrances and exits.
   Entrances and exits will unavoidably be less pointed than in proscenium staging. Except for buildings designed especially for central staging, it is rarely possible for the actor to disappear promptly from a lighted area. Some suggested ways of dealing with the problem include:

   a. To treat the aisles through which the actors enter and exit as a convention, keeping them dark and assuming that the character is offstage as soon as he is within an aisle, so that the other characters are free to resume the dialogue without waiting for him to disappear.

   b. To treat the aisles as a playing area, letting the actors speak as they walk up and down the aisles. Disadvantages of this technique are that light is then required in the aisles, part of the audience needs to swivel their bodies around into an awkward position to see the actors, and the entire audience becomes more conscious of other spectators than is desirable during these exits and entrances.

   c. To place doors on a partial wall with the audience sitting in a horseshoe around it (flexible staging) offers the best compromise in a play where entrances and exits are important.

   d. To use the doors to the auditorium for the actors, although fire laws prohibit the disguising of the "Exit" light.

   e. To rewrite some of the entrance and exit speeches so that a pointed entrance line is preceded by several throw-away lines, and a pointed exit speech is followed by several weak lines, permitting the actor to continue his movement up or down the aisle without sacrificing significant lines.

   f. To have the actors get up and down the aisles as quickly as possible, minimizing the awkward movements when they must brush past spectators and jeopardize the illusion.

8. Blocking and recording the movement.

There is no fixed nomenclature for the central stage. Some directors use directions based on:

   a. The compass — cross North, cross South East, etc.
   b. The clock — cross to 9 o'clock, 4 o'clock, etc.
   c. The sections of the auditorium, as designated on tickets — cross to B section, D section, etc.
   d. Location of furniture and objects of actors' attention — cross to the sofa, cross away from Robert, into the group, etc.

Example of blocking for central staging: (the same speech for which a suggested proscenium blocking was given in Chapter 6, III, D, page 152. A symbol such as Ꮻ should be used to show which way a character is facing.

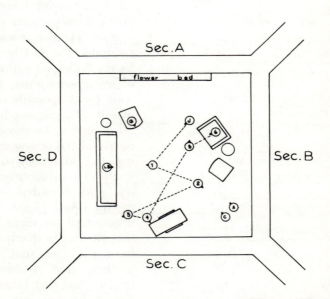

The Importance of Being Earnest, Act III.

In the proscenium composition, Lady Bracknell could be standing, for emphasis. In central staging, she and

Gwendolen would most likely be seated, and Algernon and Cecily, whose arms are around each other, standing with their backs to an aisle. The scene, in the morning room of the house, could just as effectively be played in the garden set of the previous act. Jack begins with back to the aisle between Sec. A and B.

1. X to C facing Lady Bracknell.	**JACK:** It pains me very much to have to speak frankly to you, Lady Bracknell, about your nephew, but the fact is that I do not approve at all
Turns to glare at Algy.	of his moral character. I suspect him of being untruthful.

LADY BRACKNELL: Untruthful! My nephew Algernon? Impossible! He is an Oxonian.

2. X toward Algy.	**JACK:** I fear there can be no possible doubt about the matter. This afternoon, during my temporary absence in London on an important question of romance, he obtained admission to my house by means
3. X past Algy to between D and C sections, facing aisle.	of the false pretense of being my brother. Under an assumed name he drank, I've just been informed by my butler, an entire pint bottle of my Perrier-Jouet, Brut, '89; a wine I was specially reserving for
Turns to Cecily.	myself. Continuing his disgraceful deception, he succeeded in the course of the afternoon in alienating the affections of my only
4. Moves to tea cart and picks up empty muffin dish.	ward. He subsequently stayed to tea, and devoured every single
5. X center near chair at Sec. B facing Sec. A.	muffin. And what makes his conduct all the more heartless is, that he was perfectly well aware from the first that I have no brother, that I never had a brother, and that I don't intend to
6. Sits in chair, Sec. B (toward Sec. A).	have a brother, not even of any kind. I distinctly told him so myself yesterday afternoon.

C. Voice.

Although less vocal projection is required in central staging than in a large proscenium theatre, it may be surprising to discover that *more* projection is needed in central staging than in a comparable size room used for proscenium staging. The reason is apparent: the actor's back is to part of his audience at all times, and the consonants, particularly the all-important final consonants that make for understandability, may easily be lost when the spectator neither sees accompanying facial expression nor hears the speech directly.

IV. **Problems of technical theatre-in-the-round.**

The Male Animal.

A. Scenery.
   1. Some directors of central staging have found ingenious ways of using a wall of their auditorium or an aisle between sections of the audience for bits of scenery necessary in the action — a porch on which the flower pot drops, for example, in *The Seven Year Itch*, or a wall on which a painting can hang in *The Late Christopher Bean*.

2. Doors and windows can be established by:
   a. Pantomime.
   b. Placing them at the heads of aisles.
   c. Utilizing actual entrances to the arena.
   d. Very thin skeletal outlines of the doors and windows created with 1″ x 1″ lumber or aluminum tubing.
   e. Half-doors and windows, no more than 2′ high, as in accompanying picture.
3. Mirrors and pictures on walls can be convincingly pantomimed if the actor is truthful and consistent, or they can be reduced to table size.
4. Changes of setting can be accomplished by:
   a. Having actors in the cast who play butlers, maids or lackeys shift the furniture and properties in view of the audience at intermission. The shifts must be carefully rehearsed, performed in character and without haste.
   b. Having members of the technical crew, dressed in clean and appropriate work clothes do the shifts in view of the audience at intermission.
   c. Having crew members or actors make the shifts in the dark during blackouts between scenes. They must be dressed in black, must carefully rehearse each move, and should have music to cover the noise of shifting. Complicated shifts should not be attempted in the dark, for the audience may soon grow either embarrassed or bored.
   d. Use of simultaneous settings and a change in light. The stage area can be divided into two or more areas, separated by very low wainscoting, hedges, fences or outlines of walls.

B. Properties.

In central staging, furniture and properties take over many of the functions of scenery — setting the locale, creating atmosphere, reinforcing the emphasis on the actor.

1. All furniture *must* be low — never higher than eye-level of spectators in the first row, preferably even lower. Overstuffed armchairs with wing-backs are ruled out, as are upright pianos, fireplaces, and cupboards. (Sometimes such items may be placed against a small bit of wall between sections of the auditorium.)
2. The back of the furniture must be as much in character as the front.
3. Complete authenticity in hand props is necessary. A card game would require prestacking the deck; newspapers, mixing drinks and eating scenes are given close scrutiny by the audience and leave little room for faking.[4]

---

[4]For ingenious solutions to property problems, see Kelly Yeaton, *loc. cit.*

4. When props are pantomimed, there should be a consistency and unity within the style of the production.
5. Rugs, grass mats or planters can be used to demark the borders of acting areas.
6. Tall lamps, vases and trim props should not be used.

C. Costumes.

Much of the pictorial color and style of period plays must be supplied by costume. Like properties, they must bear scrutiny at close range, front and back. Modern costumes require frequent cleaning, and removal of make-up from around collars.

D. Make-up.

Heavy character make-ups are often unconvincing in central staging. This is a serious problem for young people playing older roles. Directors in central staging tend to cast to type and rely very little upon make-up.

E. Lighting.

The time and money invested in scenery on the proscenium stage should be spent on painstaking lighting in central staging, which makes a major contribution in the creation of mood and emphasis.

1. Lighting instruments should be so placed that bounce or spill of light on the spectators is eliminated or minimized.
2. The actor's face needs to be well-lighted from all sides.
3. The switchboard needs to be so placed that the lighting crew has a view of the stage area.
4. Fluorescent paint should be used to mark aisles and any places actors need to find in the dark.
5. Blackouts or dimouts become the equivalent of the curtain.
6. Closing a drape or pulling down a shade may be suggested by the actor's pantomime accompanied by a well-timed dimdown in light. Kelly Yeaton's article in *Producing the Play* is the most valuable analysis of lighting problems in central staging.

F. Music.

Together with lighting, music serves as a substitute for a curtain in swelling a scene to climax and punctuating it with finality. The use of music has become standard in central staging, as it drowns out the noise of actors making their entrances in the dark and props being shifted. Stereophonic, multi-speaker sound systems should be used if possible.

G. Sound effects.

Authentic sound may also form a valuable substitute for the missing visual elements of spectacle. What would in proscenium theatre be only an "off-stage sound" may in central staging become a significant part of the total impact, surrounding the spectators and heightening their feeling that they are participating with the actors in the situation.

V. Flexible Staging.

A. Tailoring the theatre to the play.

Audience acceptance of central staging has opened up many exciting new possibilities for a flexible theatre in which placement of stage and audience is tailored to the requirements of each play. Walden Boyle[5] describes some of these variations which movable risers for the audience made possible at the University of California at Los Angeles — a pioneer in flexible theatre. Among the most successful are:

The Cocktail Party. University of California at Los Angeles.

1. Horseshoe staging or three-quarters round.

This plan incorporates some of the most valuable aspects of central staging with one area for scenic effects, surrounded on three sides by spectators. The University of Miami Ring Theatre was built as a flexible plant so that the audience can be grouped on three sides facing a large acting area; the fourth side (on a revolving stage) contains a shallow proscenium for scenic effects; the audience risers can also be regrouped for central or double-end staging. Long Beach, California, is the first city

[5]Boyle, *op. cit.*

to have a Community Playhouse built especially for horseshoe staging; the acting area shown below can be divided in half by lighting.

a. The fourth side in horseshoe staging is particularly valuable for doors, windows, decor, and required props which would obstruct the view in central staging.

The Long Beach (California) Community Playhouse.

b. Horseshoe staging is a modern approximation of the conditions of Shakespeare's Globe Theatre and as such lends itself to the staging of Shakespeare, with scenes alternating between the proscenium area and the three-quarters round area. The ancient Greek theatre was also three-quarters round.

2. L-shaped staging.
   With the audience on two sides at right angles, even more space is available for background settings in the proscenium manner. The L-shaped audience arrangement is as old as the first known theatres on the island of Crete.

3. Double-end staging.
   With the audience on two parallel sides, an acting area is provided in the center with scenic elements at both ends. This is well

suited to such plays as *Twelfth Night* and *Henry IV*, Part I, where the action alternates between two locales.

B. The "Dramatic Laboratory Teaching Station" is proving to be a workable answer to the problem of finding a home for the theatre arts in high schools without adequate auditoriums. Developed by Horace Robinson at the request of the Southern California District of the American Educational Theatre Association, such a room would include both a small stage with an adjustable proscenium opening and a space for arena staging. End-staging, theatre-in-the-round and horseshoe staging are all possible in this room, with the intimacy and flexibility that are desirable for young players.[6]

VI. The platform or open stage.

A. This exciting new development in theatre architecture permits the audience to sit on three sides of a platform or thrust which brings the actors into close contact with the spectators. Based on concepts of the Greek and Elizabethan theatre, it was pioneered in modern times by Frederic McConnell at the Euclid-77th Street Theatre of the Cleveland Playhouse, and found to be adaptable to a wide variety of styles and types of plays, and to permit of considerable use of pictorial scenic elements (see photograph of *The Crucible* on page 73).[7] The more recent theatres at Stratford, Ontario, and Minneapolis incorporate a much deeper thrust, use no curtain and virtually no scenic elements.

B. The Tyrone Guthrie Theatre at Minneapolis, shown in photograph, can be used with realistic props and furniture as in *The Three Sisters,* but it works equally well for an almost totally prop-less and furniture-less production of *Death of a Salesman.* It is ideally suited to the staging of classics written in pre-proscenium periods. The problem of entrances has been alleviated by the use of tunnels leading out from the platform underneath the spectators. Principles of blocking on the open stage must generally follow those of theatre-in-the-round, but with one less side of the audience with which to be concerned. Plastic, three-dimensional groupings of actors offer challenging possibilities on this stage, but as the auditoriums grow larger (the Guthrie Theatre seats 1,400) it becomes more difficult to hear the actors in any section of the house to which backs are turned during intimate scenes.

C. The Repertory Theatre of Lincoln Center in New York utilizes a similar platform in its temporary quarters, although the new Vivian

---

[6]Jack Morrison, "A Dramatic Laboratory Teaching Station for High Schools," *Secondary School Theatre Conference News,* II, 3, Summer, 1964.

[7]Frederic McConnell, "Using the Open Stage: A Ten Year Experiment at the Cleveland Playhouse," *The Theatre Annual,* XVII, 1960, pp. 48-67.

The Three Sisters, at the Tyrone Guthrie Theatre, Minneapolis.

Beaumont Theatre will incorporate both a proscenium with great depth and a thrust platform.[8] From his experience in directing in its temporary ANTA Washington Square Theatre, José Quintero wrote of the new demands which the platform stage makes upon the actor, who is forced to a "deeper kind of reality" in his playing:

> *In directing a play for the open stage, what must be avoided is blocking the view of some portion of the audience. One must be inventive to keep the play mobile, almost as if it were a "figure eight," without the movement being unmotivated or capricious. Certain areas in view of the entire audience assume varying values, such as the farthest*

---

[8]Richard and Nancy Meyer, "Lincoln Center's Bargain Theatre," *Players Magazine*, XL, 7, April, 1964, pp. 206-208.

*section. One makes the initial statement back there and then
breaks it down into its components down center.*[9]

Exercises: Reblock for central staging or the platform some of the
scenes previously studied, such as the one from *Summer
and Smoke* or *The Crucible* (Chapter 6), *The Late Christopher Bean* (Chapter 9), *Winterset* (Chapter 9), or
those from *Hedda Gabler, A Midsummer Night's Dream,
Death of a Salesman,* or *The Importance of Being Earnest*
given in Appendix D.

VII. Summary.

All the principles of good theatre apply to central staging except for
special treatment of composition, movement, and technical elements so
that each section of the audience sees part of every beat, long speech
or scene, and at least one actor's face is visible to each section at all
times.

A. Advantages and disadvantages of central staging.
  1. Advantages.
  2. Disadvantages.
B. Problems of blocking.
  1. Composition.
  2. Movement.
  3. Voice.
C. Problems of technical theatre in the round.
  1. Scenery.
  2. Properties.
  3. Costumes.
  4. Make-up.
  5. Lighting.
  6. Music.
  7. Sound effects.
D. Flexible staging.
  1. Tailoring the theatre to the play.
  2. The Dramatic Laboratory Teaching Station.
E. The platform or open stage.
  1. The Cleveland Playhouse.
  2. The Tyrone Guthrie Theatre.
  3. The Repertory Theatre of Lincoln Center.

---

[9]Barry Hyams, "A Theatre: Heart and Mind," in *Theatre: The Annual of the Repertory Theater of Lincoln Center.* Vol. I. (New York: A Repertory Theater Publication in
association with Playbill, Inc., 1964.)

Suggested Reading

ALBRIGHT, H. D., HALSTEAD, WILLIAM P., AND MITCHELL, LEE. *Principles of Theatre Art*. Boston: Houghton Mifflin Company, 1955, pp. 222-229.

BOYLE, WALDEN P. *Central and Flexible Staging*. Berkeley and Los Angeles: University of California Press, 1956.

DIETRICH, JOHN E. *Play Direction*. New York: Prentice-Hall, Inc., 1953, Chapter 22.

GOODMAN, RANDOLPH. *Arena Theatre — 1957: A bibliography*. New York: American National Theatre and Academy, Service Pamphlet, August, 1957.

HUGHES, GLENN. *The Penthouse Theatre*. New York: Samuel French, 1942.

HYAMS, BARRY (Editor). *Theatre: The Annual of the Repertory Theatre of Lincoln Center*, Vol. I. New York: Playbill, Inc., 1964.

JONES, MARGO. *Theatre-in-the-Round*. New York: Rinehart and Co., 1951.

MCCONNELL, FREDERIC. "Using the Open Stage: A Ten Year Experiment at the Cleveland Playhouse," *The Theatre Annual*, XVII, 1960, pp. 48-67.

MEYER, RICHARD AND NANCY. "Lincoln Center's Bargain Theatre," *Players Magazine*, XL, 7, April, 1964, pp. 206-208.

MORRISON, JACK. "A Dramatic Laboratory Teaching Station for High Schools," *Secondary School Theatre Conference News*, II, 3, Summer, 1964.

SOUTHERN, RICHARD. *The Open Stage*. New York: Theatre Arts Books, 1959.

WILLIAMS, DALLAS S. "A Bibliography for Arena Theatre," *Educational Theatre Journal*, X, 3, October, 1958, pp. 259-267.

YEATON, KELLY. "Arena Production," in Gassner, John (ed.), *Producing the Play*. New York: The Dryden Press, 1953. Also section on "Simplified Staging" in same volume.

Chapter 13

WHERE TO GO FROM HERE

I. Introduction.

This manual has presented many of the principles which the director in the theatre will use. Before he can master them all, however, he will need considerable practice in which he exposes the results of his work to live audiences, deepens his insight into the drama, and discovers how he works best as a director. The audience is ultimately the best teacher—not with the flattery of friends but with the laughter, the breathless silence, the restless coughing, and the applause by which the spectators communicate their feelings back to the stage. With the theory and practical exercises given in this text as a beginning in the fundamentals of play direction, the young director should broaden his background to include the following experiences:

II. Experiences the director should have.

   A. College courses in:
      1. Acting.
      2. Stagecraft.
      3. Lighting.
      4. Costuming.
      5. Make-up.

   Work in these five areas is desirable before the student begins the course in direction or play production — if not, as soon thereafter as possible.

      6. Dramatic literature and history of the theatre.

314

7. Directing — laboratory experiences in directing scenes (if possible concurrently with the fundamentals of direction course), then one-act plays and finally a full-length play.
8. Music and art appreciation.
9. Dance and movement for the stage.
10. Psychology.

B. Practical experience on productions.

There is no substitute for being involved in actual production. A student interested in *any* phase of the theatre should seek experience in *all* phases. A young person with ambition as an actor should not only welcome the opportunity to work backstage on technical crews — he also should seek out these opportunities; there is much he can learn about acting — timing, interpretation of lines and audience response — by standing in the wings as a member of a prop, lighting or stage crew. So too the student interested in creative writing should learn the theatre from backstage. Above all, a director needs to know every phase of backstage work from actual experience.

C. Attending the theatre.

It is not unheard of for a college drama major never to have seen a professional production of a play. A student of the theatre should attend the theatre regularly, seeing all kinds of productions including professional companies, musicals, children's theatre, central staging, community theatre and educational theatre. If a student (outside New York City) sees every professional company in his area, he will still see far too little theatre — much less, for example, than is available to a student in the average European city.

III. **Satisfactions for the theatre student.**

An educational program such as the one outlined offers its own rewards that amply justify its inclusion among the liberal arts. This text began by enumerating the many values which might be derived from a theatre arts experience, regardless of the future vocational aims of the student. It should conclude with a reiteration of the satisfactions which the theatre offers to all who are caught up in its magic:

A. Liberal education in depth and breadth.
1. Insight into human nature.
2. Appreciation of literature.
3. Development of critical standards.
4. Personal growth and development.
B. Appreciation for the theatre arts which offers lifelong satisfactions to a playgoer.
C. Development of personal skills which will provide lifelong avocational or recreational outlets as a participant or leader in community theatres, civic, church groups or children's theatre.

IV. Vocational opportunities for the theatre student.

A revealing survey by the Gallup Poll documented for the first time the "cultural explosion" that is taking place in this country. Appreciation for the theatre arts instilled on college campuses has created a new generation of playgoers and participants. Among cultural pursuits, the most popular in 1962 was going to a motion picture (50 per cent of Americans questioned), followed by reading a book (46 per cent). Some sports ranked next, including bowling (24 per cent), football (24 per cent), and basketball (17 per cent). But surprisingly enough, attending a stage or theatre production ranked next — some 17 per cent or 18 million adults — tied with the number that visited an art museum. This number exceeds those who played bingo or attended a symphony concert. Gallup found too, that 3 per cent or 3 million adults participated in theatre production.[1]

It is in providing leadership for these new participants and playgoers who seek the satisfactions of the theatre arts that many graduates of drama departments will find vocational opportunities. The most fertile fields lie away from Broadway and Hollywood, in the innumerable cities across the nation where the new theatre movement is growing from grass roots. As the cultural explosion expands, openings for well-trained drama directors, teachers and technical personnel will increase in the following categories:

A. Secondary schools.
1. High schools offer the most numerous opportunities for drama teachers and directors. A teacher's credential is required, and a broad background in other subjects is usually desired, as the drama program generally does not constitute a full teaching load. Although the pattern varies from state to state, many high schools find the following combinations workable:

a. Director of plays, generally combined with classes in English or speech; should have background in acting and dramatic literature.
b. Technical director, teacher of stagecraft and scene designer for productions, generally combined with other subjects in art or industrial arts. Students with preparation in this combination are at present considerably in demand.

2. Junior high schools.
Although less specialization is required, a growing number of junior high schools will have opportunities for a teacher with some training in formal drama as well as the ability to use cre-

---

[1]"Gallup Poll," *Los Angeles Times,* Feb. 24, 1963.

ative dramatics in other classes, which may include English, speech or social studies.

Students interested in preparing for the secondary field should affiliate with and obtain further information from:

Secondary School Theatre Conference, a division of the American Educational Theatre Association. For address, see the latest issue of the *Educational Theatre Journal*. The placement services listed following also service the high school field, although a student is most likely to hear of high school vacancies through the placement service of his teacher-training college.

B. Junior colleges.

As school populations grow, more and more teachers will find placement in junior (two-year) colleges in states such as California and Texas. In addition to a teacher's credential and a major in drama, a Master of Arts degree in drama is recommended in many schools and required in some. Some specialization is desirable, either in acting-directing or technical theatre.

C. Colleges and universities.

A recent study by Burnet M. Hobgood found that at present there are some 15,000 college students enrolled for theatre courses in 900 accredited colleges and universities, and that approximately 1,500 full-time teachers are employed in this instruction plus half again as many part-time instructors.[2] The Master of Arts degree usually is required for such teaching positions, and the Ph.D. degree or extensive experience in the professional theatre generally is a prerequisite for advancement on most university theatre faculties.

1. Specialization versus general background.
   Smaller colleges require an all-around theatre person able to direct, design and build scenery and costumes, to teach acting, speech and dramatic literature. The candidate with strong preparation in each of these fields will render himself more valuable to schools with limited faculties. In those colleges with a large drama faculty, however, specialization is desirable; the most common combinations include:

   a. Acting-directing, voice.
   b. History of the theatre, dramatic literature and playwriting.
   c. Technical theatre, scene design, and lighting.
   d. Costume design and construction, make-up.

---

[2]Hobgood, Burnet M., "Theatre in U. S. Higher Education: Emerging Patterns and Problems," *Educational Theatre Journal*, XVI, 2, May, 1964, pp. 142-159.

2. Placement services.
For college level positions, applicants should contact:

   a. American Educational Theatre Association, Contact placement service. (Also services high school, community and children's theatre.) For current address, see latest issue of the *Educational Theatre Journal*.
   b. Speech Association of America, Placement Service. For current address, see latest issue of *The Quarterly Journal of Speech*.
   c. The placement service of the student's college or university.
   d. Privately operated placement services.

D. Community theatres.
Throughout the country there is a mushrooming of community theatres which offer full or part-time employment to a director and sometimes a technical director as well. Academic degrees are usually less important than a person's theatre skill, his ability to get along with volunteer workers, and his enthusiasm for the theatre. Insight into the problems and challenges of building and operating a community theatre can be gained from some of the books suggested at the end of this chapter.

Students interested in preparing for this field should affiliate with and obtain further information from:

American Community Theatre Association, a division of the American Educational Theatre Association. For address see the latest issue of *Educational Theatre Journal*.

E. Children's theatre.
The children's theatre movement is developing throughout the United States and provides opportunity for part-time paid directors in some cases and volunteer directors in others. Organizations producing plays for children can be divided into:

1. Groups using volunteer adult actors.
2. Groups using children as actors.
3. Professional adult groups producing for children.
4. Recreation groups.

   This is a sizeable and growing area offering opportunity for directors. Many communities employ drama directors through the municipal recreation department. Programs offered after school and on Saturday include creative dramatics, puppetry and formal dramatics for children and teen-agers.

Students interested in preparing for this field should affiliate with and obtain further information from the Children's Theatre Confer-

Sleeping Beauty.

ence, a division of the American Educational Theatre Association. The address appears in the latest issue of *Educational Theatre Journal.*

F. Semiprofessional theatre.

There are more opportunities in this area than one might realize, and more are awaiting the imaginative director with the vision to organize such a theatre. Included in this category are many organizations offering experience for actors and backstage technicians which would be invaluable for future directors:

1. Outdoor summer pageants and historical dramas. Symphonic dramas begun by Paul Green have now spread from *The Lost Colony* at Manteo, N. C., to Williamsburg, Va., Cherokee, N. C., Berea, Ky., Blowing Rock, N. C., and the *Ramona* play at Hemet, Calif.

2. Summer Shakespeare festivals.
   Currently summer festivals offering Shakespeare include Boulder, Colorado, Ashland, Oregon, San Diego, California, Antioch, Ohio, as well as professional companies at Stratford, Ontario, and in Connecticut.

3. The so-called "off-Broadway" theatre, which now can be found in a number of cities other than New York, attempts to offer modest salaries to part or all of their company.

4. Summer theatres.
   Groups banding together to produce theatre during the summer, with either college or community affiliations, also form a growing

opportunity for directors. Often the weekly receipts determine whether the group can be called semiprofessional, professional or a nonprofit organization.

G. Professional theatre.

When a strike of Actors' Equity Association in 1960 closed down all professional theatres in the United States, there were only 731 actors at work in New York City and another 175 on the road — an incredibly tiny proportion for a nation of over 192,000,000! There are more encouraging signs, however, in the burgeoning resident theatres and repertory companies outside New York which have sprung up or which have made the transition from community or semiprofessional to professional theatres thanks to subsidies from the Ford Foundation in cities such as Houston, San Francisco, Milwaukee, Oklahoma City, Minneapolis, Washington, D. C., and Los Angeles. New York State has established an Arts Council to aid the performing arts, and the McKnight Foundation makes it possible for graduate students of drama to work as apprentices at the Tyrone Guthrie Theatre in Minneapolis. The decentralization of the professional theatre offers the most encouraging promise of vocational opportunity for talented and well-trained young people interested in management, direction, technical theatre, public relations as well as acting, and may provide the pattern which will grow into the truly national theatre of the United States.

H. Creative writing.

Of all the skills within the broad field of the theatre arts, creative writing is the least overcrowded as well as the most badly needed. Directors of theatre at every level have a responsibility to seek out and encourage new writing talent and to produce original plays when possible. The student with an aptitude for playwriting should learn the theatre firsthand as an actor, director or member of a backstage crew in addition to studying dramatic literature and the craft of playwriting. He will then find a variety of channels open to his talents — writing for the children's theatre, the high school theatre, musical comedy, possibly even television or motion pictures.

I. Television and motion pictures.

The best training for television and motion pictures is the living stage, offering the two-way communication between audience and performer which is unavailable in the other media. A strong drama major will permit the student to translate his basic skills in acting, directing, writing, costuming or scenic design into the specialized requirements of TV and cinema. Like the professional theatre, however, these fields are fiercely competitive and unstable.

V. Keeping abreast of the field.

The theatre arts are a changing field in vocational opportunities, forms of staging, dramatic literature and technical materials. The drama director needs to keep abreast of the field and should affiliate with professional organizations, receiving their journals and attending their conventions and conferences, often held locally, regionally and nationally. Among the organizations working for the betterment of the theatre and theatre artists are:

A. American Educational Theatre Association (AETA).
     Executive Office: John F. Kennedy Center for the Performing Arts, 1701 Pennsylvania Ave. NW, Washington, D.C.

     Includes: Children's Theatre Conference
                Secondary School Theatre Conference
                American Community Theatre Division

B. American National Theatre and Academy (ANTA).
     245 W. 52nd St., New York City

     Chartered by Congress to foster a national theatre in the United States, ANTA receives no governmental subsidy as yet except for its overseas tours. ANTA is the American representative to the International Theatre Institute (I. T. I.) which publishes *World Theatre,* a quarterly review available from Theatre Arts Books, 333 Sixth Ave., New York 14.

C. National Thespian Society (for secondary level).
     An organization with chapters in many high schools; publishes *Dramatics Magazine,* which is very valuable for high school drama teachers; College Hill Station, Cincinnati 24, Ohio.

D. National Collegiate Players, publishers of *Players Magazine.* Editorial Office: Department of Speech and Drama, University of Kansas, Lawrence, Kansas.

E. National Theatre Conference, an association of community and college theatre directors (membership by election only). Central Office: Tufts University, Medford, Mass.

VI. Summary.

To learn the art of directing for the theatre, the student needs a wide background of theory and practice in all phases of the theatre. These experiences offer rewards as part of a liberal education irrespective of vocational goal. There is, however, a growing need for teachers of theatre arts. The capable drama student can be reasonably assured that he can make a productive and satisfying career for himself in the educational theatre, the community theatre, or children's theatre; a very few students with exceptional gifts may be encouraged to pursue a career in the professional theatre or television; other drama students may choose to use their theatre skills for a lifelong avocational enrichment. In any case, the student who loves the theatre should look upon any opportunity to set his foot upon a stage in any role or backstage in any capacity as a challenge and a privilege — to improve his skills, to share a memorable play with an audience, and to enjoy a personally rewarding experience.

A. Experiences the director should have:
  1. College courses.
  2. Practical experiences on production.
  3. Attending the theatre.

B. Rewards for the theatre student.
  1. Liberal education in depth and breadth.
  2. Appreciation for the theatre arts.
  3. Development of lifelong avocational or recreational skills.

C. Vocational opportunities for the theatre student.
  1. Secondary schools.
  2. Junior colleges.
  3. Colleges and universities.
  4. Community theatres.
  5. Children's theatre.
  6. Semiprofessional theatre.
  7. Professional theatre.
  8. Creative writing.
  9. Television and motion pictures.

D. Keeping abreast of the field.
  1. American Educational Theatre Association.
  2. American National Theatre and Academy.
  3. National Thespian Society.
  4. National Collegiate Players.
  5. National Theatre Conference.

Suggested Reading

BOUGHTON, WALTER. "A Directory of Summer Theatres Sponsored by AETA Members, 1961." *Educational Theatre Journal*. XIII, I, March, 1961, pp. 34-45.

CHORPENNING, CHARLOTTE B. *Twenty-One Years with Children's Theatre*. Anchorage, Ky.: The Children's Theatre Press, 1954.

DAVIS, JED H., AND WATKINS, MARY JANE. *Children's Theatre: Play Production For the Child Audience*. New York: Harper and Brothers, 1960.

FISHER, CAROLINE, AND ROBERTSON, HAZEL. *Children and the Theatre*. Stanford, California: Stanford University Press, 1940.

FORKERT, OTTO MAURICE. *Children's Theatre That Captures its Audience*. Chicago: The Coach House Press, 1962.

GARD, ROBERT E., AND BURLEY, GERTRUDE S. *Community Theatre: Idea and Achievement*. New York: Duell, Sloan and Pearce, Inc., 1959.

GASSNER, JOHN. *Producing the Play*, Revised Edition. New York: The Dryden Press, 1953, Sections IV and V.

GIBSON, WILLIAM. *The Seesaw Log*. New York: Alfred Knopf, 1959.

HIRSCHFELD, BURT. *Stagestruck: Your Career in Theatre*. New York: Messner, 1963.

HOBGOOD, BURNET M. (ed.). *Directory of American College Theatre*. East Lansing, Michigan: American Educational Theatre Association, 1960. Also article, "Theatre in U. S. Higher Education: Emerging Patterns and Problems," *Educational Theatre Journal*, XVI, 2, May, 1964.

HOUGHTON, NORRIS. *Advance From Broadway*. New York: Harcourt, Brace and Co., 1941.

JONES, MARGO. *Theatre-in-the-Round*. New York: Rinehart and Co., 1951.

KAHAN, GERALD. "A Graduate Curriculum for Community Theatre Directors," *Educational Theatre Journal*, XIV, 3, October, 1962.

McCLEERY, ALBERT, AND GLICK, CARL. *Curtains Going Up*. New York: Pitman Publishing Corporation, 1939.

————. *Nonprofessional Community Theatres in the United States*. East Lansing: American Educational Theatre Association, 1952.

SAMACHSON, DOROTHY AND JOSEPH. *Let's Meet the Theatre*. New York: Abelard-Schuman, Inc., 1954.

SAVAN, BRUCE. *Your Career in the Theatre*. Garden City, N. Y.: Doubleday and Co., 1961.

SELDEN, SAMUEL (ed.). *Organizing a Community Theatre*. Cleveland: National Theatre Conference, 1945.

STEVENS, DAVID H. *Ten Talents in the American Theatre*. University of Oklahoma Press, 1957.

————. "Summer Theatre," *Theatre Arts*, XLIV, 6, June, 1960.

————. *"The Educational Theatre in Adult Education,"* American Educational Theatre Association. East Lansing, Michigan.

WARD, WINIFRED, *Theatre for Children*. Anchorage, Ky.: Children's Theatre Press, 3rd rev. ed., 1958.

WRIGHT, EDWARD A. *A Primer for Playgoers*. Englewood Cliffs, N. J., Prentice-Hall, Inc., 1958.

YOUNG, JOHN WRAY. *The Community Theatre and How It Works*. New York: Harper and Brothers, 1957.

DUTIES OF BACKSTAGE STAFF
AND CREW HEADS

Duties of Backstage Staff and Crew Heads

Note: This division of responsibilities is based on the one evolved for California State College at Long Beach. Each producing group will have its own requirements; this plan is suggested as a basis for modification to fit each group's needs.

I. **Technical Director.**
   A. Pre-production (at least 2 to 3 weeks prior to the first rehearsal).
      1. Participates in the selection of the play at a meeting of the staff.
      2. Selects designer unless he is to design sets himself. If technical director is also designer, he performs those functions listed under *Designer* in addition to those given here.
      3. Assumes responsibility for execution of scene designs after they have been finally approved by director at production conference.
      4. Prepares estimated budget for scenery, properties and set decoration
      5. Prepares for the director a scale ground plan of the sets, and supervises the layout of the ground plan on the floor of the stage or rehearsal hall with paint or masking tape. Scale ground plans also given to lighting technician, stage manager and head of property crew.
      6. Organizes and selects crew heads for:
         a. Scene construction crew.
         b. Scene painting crew.
         c. Stage crew.
         d. Property crew.
         e. Lighting crew.
         f. Sound crew.
      7. Prepares or approves requisitions for materials and supplies to be used in constructing the production.
      8. Advises director in the selection of a poster and program design which will be related to the over-all design of the production.
   B. During rehearsal period:
      1. Supervises the construction and painting crews in the building and painting of the sets according to the scale ground plans, elevations, and painter's elevations furnished by designer.
      2. Supervises the property crew in the making of a complete prop list and the obtaining of props and furniture, conferring with the director when necessary concerning size and function of pieces of furniture.
      3. Supervises lighting technician or light crew head in the planning of the light plot and the hanging of equipment.

4. Supervises maintenance of scene shop.
5. Coordinates the final rehearsal schedule with the director, arranging times when the stage will be used for setup, lighting, property trim, technical rehearsals and dress rehearsals.
6. Supervises setup of scenery, rigging, and trim props prior to dress rehearsal.
7. Supervises hanging of lights, cabling, plugging of switchboard, focus of lights and selection of gelatine colors.
8. Assembles and gives to program editor the names of all crews under his supervision for program copy, as well as credits to be included in program. Gives requests for complimentary tickets to business manager.
9. Selects curtain man from stage crew.

C. During dress rehearsal period:
1. Supervises completion of the scenery, the dressing and trimming of the sets, drapes, and backings.
2. Supervises the lighting rehearsal at which time each dimmer reading is set, approved by the director, and recorded on cue sheets.
3. On multi-set plays, assigns responsibilities to each crew member for scene shifts; conducts shift rehearsals with stage crew, props, and lights until shifts are sufficiently fast.
4. At dress rehearsals, sits out front with director and makes notes on details yet to be fixed or problems still requiring attention. Gives notes to crew heads after rehearsal.
5. Assigns responsibility for cleanup and sweeping of stage each night and storage of properties.

D. During performances:
1. Checks each night to make sure that crews are on duty, and deals with any problems that arise in connection with the running of the scenery, curtain or lights.
2. Leaves running of the show in the hands of the stage manager.
3. Completes tally of production costs, including petty cash slips to be turned in to business manager.
4. Works with the director when production pictures are taken to obtain effective groupings and a complete record of the production.

E. After final performance:
1. Supervises the strike and storing of sets, returning of all borrowed items, striking of lights, and cleanup of stage and shop.
2. Requisitions new supplies to bring shop inventories back to working level.
3. Assembles all sketches, models and working drawings for files.

II. Designer.

(Duties which may be performed by technical director or by another individual working closely under his supervision.)

A. Pre-production:
1. Reads and studies the play; attends first production conference at which director presents his interpretation of the play. Discusses possible scenic treatments with the director and technical director, particularly with reference to shifting problems.
2. Does research on architecture, furniture and décor of the period as well as the locale of the setting and style of the play.

3. Brings to second production conference (at least 2 to 3 weeks before first rehearsal) preliminary sketches and/or models with ground plans and color samples. Discusses any suggested modifications with director and technical director.
4. Revises and completes sketches and scale ground plan on the basis of discussion with director and technical director. Brings final sketches to third production conference for final approval of director.

B. During rehearsal period:
1. Explains designs, sketches or models to cast and to property crew. Discusses in detail with head of property crew what each item of furniture and trim should be.
2. Makes complete working drawings and painter's elevations for construction and painting crews.
3. Works with technical director in laying out the ground plan on the floor of stage or rehearsal hall in paint or masking tape.
4. Coordinates colors of set and furniture with costumer.
5. Mixes colors for scene painting, recording the formula, and works closely with scene paint crew in finishing work.
6. Works closely with lighting technician or light crew head in selecting gelatine colors.
7. Works closely with property crew in selecting or approving drapery materials and other trim props.

C. Dress rehearsal period:
1. Supervises the prop crew in placing trim, pictures and ornaments on the set.
2. Assists the director in placing furniture and establishing marks on the floor.
3. Works with the director and technical director at the lighting rehearsal, setting the final intensity and color of light.
4. Watches dress rehearsal with director and technical director, making notes of any details yet to be completed.
5. Assists the director during picture-taking session in order to obtain an effective photographic record of all the sets.

III. Lighting Designer or Light Crew Head.

A. Pre-production:
1. Reads and studies play; lists time of day and mood for each scene and lighting effects and motivated sources of light referred to in the text.
2. Attends production conferences or discusses with director and designer the interpretation of the play, mood, style, principal acting areas to be used, motivated light sources, and any special effects needed.
3. Turns in to technical director requisitions for gelatines low in inventory and other materials needed for special effects.
4. Gets from technical director an overlay of the scale ground plan, and studies designer's sketches.

B. During rehearsal period:
1. Prepares preliminary light plot, presenting it to technical director for his approval.

2. Confers with director, noting in his script the acting areas, mood and intensities desired for each scene of the play.
3. Discusses with technical director any problems relative to placement of instruments, particularly backing lights and cyclorama lights.
4. Hangs all instruments and connects to the switchboard, making a plot showing accurately every light and the dimmer number which controls it.
5. Prepares gelatine color frames.
6. Electrifies lamps and wall brackets gathered by prop crew if necessary.

C. During dress rehearsal period:
1. Focuses each light before or during the lighting rehearsal, with stage manager or assistant standing in each acting area as needed.
2. Lights each scene, adjusting or modifying lights at the request of director or technical director.
3. Makes sure each dimmer reading is recorded on lighting cue sheet before moving on to next cue.
4. In shows with many light cues, runs through the entire play for lights (without cast) in order to perfect operations of light crew.
5. During dress rehearsals, sits out front with director and technical director, making minor adjustments in lighting and making sure cue sheets are corrected for new readings.
6. After final dress rehearsal makes up clean cue sheets if necessary.

D. During performances:
1. Each night before the house is open, checks every light for focus, burned out lamps or faded gelatines.
2. Checks onstage lamps and brackets.
3. Makes sure house and cove lights are on when house is opened at 7:30 P.M.
4. Makes sure that lighting crew is present for duty, to run through play on cues from stage manager.
5. Watches play from auditorium rear near an intercom telephone, to correct any mistakes if necessary.
6. After performance, makes sure switchboard is dead before leaving building.

E. After final performance:
1. Puts away all special instruments, floor units; disconnects any borrowed lamps or light fixtures.
2. Turns in to technical director requisitions for replacement of lamps, lenses, gelatines, etc.
3. Turns in light plots to technical director for filing.

IV. Costumer or Costume Crew Head.

A. Pre-production.
1. Attends production conferences and discusses with director and designer the interpretation of the play, period, style and general impression which the director has in mind, and each character's costumes.
2. Does research on the period in which the play is to be costumed.

3. Brings to third production conference preliminary sketches for costumes and/or research materials which will be used as a guide in renting costumes.
4. Coordinates colors used by designer so as to avoid clashes with costumes.
5. Discusses costume sketches with director, modifying or redesigning costumes when necessary.
6. Brings revised and final sketches for all costumes to fourth production conference for final approval of director.
7. Brings tentative budget estimate for costumes to production conference for approval.

B. During rehearsal period:
   1. Schedules each actor to come to costume room for measurement.
   2. Makes up detailed costume plot.
   3. Makes preliminary survey of costume rental shops or secondhand stores to find out what is available.
   4. Checks wardrobe stock to find garments that can be used or remade.
   5. Requisitions materials and supplies to be bought.
   6. After preliminary weeding out, takes director to see what is available at rental sources (if renting).
   7. Lays out patterns, supervises cutting, and delegates responsibility for making costumes to members of costume crew (if constructing).
   8. Through stage manager, schedules actors to come in for fittings as needed (at times when actor is not due on stage).
   9. Makes final arrangements with costume rental companies for items to be rented, date to be picked up, and total cost.
   10. Maintains accurate list of sources for all costumes and accessories borrowed or rented.
   11. Assists director in scheduling a publicity photograph session at a time agreeable to newspaper photographer; plans with director for two or three of principals' costumes to be ready for picture session.
   12. Assembles and gives to program editor names of all crew members under costumer's supervision as well as credits for program.

C. During dress rehearsal period:
   1. Arranges for director to check and approve each actor in his costume prior to first dress rehearsal. (Where necessary on a large costume play, a costume parade is held at which director and costumer look at and make notes on each costume worn by actors under stage lights.)
   2. Gives cast instruction on proper wearing and care of costumes, as well as when to bring personal accessories such as shoes and stockings.
   3. Works out schedule with costume crew for dress rehearsal period, assigning responsibilities including a crew member to assist each actor who has a quick change.
   4. Arranges for check-out and in, safeguarding, cleaning or washing of all costumes during dress rehearsal and performance period.
   5. Assists actors into their costumes at dress rehearsal and helps actors in every way to be comfortable in their costumes and to wear them correctly.

COSTUME MEASUREMENT CHART

Actor .... Production ....

Address .... Character ....

Phone .... Date ....

Height .... Weight .... Bust (Chest) .... Waist .... Hip (7") ....

Hip (largest) .... Neck .... Shoulder Seam .... Shoulders (back) ....

Center Back to Wrist (elbow raised & bent) .... Sleeve Inseam ....

Upper Arm .... Lower Arm .... Wrist ....

Neck to Waist: Front .... Back .... Armscye .... Armscye to Waist ....

Waist to Knee .... Waist to Floor (over hip) .... Neck to Floor ....

Trouser Inseam .... Thigh .... Calf .... Ankle ....

Hair Color .... Length or Cut .... Hat Size ....

Brow .... Hairline to Base of Skull .... Ear to Ear (over head) ....

Glove Size .... Base of Palm to Tip of 2nd Finger .... Around Joints ....

Standard Clothing Sizes:
Shirt .... Coat .... Dress .... Stocking .... Shoe ....

Special Measurements & Notations:

COSTUME PLOT:

	Garments	Accessories	Hat	Shoes
Act I				
Act II				
Act III				

Quick Changes:

6. Sits out front with director at dress rehearsals, noting details yet to be completed or adjusted.
7. Assists director in planning production photographs and expediting picture-taking session.

D. During performances:
1. Schedules crew member to be on duty each night for emergency sewing and to assist actors.
2. Supervises check-out and check-in of costumes.

E. After final performance:
1. Supervises return of borrowed or rented costumes on first school day after close of the run.
2. Arranges for dry cleaning of costumes when necessary.
3. Assembles final figures on cost of costuming production and turns in all petty cash slips to business manager.
4. Supervises cleanup of costume room and dressing rooms.

V. **Make-up Crew Head or Supervisor.**

A. Pre-production.
1. Reads and studies play, making notes on references in the script which affect make-up or hair styles.
2. Does research, if necessary, on period and style, with particular reference to wigs, beards and hair styling.
3. Confers with director to find out effect desired for each character as to age, health, lines and shadows, beards and hair.

B. During rehearsal period.
1. Attends rehearsal as soon as play is cast to prepare make-up chart, noting facial features of actors, special problems, checking which actors can make up themselves, and giving special instructions where necessary concerning haircuts during rehearsal period. Obtains actors' head measurements when necessary for wigs.
2. Confers with electrician or lighting technician to learn predominant colors in lights.
3. Checks make-up supplies and prepares requisitions for those necessary.
4. Completes make-up chart in detail, selecting base colors, powder, and liners for each actor and putting them in individual kits. Assigns crew member to each actor who cannot make up himself.
5. Trains make-up crew in applying make-up, or recruits a crew with previous experience.
6. Works out, for director's approval, a schedule of make-up calls for actors at dress rehearsals and performances.
7. Schedules cleanup crew for make-up room.

C. During dress rehearsal period:
1. Supervises make-up of cast, getting director's approval of each make-up before powdering.
2. Corrects make-up chart, noting any changes in base or other colors so that actors will be able to do more of their own make-up.
3. Supervises hair styling.
4. Sits out front at dress rehearsal to check make-ups from first row and last row of theatre, making notes for changes.

D. During performances:
1. Makes sure that crew is on duty at specified time.
2. Supervises make-ups and checks each actor before powdering.
3. Assigns crew member for any quick changes or retouching of make-up necessary.

E. After final performance:
1. Makes sure that dressing rooms and make-up room are clean and supplies back in place.
2. Requisitions additional supplies to bring up inventory of make-up.

VI. **Stage Manager.**

A. Pre-production:
1. Makes up a *prompt book* from a script of the play. (See sample, page 95.)
2. Obtains ground plan from technical director and assists technical staff in laying out ground plan on floor of stage or rehearsal hall.
3. Assists director in selecting rehearsal furniture from prop room.
4. Makes sure that all cuts and changes are in the prompt book.

B. During early rehearsal period:
1. At first reading with the cast, obtains their names, addresses and telephone numbers, typing a duplicate copy for the director.
2. Makes sure that each actor receives a rehearsal schedule and keeps cast advised of any changes.
3. Arrives fifteen minutes ahead of all scheduled rehearsals and sets up stage with rehearsal furniture and any required rehearsal props; provides butt-cans for cigarettes backstage and enforces no-smoking rule in auditorium; clears stage of all furniture and risers at end of each rehearsal.
4. At blocking rehearsals, records in prompt book all positions of actors, rises, seatings, crosses, movement and business as evolved by director and cast.

   a. Uses abbreviations such as XDL and XUR.
   b. Relates actors' positions to furniture whenever possible — "X below sofa," "X above C table."
   c. Indicates with a line drawn from the text to the margin precisely where the movement begins in relation to the dialogue.
   d. Sketches the ground plan at least once on each page of prompt book (more often if there is much movement), indicating with initials the positions of all actors.

5. Walks through scene for any absent actor.
6. Marks in prompt book in red the name of each character at the time of each entrance, and one page prior to that, a *warning* for each character; makes sure that actors are ready for their entrances at each rehearsal.
7. Serves as liaison with costume crew head, sending actors for measurements or fittings as needed when they have time between scenes.
8. Serves as liaison with property crew head, advising him of placement of important hand props, additional props or changes in placement of props.

MAKE-UP CHART

Production .... Approved by Director ....

Character .... Actor ....

Character Analysis:

Forehead	Cheek	Mouth	Eye	Nose

Base:

Powder:

Hair & Beard:

Shadows:

Highlights:

Special:

C. During later weeks of rehearsal:
1. As actors begin to do scenes without book, prompts them *precisely* and corrects mistakes to the extent that the director wishes.
2. Obtains substitute hand props from prop room and puts them away after rehearsal.
3. Records in prompt book all *intentional pauses.*
4. Records in prompt book all light cues, sound cues, music cues and curtain cues, marking them in red with a warning one page before.
5. Lists in prompt book the names of "beginners," (actors on stage at the beginning of a scene) and where necessary delegates to assistant stage manager certain actors or chorus to be called.
6. Holds stop watch to time each scene or speech which will have a musical background.

D. During dress rehearsal period:
1. Assists director at property check-in, advising prop crew as to placement of onstage props.
2. As director and designer place the furniture, marks placement on floor or ground cloth with scene paint, one color for each different set.
3. Stands in for actors at the lighting rehearsal, assisted by assistant stage managers. Records in prompt book each light cue, its number, and when it begins.
4. Sets up stage manager's desk, with paging amplifiers and microphone, prior to first dress rehearsal.
5. Sets up telephone and doorbell kit when needed.
6. Takes complete charge backstage at dress rehearsals.
7. Enforces no-smoking rule strictly.
8. Enforces no-visitors rule backstage.
9. Maintains quiet backstage.
10. Checks prop crew head to be sure all props ready.
11. Checks to be sure all actors in place.
12. Checks sound man and gives him warnings.
13. Runs dress rehearsal like a performance. When going back over a cue, makes sure all involved are reset and ready.

E. During performances:
1. Checks in at 7 P.M.
2. Makes sure asbestos is down and house and cove lights on at 7:30.
3. Checks each actor in at 7:30 and reports any absences *immediately* to director.
4. Checks crew heads in at 7:30 and crew members at 8. Makes sure props ready.
5. Calls time to the dressing rooms at "Half-hour," "15 minutes," "10 minutes," "5 minutes," and *"Places."* Calls "Places" at 8:28 and makes sure each "Beginner" comes onstage promptly.
6. Takes up asbestos at 8:25.
7. Makes sure lights are ready.
8. *Waits* for go-ahead signal from house manager, also to start Acts II and III. When signal comes:
   a. Checks to be sure all actors in place.
   b. Calls "Worklights out."
   c. Makes sure curtain man in place.
   d. Stage lights and foots up to readings.

e. Cues music or sound (if used).
f. Calls "House out."
g. Calls "Coves out."
h. Cues curtain.
9. Prompts actors if it should be necessary.
10. Cues all lights, sound, music, curtains.
11. Notes time at the end of each act, and follows calling procedure (8) again after 8 minutes of intermission.
12. Worklights on during intermission. No visitors backstage.
13. Runs the curtain calls at end of play, calling for house lights when applause begins to wane.

VII. Property Crew Head.

A. During first weeks of rehearsal:
1. Reads and studies play.
2. Does research if necessary on the period and style of furniture and properties.
3. Confers with the director and technical director or designer.
   a. Obtains a ground plan showing location of all furniture.
   b. Notes whatever comment the director or designer makes concerning the size, style, color, or function of each piece of furniture.
   c. Notes from the designer's color sketch or model the trim props, including pictures, lamps, rugs, bric-a-brac, drapes.
4. Makes up a detailed property list (following sample illustrated) in triplicate; one copy to director, one for check list in gathering, one for check list in setup and shifting during performance. "Source," "date borrowed" and "date returned" need not be shown on the duplicate copies. Divides property list into:

   a. Furniture.
   b. Trim props.
   c. Hand props.
      (1) On stage (indicate where).
      (2) Off stage (indicate who carries it in).
5. After making the list of hand props from reading the play, noting each prop referred to and checking it against list in back of acting edition (if any), checks the list with director to make sure some properties have not been omitted or added.
6. Discusses budget with director and technical director, deciding which items will have to be bought or rented. Obtains purchase order from business manager for items approved for purchase.

B. During later weeks of rehearsal:
1. Organizes property crew. A good-sized crew will make lighter work for all. Finds out:

   a. Which crew members have automobiles.
   b. Which shopping area crew members live near or pass enroute to the theatre.
   c. Which crew members can work property crew during dress rehearsals and performances. (Ideally each crew member who learns a job during dress rehearsal should perform it at every performance. An understudy may be worked in if every prop assigned to the crew member is listed on a detail card.)

(MAKE IN TRIPLICATE)

NAME OF PLAY _____

PROPERTY PLOT

Put these columns
only on Copy 2

ACT I

FURNITURE		Source	Date Borrowed	Date Returned
1. armchair	DR	Mrs. L. E. Green	6/15	6/30
2. card table	DR	from Prop room	--	--
3. bridge lamp	DR	Olson & Brown Hardware	6/10	6/30
4. cabinet	URC	Mr. Johnson	6/11	7/1
5. 2 chairs	UR	recover 2 in Prop Rm.	--	--
6. couch	DRC cut	stock	--	--
7. end table	UR	bring from home	6/11	7/1
8. bookshelves	UL	construct		
9. lamp	UL	Olson & Brown Hardware	6/10	6/30
10. desk, kneehole	DL	rent -- Smith Studios	6/12	7/2
11. sofa	C	stock	--	--
12. hassock	DC	bring from home	6/11	7/1
13. 2 desk chairs	L	stock -- Green Room	--	--

TRIM				
1. drapes, heavy	UR	make -- material in stock	--	--
2. Venetian blinds	UR	Olson & Brown Hardware	6/11	7/1
3. 2 brackets, practical	URC	Olson & Brown Hardware	6/11	7/1
4. mirror, oval	URC	prop room	--	--
5. 2 prints	ULC	use 2 in Mr. S's office	--	--
6. 6 shelves books	ULC	prop room	--	--
7. 2 candlesticks	ULC	prop room	--	--
8. clock, electric	ULC	bring from home	--	--

HAND PROPS				
1. On table	DR			
gloves (Sue's)		actress use her own	--	--
ashtray		prop room	--	--
newspaper		bring from home	--	--
2. On sofa,	C			
raincoat (John's)		actor bring his own	--	--
book		prop room	--	--
newspaper		bring from home	--	--
3. OFF -- UL				
sack of groceries (Sue)		buy		
brief case with contract in it (Doc)		borrow from DR. G.		

2. Begins to farm out props and furniture to members of the crew to locate. Each crew member should volunteer for those items he thinks he can find. The crew head should write down the name of volunteer in pencil in "Source" column and then follow through in a few days to see if the volunteer has located them. Each crew member should be conscious of public relations — he can hurt or help his theatre and school by the way he deals with people.

3. Lists possible sources for finding properties. Tries each of the following sources in priority order before going on to the next one:

   a. The theatre's property room.
   b. Borrowing from private sources, including members of the crew, cast, and friends in the community.
   c. Constructing the property in the scene shop.
   d. Borrowing from merchants, including antique shops, salvage stores, furniture stores, department stores, etc. As an inducement, a credit in the program and complimentary tickets may be promised to cooperating merchants. Turns in list to business manager promptly.
   e. Buying the property, so as to add it to theatre's prop collection. Inexpensive used furniture can be found at such sources as:

      (1) Salvation Army
      (2) Disabled American Veterans
      (3) Veterans Salvage
      (4) Goodwill Industries
      (5) Antique shops
      (6) Junk yards

   f. Renting the property (only as a last resort).
      If an item cannot be found locally, there are rental studios in Hollywood or New York which specialize in hard-to-find items.

4. Begins making trips to locate items from the sources mentioned. Before making a commitment to obtain an item, it is wise to:

   a. Sketch the item and measure it so as to give an accurate description to designer or director. Note color carefully.
   b. Find out the price if purchase or rental being considered.
   c. Discuss dates it will be needed with the merchant.
   d. Find possible alternatives if the item isn't what the director or designer wants.

5. When items are approved by director and designer, returns to merchant or lender to make final arrangements for pickup and delivery; also which night the merchant desires complimentary tickets. Arranges with technical director for school truck to pick up furniture on last school day prior to first technical rehearsal, and to return items on first school day after close of the play.

6. Attends rehearsal when necessary to note placement and use of hand props.

7. Assembles and checks out with director and designer *every* prop and item of furniture or trim prior to first dress rehearsal, at a time to be set in advance.

C. During dress rehearsals:

1. Sets up on stage each item of furniture and trim prior to first light rehearsal. After positions approved by director, assists stage manager

in marking on floor cloth positions of each item of furniture, using different colors for each set.

2. Keeps all borrowed furniture covered during dress rehearsals and week of performance, and all valuable items locked in prop room between performances. Guns are to be kept locked in director's office.
3. Sets up a prop table backstage for all hand props. Sometimes more than one will be necessary, near each entrance through which many props are carried on. Actors should pick up props from prop table and return them there.
4. Prepares special list of actors' hand props which need to be personally checked each night with the actors — things in their pockets, etc.
5. During the setting and rehearsal of prop shifts, prepares a list of duties done by each member of the prop crew.

D. During performances:
1. Sees that all food props are purchased or prepared fresh daily.
2. Checks in no later than 7:30 P.M.
3. Sweeps stage each night.
4. Sets up furniture on its marks and all hand props. Reports to stage manager when all props checked and in place.
5. Makes sure all hand props are laid out and given to actors as necessary.
6. Makes sure crew is in place for shifts.

E. After final performance:
1. Returns all borrowed or rented items the first school day after close of play. Gives merchants a copy of program showing their credit.
2. Turns in to business manager all petty cash slips for items purchased.
3. Prepares on 3 x 5 cards alphabetical catalogue of all difficult props and source where located. Turns in to director.
4. Returns all of theatre-owned props to prop room, sorts out, and leaves prop room neat.

VIII. Stage Crew Head.

A. During rehearsal period:
1. Works under supervision of technical director in constructing and painting sets.
2. Organizes crews and delegates duties to crew members.
3. Keeps shop clean and tools put away.
4. Makes sure that curtain man is designated.

B. During dress rehearsal period:
1. Works under supervision of technical director in setting up scenery and completing final bracing, trim and detail.
2. On plays with more than one set:
   a. Works under supervision of technical director in planning how each flat will shift and where it will store.
   b. Rehearses stage crew members in shifting each set piece at a technical rehearsal prior to first dress rehearsal.
   c. Makes sure scenery shifted back to Act I before each dress rehearsal.

C. During performances:
1. Makes sure set is in place and that nothing has been damaged.
2. Makes sure curtain man on duty.
3. On plays with more than one set:

    a. Makes sure stage crew on duty.

    b. Makes sure storage areas clear prior to a shift.

    c. Makes scene shifts with crew and reports to stage manager immediately when shift is over.

    d. Takes steps to correct any delay, malfunction or fouling of scenery during shifts, or reports problem to technical director.

D. After final performance.

    1. Works under supervision of technical director in striking sets, removing hardware and dutchmen and returning set pieces to storage.

    2. Leaves stage clear and clean for next production.

IX. Sound Crew Head or Operator.

A. During rehearsal period:

    1. Reads play and confers with director, noting each sound cue and how it will be produced; divides all sounds into manual and recorded.

    2. Notes in script whether each sound cue begins and ends definitely or is a "sneak cue."

    3. Attends a rehearsal to check timing of sound cues.

    4. Obtains requisition from business manager for sound effects or musical recordings to be purchased.

    5. Sets time with director for dubbing session to transfer effects to tape.

    6. Checks with director for approval on each manual or recorded sound as found.

    7. For recorded effects, learns operation of sound control console and is checked out prior to first dress rehearsal.

B. During dress rehearsals:

    1. At the dress rehearsal designated by director, runs through sound or music cues, noting in script the volume setting which the director approves for each cue.

    2. Makes copy of master tape as a protection.

C. During performances:

    1. Reports to stage manager by 7:30 P.M. and warms up equipment.

    2. Makes sure crew members are on duty for manual effects.

    3. Takes cues either visually or by intercom from stage manager and runs sound or music effects.

    4. Makes sure equipment turned off and master tape locked in director's office each night after performance.

X. Business Manager.

A. During rehearsal period:

    1. Obtains from director the approved budget, showing amounts allocated for each category of the production.

    2. Prepares requisitions or purchase orders as requested by technical director, costumer, head of props, lights, make-up, sound or publicity crews for approval of appropriate supervisor or faculty member.

    3. Corrects purchase order requests to show actual amount spent when originally issued on an estimate.

    4. Keeps books up to date so that each crew head can know how much money he has spent.

    5. Keeps petty cash fund and turns in slips for refund.

    6. Works in close liaison with associated students' business manager to expedite last-minute purchases as dress rehearsals approach.

7. Makes sure royalty check is issued in ample time to reach play leasing company one week before opening night.

B. After final performance:
1. Tallies up expenditures in each category and prepares final statement on cost of production.
2. Prepares final statement of income from ticket sales.
3. Brings books up to date.

(NOTE: In some organizations the business manager also performs all of the following responsibilities or supervises the crews which perform them.)

XI. Publicity Crew Head.

A. During first weeks of rehearsal:
1. Confers with director on general approach to be used in publicity.
2. Assembles complete cast list with names checked for spelling.
3. Attends a rehearsal and interviews each actor, getting his previous experience, home town and street address as well as other feature material.
4. Assists director in liaison with art department or art student who is to design the poster and mailing piece; furnishes correct dates, curtain time and other information.
5. Prepares newspaper releases for both campus and off-campus newspapers but does not release them until approved by director. Campus newspaper should be given at least four articles:
   a. Release of names of cast.
   b. Feature on backstage activity including names of technical director, designer and backstage crews.
   c. Feature material on play itself and the author.
   d. Information on sale of tickets and recapitulation of previous information prior to opening night.

B. During last weeks of rehearsal:
1. Coordinates planning for newspaper photograph session, making sure that date, time and place are acceptable to photographer, director, costumer, technical director and actors designated for publicity pictures.
2. Brings publicity releases to newspaper photograph session for photographers and assists them in identifying and spelling correctly the name of each actor photographed.
3. Prepares mailing labels to send out publicity brochure or throwaway.
4. Picks up proof of mailing piece at printer's and returns it after it has been approved by director.
5. Picks up mailing pieces at printer's when finished and supervises a crew in pasting labels, folding, stapling, assembling by towns, running through postage meter and taking to post office.
6. Picks up posters when ready and supervises distribution of them on and off campus.
7. Turns in bill for mailers, posters and programs to business manager.
8. Prepares releases for local radio and television stations.
9. Arranges for other campus publicity including announcements on P. A. system in cafeteria, "Burma-shave" type signs, banners, parade of cast in costume, etc.

10. Prepares letters for director's signature to appropriate teachers of English, drama, foreign languages or social studies at various schools in area.
11. Contacts newspaper critics and invites them to opening night, arranging for complimentary tickets.
12. Prepares display cases in lobby of theatre, campus library and elsewhere featuring materials related to the play.
13. Saves clippings of all publicity for scrapbook.
14. Arranges to buy advertising space in off-campus newspapers if necessary.
15. Releases last-minute information to press as to which nights have seats still available.
16. Arranges complimentary tickets for newspaper, radio and TV personnel who have been helpful.

C. After final performance:
1. Takes down all posters and banners on campus.
2. Brings theatre scrapbook up to date by pasting in all clippings, mailing pieces, programs, pictures and reviews of play.

XII. Program Editor.

A. During rehearsal period:
1. Gets sample format from previous program.
2. Obtains names of cast from director and verifies for correct spelling; obtains names of backstage crews from technical director, costumer or director, verifying for correct spelling.
3. Obtains list of coming events with correct dates.
4. Obtains program notes, if applicable, from director.
5. Serves as liaison with program art designer as to cover, size, type, color of ink and paper stock.
6. Types final program copy for approval of director.
7. Obtains credits to be acknowledged for the loan of properties from head of prop crew and leaves space for last-minute additions.
8. Takes copy to printer and arranges to pick up proof.

B. During performance week:
1. Returns corrected proof of program to printer on Monday morning.
2. Arranges to pick up programs no later than printer's closing time on opening night and brings programs to lobby of theatre.
3. Obtains bill from printer and turns it in to business manager.

XIII. Box Office Crew Head.

A. During rehearsal period:
1. Checks with business manager to make sure tickets have been ordered from printer.
2. Arranges personnel to man the box office and schedules their hours.
3. Makes sure there is an adequate supply of all forms used in box office.
4. Racks the tickets, withholding at least two rows for "house seats."
5. Obtains $20.00 change fund in dollars, halves and quarters.
6. Instructs box office personnel in procedure for selling tickets.
7. Obtains assigned number to be punched on student body cards.

B. During period seats are on sale (week before and week of performance as a general rule).
1. Unlocks box office at proper time, checks in ticket seller and verifies amount of money in drawer.

2. Locks box office at proper time, checks out ticket seller and verifies amount of money in drawer.
3. Turns money in to Associated Students' business office, obtaining receipt which is turned over to business manager or director.
4. Contacts the secretary of the college president and deans to determine which night they wish reservations; delivers to them complimentary "house seats."
5. Makes sure seats for the press are held from "house seats."
6. Makes sure ticket reservation pads are placed at all telephones in theatre from which reservations are made when box office closed.
7. Arranges with stage manager for distribution of complimentary tickets to cast and crews according to policy established by director.
8. Advises publicity crew head or director when a night is sold out.
9. Makes sure that everyone handling tickets or reservations understands the policy on holding unpaid reservations.

C. During performances:
1. Opens box office at 7 P.M., making sure sufficient change fund on hand.
2. Attempts to handle patrons as quickly and courteously as possible.
3. After curtain is up, counts unsold seats in rack and assists house manager in doing stub count.
4. Turns money in to business manager or director — no large sums to be left overnight in box office except in the safe.

D. After final performance:
1. Turns in time sheet for payment of all box office personnel.

XIV. House Manager.

A. During rehearsal period:
1. Arranges for sufficient ushers and ticket-takers for each performance (with two stand-bys if possible).
2. Advises ushers as to dress and time for reporting.
3. Memorizes seating plan of theatre and learns from director proper procedure in seating patrons.
4. If clubs are furnishing ushers, advises program editor in time to list the clubs in the program.
5. Advises box office crew head as to number of seats to be set aside for ushers and, if desired, their escorts.
6. Obtains fresh batteries for pen lights.

B. During performances:
1. Arrives no later than 7 P.M., sets up stub boxes, programs and pen lights.
2. When ushers assemble (no later than 7:15 P.M.) shows them room in which to leave wraps and purses, and gives ushers thorough briefing on seating plan and method of seating audience; assigns ushers to each aisle and head of aisles.
3. Sees that house is open, lights on and asbestos down by 7:30 P.M.
4. Seats the audience in efficient and courteous manner.
5. Handles special situations as they arise — doctors who may wish to be on call, wheel chair patrons, people in wrong seats, etc.
6. Looks after heating and comfort of theatre.
7. Gives starting cue to stage manager by intercom telephone as soon after 8:30 P.M. as patrons are seated, seating late-comers according to policy established by director.

8. Before curtain, makes sure exit doors closed and lobby lights turned down.
9. After curtain is up, maintains quiet in lobby; answers lobby telephone.
10. During first act, does stub count and enters totals on box office tally sheet.
11. At each intermission, notes time curtain falls, turn on lobby lights and opens doors. Two minutes before end of intermission, flicks lobby lights or rings chimes to get audience back in.
12. When audience is in, gives starting cue to stage manager, turns off lobby lights and makes sure exit doors closed.
13. Remains on duty in lobby or back row of auditorium throughout play to maintain quiet and deal with emergencies.
14. Makes sure ushers turn in pen lights before leaving, and unlocks room where ushers' wraps and purses are.

LISTS OF RECOMMENDED PLAYS
FOR HIGH SCHOOLS

Recommended Full Length Plays for High Schools

Note: This list is not intended to be exhaustive, but merely suggestive. All of the plays listed have been staged successfully in high schools. Keep the list current by getting on the mailing list of the play-leasing companies which publish catalogues. The principal ones are as follows:

GENERAL:

Code

Samuel French, Inc.   French
7623 Sunset Blvd.
Hollywood 46, Calif.
or 25 W. 45th Street, New York 36

Dramatists Play Service, Inc.   DPS
14 East 38th Street
New York 16, N. Y.

Walter H. Baker Company   Baker
100 Summer Street
Boston 10, Mass.

MUSICALS:

(Some listed by above companies)
Music Theatre International
119 W. 57th St.
New York 19, N. Y.

The Rodgers and Hammerstein
   Repertory
120 E. 56th St.
New York 22, N. Y.

Tams-Witmark Music Library
115-117 West 45th St.
New York, N. Y.

Code

Dramatic Publishing
   Company   Dram PC
179 North Michigan Avenue
Chicago 1, Ill.

Harper and Row, Publishers   H-R
1911 Ridge Avenue
Evanston, Ill.
Pleasanton, Calif.
Elmsford, N. Y.

Banner Play Bureau, Inc.   BPB
619 Post Street
San Francisco 9, Calif.

PLAYS FOR CHILDREN:

The Children's Theatre Press
Cloverlot
Anchorage, Ky.

The Coach House Press
53 West Jackson Blvd.
Chicago, Ill.

Caution: Never announce a copyright play for production until you have received a letter from the authorized agent (usually one of the foregoing companies) giving you specific permission to produce the play. The royalties listed following are variable and may be reduced when groups have a small auditorium and charge little or no admission. $50-$25 means $50.00 royalty for the first performance and $25.00 for succeeding performances, but often a blanket reduction will be given if you write in advance.

Abbreviations: C — Comedy; D — Drama; F — Farce; M — Mystery; T — Tragedy.

SIX OR FEWER CHARACTERS

Play	Author	Type	No. of Characters	Sets	Leasing Company	Royalty
ANGEL STREET	Patrick Hamilton	M	3m, 2w	Int.	French	on app.
ASPERN PAPERS, THE	Michael Redgrave from Henry James' story	M	2m, 4w	Int.	French	$50. - $25.
GLASS MENAGERIE, THE	Tennessee Williams	D	2m, 2w	Int.	DPS	$50. - $25.
PAPA IS ALL	Patterson Greene	C	3m, 3w	Int.	Baker	$35.
PLAYS FOR BLEEKER STREET	Thornton Wilder	3	one-acts		French	Write
ROMANCERS, THE	Edmond Rostand	C	5m, 1w	Arena	French	None
WORLD OF CARL SANDBURG, THE	Norman Corwin	(Reading)	2m, 1w	- - -	French	$50. - $25.

SEVEN CHARACTERS

Play	Author	Type	No. of Characters	Sets	Leasing Company	Royalty
BLITHE SPIRIT	Noel Coward	F	2m, 5w	Int.	French	$50.
BRIEF MUSIC	Emmet Lavery		7w	Int.	French	$25.
HEAVEN CAN WAIT	Harry Segall	C	5m, 2w (extras)	Int. (2 add. sets)	DPS	$25. - $20.
MARRIAGE WHEEL	Joel Climenhaga	C	4m, 3w	Int.	French	$25. - $20.
MR. PIM PASSES BY	A. A. Milne	C	3m, 4w	Int.	French	$50.
RAINMAKER, THE	N. Richard Nash	C	6m, 1w	Comp. set	French	$50.
YES AND NO	Kenneth Horne	C	3m, 4w	Int.	French	$25.
YOU AND I	Philip Barry	C	4m, 3w	Int.	French	$25.

EIGHT CHARACTERS

Play	Author	Type	No. of Characters	Sets	Leasing Company	Royalty
CLAUDIA	Rose Franken	C-D	3m, 5w	Int.	French	$50.
FOOL'S PARADISE	Peter Coke	F	2m, 6w	Int.	French	$35. - $25.
JANE EYRE	Marjorie Carleton	D	3m, 5w	Int.	Baker	$15.
LO AND BEHOLD!	John Patrick	C	5m, 3w	Int.	French	$50.
MISTRESS OF THE INN	Carlo Goldoni	C	5m, 3w	Int.	Longmans	$10.
MOOR BORN	Dan Totheroh	D	3m, 5w	Int.	French	$25.
RELUCTANT DEBUTANTE, THE	William Home	C	3m, 5w	Int.	French	on app.
YOUR UNCLE DUDLEY	Howard Lindsay & Bertrand Robinson	C	4m, 4w	Int.	French	$50.

NINE CHARACTERS

Play	Author	Type	No. of Characters	Sets	Leasing Company	Royalty
FAMILY UPSTAIRS, THE	Harry Delf	C	4m, 5w	Int.	French	$25.
GREEN VALLEY	Frank Wattron	C	5m, 4w (8 extras)		H-R	$10.-$25.
HAROLD	Herman Raucher	C	7m, 2w	Ext.	French	$50.-$25.
HASTY HEART, THE	John Patrick	C-D	8m, 1w	Int.	DPS	$50.-$25.
HAY FEVER	Noel Coward	C	4m, 5w	Int.	French	$50.-$25.
HEIRESS, THE	Ruth & Augustus Goetz	D	3m, 6w	Int.	DPS	$50.-$25.
IMPORTANCE OF BEING EARNEST, THE	Oscar Wilde	C	5m, 4w	1 Ext., 2 Ints.	Baker	none
LATE CHRISTOPHER BEAN, THE	Sidney Howard	C	4w, 5m	Int.	French	$25.
LOUD RED PATRICK, THE	John Boruff	C	4m, 5w	Int. (costumes 1912)	French	on app.
NIGHT MUST FALL	Emlyn Williams	M	4m, 5w	Int.	French	$25.
NINE GIRLS	Wilfrid H. Pettit	M	9w	Int.	Dram PC	$25.
OUTWARD BOUND	Sutton Vane	C-D	6m, 3w	Int.	French	$25.
ROMANTIC AGE, THE	A. A. Milne	C	5m, 4w	Int., Ext.	French	$50.
SEE HOW THEY RUN	Philip King	F	6m, 3w	Int.	French	$25.
STARING MATCH, THE	Jerry McNeely	D	6m, 2w	Int.	French	$25.
SUN-UP	Lula Vollmer	D	2w, 7m (1 girl, extras)	Unit	DPS	$25.
THREE CORNERED MOON	Gertrude Tonkonogy	C-D	5m, 4w	Int.	Longmans	$25.
YEARS AGO	Ruth Gordon	C	4m, 5w	Int.	French	$25.-$50.
YOUNGEST, THE	Philip Barry	C	4m, 5w	Ext., Int.	DPS	$25.

TEN CHARACTERS

Play	Author	Type	No. of Characters	Sets	Leasing Company	Royalty
ALL MY SONS	Arthur Miller	D	6m, 4w	Ext.	DPS	$35.-$25.
BEYOND THE HORIZON	Eugene O'Neill	T	6m, 4w	2 Ext., Int.	DPS	$35.-$25.
BISHOP MISBEHAVES, THE	Frederick Jackson	F	3w, 7m	2 Int.	French	$25.
BROKEN DISHES	Martin Flavin	C	4w, 6m	Int.	French	$25.
BUT NOT GOODBYE	George Seaton	C	8m, 2w	Int.	French	$25.
CHARLEY'S AUNT	Brandon Thomas	F	6m, 4w	Ext., 2 Ints.	French	$25.
CLARENCE	Booth Tarkington	C	5m, 5w	2 Int.	French	$25.

TEN CHARACTERS (Continued)

Play	Author	Type	No. of Characters	Sets	Leasing Company	Royalty
DEAR BRUTUS	J. M. Barrie	D	4m, 6w	Int., Ext.	French	$35. –$25.
DEAR RUTH	Norman Krasna	C	5m, 5w	Int.	Dram PC	$25. –$35.
DIARY OF ANNE FRANK, THE	Goodrich and Hackett	D	5m, 5w	Int.	DPS	$50. –$25.
FOUR DAUGHTERS	Fannie Hurst Story	C	5m, 5w	Int.	Longmans	$25.
GREEN VINE, THE	Nan Bagby Stephens	C	5m, 5w	Int.	H–R	$1. –$25.
HEART TROUBLE	Howard Chenery	C	5m, 5w	Int.	H–R	$1. –$25.
LITTLE WOMEN	John Ravold	D	4m, 6w	Int.	Baker	$10.
MY THREE ANGELS	Sam and Bella Spewack	C	7m, 3w	Int.	DPS	$50. –$25.
PERFECT ALIBI	A. A. Milne	M	7m, 3w	Int.	French	$50.
ROADSIDE	Lynn Riggs	C	8m, 2w	Int., Ext.	French	$25.
SUMMER RASH	Rowena Blake	C	4m, 6w	Int.	Baker	none
TIME OUT FOR GINGER	Ronald Alexander	C	5m, 5w	Int.	DPS	$50. –$25.

ELEVEN CHARACTERS

Play	Author	Type	No. of Characters	Sets	Leasing Company	Royalty
BELVEDERE	Gwen Davenport	C	5m, 4w, 2c	Int.	French	$25.
BROTHER GOOSE	William Davidson	C	3m, 8w	Int.	Dram PC	$25.
CURIOUS SAVAGE, THE	John Patrick	C	5m, 6w	Int.	DPS	$35. –$25.
ESMERALDA	Burnett & Gillette	C	6m, 5w	3 Int.	French	$10.
EVER SINCE EVE	Ryerson & Clements	C	6m, 5w (extras)	Int.	French	$25.
RAISIN IN THE SUN, A	Lorraine Hansberry	D	7m, 3w, 1c	Int.	French	$50. –$25.
ROMANTIC YOUNG LADY, THE	G. Martinez–Sierra	C	5m, 6w	2 Int.	French	$50.
UNCERTAIN WINGS	Robert Hill and					
WINSLOW BOY, THE	Floyd Crutchfield	C	5m, 6w	Int.	French	$25.
	Terence Rattigan	D	7m, 4w	Int.	DPS	$50. –$25.

TWELVE CHARACTERS

Play	Author	Type	No. of Characters	Sets	Leasing Company	Royalty
ADVENTURES OF TOM SAWYER	Charles George	C	6m, 6w	Int.	Dram PC	$10.
ANTIGONE	Jean Anouilh	T	8m, 4w	Int.	French	$25.
BISHOP'S MANTLE	Marion L. Johnson	D	5m, 7w	Int.	Dram PC	$25.
CONNECTICUT YANKEE IN KING ARTHUR'S COURT, A	John G. Fuller	C	6m, 6w	Int.	Baker	$25.

TWELVE CHARACTERS (Continued)

Play	Author	Type	No. of Characters	Sets	Leasing Company	Royalty
DOUBLE DOOR	Elizabeth McFadden	D	7m, 5w	Int.	French	$25.
FAMILY CIRCLE	Anne Coulter Martens	C	5m, 7w	Int.	Dram PC	$25.
GREAT BIG DOORSTEP	Frances Goodrich and Albert Hackett	C	5m, 7w	Ext.	Dram PC	$35.
HARVEY	Mary Chase	C	6m, 6w	2 Int.	Dram PC	$50.-$25.
HE WHO HESITATES	George Savage, Jr., and John McRae	C	5m, 7w	Int.	Eldridge	$10.
ICEBOUND	Owen Davis	D	6w, 5m 1 boy or girl	Int.	Longmans	$25.
IMAGINARY INVALID, THE	Kenneth Turner and Molière	C	8m, 4w	Int.	Dram PC	none
MR. MERGENTHWERKER'S LOBBLIES	Nelson Bond	C	9m, 3w (extras)	2 Int.	French	$35.
OUT OF THE FRYING PAN	Francis Swann	C	7m, 5w	Int.	French	$25.
PYGMALION	George Bernard Shaw	C	6m, 6w	2 Int., 1 Ext.	French	$1.-$25.
SPRING FEVER	Glenn Hughes	F	6m, 6w	Int.	H-R	$25.
SPRING JOURNEY	Mona Graham and John Ware	C	7m, 5w (extras)	Int.	French	$25.
STEPHEN FOSTER	E. H. Smith	C	7m, 5w	Int.	DPS	$10.
WE SHOOK THE FAMILY TREE	Perry Clark	C	7m, 5w	Int.	Dram PC	$25.

THIRTEEN CHARACTERS

Play	Author	Type	No. of Characters	Sets	Leasing Company	Royalty
ALL IN THE FAMILY	Theodore Hatlen	C	7m, 6w	Int.	H-R	$25.
ANASTASIA	Guy Bolton	D	8m, 5w	Int.	French	$50.
DOCTOR IN SPITE OF HIMSELF, THE	Molière, adapted by Barnard Hewitt	F	8m, 5w	3 Ext.	H-R	none
JANE EYRE	Charlotte Bronte, Jane Kendall	D	4m, 9w	Int.	Dram PC	$25.
JANUARY THAW	William Roos	C	7m, 6w	Int.	Dram PC	$35.
JUNE MAD	Florence Ryerson and Colin Clements	C	7m, 6w	Int.	French	$25.
LITTLE SHEPHERD OF KINGDOM COME	Charles George	C-D	5m, 8w	Int.	Baker	$10.

THIRTEEN CHARACTERS (Continued)

Play	Author	Type	No. of Characters	Sets	Leasing Company	Royalty
MR. BARRY'S ETCHINGS	Walter Bullock and Daniel Archer	C	7m, 6w	Int.	DPS	$25.
RIVALS, THE	Richard B. Sheridan	C	7m, 6w	Multiple	Baker	none
SERVANT OF TWO MASTERS, THE	Goldoni, C. (in Eric Bentley, The Classic Theatre)	F	10m, 3w	Exts., Ints.	French	$25.-$20.
SEVEN KEYS TO BALDPATE	George M. Cohan	M	4m, 9w	Int.	French	$25.
SEVEN NUNS AT LAS VEGAS	Natalie White	C	2m, 11w	Int.	DPS	$25.
THAT BREWSTER BOY	Pauline Hopkins	C	6m, 7w	Int.	French	$25.
TWELFTH NIGHT	William Shakespeare	C	3w, 10m	Multiple	French	none

FOURTEEN CHARACTERS

Play	Author	Type	No. of Characters	Sets	Leasing Company	Royalty
CRADLE SONG	G. Martinez–Sierra	D	4m, 10w	2 Ints.	French	$50.
DATE WITH JUDY, A	Aleen Leslie	C	5m, 9w	Int.	Dram PC	$35.
DINNY AND THE WITCHES	William Gibson	C	8m, 6w	Ext.	DPS	$25.
DOG SITTERS, THE	Mary Chase	C	7m, 7w	Int.	DPS	$35.-$25.
EASTWARD IN EDEN	Dorothy Gardner	D	8w, 6m	Int.		
I HAVE FIVE DAUGHTERS	Margaret Macnamara	C	4m, 10w	Int. (extra drop)	Longmans	$25.
AN ITALIAN STRAW HAT	Labiche and Marc–Michel	C	9w, 5m (extras)	4 Int., 1 Ext.	Baker	$15.
JENNY KISSED ME	Jean Kerr	C	4m, 10w	Int.	French	$25.
LOST HORIZON	James Hilton	D	7m, 7w	Int.	DPS	$35.-$25.
MIRACLE WORKER, THE	William Gibson	D	7m, 7w	Unit	Dram PC	$25.
ON BORROWED TIME	Paul Osborn	D	11m, 3w	1 Ext.	French	$50.-$25.
ROLLING HOME	John Hunter Booth	D	4w, 10m	Int.	DPS	$35.-$25.
SABRINA FAIR	Samuel Taylor	D	7m, 7w	Ext.	French	$25.
SENSE AND SENSIBILITY	Jane Kendall	C	5m, 9w	Ext.	DPS	$50.-$25.
SEVEN SISTERS	Edith Ellis	C	6m, 8w	Int.	Dram PC	none
SEVENTEEN	Booth Tarkington	C	6w, 8m	Ext., 2 Int.	French	$25.

FIFTEEN CHARACTERS

Play	Author	Type	No. of Characters	Sets	Leasing Company	Royalty
BERKELEY SQUARE	John L. Balderston	D	7m, 8w	2 Int.	French	$25.
BOURGEOIS GENTLEMAN, THE	Molière	C	11m, 4w (extras)	Int.	Modern Library	on app.
FIGHTING LITTLES, THE	Caroline Francke	C	5m, 10w	Int.	French	$25.
HAPPIEST MILLIONAIRE, THE	Kyle Crichton	C	9m, 6w	Int.	DPS	$50. – $25.
KISS AND TELL	F. Hugh Herbert	C	9m, 6w	Int.	DPS	$35. – $25.
KNOCK, (DR.)	Jules Romains	C	9m, 6w	2 Int., Inset	French	$25. – $20.
LUTE SONG (Chinese)	Adapted by Irwin and Howard	D	9m, 6w	1 basic	Dram PC	$35.
MEN ARE LIKE STREET CARS	G. and S. Lorimer	C	5m, 10w	Int.	Dram PC	$25.
MOTHER IS A FRESHMAN	Perry Clark	C	9w, 6m	Int.	Dram PC	$25.
QUALITY STREET	J. M. Barrie	C	6m, 9w (extras)	2 Int.	French	$35.
RAMSHACKLE INN	George Batson	M	9m, 6w	Int.	DPS	$25.
ROBIN HOOD	Owen Davis	D	10m, 5w	Int., Ext.	French	$25.
STRANGE BOARDERS	George Batson and Jack Kirkland	C-M	8m, 7w	Int.	DPS	$25.
TWELVE ANGRY MEN	Reginald Rose	D	15m or 15w	Int.	Dram PC	$35.

SIXTEEN CHARACTERS

Play	Author	Type	No. of Characters	Sets	Leasing Company	Royalty
CHEAPER BY THE DOZEN	Perry Clark	C	9m, 7w	Int.	Dram PC	$35.
LIFE WITH FATHER	Howard Lindsay and Russel Crouse	C	8m, 8w	Int.	DPS	$50. – $25.
LIFE WITH MOTHER	Howard Lindsay and Russel Crouse	C	8m, 8w	Int.	DPS	$50. – $25.
MEET ME IN ST. LOUIS	Perry Clark	C	8m, 8w	2 Int.	Dram PC	$25.
MATCHMAKER, THE	Thornton Wilder	C	7m, 9w	Int. (cost. 1880)	French	on app.
MIDGIE PURVIS	Mary Chase	F	9m, 7w	3 Int.	DPS	$50. – $25.
MISER, THE	Molière	C	11m, 5w	Int. (costumes)	Modern Library	on app.
PRIDE AND PREJUDICE	Jane Austin	C	5m, 11w	Int.	Dram PC	$25.
YOU CAN'T TAKE IT WITH YOU	Moss Hart and George S. Kaufman	C	9m, 7w (extras)	Int.	DPS	$25.

SEVENTEEN CHARACTERS

Play	Author	Type	No. of Characters	Sets	Leasing Company	Royalty
AND CAME THE SPRING	Marijane and Joseph Hayes	C	9m, 8w	Int.	French	$25.
BACHELOR BORN	Ian Hay	C	11m, 6w	Int.	French	$25.
BARRETTS OF WIMPOLE STREET, THE	Rudolph Besier	D	12m, 5w	Int.	DPS	$50.-$25.
BEST FOOT FORWARD	John Cecil Holm	C	10m, 7w	Int.	Dram PC	$35.
CLOUD SEVEN	Max Wilk	C	9m, 8w	Int.	DPS	$35.-$25.
COMEDY OF ERRORS	William Shakespeare	F	13m, 4w			
DON'T TAKE MY PENNY	Anne Coulter Martens	C	8m, 9w	Int.	Dram PC	$10.
FATHER OF THE BRIDE	Caroline Francke	C	10m, 7w (extras)	Int.	DPS	$35.-$25.
GEORGE WASHINGTON SLEPT HERE	Kaufman & Hart	C	9m, 8w	Int.	DPS	$25.
HARRIET	Ryerson and Clements	C-D	7m, 10w	3 Ints.	French	$50.
JUNIOR MISS	Jerome Chodorov and Joseph Fields	C	11m, 6w	Int.	DPS	$35.-$25.
OFF A PEWTER PLATTER	Robert and Lillian Masters	C	6m, 11w	Int.	French	$25.
ONE FOOT IN HEAVEN	Anne Coulter Martens	C	8m, 9w	Int.	Dram PC	$25.
OUR HEARTS WERE YOUNG AND GAY	Jean Kerr	C	8m, 9w	Int.	Dram PC	
R. U. R.	Karel Capek	D	13m, 4w	2 Ints.	French	$25.
SWAN, THE	Ferenc Molnar	D	9m, 8w (extras)	Int.	Longmans	$25.

EIGHTEEN OR MORE CHARACTERS

Play	Author	Type	No. of Characters	Sets	Leasing Company	Royalty
ABE LINCOLN IN ILLINOIS	Robert M. Sherwood	D	25m, 7w	7 Ints., 3 Ext.	DPS	$25.
ACCIDENTAL HERO	Phyllis Woodruff Sapp	F	12m, 11w		Eldridge	none
ADMIRABLE CRICHTON, THE	J. M. Barrie	C	13m, 12w	Ext., 2 Int.	French	$35.-$25.
ALICE IN WONDERLAND	Charlotte Chorpenning	C	14m, 4w	1 Int., 1 Ext.	Dram PC	$10.-$25.
ALMANAC OF LIBERTY	Reginald Rose	D	11m, 11w	Int.	Dram PC	$35.
ANDROCLES AND THE LION	George Bernard Shaw	C	16m, 2 w	Multiple	Baker	$25.
AS YOU LIKE IT	William Shakespeare	C	16m, 4w	Various		none

EIGHTEEN OR MORE CHARACTERS (Continued)

Play	Author	Type	No. of Characters	Sets	Leasing Company	Royalty
ASK ANY GIRL	Winifred Wolfe	C	5m, 12w (extras)	Int.	Dram PC	$35.
BEGGAR ON HORSEBACK	Connelly & Kaufman	C	16m, 5w	Multiple	French	$50.-$25.
BERNARDINE	Mary Chase	C	13m, 6w	4 Int., 1 Ext.	DPS	$50.-$25.
BOY WITH GREEN HAIR, THE	F. Andrew Leslie	C	16m, 4w	Unit	DPS	$35.-$25.
CRUCIBLE, THE	Arthur Miller	D	10m, 10w	Unit	DPS	$50.-$25.
DAVID COPPERFIELD	John Ravold	D	10m, 9w	Int.	French	$10.
DINO	Reginald Rose	D	7m, 11w		Dram PC	$35.
DISRAELI	Louis N. Parker	D	14m, 6w	Int.	Baker	$25.
FATHER OF THE BRIDE	Caroline Francke	C	11m, 7w			
GOOD MORNING MISS DOVE	William McCleery	D	12m, 10w (extras)	Int.	DPS	$35.-$25.
GROWING PAINS	Aurania Rouverol	C	8m, 10w	6 Insets	French	$35.-$25.
HOOSIER SCHOOLMASTER	Lee Norvelle	C	18m, 8w	Int.	French	$25.
HOUSE OF THE SEVEN GABLES	Wall Spence	D	11m, 11w	Int.	H-R	$1.-$25.
INHERIT THE WIND	Lawrence & Lee	D	21m, 6w	Unit	French	$10.
INSPECTOR GENERAL, THE	Nikolai Gogol	F	19m, 9w	2 Int.	DPS	$50.-$25.
					Baker or French	$15.
I REMEMBER MAMA	John Van Druten	C	9m, 13w	1 Int.	DPS	$25.
JOHN BROWN'S BODY	Stephen Vincent Benet	(Reading)	Variable		DPS	$50.-$25.
A KISS FOR CINDERELLA	J. M. Barrie	C	11m, 10w (extras)		French	$50.-$25.
LADIES OF THE JURY	Fred Ballard	C	12m, 10w	4 Int., Ext.	French	$35.
LILIOM	Ferenc Molnar	D	17m, 5w	2 Int.	French	$50.
MADWOMAN OF CHAILLOT, THE	Jean Giraudoux	C	17m, 8w	1 Int., 4 Ext.	French	$25.
MAN WHO CAME TO DINNER, THE	Moss Hart and George S. Kaufman	C	15m, 9w (extras)	1 Int., 1 Ext.	DPS	$50.-$25.
"ME, CANDIDO!"	Walt Anderson	C-D	9m, 8w	Int.	DPS	$25.
A MIDSUMMER NIGHT'S DREAM	William Shakespeare	C	11m, 10w	Unit	DPS	$35.-$25.
NIGHT OF JANUARY 16	Ayn Rand	C-M	11m, 10w (extras)	Multiple		none
1984 (GEORGE ORWELL)	Owens & Miles	D	6m, 14w	Int.	Baker	$10.
				Int.	Dram PC	$35.

EIGHTEEN OR MORE CHARACTERS (Continued)

Play	Author	Type	No. of Characters	Sets	Leasing Company	Royalty
NO MORE FRONTIER	Talbot Jennings	D	27m, 5w	3 Int.	French	$25.
ONIONS IN THE STEW	Betty McDonald	C	7m, 11w (extras)	Int.	Dram PC	$35.
OUR AMERICAN COUSIN	Tom Taylor	C	12m, 6w	Int.	Dram PC	$35.
OUR TOWN	Thornton Wilder	D	17m, 7w	Bare	French	$25.
PRIDE AND PREJUDICE	Mrs. Steele MacKaye	C	10m, 10w	3 Int., Ext.	French	$25.
PROLOGUE TO GLORY	E. P. Conkle	D	14m, 7w (extras)	Int.	French	$25.
REBEL WITHOUT A CAUSE	from film	D	12m, 10w	Bare	Dram PC	$35.
REMARKABLE INCIDENT AT CAR- SON CORNERS, THE	Reginald Rose	D	13m, 13w	Int.	Dram PC	$25.
REMEMBER THE DAY	Higley and Dunning	D	13m, 12w	simple	H-R	$25.-$10.
SHE STOOPS TO CONQUER	Oliver Goldsmith	C	15m, 4w	2 Int., Ext.	Baker	none
SKIN OF OUR TEETH, THE	Thornton Wilder	D	5m, 5w (extras)	1 Int., 1 Ext.	French	$50.-$25.
STAGE DOOR	Edna Ferber and George S. Kaufman	C	11m, 21w	2 Int.	DPS	$25.
THAT'S MY COUSIN	Kurtz Gordon	C	8m, 10w (extras)	Int.	DPS	$25.
TAMING OF THE SHREW, THE	William Shakespeare	C	18m, 6w	7 scenes		none
TEAHOUSE OF THE AUGUST MOON	John Patrick	C	18m, 8w 3 ch., 1 goat	Int., Ext.	DPS	$50.-$25.
WARRIOR'S HUSBAND, THE	Julian Thompson	C	8m, 13w	Int., 2 Exts.	French	$25.
WHAT A LIFE	Clifford Goldsmith	C	8m, 10w (extras)	Int.	DPS	$25.
WONDERFUL ADVENTURES OF DON QUIXOTE	Conrad Seiler	C	12m, 10w	Exts.	DPS	$25.
YELLOW JACK	Sidney Howard	D	26m, 1w	Unit	DPS	$25.

SOME RECOMMENDED ONE-ACT PLAYS FOR HIGH SCHOOL

Play	Author	Type	No. of Characters	Sets	Leasing Company	Royalty
AFFECTED YOUNG LADIES, THE	Molière	C	6m, 3w	Int.	French	none
ANTIC SPRING	Robert Nail	C	3m, 3w	None	French	$5.
APOLLO OF BELLAC, THE	Giraudoux	C	9m, 3w	Int.	French	$25.

SOME RECOMMENDED ONE-ACT PLAYS FOR HIGH SCHOOL (Continued)

Play	Author	Type	No. of Characters	Sets	Leasing Company	Royalty
BALCONY SCENE	Donald Elser	D	4m, 4w	Int.	H-R	$5.
BISHOP'S CANDLESTICKS, THE	N. McKinnel from Victor Hugo	D	3m, 2w	Int.	French	$5.
BLOOD OF THE MARTYRS	Percival Wilde	D	15m, 2w	Int.	Baker	$10.
BOOR, THE	Chekhov	C	2m, 1w	Int.	French	none
BOX AND COX	J. M. Morton	F	2m, 1w	Int.	French	none
BOY ABE, THE	Betty Smith	C	6m, 6w	Int.	Baker	none
CASE OF THE CRUSHED PETUNIAS	Tennessee Williams	C	2m, 2w	Int.	DPS	$10.
CHINA-HANDLED KNIFE, A	E. P. Conkle	C	6m, 4w	Int.	Baker	$5.
CUP OF TEA, A	Katherine Mansfield	D	2m, 4w	Int.	Dram PC	$10. or $5. #
DANCERS, THE	Horton Foote	D	3m, 7w	Ints.	DPS	$15.
DARK RIDER	Robert Finch	D	6m	Int.	H-R	$5.
DEAR DEPARTED, THE	Stanley Houghton	C	3m, 3w	Int.	French	$5.
DESERT SHALL REJOICE, THE	Robert Finch	D (Xmas)	7m, 2w	Int.	French	$5.
DEVIL AND DANIEL WEBSTER, THE	Stephen V. Benet	C	6m, 1w (extras)	Int.	DPS	$5.
DUST OF THE ROAD	Kenneth S. Goodman	D (Xmas)	3m, 1w	Int.	Baker	$5.
DUST IN YOUR EYES	Labiche & Martin	C	7m, 6w	2 Ints.	DPS	$10. or $5. #
EVERYMAN	Anonymous	D	11m, 6w	Int.	French	$25. -$15.
FIFTEENTH CANDLE, THE	Rachel Field	D	2m, 3w	Int.	French	none
FEATHERTOP	Nathaniel Hawthorne	D	7m, 3w	Unit	DPS	$5.
FIXIN'S	Erma and Paul Green	D	2m, 1w	Int.	French	$10.
FLATTERING WORD, THE	George Kelly	C	2m, 3w	Int.	French	$5.
FLORIST SHOP, THE	Winifred Hawkridge	C	3m, 2w	Int.	Baker	$10.
FOUR ON A HEATH	Foster Fitz-Simons	D	4m	Ext.	H-R	$10.
GAME OF CHESS, THE	Kenneth S. Goodman	D	4m	Int.	Baker	$5.
GIANTS' STAIR, THE	Wilbur Daniel Steele	D	2m, 2w	Int.	French	$5.
GRENACHIKA	Merle B. Young	C	2m, 1w	Int.	H-R	$5.

SOME RECOMMENDED ONE-ACT PLAYS FOR HIGH SCHOOL (Continued)

Play	Author	Type	No. of Characters	Sets	Leasing Company	Royalty
HAPPY JOURNEY TO CAMDEN AND TRENTON, THE	Thornton Wilder	C	3m, 3w	None	French	$10.
HEAT LIGHTNING	Robert F. Carroll	D	2m, 1w	Int.	French	$5.
HERITAGE OF WIMPOLE STREET	Robert Knipe	D	1m, 3w 1 boy			
HIGH WINDOW	Verne Powers	D	2m, 3w	Int.	Baker	$5.
HYACINTH HALVEY	Lady Gregory	C	3m, 2w	Int.	H-R	$5.
'ILE	Eugene O'Neill	D	5m, 1w	Ext.	French	$5.
I'M A FOOL	Sherwood Anderson	C	4m, 4w	Int.	DPS	$5.
IN THE SUDS	Medieval French	F	1m, 2w	Int.	Dram PC	$10. or $5. #
IN THE ZONE	Eugene O'Neill	D	9m	Int.	H-R	none*
INFANTA	L. Olfson from Wilde	D	2m, 3w	Int.	DPS	$5.
JUST WOMEN	Colin Clements	C	7w	Int.	H-R	none*
LADIES ALONE	Ryerson and Clements	C	3w	Int.	French	none
LADY OF THE MARKET PLACE	Charlotte I. Lee	D (Xmas)	3m, 14w	Ext.	French	$5.
LAST OF THE LOWRIES, THE	Paul Green	D	1m, 3w	Int.	H-R	none*
LAST TRIP OUT	Walter Hackett	T	2m, 5w	Int.	French	$5.
LAWYER LINCOLN	Chase Webb and B. Smith	C	4m, 5w	Int.	Baker	$5.
LITTLE FATHER OF THE WILDERNESS, THE	A. Strong and Lloyd Osbourne	D	6m, 1w	Int.	H-R	$5.
LONG CHRISTMAS DINNER, THE	Thornton Wilder	D	5m, 7w	Int.	French	$10.
LOST ELEVATOR, THE	Percival Wilde	C	6m, 5w	Int.	French	$10.
LOVE AND HOW TO CURE IT	Thornton Wilder	C	2m, 2w	Bare Stage	French	$10.
MAID OF DOMREMY, THE	Joe Corrie	D	4m, 3w	Int.	Baker	$5.
MAN IN THE BOWLER HAT, THE	A. A. Milne	C	4m, 2w	Int.	Baker	$10.
MAN WHO DIED AT TWELVE O'CLOCK	Paul Green	F	2m, 1w	Int.	French	$5.
MAN WHO MARRIED A DUMB WIFE	Anatole France	F	7m, 3w	Int.	French	$25.

SOME RECOMMENDED ONE-ACT PLAYS FOR HIGH SCHOOL (Continued)

Play	Author	Type	No. of Characters	Sets	Leasing Company	Royalty
MARRIAGE PROPOSAL, A	Chekhov	F	2m, 1w	Int.	Baker	none
MASTER PIERRE PATHELIN	Medieval French	F	5m, 1w	Multiple	—**	
MINOR MIRACLE	Verne Powers	D	4m	Raft	H-R	$10. or $5. #
MINUET, A	Louis N. Parker	D	2m, 1w	Int.	French	$10.
MONKEY'S PAW, THE	W. W. Jacobs and L. Parker	M	4m, 1w	Int.	French	$10.
NIGHT AT AN INN, A	Lord Dunsany	M	8m	Int.	Baker	$10.
NINE DAYS QUEEN, A	Rachel Field	D	5m, 2w	Int.	French	$5.
NO 'COUNT BOY, THE	Paul Green	C	2m, 2w	Ext.	French	$5.
ONE EGG	Babette Hughes	F	2m, 1w	Int.	French	$5.
PASSING OF CHOW CHOW, THE	Elmer Rice	C	2m, 1w	Int.	French	$10.
PEPPER AND SAND	Emlyn Williams	C	1m, 1w	Int.	Baker	$5.
PINK AND PATCHES	Margaret Bland	C	1m, 3w	Ext.	French	$10.
POOR AUBREY	George Kelly	C	1m, 3w	Int.	Baker	$10.
PURPLE DOORKNOB, THE	Walter P. Eaton	C	3w	Int.	French	$5.
QUEENS OF FRANCE	Thornton Wilder	C	1m, 3w	Int.	French	$10.
RED VELVET GOAT, THE	Josephina Niggli	C	4m, 5w (extras)	Int.	French	$10.
RIDERS TO THE SEA	John M. Synge	T	1m, 3w	Ext.	French	$5.
RISING OF THE MOON, THE	Lady Gregory	D	4m	Ext.	Baker	$10.
ROMANCE OF THE WILLOW PATTERN	Ethel Van Der Veer	C	3m, 1w	Chinese	French	$5.
SAY IT WITH FLOWERS	Ada K. Runner	C	9w	Int.	French	$5.
SECOND SHEPHERD'S PLAY	Medieval	C (Xmas)			French	none
SIRE DE MALETROIT'S DOOR, THE	L. Langner from Stevenson	D	4m, 3w 3m, 1w (extras)	Multiple		
SO WONDERFUL (IN WHITE)	N. Richard Nusbaum	D	9w	Int.	French	$10.
SOLDADERA	Josephina Niggli	D	1m, 7w	Ext.	French	$5.
SORRY, WRONG NUMBER	Lucille Fletcher	D	3m, 4w	Int.	DPS	$10.

SOME RECOMMENDED ONE-ACT PLAYS FOR HIGH SCHOOL (Continued)

Play	Author	Type	No. of Characters	Sets	Leasing Company	Royalty
SPARKIN'	E. P. Conkle	C	1m, 3w	Int.	French	$5.
SPECIAL GUEST	Donald Elser	D	3m, 2w	Int.	H-R	$5.
SPREADING THE NEWS	Lady Gregory	C	7m, 3w	Ext.	French	$5.
STRONGER SEX, THE	Conrad Seiler	C	3m, 2w	None	DPS	$10.
SUBWAY CIRCUS	William Saroyan	C	Variable	Multiple	French	$10.
SUGAR AND SPICE	Ryerson and Clements	C	2m, 3w	Int.	French	$5.
SUMMER COMES TO THE DIAMOND O	Robert Finch	C	8m	Int.	H-R	$5.
SUNDAY COSTS FIVE PESOS	Josephina Niggli	C	1m, 4w	Ext.	French	$5.
TOOTH OR SHAVE	Josephina Niggli	C	2m, 2w	Ext.	French	$5.
TRIFLES	Susan Glaspell	D	3m, 2w	Int.	Baker	$10.
TRYSTING PLACE, THE	Booth Tarkington	C	4m, 3w	Int.	French	$10.
TWELVE POUND LOOK, THE	James M. Barrie	C	2m, 2w	Int.	Baker	$10.
WHAT'S WRONG WITH THE GIRLS	Conrad Seiler	C	4m, 3w	None	DPS	$10.
WHERE THE CROSS IS MADE	Eugene O'Neill	T	6m, 1w	Int.	DPS	$5.
WHY I AM A BACHELOR	Conrad Seiler	F	2m, 4w	None	DPS	$5.
WHY THE CHIMES RANG	Elizabeth McFadden	D	3m, 1w (extras)	Multiple	French	$5.
WONDER HAT, THE	Kenneth S. Goodman	C	3m, 2w	Ext.	French	$10. or $5.
WURZEL-FLUMMERY	A. A. Milne	C	3m, 2w	Int.	French	$10.
YOUNG LADY OF PROPERTY, A	Horton Foote	D	3m, 6w	Multiple	DPS	$15.
YOUNG MAN'S FANCY	Hilda Manning	C	3m, 3w	Int.	French	$5.

Anthologies of One-Act Plays

A Suggested List for Junior High Schools and High Schools

ARBUTHNOT, MAY H. *Time for Fairy Tales Old and New.* Scott, Foresman and Co., 1952.

BARROWS, MARJORIE WESCOTT. *Drama I.* New York: Macmillan Co., 1962.

BRINGS, LAWRENCE M. *The Golden Book of Christmas Plays.* Minneapolis: T. S. Denison & Co., 1962.

BULLARD, CATHARINE. *One-Act Plays for Junior High School.* New York: Henry Holt & Co., 1937.

BURACK, A. S. *Christmas Plays for Young Actors.* Boston: Plays, Inc., 1950.

————. *One Hundred Plays for Children.* Boston: Plays, Inc., 1949.

————. *A Treasury of Holiday Plays for Teen-agers.* Boston: Plays, Inc., 1963.

CERF, BENNETT, AND CARTMELL, VAN H. *Thirty Famous One-Act Plays.* Modern Library, 1949.

————. *24 Favorite One-Act Plays.* Doubleday, 1959.

DuBOIS, GRAHAM. *Plays for Great Occasions.* Boston: Plays, Inc., 1951.

FENNER, PHYLLIS, AND HUGHES, AVAH. *Entrances & Exits: A Book of Plays for Young Actors.* New York: Dodd, Mead & Co., 1960.

FISHER, AILEEN. *Health and Safety Plays and Programs.* Boston: Plays, Inc., 1953.

————. *Christmas Plays and Programs.* Boston: Plays, Inc., 1960.

————, AND RABE, OLIVE. *Patriotic Plays and Programs.* Boston: Plays, Inc., 1956.

GRIFFITH, FRANCIS, AND MERSAND, JOSEPH. *Modern One-Act Plays.* New York: Harcourt Brace & Co., 1950.

HACKETT, WALTER. *Radio Plays for Young People.* Boston: Plays, Inc., 1950.

HARK, MILDRED, AND McQUEEN, NOEL. *Twenty-Five Plays for Holidays.* Boston: Plays, Inc., 1952.

————. *Modern Comedies for Young Players.* Boston: Plays, Inc., 1951.

————. *Special Plays for Special Days.* Boston: Plays, Inc., 1947.

HOWARD, VERNON. *Short Plays From the Great Classics* (for young actors and actresses). New York: Sterling Pub. Co., 1960.

KAMERMAN, SYLVIA E. *A Treasury of Christmas Plays.* Boston: Plays, Inc., 1958.

KISSEN, FAN. *The Bag of Fire.* Houghton Mifflin Co., 1949.

————. *The Straw Ox.* Houghton Mifflin Co., 1948.

KONICK, MARCUS. *Plays for Modern Youth.* New York: Globe Book Co., 1961.

KOZLENKO, WILLIAM. *One Hundred Non-Royalty One-Act Plays.* New York: Grosset & Dunlap, 1940.

LEVERTON, GARRETT H. *On The Air.* New York: Samuel French, 1944.

MAYORGA, MARGARET. *Twenty Short Plays on a Royalty Holiday,* 3 Vols. New York: Samuel French, 1940, 1943, 1950.

MILLER, HELEN L. *Holiday Plays for Teen-Agers.* Boston: Plays, Inc., 1952.

————. *On Stage for Teen-Agers.* Boston: Plays, Inc., 1950.

————. *Easy Plays for Boys and Girls.* Boston: Plays, Inc., 1963.

————. *Plays for Living and Learning.* Boston: Plays, Inc., 1955.

MOSES, MONTROSE J. *A Treasury of Plays for Children.* Boston: Little, Brown and Co., 1924.

NAGELBERG, M. M. *Drama in Our Time.* New York: Harcourt Brace & Co., 1948.

NOLAN, PAUL T. *Round-The-World Plays for Young People.* Boston: Plays, Inc., 1961.

PARADIS, MARJORIE B. *One-Act Plays for All-Girl Casts.* Boston: Plays, Inc., 1952.

PHILIPS, EDITH M. *Book and Library Plays,* 2 Vols. H. W. Wilson Co., 1939 and 1941.

Plays: The Drama Magazine for Young People. Boston: Plays, Inc., 8 Arlington St.

Plays for Living. Family Service Association of America, 44 E. 23rd St., New York.

POWERS, VERNE E. *Plays for Players and a Guide to Play Production*. Evanston, Ill., Row Peterson Co., 1957.

PRICE, OLIVE. *Plays of Far Places*. Boston: Baker's Plays, 1936.

RICHMOND, SAMUEL S. *Career Plays for Young People*. Boston: Plays, Inc., 1949.

SHAY, FRANK. *Fifty More Contemporary One-Act Plays*. New York: D. Appleton and Co., 1928.

SMITH, BETTY, and others. *A Treasury of Non-Royalty One-Act Plays*. Garden City, N. Y.: Garden City Books, 1945.

SPER, FELIX. *Modern Short Plays*. New York: Globe Book Company, 1952.

STEVENSON, AUGUSTA. *The Black Pearl and Other Plays*. Boston: Houghton Mifflin Co., 1940.

WEBBER, JAMES, AND WEBSTER, HANSON. *One-Act Plays for Secondary Schools*. Boston: Houghton Mifflin, 1923.

WOOLSEY, JANETTE, AND SECHRIST, ELIZABETH. *It's Time to Give a Play*. Philadelphia: Macrae Smith Company, 1955.

ZACHAR, IRWIN J. (Ed.) *Plays As Experience*: *One-Act Plays for the Secondary School*. New York: Odyssey Press, 1962.

LIST OF RECORDINGS FOR TEACHING VOICE, SPEECH AND DIALECTS

List of Recordings for Teaching Voice, Speech and Dialects

Author	Title	Record Label
Albee, Edward	WHO'S AFRAID OF VIRGINIA WOOLF?	Columbia DOL 287
ANTA Albums of Stars:	Great Moments from Great Plays Vol. 1 VICTORIA REGINA, Helen Hayes YEARS AGO, Frederick March, Florence Eldridge THE SKIN OF OUR TEETH, March and Eldridge HEDDA GABLER, Eva LeGallienne, Philip Bourneuf KING RICHARD II, John Gielgud	Decca DL 9002
	Vol. 2. THE BARRETTS OF WIMPOLE STREET, Katharine Cornell, Brian Ahern THE FARMER TAKES A WIFE, Henry Fonda, Julie Harris THE SEAGULL, Edith Evans, Torin Thatcher THE LITTLE FOXES, Tallulah Bankhead, Kent Smith	Decca DL 9009
Art of Ruth Draper		RCA Victor LM 1859
Beckett	WAITING FOR GODOT, Bert Lahr, E. G. Marshall	Columbia 02L 238
Benet	JOHN BROWN'S BODY, Tyrone Power, Judith Anderson, Raymond Massey	Columbia OSL 181
Besier	THE BARRETTS OF WIMPOLE STREET, Katharine Cornell, Anthony Quayle	Caedmon TC 1071
Chekhov	UNCLE VANYA, Sir Laurence Olivier	Philips, 640
Coward	PRIVATE LIVES, TONIGHT AT 8:30, Noel Coward, Gertrude Lawrence	RCA Victor LCT 1156
Coward	NOEL COWARD DUOLOGUES, (BRIEF ENCOUNTER, BLITHE SPIRIT), Noel Coward, Margaret Leighton	Caedmon TC 1069

Author	Title	Record Label
Eighteenth century comedy	THE SCHOOL FOR SCANDAL, THE RIVALS, THE BEAUX STRATEGM, THE WAY OF THE WORLD, Edith Evans, John Gielgud	Angel, 35213
Eliot	THE COCKTAIL PARTY, Alec Guiness, Cathleen Nesbit	Decca DX 100
Eliot	MURDER IN THE CATHEDRAL, Robert Donat and Old Vic Co.	Angel 35043-4
Fletcher	SORRY, WRONG NUMBER, Agnes Moorehead	Decca DL 9062
Fry	THE LADY'S NOT FOR BURNING, John Gielgud, Pamela Brown	Decca DX 110
Ibsen	HEDDA GABLER, Eva LeGallienne	Theatre Masterworks GRC 861
Jeffers	MEDEA, Judith Anderson	Decca DL 9000
Levitt	THE ANDERSONVILLE TRIAL, Albert Dekker, Herbert Berghof	20 Cent. Fox S4000
Marlowe	THE TRAGICAL HISTORY OF THE LIFE AND DEATH OF DR. FAUSTUS, Frank Silvera and cast	Caedmon TC 1033
McLeish	J. B.	RCA Victor LD 6075
Miller	DEATH OF A SALESMAN, Thomas Mitchell, Mildred Dunnock, Arthur Kennedy and cast	Decca DX 102
O'Casey	JUNO AND THE PAYCOCK, Siobhan McKenna and cast	Angel 3540
O'Casey	PICTURES IN THE HALLWAY	Riverside 7006-7
O'Neill	STRANGE INTERLUDE	Columbia DOL 238
Rostand	CYRANO DE BERGERAC, Jose Ferrer and cast	Capitol 5283
Sartre	NO EXIT, Betty Field and cast	Riverside RLP 7004-5
Shakespeare	THE AGES OF MAN, John Gielgud	Columbia OL 5390
Shakespeare	Styles in Shakespearean Acting, 1890-1950	(tape) AETA, Michigan State Univ
Shakespeare	AS YOU LIKE IT, Dublin Gate Production	Spoken Word SWA 4
Shakespeare	HAMLET, John Gielgud and Old Vic Company	Victor 6404
Shakespeare	HAMLET, Maurice Evans	Columbia Masterworks, M 340
Shakespeare	HAMLET, Laurence Olivier and cast	RCA Victor LCT 5
Shakespeare	HAMLET, Paul Scofield, Diana Wynyard. Shakespeare Recording Society	Caedmon, SR 232

Author	Title	Record Label
Shakespeare	KING HENRY VIII, Dame Sybil Thorndike, Sir Lewis Casson and cast	London LL 578
Shakespeare	JULIUS CAESAR, Orson Welles and Mercury Theatre	Columbia Entre EL 52
Shakespeare	JULIUS CAESAR, Marlowe Society	London A 4334
Shakespeare	KING HENRY V, Laurence Olivier	RCA Victor LM 1924
Shakespeare	KING RICHARD II, Maurice Evans and cast	Columbia RL 3107
Shakespeare	KING RICHARD II, Shakespeare Memorial Theatre Festival Company	Memorial Theatre Series BA 3
Shakespeare	KING RICHARD III, Sir Laurence Olivier, film sound track	RCA Victor LM 1940
Shakespeare	KING RICHARD III, John Gielgud, Laurence Olivier, Sir Cedric Hardwick and cast	Victor LM 6126
Shakespeare	MACBETH, Marlowe Society Professional Players	London A 4343
Shakespeare	MACBETH, Alec Guiness, Pamela Brown and Old Vic Company	Victor LM 6010
Shakespeare	MACBETH, Living Shakespeare, Inc.	N8OY 8835
Shakespeare	MERRY WIVES OF WINDSOR, Stratford Memorial Theatre Festival Company	Memorial Theatre Series BA 1
Shakespeare	A MIDSUMMER NIGHT'S DREAM, Old Vic Company	RCA Victor LM 1863
Shakespeare	MUCH ADO ABOUT NOTHING, Rex Harrison, Rachel Roberts	Shakespeare Recording Society 206
Shakespeare	OTHELLO, Paul Robeson, Jose Ferrer and cast	Columbia SL 153
Shakespeare	ROMEO AND JULIET, Claire Bloom, Alan Badel and Old Vic Company	Victor LM 2064
Shakespeare	ROMEO AND JULIET, Eva LeGallienne and cast	Atlantic 401
Shakespeare	THE TEMPEST, Raymond Massey and cast	Polymusic 3001-2
Shakespeare	THE TEMPEST, Stratford Memorial Theatre Festival Company	Memorial Theatre Series BA 2
Shakespeare	TWELFTH NIGHT, Siobhan McKenna, John Neville, Paul Scofield. Shakespeare Recording Society.	Caedmon SRS 213
Shaw	THE APPLE CART, Noel Coward and Margaret Leighton	Caedmon TC 1094
Shaw	DON JUAN IN HELL, Charles Laughton, Agnes Moorehead, Charles Boyer, Sir Cedric Hardwick	Columbia SL 166
Shaw	SAINT JOAN, Siobhan McKenna and cast	RCA Victor LOC 6133

Author	Title	Record Label
Sheridan	THE RIVALS, Dame Edith Evans, Pamela Brown, Michael MacLiammoir	Caedmon TC 2020
Sheridan	THE SCHOOL FOR SCANDAL, Dame Edith Evans, Claire Bloom and cast	Angel 35292
Sophocles	OEDIPUS REX, Douglas Campbell and cast	Caedmon TC 2012
Sophocles	OEDIPUS REX	Harry Partch Trust Fund
Sophocles	OEDIPUS REX, Amherst College Students	Folkways 9862
Sophocles	ANTIGONE, McGill University Students	Folkways 9861
Synge	THE PLAYBOY OF THE WESTERN WORLD, Cyril Cusack, Siobhan McKenna and cast	Angel 3547
Synge	RIDERS TO THE SEA and IN THE SHADOW OF THE GLEN, Radio Eireann Productions	Spoken Arts 743
Thomas	UNDER MILK WOOD, Richard Burton, Hugh Griffith	Westminster Argo WN 2202 RG 21
	WELLSPRINGS OF DRAMA, THE (Medieval Religious Drama)	Caedmon
	Vol. 1 QUEM QUAERITIS, NOAH, ROBIN HOOD, ABRAHAM AND ISAAC	TC 1030
	Vol. 2 EVERYMAN, Burgess Meredith and cast	TC 1031
	Vol. 3 SECOND SHEPHERD'S PLAY, RALPH ROISTER DOISTER, GAMMER GURTON'S NEEDLE, A MERRY PLAY	TC 1032
	Vol. 4 DR. FAUSTUS	TC 1033
Wilde	THE IMPORTANCE OF BEING EARNEST, John Gielgud, Dame Edith Evans, Pamela Brown and cast	Angel 3504B
	THE IMPORTANCE OF BEING EARNEST, Margaret Rutherford, John Gielgud	Decca DU 90012 A
Tennessee Williams,	THE GLASS MENAGERIE, Montgomery Clift, Julie Harris, Jessica Tandy, David Wayne	Theatre Recording Society
Yeats	THE COUNTESS CATHLEEN, Siobhan McKenna and cast	Tradition TLP 501

RECORDINGS FOR THE STUDY OF DIALECTS

	ACCENT ON ACCENTS, No. 1, Gertrude Walsh, Ed.	Alcone, ST 281
British	BRITISH DRAMA LEAGUE recordings, including Cockney, Welsh, Yorkshire, Sussex, Scottish border.	Linguaphone Institute, 30 Rockefeller Plaza, New York 20

Author	Title	Record Label
	NOEL COWARD DUOLOGUES	Caedmon TC 1069
	ENGLISH DIALECT RECORDING, Wallace House	Folkways 33 FP 99
Cockney	NOEL AND GERTIE	RCA Victor LCT 1156
Irish	SEAN O'CASEY READING FROM HIS WORK	Caedmon TC 1012
	RIDERS TO THE SEA and IN THE SHADOW OF THE GLEN, Radio Eireann Players	Spoken Arts 743
Scottish	SCOTS BORDER BALLADS, George S. Emmerson	Thomas Tenney Records TC 1001
	SONGS AND POEMS OF ROBERT BURNS, spoken by Ian Gilmour and Meta Forrest	Angel 35256
Southern	PAUL GREEN READING FROM IN ABRAHAM'S BOSOM AND ROLL SWEET CHARIOT	Spoken Arts 719, West-minster XTV 25173
	WILLIAM FAULKNER READING FROM HIS WORKS	MGM E3617 ARC
Welsh	DYLAN THOMAS READING FROM HIS POETRY	Caedmon TC 2006 B

SCENES AND EXERCISES

THE TEMPEST
William Shakespeare

Act V, Scene I
(John Gielgud, The Ages of Man, Columbia OL 5390)

PROSPERO: Ye elves of hills, brooks, standing lakes and groves,
                 And ye that on the sands with printless foot
                 Do chase the ebbing Neptune and do fly him
                 When he comes back; you demi-puppets that
                 By moonshine do the green sour ringlets make,
                 Whereof the ewe not bites, and you whose pastime
                 Is to make midnight mushrooms, that rejoice
                 To hear the solemn curfew; by whose aid,
                 Weak masters though ye be, I have bedimm'd
                 The noontide sun, call'd forth the mutinous winds,
                 And 'twixt the green sea and the azured vault
                 Set roaring war: to the dread rattling thunder
                 Have I given fire and rifted Jove's stout oak
                 With his own bolt; the strong-based promontory
                 Have I made shake and by the spurs pluck'd up
                 The pine and cedar: graves at my command
                 Have walked their sleepers, op'd, and let 'em forth
                 By my so potent art. But this rough magic
                 I here abjure; and, when I have required
                 Some heavenly music, which even now I do,
                 To work mine end upon their senses that
                 This airy charm is for, I'll break my staff,
                 Bury it certain fathoms in the earth,
                 And deeper than did ever plummet sound
                 I'll drown my book.

HEDDA GABLER
by
Henrik Ibsen

Act II
(Eva LeGallienne, ANTA Album #1, Decca DL 9002)

BRACK: What was that you said about a hat?
HEDDA: Oh, it was something that happened this morning. Miss Tesman took off her hat and put it down there on the table and I pretended to think it was the servant's.

BRACK: Why, my dear Mrs. Hedda, how could you do such a thing to that nice old lady?

HEDDA: My dear Judge, I really don't know — I suddenly get impulses like that, and I simply can't control them; I don't know how to explain it myself.

BRACK: You're not really happy — I think that's the explanation.

HEDDA: I can't imagine why I should be — happy. Can you tell me?

BRACK: Well, to begin with, you are in the very house you always longed to live in.

HEDDA: Oh, you believe in that fairy tale?

BRACK: Fairy tale? Wasn't it true then?

HEDDA: I'll tell you how that happened. You see, last summer I made use of Tesman to see me home from parties.

BRACK: Yes, unfortunately my way lay in a different direction.

HEDDA: Yes, you were going in a different direction then, weren't you Judge?

BRACK: Shame on you Mrs. Hedda! And so, you and Tesman — ?

HEDDA: Well, one evening we happened to pass by this house and Tesman was turning and twisting and he couldn't think of anything to say; I really felt sorry for the poor learned wretch.

BRACK: Sorry? You?

HEDDA: Yes, I really did, I felt sorry for him. And so — just to make conversation to help him out a bit — I was foolish enough to say what a charming house this was and how I should love to live in it.

BRACK: No more than that?

HEDDA: Not that evening.

BRACK: But afterwards?

HEDDA: Afterwards — afterwards my foolishness was not without consequences.

BRACK: Unfortunately, that happens all too often.

HEDDA: Yes, thanks. So you see it was this fictitious enthusiasm for Secretary Falk's villa that really brought Tesman and me together. That was the immediate cause of our engagement, our wedding, our wedding journey, and all the rest of it. Well, my dear Judge they say — as you make your bed so you must lie.

BRACK: This is really priceless! Then you didn't really care a rap about the house?

HEDDA: God knows I didn't.

BRACK: Still, now that we've made it so attractive and comfortable for you —

HEDDA: To me it smells of lavender and dried rose-leaves — what might be called the Aunt Julia atmosphere. Oh, my dear Judge, my dear Judge — how incredibly I shall bore myself here.

MEDEA
Robinson Jeffers

Act I
(Decca DAU-12 or DL 9000)

Judith Anderson's pauses marked as indicated:

MEDEA: I will look at the light of the sun, this last time. || I wish from that blue sky the white wolf of lightning
Would leap, and burst my skull and my brain, || and like a burning babe cling to these breasts || . . . (She checks and looks fiercely at the women below.)

Someone is here? || (Her hostile eyes range back and forth; she sees
    the women clearly now, and assumes full self-control.
    Her voice is cautious and insincere.) I did not know I had
    visitors. || . . . Women of Corinth: |
If anything has been spoken too loudly here, | consider
That I believed I was alone; | and I have some provocation. || You've
    come — let me suppose
With love and sympathy — to peer at my sorrow. | I understand well
    enough
That nothing is ever private in a Greek city; | whoever withholds
    anything
Is thought sullen or proud || . . . (with irony) undemocratic
I think you call it. || This is not always just, | but we know that
    justice, at least on earth,
Is a name, not a fact || and as for me, | I wish to avoid any appearance
Of being . . . proud. | Of what? | Of affliction? || I will show you my
    naked heart. || You know that my lord Jason
Has left me and made a second marriage, with the bright-haired child
Of wealth and power. | I too was a child of power, but not in this
    country; | and I spent my power
For love of Jason. I poured it out before him like water, | I made him
    drink it like wine. | I gave him
Success and fame; | I saved him his precious life; not once, many
    times. || You may have heard what I did for him: ||
I betrayed my father for him, | I killed my brother to save him; I
    made my own land to hate me forever; |
And I fled west with Jason in the Greek ship, under the thunder of
    the sail, weeping and laughing, |
That huge journey through the Black Sea and the Bosphorus,
    Where the rocks clang together, | through the Sea of Marmora,
And through the Hellespont, watched by the spearmen of wealthy
    Troy, | and home to Greek water: || his home, || my exile, ||
My endless exile. || And here I have loved him and borne him sons; |
    and this . . . man . . .
Has left me and taken Creon's daughter, to enjoy her fortune, | and
    put aside her soft yellow hair
And kiss her young mouth. || (Medea stands rigid, struggling for
    self-control.)

Key: | = Brief pause for breath
      || = Full pause

AN EXERCISE IN MOVEMENT

From Shakespeare's *A Midsummer Night's Dream*
Period and Costumes: Grecian
Mood: Romantic and comic.
Style: Larger than realism.

Characters: Lysander — a young man in love with Hermia.
            Hermia — a young girl in love with Lysander but ordered by her father
                   to marry Demetrius.
            Helena — a young girl, in love with Demetrius but jilted by him.
            Demetrius — a young man in love with Hermia.

Setting: a forest. Risers upstage, UC a large rock, ULC a stylized tree, UL a riser with a winding path leading off-stage, UR a tree trunk which is hollow, DR a low riser with a bank of flowers. (See picture on page 261.)

Ground Plan:

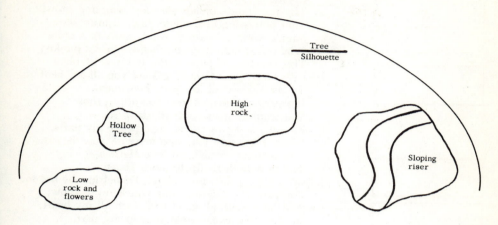

Oberon, King of the Fairies has seen Helena hopelessly pursuing the unresponsive Demetrius through the forest, and tries to help by ordering Puck to anoint Demetrius' eyes with the magic love-juice that will make him love the first person he sees on awakening. Puck by mistake anoints Lysander's eyes, and on awakening he falls in love with Helena, abandoning Hermia. To remedy things, Oberon also anoints Demetrius' eyes, and withdraws to the top of the rock with Puck to watch the consequences, Puck exclaiming, "Lord, what fools these mortals be!" Demetrius is asleep on the L riser.

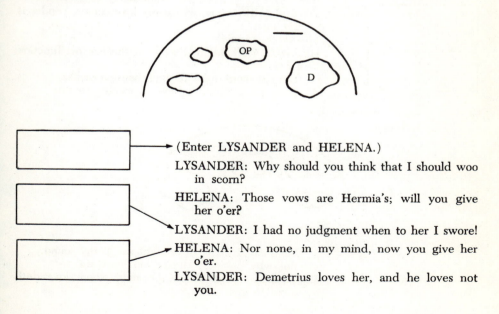

(Enter LYSANDER and HELENA.)

LYSANDER: Why should you think that I should woo in scorn?

HELENA: Those vows are Hermia's; will you give her o'er?

LYSANDER: I had no judgment when to her I swore!

HELENA: Nor none, in my mind, now you give her o'er.

LYSANDER: Demetrius loves her, and he loves not you.

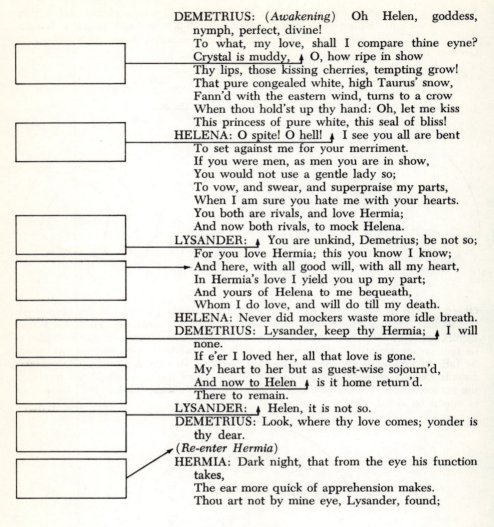

DEMETRIUS: (*Awakening*) Oh Helen, goddess, nymph, perfect, divine!
To what, my love, shall I compare thine eyne?
Crystal is muddy, ⚹ O, how ripe in show
Thy lips, those kissing cherries, tempting grow!
That pure congealed white, high Taurus' snow,
Fann'd with the eastern wind, turns to a crow
When thou hold'st up thy hand: Oh, let me kiss
This princess of pure white, this seal of bliss!
HELENA: O spite! O hell! ⚹ I see you all are bent
To set against me for your merriment.
If you were men, as men you are in show,
You would not use a gentle lady so;
To vow, and swear, and superpraise my parts,
When I am sure you hate me with your hearts.
You both are rivals, and love Hermia;
And now both rivals, to mock Helena.
LYSANDER: ⚹ You are unkind, Demetrius; be not so;
For you love Hermia; this you know I know;
And here, with all good will, with all my heart,
In Hermia's love I yield you up my part;
And yours of Helena to me bequeath,
Whom I do love, and will do till my death.
HELENA: Never did mockers waste more idle breath.
DEMETRIUS: Lysander, keep thy Hermia; ⚹ I will none.
If e'er I loved her, all that love is gone.
My heart to her but as guest-wise sojourn'd,
And now to Helen ⚹ is it home return'd.
There to remain.
LYSANDER: ⚹ Helen, it is not so.
DEMETRIUS: Look, where thy love comes; yonder is thy dear.
(*Re-enter Hermia*)
HERMIA: Dark night, that from the eye his function takes,
The ear more quick of apprehension makes.
Thou art not by mine eye, Lysander, found;

Mine ear, I thank it, brought me to thy sound.
But why unkindly didst thou leave me so?
LYSANDER: Why should he stay, whom love doth press to go?

HERMIA: What love could press Lysander from my side?

LYSANDER: Lysander's love, that would not let him bide —

Fair Helena, ⸋ who more engilds the night
Than all yon fiery O's and eyes of light.
Why seek'st thou me? Could not this make thee know,
The hate I bare thee made me leave thee so?

HERMIA: You speak not as you think; it cannot be.

HELENA: Lo, she is one of this confederacy!
Now I perceive they have conjoin'd all three
To fashion this false sport, in spite of me.
Injurious Hermia, most ungrateful maid!
Have you conspired, have you with these contrived
To bait me with this foul derision?

HERMIA: I understand not what you mean by this.

HELENA: Aye, do, persever, counterfeit sad looks,
Make mouths upon me when I turn my back;
Wink each at other; hold the sweet jest up.
This sport, well carried, shall be chronicled.
If you have any pity, grace, or manners.
You would not make me such an argument.
But fare ye well; 'tis partly my own fault;
Which death or absence soon shall remedy.

LYSANDER: Stay, gentle Helena; hear my excuse:
My love, my life, my soul, fair Helena!

HELENA: O excellent!

LYSANDER: Helen, I love thee; by my life, I do:
I swear by that which I will lose for thee,
To prove him false that says I love thee not.

DEMETRIUS: ⸋ I say I love thee more than he can do.

LYSANDER: ⸋ If you say so, withdraw, and prove it too.

DEMETRIUS: ⸋ Quick, come!

HERMIA: ⸋ Lysander, whereto tends all this?

LYSANDER: Away, you Ethiope!
Hang off, thou cat, thou burr! vile thing, let loose,
Or I will shake thee from me like a serpent!

HERMIA: Why are you grown so rude? What change is this? Sweet love —

LYSANDER: Thy love! out, tawny Tartar, out!
Out, loathed medicine! hated potion, hence!

HERMIA: Do you not jest?

HELENA: Yes, sooth and so do you.

HERMIA: ⸋ Oh, me, you juggler! you canker-blossom,
You thief of love! what, have you come by night
And stolen my love's heart from him?

HELENA: Fie, fie! you counterfeit, you puppet, you!

HERMIA: Puppet? Why so? aye, that way goes the game.
Now I perceive that she hath made compare

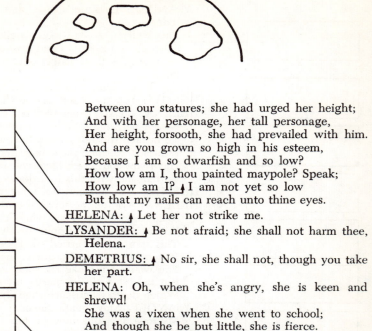

Between our statures; she had urged her height;
And with her personage, her tall personage,
Her height, forsooth, she had prevailed with him.
And are you grown so high in his esteem,
Because I am so dwarfish and so low?
How low am I, thou painted maypole? Speak;
How low am I? ↓ I am not yet so low
But that my nails can reach unto thine eyes.

HELENA: ↓ Let her not strike me.

LYSANDER: ↓ Be not afraid; she shall not harm thee, Helena.

DEMETRIUS: ↓ No sir, she shall not, though you take her part.

HELENA: Oh, when she's angry, she is keen and shrewd!
She was a vixen when she went to school;
And though she be but little, she is fierce.

HERMIA: Little again! nothing but low and little!
Why will you suffer her to flout me thus? ↓
Let me come to her.

LYSANDER: Get you gone, you dwarf;
You minimus, of hindering knot-grass made;
You bead, you acorn.

DEMETRIUS: You are too officious
In her behalf that scorns your services.
→ Let her alone.

LYSANDER: Now she holds me not;
→ Now follow, if thou darest, to try whose right
of thine or mine, is most in Helena.

DEMETRIUS: Follow! ↓ nay, I'll go with thee, cheek by jowl.
(*Exeunt LYSANDER and DEMETRIUS*)

HERMIA: You, mistress, ↓ all this coil is 'long of you.
Nay, go not back.

HELENA: ↓ I will not trust you, I,
Nor longer stay in your curst company.
Your hands than mine are quicker for a fray,
My legs are longer, though, ↓ to run away.
(*HELENA Exits*)

HERMIA: I am amazed, ↓ and know not what to say.
(*HERMIA Exits*)

EXERCISE FOR TOPPING, CLIMAX, AND VOCAL INTERPRETATION
DEATH OF A SALESMAN

Example of skillful topping, undercutting, and building to climax. From *Death of a Salesman*, by Arthur Miller, near the end of Act. I.

Scene is reproduced without punctuation, as read on Decca DX-102 LP Record, Side 2, 1″ from inside, 9007, by Thomas Mitchell, Arthur Kennedy, Mildred Dunnock, Cameron Mitchell. Listen to the recording several times, then mark the script as indicated for emphatic words, rising and falling inflections, pauses, topping and undercutting.

Code for marking vocal interpretation:

Emphasis

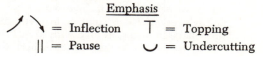

/ \ = Inflection   T = Topping

|| = Pause   ∪ = Undercutting

Biff: I'm — I'm leaving early tomorrow
Happy: He's going to see Bill Oliver   Pop
Willy: Oliver   For what
Biff: He always said he'd   stake me   and I'd like to go into business   so maybe I can take him up on it
Linda: Isn't that wonderful
Willy: Don't interrupt   What's wonderful about it   Fifty men in the city of New York who'd stake him   Sporting goods
Biff: I guess so   I know something about it and
Willy: He knows something about it   You know sporting goods better than Spalding   for God's sake   How much is he giving you
Biff: I don't know   I didn't even see him yet   but
Willy: Then what're you talkin' about
Biff: Well   all I said was I'm gonna see him   That's all
Willy: Ah you're counting your chickens again
Biff: Oh   Jeez   I'm going to sleep
Willy: Don't curse in this house
Biff: Since when did you get so clean
Happy: Wait a . . .
Willy: Don't use that language to me   I won't have it
Happy: Wait a minute   I got an idea   I got a feasible idea   Come here Biff   let's talk this over now   let's talk some sense here   When I was down in Florida last time I thought of a great idea to sell sporting goods   It just came back to me   You and I   Biff   we have a line   the Loman Line   We train a couple of weeks and put on a couple of exhibitions   see
Willy: That's an idea
Happy: Wait   We form two basketball teams   see   Two waterpolo teams   We play each other   It's a million dollars worth of publicity   Two brothers   see   The Loman Brothers   Displays in the Royal Palms   all the hotels   And banners over the ring   and the basketball court   "Loman Brothers"   Baby we could sell sporting goods
Willy: That is a one-million-dollar idea
Linda: Marvelous

AN EXERCISE IN TEMPO AND CLIMAX

From Oscar Wilde's *The Importance of Being Earnest*
(Angel Record, 3504 B)

Period and Costumes: Elegant Edwardian England
Mood: High comedy with a sense of the absurd
Style: Artificial, stylized realism
Characters:

    Lady Bracknell............an overbearing matron
    Gwendolen ....her daughter, in love with Jack
    Jack Worthing ....a debonair young man about town
    Algernon.....................his friend, the nephew of Lady Bracknell
    Cecily ....the ward of Jack and in love with Algy
    Miss Prism.................Cecily's governess, a spinster in love with Rev. Chasuble
    Rev. Chasuble...........the village minister, in love with Miss Prism
  Setting: The morning room of the house in the country where Cecily lives.

(Enter MISS PRISM hurriedly.)

MISS PRISM: I was told you expected me in the vestry, dear Canon. I have been
    waiting for you there for an hour and three-quarters.
    (Catches sight of LADY BRACKNELL, who has fixed her with
    a stony glare. MISS PRISM grows pale and quails. She
    looks anxiously round as if desirous to escape.)
LADY BRACKNELL: (In a severe, judicial voice.) Prism! (MISS PRISM bows her
    head in shame.) Come here, Prism! (MISS PRISM approaches in a humble
    manner.) Prism! Where is that baby? (General consternation. THE CANON
    starts back in horror. ALGERNON and JACK pretend to be anxious to shield
    CECILY and GWENDOLEN from hearing the details of a terrible public
    scandal.) Twenty-eight years ago, Prism, you left Lord Bracknell's house,
    Number 104, Upper Grosvenor Street, in charge of a perambulator that con-
    tained a baby, of the male sex. You never returned. A few weeks later, through
    the elaborate investigations of the Metropolitan police, the perambulator was
    discovered at midnight, standing by itself in a remote corner of Bayswater.
    It contained the manuscript of a three-volume novel of more than usually re-
    volting sentimentality. (MISS PRISM starts in involuntary indignation.) But the
    baby was not there! (Everyone looks at MISS PRISM.) Prism, where is that
    baby? (A pause)
MISS PRISM: Lady Bracknell, I admit with shame that I do not know. I only wish
    I did. The plain facts of the case are these. On the morning of the day you
    mention, a day that is forever branded on my memory, I prepared as usual
    to take the baby out in its perambulator. I had also with me a somewhat old,
    but capacious hand-bag in which I had intended to place the manuscript of a
    work of fiction that I had written during my few unoccupied hours. In a mo-
    ment of mental abstraction, for which I never can forgive myself, I deposited the
    manuscript in the bassinette, and placed the baby in the hand-bag.
JACK: (Who has been listening attentively.) But where did you deposit the
    hand-bag?
MISS PRISM: Do not ask me, Mr. Worthing.
JACK: Miss Prism, this is a matter of no small importance to me. I insist on
    knowing where you deposited the hand-bag that contained that infant.
MISS PRISM: I left it in the cloak room of one of the larger railway stations in
    London.
JACK: What railway station?
MISS PRISM: (Quite crushed.) Victoria. The Brighton line. (Sinks into a chair.)

JACK: I must retire to my room for a moment. Gwendolen, wait here for me.

GWENDOLEN: If you are not too long, I will wait here for you all my life.

(Exit JACK in great excitement.)

CHASUBLE: What do you think this means, Lady Bracknell?

LADY BRACKNELL: I dare not even suspect, Dr. Chasuble. I need hardly tell you that in families of high position strange coincidences are not supposed to occur. They are hardly considered the thing.

(Noises heard overhead as if some one was throwing trunks about. Every one looks up.)

CECILY: Uncle Jack seems strangely agitated.

CHASUBLE: Your guardian has a very emotional nature.

LADY BRACKNELL: This noise is extremely unpleasant. It sounds as if he was having an argument. I dislike arguments of any kind. They are always vulgar, and often convincing.

CHASUBLE: (Looking up.) It has stopped now. (The noise is redoubled.)

LADY BRACKNELL: I wish he would arrive at some conclusion.

GWENDOLEN: This suspense is terrible. I hope it will last.

(Enter JACK with a hand-bag of black leather in his hand)

JACK: (Rushing over to MISS PRISM.) Is this the hand-bag, Miss Prism? Examine it carefully before you speak. The happiness of more than one life depends on your answer.

MISS PRISM: (Calmly) It seems to be mine. Yes, here is the injury it received through the upsetting of a Gower Street omnibus in younger and happier days. Here is the stain on the lining caused by the explosion of a temperance beverage, an incident that occurred at Leamington. And here, on the lock, are my initials. I had forgotten that in an extravagant mood I had had them placed there. The bag is undoubtedly mine. I am delighted to have it so unexpectedly restored to me. It has been a great inconvenience being without it all these years.

JACK: (In a pathetic voice.) Miss Prism, more is retored to you than this hand-bag. I was the baby you placed in it.

MISS PRISM: (Amazed.) You?

JACK: (Embracing her.) Yes . . . mother!

MISS PRISM: (Recoiling in indignant astonishment.) Mr. Worthing! I am unmarried!

JACK: Unmarried! I do not deny that is a serious blow. But after all, who has the right to cast a stone against one who has suffered? Cannot repentance wipe out an act of folly? Why should there be one law for men, and another for women? Mother, I forgive you. (Tries to embrace her again.)

MISS PRISM: (Still more indignant.) Mr. Worthing, there is some error. (Pointing to LADY BRACKNELL.) There is the lady who can tell you who you really are.

JACK: (After a pause.) Lady Bracknell, I hate to seem inquisitive, but would you kindly inform me who I am?

LADY BRACKNELL: I am afraid that the news I have to give you will not altogether please you. You are the son of my poor sister, Mrs. Moncrieff, and consequently Algernon's elder brother.

JACK: Algy's elder brother! Then I have a brother after all. I knew I had a brother! I always said I had a brother! Cecily, — how could you have ever doubted that I had a brother? (Seizes hold of ALGERNON). Dr. Chasuble, my unfortunate brother. Miss Prism, my unfortunate brother. Gwendolen, my unfortunate brother. Algy, you young scoundrel, you will have to treat me with more respect in the future. You have never behaved to me like a brother in all your life.

ALGERNON: Well, not till to-day, old boy, I admit. I did my best, however, though I was out of practice. (Shakes hands.)

GWENDOLEN: (TO JACK.) My own! But what own are you? What is your Christian name, now that you have become some one else?

JACK: Good heavens! . . . I had quite forgotten that point. Your decision on the subject of my name is irrevocable, I suppose?

GWENDOLEN: I never change, except in my affections.

CECILY: What a noble nature you have, Gwendolen!

JACK: Then the question had better be cleared up at once. Aunt Augusta, a moment. At the time when Miss Prism left me in the hand-bag, had I been christened already?

LADY BRACKNELL: Every luxury that money could buy, including christening, had been lavished on you by your fond and doting parents.

JACK: Then I was christened! That is settled. Now, what name was I given? Let me know the worst.

LADY BRACKNELL: Being the eldest son you were naturally christened after your father.

JACK: (Irritably.) Yes, but what was my father's Christian name?

LADY BRACKNELL: (Meditatively.) I cannot at the present moment recall what the General's Christian name was. But I have no doubt he had one. He was eccentric, I admit. But only in later years. And that was the result of the Indian climate, and marriage, and indigestion, and other things of that kind.

JACK: Algy! Can't you recollect what our father's Christian name was?

ALGERNON: My dear boy, we were never even on speaking terms. He died before I was a year old.

JACK: His name would appear in the Army lists of the period, I suppose, Aunt Augusta?

LADY BRACKNELL: The General was essentially a man of peace, except in his domestic life. But I have no doubt his name would appear in any military directory.

JACK: The Army Lists of the last forty years are here. These delightful records should have been my constant study. (Rushes to bookcase and tears the books out.) M. Generals . . . Mallam, Maxbohm, Magley, what ghastly names they have — Markby, Migsby, Mobbs, Moncrieff! Lieutenant 1840, Captain, Lieutenant-Colonel, Colonel, General 1869, Christian names, Ernest John (Puts book very quietly down and speaks quite calmly.) I always told you, Gwendolen, my name was Ernest, didn't I? Well, it is Ernest after all. I mean it naturally is Ernest.

LADY BRACKNELL: Yes, I remember that the General was called Ernest. I knew I had some particular reason for disliking the name.

GWENDOLEN: Ernest! My own Ernest! I felt from the first that you could have no other name!

JACK: Gwendolen, it is a terrible thing for a man to find out suddenly that all his life he has been speaking nothing but the truth. Can you forgive me?

GWENDOLEN: I can. For I feel that you are sure to change.

JACK: My own one!

CHASUBLE: (To MISS PRISM.) Laetitia! (Embraces her.)

MISS PRISM: (Enthusiastically.) Frederick! At last!

ALGERNON: Cecily! (Embraces her.) At last!

JACK: Gwendolen! (Embraces her.) At last!

LADY BRACKNELL: My nephew, you seem to be displaying signs of triviality.

JACK: On the contrary, Aunt Augusta, I've now realized for the first time in my life the vital Importance of Being Earnest.

TABLEAU

CURTAIN

SUPPLEMENTARY BIBLIOGRAPHY

Supplementary Bibliography

(The following selected list of books is intended as a foundation for those without previous experience in the fields indicated. Titles listed in the suggested reading for each chapter are not repeated here.)

Drama in the Junior High School

BURGER, ISABEL B. *Creative Play Acting*. New York: A. S. Barnes and Co., 1950.

GILES, H. H. (Editor). *Playwrights Present: Problems of Everyday Life*. New York: Harper and Brothers, 1942.

HUTCHINSON, WILLIAM. *A Child's Book of the Theatre*. New York: Maxton Publishers, 1956. (Well illustrated — excellent for students.)

WARD, WINIFRED. *Creative Dramatics in the Upper Grades and Junior High School*. New York: Appleton-Century, 1930. (See also *Playmaking with Children*, 1957.)

WEISS, M. JERRY. *Guidance Through Drama*. New York: Whiteside, Inc., and William Morrow and Co., 1954.

Drama in the High School

BARNES, GRACE, AND SUTCLIFFE, MARY JEAN. *On Stage, Everyone*. New York: Macmillan and Co., 1954.

BOYLSTON, HELEN DORE. *Carol Goes Backstage*. Boston: Little, Brown and Co., 1941. (A novel dealing with the theatre.)

Course of Study, Secondary School Theatre Conference of the American Educational Theatre Association, 1963.

DAVIS, EUGENE C. *Amateur Theatre Handbook*. New York: Greenberg Publishers, 1945.

DEUTSCH, SALLY. *All-Star Cast: A Footlight Anthology*. Chicago: Ziff-Davis Publishing Co., 1947. (Short stories dealing with the theatre.)

FRANKLIN, MIRIAM. *Rehearsal: The Principles and Practice of Acting for The Stage*. Englewood Cliffs, N. J.: Prentice Hall, Inc., 1963.

HODGE, C. WALTER. *Shakespeare and the Players*. London: Ernest Benn, Ltd., 1950.

LOWNDES, POLLY ROBBINS. *Creative Assemblies*. Minneapolis, Minn.: T. S. Denison and Co., 1961.

MILLER, HELEN LOUISE. *Pointers on Producing the School Play*. Boston: Plays, Inc., 1960.

OMMANNEY, KATHERINE ANNE. *The Stage and the School*. New York: McGraw-Hill Book Co., 3rd edition, 1960.

SAMACHSON, DOROTHY AND JOSEPH. *The Dramatic Story of the Theatre*. New York: Abelard, Schuman Ltd., 1955.

Play Production

(With chapters on each of the backstage crafts)

CRAFTON, ALLEN, AND ROYER, JESSICA. *The Complete Acted Play: From Script to Final Curtain*. New York: F. S. Crofts and Co., 1946.

DOLMAN, JOHN JR. *The Art of Play Production*. New York: Harper and Brothers, revised edition, 1946.

GASSNER, JOHN. *Producing the Play*. New York: The Dryden Press, 1953.

HEFFNER, HUBERT C., SELDEN, SAMUEL, AND SELLMAN, HUNTON D. *Modern Theatre Practice*. New York: Appleton-Century-Crofts, 4th edition, 1959.

HEWITT, BARNARD, FOSTER, J. F., AND WOLLE, MURIEL SIBELL. *Play Production: Theory and Practice*. Chicago: J. B. Lippincott Co., 1952.

NELMS, HENNING. *Play Production*. New York: Barnes and Noble, Inc., 1950.

Scenery

BUERKI, F. A. *Stagecraft for Nonprofessionals*. Madison: University of Wisconsin Press Paperback, 1962.

BURRIS-MEYER, HAROLD, AND COLE, EDWARD C. *Scenery for the Theatre*. New York: Little, Brown and Co., 1938.

CORNBERG, SOL, AND GEBAUER, EMANUEL L. *A Stage Crew Handbook*. New York: Harper and Brothers, 1941.

GILLETTE, ARNOLD S. *Stage Scenery: Its Construction and Rigging*. New York: Harper and Brothers, 1960.

HAKE, HERBERT V. *Here's How*. Evanston, Ill.; Row, Peterson and Co., 1942.

LARSON, ORVILLE K. *Scene Design for Stage and Screen*. East Lansing: Michigan State University Press, 1961.

LOUNSBURY, WARREN C. *Backstage from A to Z*. Seattle: University of Washington Press, 1959.

PARKER, W. OREN, AND SMITH, HARVEY K. *Scene Design and Stage Lighting*. New York: Holt, Rinehart and Winston, 1963.

PHILIPPI, HERBERT. *Stagecraft and Scene Design*. Cambridge, Mass.: The Riverside Press, 1953.

SELDEN, SAMUEL, AND SELLMAN, HUNTON D. *Stage Scenery and Lighting: A Handbook for Nonprofessionals*, 3rd edition, New York: Appleton-Century-Crofts, 1959.

SIMONSON, LEE. *The Art of Scenic Design*. New York: Harper and Brothers, 1950.

STAHL, LEROY. *Simplified Stagecraft Manual*. Minneapolis: T. S. Denison Co., 1962.

Properties

ARONSON, JOSEPH. *The Encyclopedia of Furniture*. New York: Crown Publishers, 1938.

CONWAY, HEATHER. *Stage Properties*. London: H. Jenkins, Ltd., 1960.

GOULD, G. G. *The Period Furniture Handbook*. New York: Dodd, Mead and Co., 1928.

MEYER, FRANZ S. *A Handbook of Ornament*. Chicago: Wilcox and Follett, rev. ed., 1946.

PHILIPPI, HERBERT. *Stagecraft and Scene Design*. Cambridge, Mass.: The Riverside Press, 1953.

Lighting

BOWMAN, WAYNE. *Modern Theatre Lighting*. New York: Harper and Brothers, 1950.

FUCHS, THEODORE. *Stage Lighting*. Boston: Little, Brown and Co., 1929.

McCANDLESS, STANLEY R. *A Method of Lighting the Stage*. New York: Theatre Arts, Inc., 3rd edition, 1947.

RUBIN, JOEL E., AND WATSON, LELAND H. *Theatrical Lighting Practice*. New York: Theatre Arts Books, 1954.

SELDEN, SAMUEL, AND SELLMAN, HUNTON D. *Stage Scenery and Lighting*: A Handbook for Nonprofessionals. New York: Appleton-Century-Crofts, 3rd ed., 1959.

Costume

BARTON, LUCY. *Historic Costume for the Stage*. Boston: Walter H. Baker Company, 1935.

BROOKE, IRIS. *Costume in Greek Classic Drama*. New York: Theatre Arts Books, 1962.

DAVENPORT, MILLIA. *The Book of Costume*, 2 vols. New York: Crown Publishers, 1948.

GORSLINE, DOUGLAS. *What People Wore*: A Visual History of Dress from Ancient Times to 20th Century America. New York: Viking Press, 1952.

LAVER, JAMES (Editor). *Costume of the Western World*, 6 vols. London: George C. Harrap and Company, 1951.

WALKUP, FAIRFAX P. *Dressing the Part*, revised edition. New York: Appleton-Century-Crofts, 1950.

Make-Up

BAIRD, JOHN. *Make-up*. New York: Samuel French, 1930.

CORSON, RICHARD. *Stage Make-up*. New York: D. Appleton-Century-Crofts, Inc., 3rd edition, 1960.

FACTOR, MAX. *Hints on the Art of Make-Up*. Hollywood: Max Factor Studios, 1936.

STRAUSS, IVARD. *Paint, Powder and Make-up*. New Haven: Sweet and Son, 1936.

STRENKOVSKY, SERGE. *The Art of Make-Up*. New York: E. P. Dutton and Co., 1937.

Sound

BURRIS-MEYER, HAROLD, AND MALLORY, VINCENT. *Sound in the Theatre*. Mineola, New York: Radio Magazine, Box 629, 1959.

NAPIER, FRANK. *Noises Off*: A Handbook of Sound Effects. London: Frederick Miller, Ltd., 1936.

TURNBULL, ROBERT B. *Radio and Television Sound Effects*. New York: Rinehart and Co., 1951.

Films and Filmstrips

A Suggested List for Teaching Theatre

For full lists, see *Educational Theatre Journal*, XV, 1, March 1963 and XV, 3, October, 1963.

Basic Stage Movement. Filmstrip series, by J. F. Foster, B. & W. Manual. Part I: Movement: The Basis of Theatre; Part II: Symbolic Movement; Part III, The Stage as a Picture. Stanley Bowmar Co., Valhalla, N. Y. $3.50 each.

Behind the Scenes at a Theatre. Filmstrip, B & W. Manual. Edited by Richard Southern. Stanley Bowmar Co., Valhalla, N. Y. $3.50 each.

Development of the Physical Theatre, The. (V Cent. BC to XX Cent. AD), by James H. Butler and Desmond P. Wedberg. Filmstrip, B & W. Comma, Hollywood, $3.50.

Elementary Stage Make-Up. Set of 4 filmstrips. Comma. $22.00.

Elementary Set Design. Set of 5 filmstrips. Comma. $27.50.

Four Ways to Drama. Sound film; same play in arena theatre, radio, television and motion pictures. UCLA. $120.

Great Actresses of the Past. Silent film, 5 reels. Rejane, Bernhardt, Fiske, Duse. Museum of Modern Art. $10.00 rental.

Great Plays in Rehearsal. Directed by Eric Salmon at Univ. of Wisconsin. Kinescope, B & W. 1 hour each: *Candida, Misanthrope, Masterbuilder, Oedipus, Caesar, Government Inspector, Merchant of Venice, Miss Julie, The Family Reunion.* NET Film Service, Indiana University, Bloomington, Ind. $8.00 each, rental.

Greek and Roman Theatres of the Ancient World. Color filmstrips by James H. Butler. Epidauros, Dionysus, Priene, Orange. Comma, Hollywood, $32.50 set of 5.

History of Costume. Color Filmstrips. Part I, Men's, Part II, Women's, by Fred Kuwalski. Comma, Hollywood, Set. $11.00.

History of the English Theatre. B. & W filmstrips, edited by Richard Southern. Playhouse, 2 parts, Machinery, Scenery, Costume, 2 parts. Stanley Bowmar Co. $3.50 each.

Julius Caesar (The Forum Scene) With Charlton Heston. B and W sound film. International Film Bureau. $95.00, rental, $7.50.

Lighting for the Theatre. 3 color filmstrips, by William Todt and William C. White. Comma, 1535 Ivar Ave., Hollywood 28, Calif. $16.50 set.

Make-up for the Theater. Color sound film. UCLA. $125 purchase, $4.00 rental.

Making Theatrical Wigs, B and W sound film, 11 min. UCLA. $55.00, rental, $4.00.

Marcel Marceau: In the Park. B and W sound film. 14 mins. Brandon Films, 200 W. 57th St., New York City. $100, rental, $7.50.

Mask of Comedy (Commedia dell'arte). Color sound film. Pizzo Films, 80 Fairway Drive, Daly City, California.

Molière. B & W filmstrip. Manual (in French). Gessler Publishing Co. Hastings-on-Hudson, N. Y. $3.

On Stage Tonight. B and W sound film. International Film Bureau, 22 min. $95.00, rental, $7.50.

One Way to Build a Flat. B & W sound film. UCLA, Extension Division Film Library.

Producing a Play. Series of color filmstrips. Produced at Goodman Theatre. Acting Problems, Character Make-up for Boys, Straight Make-up for Boys, Make-up for Girls, Designing a Set, Building a Set, Managing a Show, The Stage Manager. International Film Bureau, 332 South Michigan Ave., Chicago 4, Ill. $4.50 each.

Salute to the American Theatre, A. Kinescope, B & W sound. Scenes from *The Octoroon, Waiting for Lefty, The Male Animal, Call me Mister, Home of the Brave, South Pacific, The Crucible, Raisin in the Sun.* Narrator, Franchot Tone. Anti-Defamation League of B'nai B'rith, 515 Madison Ave., New York 22, Nominal rental.

Scenery Construction. Set of 7 color filmstrips, Comma. $38.50.

Scenes from "Cyrano." Sound film, with Walter Hampden. Library Films, 25 W. 45th St., New York 19. $30.00 purchase.

Seventeenth Century Acting Technique. B & W silent film. Yale University Dept. of Drama.

Shakespearean Production in England. Series, B & W filmstrips. Part I, 1700-1800. Part VII, *Hamlet.* Stanley Bowmar Co., Valhalla, N. Y. $3.50 each.

Shakespeare's Theatre: The Globe Playhouse. B & W sound film. UCLA, $100, rental, $5.00.

Showtime. B & W sound film. Wisconsin Idea Theatre. University of Wisconsin. $2.50 rental.

Sophocles' Electra. Color filmstrip by James H. Butler. Comma, Hollywood. $5.50.

Stagecraft Series. Color filmstrips. Simplified Staging, Stage Settings, Simplified Stage Lighting. National Film Board of Canada, 400 W. Madison St., Chicago. $5.00 each.

Theatre in Action. B & W sound film. Semi-documentary on community theatre. Fort Wayne Civic Theatre, Fort Wayne, Indiana.

Voice, The. B & W sound film. Encyclopaedia Britannica Films. $45.00; rental, $2.50.

Working Aids for the Theatre Technician. Set of 3 filmstrips. Comma. $16.50.

Yesterday's Actors. B & W film with Edwin Burr Pettet. Comma. $150, rental, $7.50.

Illustration Credits

(California State College at Long Beach productions directed
by the author except when otherwise indicated.)

FRONTISPIECE

The Servant of Two Masters, California State College at Long Beach. Designer, Milton Howarth, Costumes, Herbert L. Camburn, Coleman Photography.

CHAPTER 1

The School for Wives, staged with *The Critique of The School for Wives,* California State College at Long Beach. Designer, Milton Howarth, Costumes, Inge Schmidt. Coleman Photography.

The Lark, California High School, Whittier, Calif. Staged in gymnasium on a platform without front curtain. Jean Prinz Korf, Director and Designer. Technical Director, George Bedford. Photo by Preston E. Mitchell.

The Emperor Jones, College of Idaho, John Ford Sollers, Director and Designer.

Antigone, Millikan High School, Long Beach, Calif. Al Randall, Director.

Bernardine, University of Oregon. Director, Frederick Hunter, Designer, Howard L. Ramey.

CHAPTER 2

The Crucible, California State College at Long Beach. Designer, John H. Green. Photo by Coleman.

Noah, New York production. Director, Jerome Mayer. Designer, Cleon Throckmorton, animals and masks by Remo Bufano. Vandamm Photo.

Death of a Salesman, Santa Monica City College, Calif. Director, Bert Holland, Designer, Elmer Bladow, Photo by Bob Reed.

CHAPTER 4

Death of a Salesman, produced by Kermit Bloomgarden and Walter Fried, New York. Director, Elia Kazan, Designer, Jo Mielziner. Photo by Eileen Darby-Graphic House.

Inherit the Wind, Manual Arts High School, Los Angeles. Director, Reuben G. Plaskoff, Designer, David Aprato. Weaver Photo Service.

Oregon Shakespeare Festival Theatre, Ashland, Oregon.

Pillars of Society, California State College at Long Beach (temporary stage, 11' deep to center fire door). Designer, Maxine Merlino. Coleman Photo.

Greek theatre at Epidauros. Steps leading to shallow stage can be seen at right. Photograph by author.

Reconstruction of the Shakespearean theatre. Globe model made by John Cranford Adams and Irwin Smith. Photographer, Wendell Kilmer.

The House of Connelly, Carnegie Institute of Technology. Director, Mary Morris, Designer, Milton Howarth.

Dead End, New York production staged by the author, Sidney Kingsley. Designer, Norman Bel Geddes. Photo courtesy New York Public Library, Theatre Collection.

The Importance of Being Earnest, University of Minnesota. Directed and designed by Wendell Josal. Costumes by Robert Moulton. Univ. Photographic Lab.

Look Homeward, Angel. California State College at Long Beach. Milton Howarth, Designer. Herbert L. Camburn, Costumer. Coleman Photo.

J. B., New York production. Director, Elia Kazan, Designer, Boris Aronson. Photo courtesy New York Public Library, Theatre Collection, George Freedley, Curator.

Knights of the Round Table, School of Drama, Yale University. Director, Frank McMullan, Designer, Frank Bevan.

The Inspector-General, University of Nebraska. Director, John F. Wenstrand, Designer, Jerry Bass. Photo by Univ. of Nebraska Photo Productions.

Desire Under the Elms, Stanford University. Director, Nicholas Vardac, Designer, Wendell Cole. Photo by Stanford Univ. Photographic Dept.

A Clearing in the Woods, New York production. Director, Joseph Anthony, Designer, Oliver Smith. Photo by Vandamm.

Le Bourgeois Gentilhomme, Yale University. Director, Halsted Welles, Designer, Donald Oenslager, Costumer, Frank Bevan. Commercial Photo Service.

The Visit, New York production starring Alfred Lunt and Lynn Fontanne. Director, Peter Brook, Designer, Ted Otto. Photo by Vandamm.

The Crucible, Cleveland Playhouse, Euclid-77th Street Theatre. Frederic McConnell, Director, William A. McCreary, Designer. Photo by Hastings-Willinger and Associates.

The Private Life of the Master Race, Hunter College. Director, Bernard Dukore, Designer, Robert Guerra. Photo by Michael Teres.

Rhinoceros, California State College at Long Beach. Milton Howarth, Designer, Herbert L. Camburn, Costumes. Photo by Coleman.

Romeo and Juliet, California State College at Long Beach. Designer, Milton Howarth, Costumes, Inge Schmidt. Photo by Coleman.

John Brown's Body, California State College at Long Beach. Designer, Milton Howarth, Costumes, Herbert L. Camburn. Photo by Coleman.

Another Way Out, California State College at Long Beach. Directed by Bob Hanrahan. Designer, Eugene Pyeatte, Photo by Coleman.

The Taming of the Shrew, University of Minnesota. Director, Frank M. Whiting, Designer, Wendell Josal. Photo by Photographic Laboratory, U. of Minn.

Hamlet, New York production, directed and designed by Norman Bel Geddes. Photograph courtesy New York Public Library Theatre Collection.

Cosi Fan Tutte, University of Kansas. Director, John Newfield, Designer, Milton Howarth.

You Can't Take It With You, California State College at Long Beach. Designer, John H. Green. Photo by Coleman.

Hedda Gabler, California State College at Long Beach. Designer, Milton Howarth, Costumes, Herbert L. Camburn. Coleman Photo.

The Little Foxes, California State College at Long Beach. Director, Stanley Kahan, Designer, Milton Howarth, Costumes, Herbert L. Camburn. Photo by Coleman.

Antigone, California State College at Long Beach. Designer, Victor Smith. Photo by Coleman.

The Winter's Tale, Experimental Theatre, Vassar College. Director, George B. Dowell, Designs by John Kurten, suggested by Botticelli. Photo by Ramon Traver.

CHAPTER 5

Coleman Photography, Long Beach, California.

Of Thee I Sing, University of California at Los Angeles. Director, Samuel Selden, Designer, John Jones.

The Last Supper, Leonardo da Vinci.

Antigone, University of Southern California. Director, James H. Butler, Designer, Marcus Fuller. S. C. Photo.

Lysistrata, California State College at Long Beach. Director, Alec Finlayson, Designer, Milton Howarth, Costumes by Herbert Camburn. Coleman Photo.

The Diary of Anne Frank, California State College at Long Beach. Designer, Milton Howarth. Coleman Photography.

The Time of Your Life, California State College at Long Beach. Designer, Harold Alexander. Coleman Photography.

The Happy Time, California State College at Long Beach. Designer, John H. Green. Coleman Photography.

Dark of the Moon, Director, W. David Sievers, Designer, Anne McFadden. Idyllwild Arts Foundation. Photo by Stelios Roccos.

The Twin Menaechmi, University of Southern California. Director, James H. Butler, Designer, John E. Blankenchip.

A Marriage Proposal, California State College at Long Beach. Designer, Norma Thormodson. Photo by Virginia Mead.

Libel! New York production. Director, Otto Preminger, Designer, Raymond Sovey. Photo by Vandamm.

A Dream Play, University of Illinois. Director, Charles Shattuck.

The Miser, Southwest Missouri State College, Springfield, Mo. Director, Robert K. Gilmore.

The Affected Young Ladies, California State College at Long Beach. Designer, Milton Howarth, Costumer, Inge Schmidt. Photo by Coleman.

Armida Abandoned by Rinaldo, by Tiepolo. Courtesy of The Art Institute of Chicago. Gift of James Deering.

Prisoners from the Front, by Winslow Homer. Courtesy of The Metropolitan Museum of Art, New York. Gift of Mrs. Frank B. Porter, 1922.

Amahl and the Night Visitors, California State College at Long Beach. Musical Direction, David Vasquez. Designer, John H. Green, Coleman Photo.

Why are you angry? by Paul Gauguin. Courtesy of The Art Institute of Chicago, Mr. and Mrs. Martin A. Ryerson Collection.

Haystacks in Snow, by Claude Monet. Courtesy of The Metropolitan Museum of Art, Bequest of Mrs. H. O. Havemeyer, 1929. The H. O. Havemeyer Collection.

The Card Players, Paul Cezanne. Stephen C. Clark Collection, New York.

A Rainy Day In Camp, Winslow Homer. Courtesy of The Metropolitan Museum of Art, Gift of Mrs. William F. Milton, 1923.

The Dance Foyer at the Opera, by Edgar Degas.

Coleman Photography.

The County Election, George C. Bingham. Collection City Art Museum of St. Louis.

CHAPTER 6

The Barretts of Wimpole Street, California State College at Long Beach, with guest artist Julie Haydon as Elizabeth. Designer, John H. Green, Costumer, Rosemary Stevens. Photo by Wes Wendland.

Dark of the Moon, Idyllwild Arts Foundation. Director, W. David Sievers. Photo by Stelios Roccos.

Summer and Smoke, California State College at Long Beach. Designer, John Nicholson. Coleman Photography.

CHAPTER 7

Morris Carnovsky in *King Lear,* Theatre Group, UCLA. John Houseman, Director, Oliver Andrews, Designer. Costumes by Dorothy Jeakins. Photo by Ivor Protheroe.

CHAPTER 8

Summer and Smoke, California State College at Long Beach. Designer, John Nicholson.

El Greco, *Portrait of a Man.* Metropolitan Museum of Art, New York.

CHAPTER 9

The Late Christopher Bean, California State College at Long Beach. Designer, Anne McFadden. Photo by Pictorial House, Bellflower.

Othello, California State College at Long Beach. Designer, Milton Howarth, Costumes, Herbert L. Camburn. Photo by Coleman.

A Moon for the Misbegotten, California State College at Long Beach. Designer, Milton Howarth. Photo by Coleman.

CHAPTER 10

Photo by Coleman.

CHAPTER 11

A Midsummer Night's Dream, California State College at Long Beach. Designer, John H. Green. Costumes by Aline Gronendyke. Photo by Coleman.

Photos by Coleman.

CHAPTER 12

The Iceman Cometh, Arena Stage, Washington, D. C. Director, F. Cowles Strickland. Designer, Curtis Cowan.

The Male Animal, California State College at Long Beach Summer Tent Theatre. Director, F. Cowles Strickland, Designer, Herbert L. Camburn. Photo by Coleman.

The Cocktail Party, University of California at Los Angeles. Director, Walden Boyle, Designer, John Jones.

The Long Beach (California) Community Playhouse. Photo by Hubert A. McClain.

The Three Sisters, Tyrone Guthrie Theatre, Minneapolis, Minn. Director, Tyrone Guthrie, Designer, Tanya Moiseiwitsch.

CHAPTER 13

Sleeping Beauty, California State College at Long Beach. Director and Costume Designer, Herbert L. Camburn. Settings by Milton Howarth. Photo by Coleman.

INDEX

Date Due

Oc 23 68			
Ag 25 69 P			
JA 24 72			

Demco 38-297